LOVE AND POETRY IN THE MIDDLE EAST

LOVE AND POETRY IN THE MIDDLE EAST

Love and Literature from Antiquity to the Present

Edited by
Atef Alshaer

I.B. TAURIS
LONDON • NEW YORK • OXFORD • NEW DELHI • SYDNEY

I.B. TAURIS
Bloomsbury Publishing Plc
50 Bedford Square, London, WC1B 3DP, UK
1385 Broadway, New York, NY 10018, USA
29 Earlsfort Terrace, Dublin 2, Ireland

BLOOMSBURY, I.B. TAURIS and the I.B. Tauris logo are trademarks of Bloomsbury Publishing Plc

First published in Great Britain 2022
This paperback edition published 2023

Copyright © Atef Alshaer, 2022

Atef Alshaer and contributors have asserted their right under the Copyright, Designs and Patents Act, 1988, to be identified as Author of this work.

Copyright Individual Chapters © 2021 Atef Alshaer, Mark Weeden, Andrew George, Robert Anderson, Tamar S. Drukker, Huma Baig, Laurent Mingon, Mariwan Kanie, Seyedeh Paniz Musawi Natanzi

For legal purposes the Acknowledgements on p. xii constitute an extension of this copyright page.

Series design by Adriana Brioso
Cover image: King Shahryar and his wife Scheherazade, telling the tales of One Thousand and One Nights, statue by Mohammed Ghani Hikmat, Baghdad, Iraq.
(© Rasoul Ali/Alamy Stock Photo)
Cover image: Moroccan Tiles (© JayKay57 / Getty Images)

All rights reserved. No part of this publication may be reproduced or transmitted in any form or by any means, electronic or mechanical, including photocopying, recording, or any information storage or retrieval system, without prior permission in writing from the publishers.

Bloomsbury Publishing Plc does not have any control over, or responsibility for, any third-party websites referred to or in this book. All internet addresses given in this book were correct at the time of going to press. The author and publisher regret any inconvenience caused if addresses have changed or sites have ceased to exist, but can accept no responsibility for any such changes.

A catalogue record for this book is available from the British Library.

A catalog record for this book is available from the Library of Congress.

ISBN: HB: 978-0-7556-4094-2
PB: 978-0-7556-4098-0
ePDF: 978-0-7556-4095-9
eBook: 978-0-7556-4096-6

Typeset by Deanta Global Publishing Services, Chennai, India

To find out more about our authors and books visit www.bloomsbury.com and sign up for our newsletters.

In memory of Professor Robert Anderson
1927–2015

CONTENTS

List of contributors	ix
Acknowledgements	xii

LOVE AND POETRY IN THE MIDDLE EAST: FROM ANTIQUITY
TO THE PRESENT
    Atef Alshaer   1

Chapter 1
POWER-PLAYS: TYPES OF LOVER AND TYPES OF LOVE IN AKKADIAN
FROM THE THIRD AND SECOND MILLENNIA BC
    Mark Weeden   12

Chapter 2
'BE MY BABY' IN BABYLONIA: AN AKKADIAN POEM OF
ADOLESCENT LONGING
    Andrew George   57

Chapter 3
ANCIENT EGYPTIAN LOVE POETRY
    Robert Anderson   66

Chapter 4
THE LOVE OF JACOB AND RACHEL IN MODERN HEBREW POETRY
    Tamar S. Drukker   87

Chapter 5
AN ARAB AND ISLAMIC VIEW OF LOVE: THE POETRY OF THE *'UDHRĪ S*
    Atef Alshaer   101

Chapter 6
A COMPARISON BETWEEN THE IDEAS OF LOVE FOUND IN
AL-GHĀZĀLĪ'S *THE ALCHEMY OF HAPPINESS* AND THE FIRST
VOLUME OF RUMI'S *MASAVI-YI MA'NAVI*
    Huma Baig   131

Chapter 7
UNVEILING DESIRE: LOVE IN MODERN TURKISH POETRY
    Laurent Mignon   151

Chapter 8
LOVE, BELOVED AND ADORER: KURDISH *GHAZAL* POETRY IN THE
NINETEENTH CENTURY AS A SPACE FOR MORAL PROTEST
    Mariwan Kanie   169

Chapter 9
THE POLITICS OF MADNESS AND LOVE IN NEW IRANIAN POETRY IN
THE 1950S–60S: THE LEGACY OF *MAJNŪN IN SHE'RE NOW*: AHMAD
SHAMLU AND FOROUGH FARROKHZAD'S LOVE POETRY
    Seyedeh Paniz Musawi Natanzi   188

Chapter 10
LOVE AND CONFLICT IN MODERN ARABIC POETRY: THE CASE OF
NIZAR QABBANI AND MAHMOUD DARWISH
    Atef Alshaer   213

Selected references   243
Index   251

CONTRIBUTORS

Atef Alshaer is a senior lecturer in Arabic and Cultural Studies at the University of Westminster. He was educated at Birzeit University in Palestine and the School of Oriental and African Studies, University of London, where he obtained his PhD and taught for a number of years. He is the author of several publications in the fields of language, literature and politics, including *Poetry and Politics in the Modern Arab World*, 2016; *The Hizbullah Phenomenon: Politics and Communication* (with Dina Matar and Lina Khatib), 2014; *A Map of Absence: An Anthology of Palestinian Writing on the Nakba*, 2019. Alshaer regularly contributes to academic and media outlets, including the BBC, Independent, I-Newspaper, Electronic Intifada, Radio Monocle, al-Arabi al-Jadid and Aljazeera. He also writes and translates poetry.

Andrew George studied Assyriology at the University of Birmingham (1973-9) and for a while kept a public house in Darlaston. He wrote his doctoral dissertation on 'Babylonian Topographical Texts' under the supervision of W. G. Lambert (1985). Since 1983 he has taught Akkadian and Sumerian language and literature at SOAS, University of London, where he is now Professor of Babylonian. His specialisms are Babylonian literature, religion and intellectual culture. He has been elected Honorary Member of the American Oriental Society (2012). He is a former visiting professor at the University of Heidelberg (2000), Member of the Institute for Advanced Study in Princeton (2004-5) and Research Associate at Rikkyo University, Tokyo (2009). He was founding chairman of the London Centre for the Ancient Near East (1995-2000) and for seventeen years co-editor of the archaeological journal Iraq (1994-2011). His best-known books are a critical edition of the *Babylonian Gilgamesh Epic for OUP* (2003) and a prize-winning translation of *The Epic of Gilgamesh for Penguin Classics* (2000). Most recently he has published six volumes of new texts from cuneiform tablets now in Norway.

Huma Baig: After completing a BA in Islamic Studies from the School of Oriental and African Studies (SOAS), Huma went on to enhance her writing skills through an MA in Journalism. She now works as a press officer in the public sector and enjoys freelance writing for national magazines. A strong believer that the intellectual history of Islam is never discussed enough and often speaks on Muslim social issues.

Laurent Mignon is Associate Professor of Turkish language and literature at the University of Oxford, a Fellow of St Antony's College and Affiliate Professor at the Luxembourg School of Religion and Society. His research focuses on the minor literatures of Ottoman and Republican Turkey, in particular Jewish literatures, as well as the literary engagement with non-Abrahamic religions during the era straddling the Ottoman Empire and the Turkish Republic. He is the author of, among others, *Uncoupling Language and Religion: An Exploration into the Margins of Turkish Literature* (Boston, 2021).

Mark Weeden (PhD SOAS University of London) concentrates his research on the ancient written cultures of northern Syria and Anatolia, particularly cuneiform and Anatolian Hieroglyphic. He is Associate Professor in Ancient Near Eastern Languages at the Department of Greek and Latin at University College London. The editor-in-chief of the Ancient Near East section of Brill's Handbook of Oriental Studies series and co-editor of the journal Iraq, his books include Hittite Logograms and Hittite Scholarship (Harrassowitz, 2011) and, edited together with Lee Ullmann, Hittite Landscape and Geography (Brill, 2017). He is an epigrapher for various archaeological projects in Turkey.

Mariwan Kanie is a lecturer in Arabic studies at the Faculty of Humanities (University of Amsterdam). He teaches political, intellectual, and literary history of the Middle East and the modern Arab world. In addition to his academic publications in English and Dutch he has published many books in Kurdish in Iraqi Kurdistan. His book 'Complex Identities' won the prize of the best non-fiction in 2004, this prize is issued by the Kurdish Ministry of Culture in Iraqi Kurdistan. Some of his publications are translated into Persian and Arabic. Some of his latest publications are: Kanie, M. (2017). Young Saudi Women Novelists: Protesting Clericalism, Religious Fanaticism and Patriarchal Gender Order. *Journal of Arabian Studies*, 7(2), 283–299. And Kanie, M (2018). Chapter 3: "Bringing about the non-citizen in Iraq: a genealogical approach". In: Nils A. Butenschøn and Roel Meijer (eds). *The Middle East in transition: the centrality of citizenship*. orthampton, MA: Edward Elgar Publishing, 72–90.

Seyedeh Paniz Musawi Natanzi has a PhD in Gender Studies from SOAS (School of Oriental and African Studies), University of London. Her doctoral research examined "The War Mode of Visual Art Production: A Feminist Geopolitical Analysis of Art-Producing Masculinities in Kabul from 2014-2018". Currently, Paniz is working in Kabul as a researcher and consultant in the field of arts, gender and diversity, labour and migration in the process of state-building, reconstruction and war in Afghanistan. She has published amongst others in the international feminist art journal *n.paradoxa*, the Centre for a Feminist Foreign Policy, Art Represent, Art Now Pakistan, Feminist Review and as a Pandemic Researcher with the Aga Khan University's Institute for the Study of Muslim Civilisations.

Robert Anderson was a graduate of Classics and Egyptology from Cambridge. He wrote more than a dozen books in these fields. He was also a prolific reviewer in journals devoted to his twin specialisms of music and Egyptology. He was a one-time reviewer for *The Times* and associate editor of the *Musical Times*, as well as

Hon. Secretary of the Egypt Exploration Society. Robert set up the Robert Anderson Research Trust in 1982, which has granted many scholarships to students for short study trips in the UK, particularly to students from Egypt and Eastern Europe. Robert was awarded two honorary doctorates and a professorship. He passed away at the age of eighty-eight in 2015.

Tamar S. Drukker studied at the Hebrew University and completed her PhD at the University of Cambridge. She teaches Hebrew language and literature and Israeli culture at SOAS University of London. Her research interests are modern Hebrew literature, especially in its representation of war and trauma. Among her recent publications are essays on Avigdor Hameiri's prose of the Great War, on Haim Gouri's poetry and on the prose of Aharon Appelfeld.

ACKNOWLEDGEMENTS

This volume would not have been possible without the patient cooperation of several colleagues. I am grateful to all the dedicated contributors who took part in this volume. Mark Weeden deserves special thanks for his encouragement, trust and assistance with the project. Thanks are also due to Professor Caroline Rooney at the University of Kent and Dr Mohammad Moussa at the University of Istanbul Sabbahattin Zaim University in Turkey. Their friendship and positive engagement with the introduction was encouraging and assuring.

Professor Robert Anderson, a scholar of Classics and Egyptology and a contributor to this volume, passed away as I was preparing the book for submission back in 2015. Robert was a dear friend. The warmth of our friendship and our discussions, be they intellectual or social, will always remain important to me. Staying in his house for more than ten years enriched me in more ways than one. Robert passed away at the age of eighty-eight. By then, he had written more than a dozen scholarly works and authored hundreds of book, film, opera and music reviews for a number of publications, in addition to other enormous philanthropic and scholarly undertakings. He served for many years as honorary secretary of the Egypt Exploration Society and was a one-time music reviewer for the *Times* and associate editor of the *Musical Times*. His charitable spirit, generously supporting students from many corners of the earth, particularly from his beloved Egypt, Eastern Europe, Russia and England, marked his indomitable character and dedication to others. I note his contribution to this volume on the love poetry of ancient Egyptian and register my deep gratitude to him with love and respect.

I started writing this book when I was teaching at SOAS and continued while at the University of Westminster, where I am now a senior lecturer in Arabic Language and Culture. Many colleagues from both universities deserve to be appreciated. In particular, I am grateful to my colleagues in the formerly known as the Department of Modern Languages and Cultures at the University of Westminster, now part of the wider School of Humanities.

I always carry feelings of gratitude and warmth towards my old friend Alison Phillips. Alison represents love at its most sincere possibility. Whenever I visited her in her house overlooking the breathtakingly beautiful surroundings of Loch Rannoch in Scotland, I felt the generosity, humility, peace and love that Alison effortlessly exudes. Alison supported me in my education in the UK, and I can never express how immensely grateful and moved I am by her humanity. Equally, I would like to register and reiterate my gratitude to Ursula Pretzlik, her husband and my dear friend Nick Pretzlik, who sadly passed away in 2004 – and also to their son, my dear friend Luke, who passed away in 2014. Alison, Nick and Ursula were indispensable to my education and life here in the UK. Heartfelt thank you.

The last few years afforded me a chance to meet my immediate family members, whether in Gaza or in the diaspora, although not all of them. I did not see most of them for nearly twenty years until I did when I visited my family in Gaza at the end of 2018, due to the restrictions imposed on travel to Gaza since I left Gaza to study at Birzeit University in the West Bank in 1999. Words cannot register how moved I was to see my family, relatives and my birthplace and all the surrounding areas in Gaza/Rafah where I grew up. I regret deeply that I cannot have these encounters regularly and that I am forced to lead an exilic life deprived of the love and warmth of my extended family.

I feel happy and lucky that this volume is on poetry and love, which I would like to extend to my family in Gaza, Palestine. I am confident that a commitment to love, the best of human values, will see all of us through.

And, finally, I would like to express my love to my beloved wife, Maram, and our darling daughter Layla and our newly born son Ahmad. Heaven is always one step closer with you, Layla and Ahmad.

LOVE AND POETRY IN THE MIDDLE EAST
FROM ANTIQUITY TO THE PRESENT

Atef Alshaer

The heartbreak of love sings.

Gibran Khalil Gibran[1]

This desire for interpersonal fusion is the most powerful striving in man. It is the most fundamental passion, it is the force which keeps the human race together, the clan, the family, the society. The failure to achieve it means insanity or destruction – self-destruction or destruction of others. Without love, humanity could not exist for a day.

Eric Fromm[2]

كما تحبُّ تكونُ
As you love, so will you be.

Naguib Mahfouz[3]

Introduction

The Middle East has been a remarkable seat for cultural and political happenings with everlasting consequences. Perhaps less appreciated about this region is its enduring tradition of poetry, and indeed literature more widely, particularly that of love. Such poetry has been central to all Middle Eastern cultures past and present. It is hard to imagine one Middle Eastern country without its stories of love which are threaded into poems and aphorisms, some of which have travelled wide and far to touch and affect other cultures and literary traditions. One significant value of this poetry, and literature more generally, is that it reveals so much about these societies, particularly in relation to their day-to-day life where life matters most essentially. Despite the fact that global, mainly Western, media have often depicted violence and conflict as if it was always intrinsic to the Middle East, the reality of the region and its people is more layered than this crude and reductive depiction. The worldwide historic significance of this region in terms of its achievements, be they literary, philosophical or scientific, outshines any political and societal strife that has plagued this region for far too long. The theme of love in Middle Eastern cultures and literatures has always been significant, suggesting the necessity of love to them in ways that transcend politics in its often oppressive and depressive consequences.

This is not to underestimate the insurmountable challenges of the Middle East, which is beset by internal and external problems. Common to this region is the largely autocratic, and increasingly brutal, regimes which preside over its states and largely vibrant peoples. Moreover, the colonized state of Palestine by Israel with the latter's inhumane attitudes towards the Palestinians and its derisory view of Arabs at large is central to these challenges. More broadly, the Middle East is locked into conflicts involving various Arab countries and other regional powers. Hence, it is only rational for one to conclude that this region has been a hotbed of instability for far too long, also abetted by superpowers such as the United States and Russia and others. The tragedy of the Middle East as far as its violent conflicts and unsafe conditions for reasonable human existence are concerned is real and lamentable. Yet this does not override the equally powerful fact that the Middle Eastern societies are inheritors of living pasts, aspects of which have been repeated and innovated upon in the present, and that they have been resilient, creative and shown much vivacity and an admirable will to life. To quote Caroline Rooney, 'what is significant here is that there is insufficient realisation that the political actors and the political arena of a state cannot automatically be assumed to represent the people as a nation with their national and regional cultures.'[4] This is particularly the case when most, if not all, Middle Eastern nations have been oppressive towards their own citizens, with the latter 'acting as if . . .,'[5] to use Lisa Wedeen's phrase, they are loyal to the state and its leadership. Whereas in reality their lives run at quite a marked distance from the formal and informal apparatus of the state, which is not democratic, and most importantly, it does not provide a safe space for secure citizenry conduct.

Poetry is indeed one of these aspects about the Middle East which has not only survived and reflected various vagaries of the region throughout the ages but also provided a perspective and remained an important existential medium through which lives are lived and relations are consolidated.[6] Practitioners of literature have often delved beneath the rough surface where politics seems to determine the outlook and perception of the Middle East, portraying societies in verse and prose with depth and insight that political coverage and analysis can hardly match. This background can be further explained through a brief history to explain how the medium of poetry developed in the Middle East. It did so from rudimentary beginnings in the ancient plains of Iraq and pharaonic Egypt, which feature prominently in this book as the first civilizations to celebrate human love in verse in the region, and perhaps the world. Ancient Iraq and ancient Egypt are the world's earliest civilizations whose celebrations of love in verse have survived in writing. Writing begins in southern Iraq in largely egalitarian city-states, but the writing down of literature and poetry is first found in the third millennium BC in Iraq, Syria and Egypt, when institutions of kingship are growing up along with archival and school institutions that preserve a written record on clay tablets in cuneiform script or in mortuary contexts with hieroglyphs on stone and papyrus. Through the explosion of written culture in the earlier second millennium BC centred around Babylon in ancient Iraq, considerably more of the rich poetic record is preserved, as also happened in Middle and then New Kingdom Egypt. Later, in the first millennium BC, we find the beginnings of Empires as one might recognise them today in Assyria, Babylon and then Persia, with their large archives and libraries where knowledge was gathered and curated.[7] In the shadow of these states there developed the Jewish tradition, which officially inaugurated the march of monotheistic creeds, and love poems from that tradition reflect clearly the importance of love poetry in speaking of and for human relations in relation to human beings themselves and to God. Perhaps most significantly, the Islamic tradition, following on from the Christian tradition, spawned a new era of love poetry in the region, as new concepts were introduced, which expanded upon earlier concepts underpinning human relations, including love.

It is with the Arab tradition in pre-Islamic time and later on with the expansion of the Islamic faith and empire that we detect the ascendance of poetry as a medium of esteem and illumination, notwithstanding the fact that poetry witnessed what amounts to suspension in the early years of Islamic faith. Islam, through the revelation of Prophet Mohammad, introduced and emphasized the prose of the Qur'an and the sayings of Prophet Mohammad as the foundational sources and texts of the Islamic faith, and side-lined poetry. While Islam did not ban poetry per se, it effectively cast a shadow over its worthiness and seriousness. However, it did not take long for this to change when the Umayyad Empire (661–750), with its seat in Damascus, assumed power, and poetry regained its former glory as an unstoppable force of expression, prestige and revelation in its own right. The Umayyad era gave way to another extraordinarily rich poetic tradition during the Abbasid era (750–1258), where love poetry figured prominently among the literary themes.[8] In particular, these two significant periods ushered in new genres of love poetry, ranging from the pure and unconsummated-based love poetry to the lewd and flagrant, linking with and echoing pre-Islamic genres, as well as advancing on them. The significance of this poetry here is that it has for several centuries served as the standard and background for other poetic and literary traditions, influenced by the then expanding Islamic empire.

Love stories such Majnun Layla, which proliferated in Arabia in the seventh century, spread to Persian poetry and later to the Mughal Empire of India, acquiring new dimensions and features in each of these traditions. Therefore, what can be described as the expansion of poetry beyond the confines of the Arabian Peninsula is concomitant with the spread of Islam in these areas. To this end, the case of Arabic poetry in general is mainly linked to three principal new paradigm shifts in what came to be known later in the nineteenth century as 'the Middle East',[9] including Turkey and Iran: the spread of Islam, the Arabization process which would subsequently underpin the formation of the Arab world, and the burgeoning of philosophy and poetry in the world of Islam within new cultures beyond Arabia where Islam originated. These later fields were also enthusiastically practised in regions which did not adopt Arabic per se but embraced the cultural products of Arabic in their cultures and languages, including Persian, Hindi and later on Ottoman and Urdu languages, among others.

With the Ottoman Empire, the influence of Arabic poetry and the significance it once held over several cultures faded. The Ottoman Empire represented the first time that Arabic was not the main language through which an entire empire communicated and celebrated its cultural achievements. Although the Ottoman Empire adopted the Arabic script, Ottoman Turkish (Osmanlica) as a language was also privileged, and Islam itself naturally took new Ottoman characteristics, which ultimately marginalized Arabic, albeit perhaps unintentionally. Arabic was still an esteemed language within the empire by virtue of its Islamic association, but it was no longer the central language in which people, such as authors from Persian and Turkic origins, aspired to write. In fact, writers from Persian backgrounds such as Saadi (1210–91) and Hafiz (1315–90) wrote almost exclusively in Persian and became celebrated poets in Persia, innovating upon an already existing rich canon of love and worldly poetry in Farsi, unlike in previous periods when many authors from Persian origins wrote also in Arabic, such as Ibn Sina (Avicenna, 980–1037), al-Ghāzālī (1058–37) and Rumi (1207–73) and others. Arabic ceased to be the lingua franca of the Islamic world, as it once was, even though many lexical items and expressions entered most of the languages that came into contact with Islamic cultures. Therefore, it is appropriate to refer to an epistemological and cultural rupture during the Ottoman Empire within Islamic culture as once held together by Arabic as the lingua franca of the region.[10]

Nonetheless, nothing of what has been written so far can be said in the absolute and without qualification of some sort. All Islamic regions, even if they did not adopt Arabic as their language or script, still revered Arabic and embedded the Arabic Qur'an in the fabric of their languages and literary traditions. It is also the case that all these languages, Arabic, Persian and Turkish, influenced and borrowed from each other; and it was not all one-way influence towards Arabic, although the latter was the main language of the Islamic faith. Yet, it is equally true that the Ottoman Empire represented a new world order with all that it entails in terms of projecting its might and culture without the literary package of earlier cultures over which it now presided.

It is only in the nineteenth century with the resurgence of Arab and other nationalisms that Arabic, Persian, Turkish and other poetries started to reassert themselves, ushering in a new period for poetry in this diverse as well as similar region. This poetry is decidedly embossed within the new emerging nationalist sentiments along clearly demarcated ethnic lines, Arab, Turkish and Persian, among others. To this end, the collapse of the Ottoman Empire represented and ended the last vestige of tangible unity as buttressed by the Islamic faith as a spiritual as well as political entity, ending the age of grand Islamic Empires. Nationalism coloured every aspect of life in these societies, although certain figures and entities continued to long for a return to a unified Islamic frame of governance as embodied in the Caliphate system. Yet interestingly, although Turkish nationalism pivoted westwards towards Europe to launch its modern itself, these nationalisms, Arab, Turkish and Persian, continued to appeal to their past achievements and poetic traditions. They revived them in the modern period, but each in light of their literary past, which happened to have crisscrossed with Islamic literary traditions, which Arabic mainly represented. These nationalisms, as much as they were at times antagonistic to each other, still appealed to allegedly discreet pasts in divergent as well as convergent ways. For indeed, there have never been discreet Arab or Persian or Turkish cultures, impervious to the surrounding cultures. These cultures have more often than not been related and have influenced each other, and particularly so after the rise of Islam. Yet, nationalism in the modern period from the nineteenth century onwards made them look to their pasts as if they were discreet and delinked from each other. Meanwhile, it is noteworthy that such a focus on nationalism as the foreground of the modern nation state in the Middle East is not uncommon among what Anderson has already called in his celebrated phrase 'imagined communities', as facilitated by print capitalism.[11]

Most importantly, this period witnessed the use of Western literary motifs inspired by Western influences in each of the said poetic traditions. This took place directly or indirectly, as most of the contemporary Middle Eastern nations were colonized by the British or French Empires. Arabic ceased to be significant or majorly relevant beyond the religious spheres for societies such as the modern Turkish and later Iranian society. All these traditions independently looked to advancements in philosophy, literature and psychology and other related fields in the West for inspiration to their writings. This is not the first time that these cultures were influenced by Western traditions, as earlier Greek and Latin sources also inspired several Arabic writings. But this period in terms of political power was decidedly European, and later on also American, both influencing most cultures in the world. Thus, as the old world of Islam made modern Europe, modern Europe made the modern world; in that, neither could be what it is today, for good or ill, without the other. This latter point would take much time to elucidate, but suffice to register the point that in medieval times as Europe fell to forces of obscurantism and sorcery, shunning science, philosophy and rational thought generally, it was Arab and Persian luminaries who kept the flame of rational thought alive, translating earlier documents from Greek and also advancing upon them. These developments were later picked up by Western thinkers, adopting scientific methods employed in the Muslim world and advancing upon them as well; thus, the modern world of Europe was established, leading to no less than a worldwide revolution in literature, science and philosophy. The European revolution in the world of literature is particularly relevant in relation to the development of the novel. This form, although not entirely new to the Middle East as classical Arabic literature abounds with examples of fine episodic fictional writings and tales, arguably embryonic to the European novel, still developed and reached unprecedented heights under largely Western aegis. Subsequently, it became a prominent literary form in various languages and in the culture of the Middle East, to the point where poetry seems to occupy a second-best literary form compared to where it was before.

As far as poetry is concerned, the influence of Arabic on other Middle Eastern languages is clear, but also on European poetry and literature more broadly. Suffice to refer to the well-known phenomenon of ghazal poetry, these pre-Islamic love poems from the Arabian Peninsula that travelled wide and far in world cultures. Bauer and Neuwirth make the point succinctly, albeit perhaps timidly, 'due to extensive migration it spread over a vast geographical space of multiple literary languages from Arabic it migrated via Persian into Turkish and the languages of India, in Spain into Hebrew via Arabic and finally, transmitted via Persian models, it even emerged in the poetic canon of German literature'.[12,]

Therefore, to reiterate an earlier point, poetry has served as a reservoir of evocative knowledge with widespread appreciation across Middle Eastern cultures. Here poetry can be said to be 'love's closest language',[13] as it provides an abiding source of intimacy, togetherness, equality and knowledge, making it suitable to be adopted and shared; its latent energy speaks to the human spirit which more often than not seeks a sublime form of expression to manifest it. Poetry expresses the intimate universality of love as an essential sentiment that binds and links people to each other as underlined initially by that force of attraction and togetherness that both love and poetry symbolize. The survival and popularity of poetry in Middle Eastern cultures for so many centuries serve an unquestionable testament to how powerful and influential a medium it has been, as well as how original and timeless that it has travelled between cultures to signify connectedness within culture and among all cultures.[14] Something that started in ancient Iraq and Egypt almost 5,000 years ago could travel, develop and move people to this day[15] so as to be recited in squares of revolutions, in people's houses, in daily conversations, in prison cells, literary forums and places of education, suggest that neither love nor poetry can part ways with each other, for wherever love exits poetry exists as well. They both stem from the same root, namely the human need for intimate expression and for togetherness. Yet, it should be said that neither love nor poetry is free of limitation. By their very nature, they are urges of instinct and cultivations of cultural revelation at their best and worst manifestations as well. The Lebanese poet Gibran Khalil Gibran gives an insightful definition of love, which could as well apply to poetry. For Gibran, love is 'an awakening that has death and life, that generates a dream stranger than life, and deeper than death'.[16]

Having painted in rather broad brushes the development of love poetry in the Middle East and its intersection with political and societal issues, it is time to highlight the spirit and structure of this book. The book analyses poetry in various ancient and contemporary languages of the Middle East, including Akkadian, Sumerian, ancient Egyptian, Classical and Modern Standard Arabic, Persian, Hebrew, Turkish and Kurdish. The book also includes literary materials that have been discovered and highlighted for the first time. With the theme of love in perspective, it covers the region from its early beginnings, from the third millennium BC on to the twenty-first century. Each of these languages is represented through one or two chapters, covering and exploring the theme of love in their poetry. The poetic materials from ancient languages that survive today, namely Arabic, Persian, Hebrew, Turkish and Kurdish, are studied with a focus on the present but include references to the past. The chapters reflect the discursive evolution of the theme of love and the sensibilities, styles and techniques used to convey it. The ingenious love poems in ancient poetry give way to complex and varied reflection of human sentiments in the medieval languages; and the modern period is further reflective of the historical resonance of love and the complexities and nuances of present times.

By shedding light on love and interpreting its embeddedness and symbolism in human relations, the book demonstrates the perennial energy of love and its associations with universal and cultural-specific dimensions. To this end, the chapters project similar conversations and cross-fertilization of invocations and manners of expressions between various and interrelated traditions. The poetic materials studied in the book show the shared and sometimes subjective concerns and poetic forms of love stories, thus demonstrating the unity of the human psyche when faced with universal or extreme situations.[17] Each literary tradition shows its own specific aspects and manners of versing, which form part of the broader human story and history of love.

This volume of love poetry from Middle Eastern literature is representative but not exhaustive. The historically broad sweep of the book, starting with ancient poetry from today's Iraq and Egypt to today's Palestine, Turkey, Iran and Kurdistan and others, is in keeping with the intention of the book to show the long pervasiveness of love as a preoccupation of the region. There are poetic materials yet to be studied and mined for further information and insights. Except for general references and one chapter on divine love (Chapter 5), contributors to this book focused on heterosexual love; whereas there are interesting worthwhile materials in Middle Eastern literatures, which cover the spectrum of love beyond that of man and woman.[18] Though there has been a growing body of literature on love in general, this literature remains largely speculative and didactic. This demonstrates the difficulty of theorizing love. Indeed, to define love in any strict sense is to define life, a task which will always remain tentative and incomplete. There are as many forms and experiences of love as there are human beings and relations between them. Whether one speaks of romantic love, love for friends and associates or universal love, these are general patterns that capture but by no means entirely cover it and its variations. Meanwhile, poets and artists remain the original dissectors of the human heart, soul and imagination with their profound access to insight from the wellspring of emotions and desires. This applies to poets and artists of the past and today.

Furthermore, this book is chronologically arranged. It begins with a chapter on Akkadian poetry. Mark Weeden opens with an illuminating explanation of the nature of love poetry and the social construction that underpins the understanding of love and the making of love poetry in general. This is followed by a discussion of the genre of love poetry in Akkadian, which is limited when compared with other languages such as Arabic and Persian. Weeden identifies the Akkadian term '*Irtum*', which he translates as 'breast (-song)', as a principal term standing for love songs, although its original application is not clear. Weeden makes a preliminary division of love poems into three categories:

(1) poetic spells of love magic, which are designed to have an effect on a beloved as an object of desire; (2) cultic poems, belonging to the type of so-called 'divine love lyrics' which appear to be articulated by divine beings or their human representatives as part of state ritual; (3) personal or so-called 'secular' love poetry, which appears to have none of the above magical or divine aspects.

However, he finds the applicability of these modern divisions to be somewhat permeable.

Weeden's astutely researched chapter is followed by one from the great scholar of Babylonian Studies, Andrew George, which offers a focused study of a newly discovered poem from the early second millennium BC. Therein an adolescent young Babylonian girl in ancient Mesopotamia is attempting to win the love of a shepherd lad, casting a magical spell on him through incantation. Through this ancient poem, which, as explained by the scholar, is echoed in modern Western popular songs, George shows how the adolescent girl is 'a very ancient example of an archetypal character that today populates popular song but is perhaps found universally in human culture'.

Another chapter from the ancient world is presented by the extraordinary Egyptologist Robert Anderson who, to my profound regret, passed away as I was writing this chapter. Robert Anderson takes us on a journey into ancient Egyptian love poetry. He shows how the aristocracy practised love and how that love was memorialized in poetry on tombs and spectacular monuments built to honour a beloved and exalt her name. The expressions of love in ancient Egyptian can be found in what Anderson identifies as the *Pyramid Texts*. These, according to the scholar, are 'inscribed on pyramid walls from the Fifth to the Sixth Dynasties, based on ideas probably current from very ancient times, to ease the passage of the dead king to the abode of the gods in the heavens above'. Anderson concludes by making the link between ancient Egyptian poetry and that of love poetry in the Old Testament, particularly as manifested in the *Song of Songs*. The rich metaphors and depth of the love portrayal in the Old Testament contrast with the terse and concise and ultimately limited depiction of love in ancient Egyptian, but the sensuous dimensions of love are rendered exquisitely in both traditions.

In her chapter, Tamar S. Drukker, SOAS's senior lecturer of Jewish Studies, reflects on Israeli Jewish poets who relate their love poems to the Old Testament and the story of Rachel and Jacob, the first love tale in the Hebrew tradition. That love story which deals with love at first sight, anticipation, fulfilment and tragedy offers many lessons in love and human relations in general to several poets. Drukker demonstrates the mutations that the image of Rachel and the story in question have undergone in modern Israeli poetry. Thus, while the ancient Hebrew model is sought, 'it is also questioned and subverted'.

The following chapter by Atef Alshaer explains the conceptual shift underpinning the writing of love poetry between the pre-Islamic and Islamic periods. It particularly focuses on the ʿUdhrī poets with their devoted love for women and its tragic twists and end. Yet, instead of explaining this tragedy in psychological terms, Alshaer focuses on how their moving poetry represents a conversation with Islam and the Islamic norms of society. In fact, one of the cardinal premises of this poetry is the rejection of the lover by the tribe or the father of the beloved, not the beloved herself. In this historical context, the emerging community of Muslims was struggling with tribal structures and coming to grips with the persisting social inequality sanctioned by Islam. To this end, the ʿUdhrī poets, particularly Majnūn Layla and Jamīl Buthaina of the Umayyad eighth century who had continuously inspired poets from the Persian, Turkish and Kurdish traditions, are perhaps among the first (romantic) dissenters and revolutionaries of Islam who inspired Sufi poets and other thinkers. They nuanced our understanding of the divine and its relation to human beings. They are pioneers in practising the *adāb*, manners of conversation with the principal sources of Islam, including the Qur'an and the *Ḥadīth* tradition. Through subversion and the psychological understanding rooted in their experiences as genuine lovers, they enlarged the uses and meanings of Islam. These are amenable to continuous revisions, shift in meanings and changes, allowing religion to converse with other points in human history and affect changes.

Setting the scene for poetry in the classical period, Huma Baig meticulously analyses two texts on love from the Arabic and Persian traditions. Both texts, al-Ghāzālī's *The Alchemy of Happiness* and Rumi's *Mathnawi*, are canonical texts on love in the traditions in questions that emerged in the twelfth and thirteenth century, respectively. The writings of those authors have continuously exerted far-reaching influence on poets and writers from the East and West; and they continue to be consulted, debated and revered. Both al-Ghāzālī and Rumi are concerned to establish unity with and experience the divine. Although their approaches to this unity differ, they are both in dialogue with an Islamic tradition expanding and developing as they practise and think through the lens of human love and the ultimate grace that resides in the love and the realization of God. For al-Ghāzālī, the path to God is paved with rationality and knowledge and is assured through worship and submission. For Rumi, God is embedded in the very relations of people; and when love reigns between them, God is present and exalted; God is present in every moment of the present and not only in the future as al-Ghāzālī implies. For Rumi, the way to love is physically and spiritually experienced, where the human becomes a willing atom of love in the orbit of divine presence filled with longing and sensual joys. Thus, as Huma writes, 'love of God can be seen through many avenues: through knowledge, through longing, through worship and through a perfected human.'

In her chapter, Paniz Musawi shows the shortcoming of psychoanalytic interpretations in the context of her study of two illustrious twentieth-century poets of Iran, namely Ahmad Shamlu and Farrokhzad. Both poets offer subverted and

Chapter 1

POWER-PLAYS

TYPES OF LOVER AND TYPES OF LOVE IN AKKADIAN FROM THE THIRD AND SECOND MILLENNIA BC*

Mark Weeden

Love and love poetry: Gender and convention, genre and reality

There seems to be something self-contradictory about the very notion of love poetry. The poet Adrienne Rich comments on the inherent dissonance between the lived and the verbalized that is involved in writing love poetry at all in her 1978 collection of poems, *The Dream of a Common Language*:

> What kind of beast would turn its life into words?
> What atonement is all this about?
> – and yet, writing words like these, I'm also living.
> Is all this close to the wolverine's howled signals
> that modulated cantata of the wild?
> or when away from you I try to create you in words,
> am I simply using you, like a river or a war?[1]

This dichotomy of the direct experience of intimacy between humans as against the practice of expressing it in words is expanded during the rest of the poem to encompass other examples of the relationship between verbal art and wordless action, which form a direct chain to the most pressing questions of political existence. The love relationship presents the focus where this thought is most immediately and clearly expressed. Rich's poem triumphantly and bitterly meshes the personal and the universal leaving us feeling emotionally decompressed. The worry is that to write about someone, a beloved, in the first place is to turn that person into an object, to deny ourselves the possibility of autonomy. When talking about love and what it means to write poetry about it, contrary to the intuitive and socially dominant view that it is a purely personal and private affair, we find ourselves very quickly in the realm of the social and political. This is not surprising: we are talking about relationships between human beings.

The cultural critic Roland Barthes in his work *A Lover's Discourse* felt that he was unable to offer an analysis of love as a form of cultural activity; he was only able to give his own personal examples of the discourse or discourses associated with it.[2] The resulting late-night paranoias and internal monologues frequently revolve around the

6   For more on this, see Atef Alshaer, *Poetry and Politics in the Modern Arab World* (London: Hurst Publishers & Co, 2016).
7   I am grateful to Mark Weeden for the information and explanation provided in this paragraph concerning the development of writing and poetry tradition in the ancient world of Iraq and Egypt (personal communication, 27 July 2021).
8   See Stefan Sperl, *Introduction: Classical Traditions and Modern Meanings* (Leiden: Brill, 1996), 1–15.
9   The term 'Middle East' is fraught with contention, as it was coined and propagated by colonialists, and often with orientalist overtones to justify conquest and imperial hegemony. Yet, it has become a firmly established construct denoting the Arab World, Iran and Turkey, in particular. Be that as it may, it is still worthwhile to quote Karen Culcasi's instructive reference concerning the term 'Middle East': 'although ambiguity about what constitutes the region certainly exists, and many atlases and scholars recognize that there is no clear definition of the region . . . the varied definitions and delineations used to make this series of summary maps indicate that the region does indeed exist.' See Karen Culcasi, 'Constructing and Naturalizing the Middle East, Geographical Review', *American Geographical Society* 100, no. 4 (October 2010): 538–97, 589.
10 For a more comprehensive view of the Ottoman Empire, see Caroline Finkel, *Osman's Dream: The Story of the Ottoman Empire 1300–1932* (London: John Murray, 2005).
11 Benedict Anderson, *Imagined Communities* (London: Verso Books, 1991).
12 Though this volume refers to many love poems which are part of the tradition of Middle Eastern ghazal poetry, it will not discuss them chronologically. This genre has been studied relatively well. The purpose of this volume is to offer examples from various Middle Eastern languages so as to draw attention to the richness and depth of love as a theme in Middle Eastern poetry and culture more broadly. Nonetheless, it is worth highlighting that ghazal poetry began in the fifth century in Arabic within the context of the poly-thematic poems in Arabia which were common then. Subsequently, the ghazal as independent love poems emerged and flourished during the Umayyad period. Yet, as Bauer and Neuwirth write, 'the most important step in the spread of the ghazal was unquestionably that from Arabic into Persian, for not only did many of the most important poets write in this language, but, furthermore, it was mainly through Persian literature that the ghazal was brought into other language areas.' Thomas Bauer and Angelica Neuwirth, *Introduction: Ghazal as World Literature, Transformation of a Literary Genre: Why the Ghazal?* (Leiden: Verlago, 1996), 14; Bauer and Neuwirth, *Introduction*, 9.
13 This phrase is taken from Caroline Rooney's personal correspondence with me, 16 November 2020.
14 For further literature, see Johan Christoph Bürgel, 'Theories About Love: How Love Manifests in Islamic Culture', in *Art &Thought: Fikrun Wa Fann*, ed. W. Stefan (Goethe-Institute, e.V, no. 86 (11), August–October, 2007), 23.
15 See also an interesting article on the modern manifestation of love in the 'Middle East: Love in the Middle East: Contradictions of Romance in the Facebook World', by Roger Friedland, Janet Afray, Paolo Gardinali and Cambria Naslund, in *Critical Research on Religion* 4, no. 3 (2016): 229–58.
16 In Sherfan, *Khalil Gibran*, 36.
17 See Stefan Sperl, '"O City Set Up Thy Lamen": Poetic Responses to the Trauma of War', in *Poetry and Warfare in the Middle East*, ed. H. Kennedy (London: I.B. Tauris, 2013), 1–39.
18 There are other important love poems which are not based on heterosexual relations. The example of the ninth-century poet Abu Nuwas is usually conjured up in contexts of homoerotic sexual love in Middle Eastern poetry. He was the most versatile in terms of love poetry. For a good treatment of his love poetry, see Jakkō Hameen-Antilla, 'Abu Nuwas and Ghazal as a Genre', in *Ghazal as World Literature, Transformations of a Literary Genre*, ed. Thomas Bauer and Angelika Neuwirth (Baden: Ergon Verlag, 2005), 87–107.

and the Palestinian poet Mahmoud Darwish. Alshaer focuses on the modernist sensibility with which their poetry of love is marked and the sociopolitical challenges of the Arab world and the Arab-Israeli conflict inflicting the particular instances and views of love. Within the newly emerging free verse Arabic poetry, the chapter demonstrates how the poetry of Nizar Qabbani emphasized and celebrated love in its physical aspects, ushering in a sexual revolution and sensibility so far suppressed – scantily referenced in modern Arabic poetry. If Nizar Qabbani pioneered the sensationalizing of love poetry reinforcing the need for openness in human relations and sincerity in expressing them, Mahmoud Darwish expressed love to his first Israeli Jewish girlfriend in an exquisite way that yet showed the tensions and dilemmas of love borne within and amidst conflict. Darwish's later reflection on love is philosophically minded, imbued with sensual and lyrical delight and expansiveness. The love poetry at hand is postmodernist in showing the agency of lovers and the inevitability, as well as fluidity of love. This love is negotiated through the concerns of sociopolitical dynamics, as well as human thought and desires. Yet love remains infinite, unparalleled in its power to conjure up insight and to incite change. In this respect, love is superior to death in its grip and endlessness. Here, love can be viewed as a felt method which entails constructive and critical dimensions, sacred and secular terrains, along a continuum of sentimentality intended to engage and speak to the intricacies of the human heart.

In conclusion, the ten chapters contained within this book offer a fresh way of looking at the Middle East and its historic and cultural wealth through the common sentiment of love that unites all human beings. Love reveals human nature in its visceral construction and the human capacity for endurance and transcendence at their deepest. The readers can trace, compare and juxtapose old texts with new ones and be exposed to a variety of approaches and styles concerning the analysis of love literature from the Middle East. They can also compare these texts and methods with other literary materials familiar to them from their languages and cultures. In addition to contributing to our knowledge and understanding of love and poetry, such scholarly and creative endeavours, as sketched here, can expand and emphasize our common humanity to which love in all its shades and variations is central. It is, thus, hoped that this book addresses the lacuna on Middle Eastern love literature and inspires further studies on love, this ultimate jewel among all sentiments.

Notes

1   Gibran Khalil Gibran in Andrew Dib Sherfan, *Khalil Gibran: The Nature of Love* (New York: Philosophy Library, 1971).
2   Eric Fromm, 'The Art of Loving: The Theory of Love', in *Art & Thought: Fikrun Wa Fann*, ed. Stefan (Goethe-Institute, e.V, no. 86 (11), August–October, 2007), 7.
3   Naguib Mafouz, *Aṣdā' al-Dhākkirah al-Dhātiyyah* (Egypt: Dār al-Shrouq, 2006), 173.
4   Personal communication with Caroline Rooney as part of her response and reading to this introduction, 16 November 2020.
5   Lisa Weeden, *Ambiguities of Domination: Politics, Rhetoric, and Symbols in Contemporary Syria* (Chicago: Chicago University Press, 1999), 6.

extended understanding of the tradition of Persian love poetry. They use the iconic story of Majnūn Layla, which was developed by Nizami in the twelfth century, from the original Arabic that existed since the eighth century to extend the notion/s of madness and its association with obsessive love. Thus, Farrokhzad becomes the Majnūnah, the mad woman whose madness is invested in the writing of love poetry, and poetry in general; and her love extends to include other human links as symbolized by the mother, son and other bonds. The subject of madness is not only the human beloved but also an activity with psychological consequences endowed with revelation, beauty and agency, as is poetry in the case of the renowned Iranian poet Farrokhzad. Musawi presents a critically sophisticated understanding of the Persian and indeed Islamic tradition of love poetry as it is used in the new Iranian love poetry and best exemplified by the two poets in question.

Laurent Mignon's chapter, 'Unveiling Desire: Love in Modern Turkish Poetry', shows the effects of the post-*Tanzimat* era of Turkish literature since the twentieth century on literature and sensibility in general. At that time, a transformation took place which changed the soul of Turkish poetry from one steeped in homoeroticism and mysticism to one brimming with questioning and sensuality that asserts the independence of lovers and celebrates heterosexual love. The important innovative Turkish poets demonstrate the change that Turkish poetry underwent in the nineteenth and twentieth century, namely in the writings of Yahya Kemal, Nâzım Hikmet, Orhan Veli and Cemal Sureya. Each of those poets introduced and added novel dimensions to Turkish poetry, particularly with the founding of the new state in 1923 and the monumental cultural and political changes that took place concomitantly. The new poetry of love in Turkey presents a realistic and innovative portrayal of love as underpinned by the subjective experience of the poets themselves and social forces they were engaging in their poetry, defined by modernist attitudes with regard to form and the content. In the new poetry, the poets invoke the independence of the beloved and the extension of love to humanity, as well as the elevation of ordinary love with its sexual bliss and the warmth of human bonds that materialize and concretize human existence. As Mignon writes, 'each of those poets was crossing lines, challenging the official legality or the wished-for legalities of others'.

Mariwan Kanie explains the transformation in the love poetry of Kurdish literature of the twentieth century, as seen through the lenses of the *'ashiq* (lover or adorer), the *ma'shuq* (beloved) and *'ishq* (adoration) by looking at the works of three Kurdish poets from the nineteenth century, namely Nali (1797–1855), Salim (1800–66) and Kurdi (1809–49). The three learned poets came from the area of Sulaymaniyah in today's northern Iraq. They were influenced by the famed Ghazal love poetry in the Persian tradition and benefitted from the Sufi tradition; but their poetry was secularized and broadened in order to take pride in their place, among the poetry of the big languages of the regions, Arabic, Turkish and Persian. The poets were mostly influenced by the latter tradition; and their poetry was concerned with human love and the beloved was often a woman. Unlike the Sufis who infused their poetry with religious symbolism blurring the lines between human and divine love, 'the experience of love in the Kurdish *ghazal* poetry in the nineteenth century', as Kanie suggests, 'has a stronger secular dimension compared to Sufi poetry, while a spiritual interpretation of the experience of love in this poetry is still possible.'

The last chapter by Atef Alshaer studies the love poetry of two iconic Arab poets in the second half of the twentieth century, namely the Syrian poet Nizar Qabbani insecurities that are concomitant with making oneself vulnerable to another person. They are, I would imagine, recognizable to most adult humans at least in the Western world during the late twentieth to early twenty-first centuries of the modern era at the same time as being disturbingly personal. Disturbing because the almost solipsistic nature of the discourse seems to be unassimilable, by definition inimitable, even catatonic. Yet it concurrently insists on claiming to possess universal comprehensibility.

Indeed, Barthes manages to situate even the most personal and self-affirming aspects of the discourse of love within the context of a series of patterns of behaviour, models for being in love, which condition and define our experience of the phenomenon, in his own case mainly constituted by the books he has read and the conversations he has had with his friends.[3] Similar to his view of text as a tissue of previously spoken and written fragments defying a single authorial point of origin, so the experience of love itself becomes a re-living and repeat with variation of what others do or have done in the same situation, only identifiable as such due to its public cultural anatomy, which Barthes makes explicit and lays bare in agonizing detail.[4]

The introduction of the notion of 'performativity' into the field of gender studies by Judith Butler, the idea backed by ethnographic research that our sexual identities consist of learned and repeatedly rehearsed roles rather than essential categories, appears to relate in an interesting way to Barthes's presentation of the discourse of the lover, whatever his or her sexuality.[5] Love may be inscribed and expressed in gender terms as much as by means of many other patterns or clusters of characteristics that can be used to describe human beings, but gender and its entanglement with power remain a crucial feature of love poetry. Lauren Berlant makes a certain type of heterosexual love into the affective correlate of the repeated rehearsal of gender roles, returning again and again to the same ritualized power-complexes, and suggests its function as an important aspect of social cohesion, the reproduction of a particular way of life entailing the exclusion of other sexual possibilities.[6] The pivotal role played by emotional life in society and politics that Berlant outlines has paved the way for a burgeoning field of studies in the relationship between love poetry and political culture.[7]

Between the claimed but patently self-negated immediacy of written love discourse and the ritualized cultural form that love practice takes in society, love poetry forms a fascinating lens through which to reflect on the values and hierarchies that cultural identity is constructed around, despite itself being the verbal art form perhaps most enmeshed in apparently artificial, traditional convention. Modern scholarship on republican and early imperial Roman love poetry, for example, has addressed the degree of 'reality' that can be accorded to the world of experience depicted in the poems, without a definitive decision on the issue being likely to be achieved or even being desirable.[8] The discussion has been concerned with the extent to which particular poetic tropes and figures, for example, the lover dominated and enslaved by his beloved, can be ascribed to modes of living of the period or to participation in the type of discourse that is love poetry. The particular relationship of subservience to the beloved which was cultivated by the Roman authors Propertius and Tibullus in their poems, for example, not only had resonance within and was defined by the world of poetry, but it marked a clear area of social space in their material lives, which were themselves informed by their literary experience. The question of power and its negotiation, whether interpersonal or social, in a literary fantasy or a political reality, was and is of significance in discussing the literary form that is love poetry.

The above-mentioned considerations are of importance in my view when considering some of the love poetry of the third and second millennia BC from ancient Iraq. Love poems, thus the thesis behind my approach, present the lover as participating in and helping to form a literary role that is framed as part of a hierarchical social, religious and political system. The lover is cast in an archetypal role, which he or she shares with divine figures who have typified it, whose worship is constituted by rituals celebrating it, and figures of authority, who similarly play or inhabit that role. Royal figures are mentioned relatively frequently in the transmitted love literature we have, acting as an index, thus this interpretation, for the social performative context of the poetry. Lovers play roles throughout Akkadian love poetry, and those roles involve positioning the lover in various relations of power, whether aggressive, submissive or mutual, to the beloved, to the social order and to the divine world.

Defining genre then and now

Akkadian love poetry is so rare a literary form that specimens of it have occasionally been heralded as new genres in and of themselves.[9] For this reason we should pause to think a little about what we mean when we talk of genre. Literary genre is a concept defining the range of expectations that the consumer of literature might form of a piece of work due to its subject matter, linguistic register or formal criteria such as metre or verse structure. Literary theory has reserved some criticism for this concept.[10] Certainly, literary genres are not hermetically sealed boxes of characteristics, but it is difficult to imagine approaching literature without making some generic classifications on the basis of what one has already experienced of text.[11] Nowadays, there are mainly formal categories such as tragedy, comedy, epic, lyric, novel; mainly content-related ones such as fiction, fantasy, romance, horror, science-fiction; mainly situational ones such as place or purpose of performance, the places and times where one would expect to encounter certain types of art, related to the function for which verbal art is used in a society. Furthermore, genre is intimately bound up with the notion of character and stereotype, again to be understood as little more than a set of expectations that are associated with a particular type of literary figure in a specific genre: the hero in an epic, the fool in a farce, the lover in a lyric poem, for some obvious examples.

Often it might appear that genres, their sub-genres and indeed super-ordinate categories or 'super-genres' only exist as imaginary models to be broken and subverted, a standard which is most clearly defined in the negative.[12] Any account of genre has to be able to encompass its flexibility, to take account of aspects such as genre-subversion, genre-bending and genre-enrichment, to use some recent and not so recent terminology.[13] There is also a distinction between the genre rules that are adopted or broken by the author of a work and those that are projected onto it during its reception and consumption, which may in different periods be entirely varied.[14] The main prerequisite for identifying the expectations which the use of a particular genre element might be expected to awake in a recipient, sometimes referred to as the text's 'genre ideology', is that we have access to enough samples of literary works that belong to the same category as well as to information about the cultural context in which they were produced or consumed. In the case of modern poetry this is not such a problem because we assume, often wrongly and arrogantly, that we inhabit what is basically the same world of experience as the author. When discussing pre-modern poetry, we are confronted at first sight by a more alien world, one that needs to be carefully explored before we can pretend to feel at home in it.

There are a number of methods for identifying genres in pre-modern literature. First, we can research the specific cultural context in which the literary work was supposed to be consumed. This does not have to be a historical task requiring a large amount of reconstruction, although this process is of course important. Often we can obtain a basic orientation by examining the material conditions of use and transmission, particularly if the works are attached to archaeological artefacts, be they inscriptions or manuscripts, which have their own history and context. We can pay attention to the terminological divisions and categories made by other ancient texts, which frequently themselves need to be decoded and interpreted through careful analysis of use-context. Then we can observe regularities in structure, lexicon, style or themes that seem to occur in a particular type of literature. Clearly, however, the cognitive process of dividing pre-modern literary data into types in the first place is ultimately rooted in our own modern experience of literature, however much we may try to impose controls and limit the variables on our judgements.

This is, at the same time, an important caveat to be remembered when we try to approach or understand pre-modern literature: investigating the contemporary meaning of a work is inherently connected with the attempt to understand ourselves, whoever we may be. With pre-modern love poetry, we are dealing with a literary genre or set of related genres to which we have no direct access. Yet studies of genre and convention in pre-modern love poetry have thrived due to the fact that they have proven relatively easy to identify. In the case of Roman, ancient Greek or medieval Arabic, Persian or Turkish love poetry, this is mainly because we have reasonably large numbers of samples with which to work as well as native and contemporary traditions if not of literary criticism then at least of associated disciplines such as rhetoric and grammar.[15]

The poets themselves in these later traditions are also sometimes explicit about the genre definitions they use, such as the Roman poet Ovid who tells us he was preparing to write a military epic in hexameters when Cupid removed a metrical foot from his second line and turned it into an elegiac couplet, the metre of love poetry.[16] Closer to ancient Iraq geographically, in early Arabic poetry the strict application of formal rules of language, metre and accompanying themes from the earliest attested examples indicates awareness of genre categories.[17] This was borne out when medieval Arab theoreticians in the early ninth century AD/third century AH started to classify poems according to the intentions of their poets, as being part of a concrete communicative context. The term used is ġaraḍ, plural aġrāḍ, 'aim, purpose', one of the most usual equivalents to the Western category of 'genre' in Arabic literary theory, with a focus on dynamic intention in a concrete situation rather than classifying an item as belonging to a category.[18] One of the basic genres from the beginning of Arabic poetry is the nasīb, the love poem, frequently lamenting a lost love and emphasizing separation from the beloved. For Akkadian love poetry the situation is quite different. Not only do we have very little in the way of explicitly theoretical works that write about literature, which does not mean that they did not exist orally, we also have very little poetry that can be assembled under the heading of the love poem.[19]

Akkadian and Akkadian love poetry: Problems of definition

The Akkadian language was written in the cuneiform script in ancient Iraq and Syria between around 2500 BC as far as the first century AD. At first, it was written largely logographically using Sumerian word-signs at sites such as Tell Abu Ṣalābīkh in Iraq and similarly but more phonetically at Ebla in northern Syria. The use of cuneiform to write Akkadian is thus attested almost over the whole history of the script, which was developed in the late fourth millennium BC probably in order to write Sumerian and other local languages. Akkadian had likely died out sometime before the last cuneiform document was written, although precisely how long before is unclear. The persistence of diachronic syntactic change in everyday documents has been held to be evidence that the language was still in use until the second century BC.[20] Certainly from the eighth century BC onwards it is clear that Aramaic was being used as a lingua franca across ancient Iraq and beyond and that Akkadian was becoming a more learned idiom with prestigious associations.[21]

Sumerian, on the other hand, appears to have died out towards the beginning of the second millennium BC, although it continued in use as the language of learning for the rest of the history of cuneiform. If you learnt to write, you learnt Sumerian in some form or other. The interaction of the Akkadian language with Sumerian ranges from aspects of shared grammar and syntax likely to have been due to prolonged bilingualism in southern Iraq during the third millennium BC to a sharing of cultural material indicative of a lack of distinct cultural barriers and absence of exclusivity in the implementation of different forms of cultural activity and institutions: mixed Sumerian-Akkadian onomastics within families, similar gods housed in the same temples, the use of Sumerian to write Akkadian, similar phraseology for everyday activities in different languages are some of the markers of this multilingual situation. The fascinating amalgam that is Sumero-Akkadian culture has yet to be meaningfully comprehended as a cultural form. It is not to be assumed that Akkadian poetic forms are always based on Sumerian models, although this often seems to be the easiest interpretation of the data. From a methodological perspective, Akkadian poetic forms need to be investigated on their own before any comparison with Sumerian should be made.

Another distinction which one needs to bear in mind when approaching Akkadian poetry is the division into the dialects of Babylonian in southern Iraq and Assyrian in the north. Babylonian seems to have the main linguistic affinity with the dialect of the language spoken in the south also during the third millennium BC, but it is during the earlier part of the second millennium BC that Babylonian emerges as the main literary vehicle of the Akkadian language, along with the territorial ascendancy of dynasties rooted in the city-states of southern and central Iraq.[22] The Assyrian dialect, in which 'literary' productions are initially limited to popular incantations or spells but also royal inscriptions with some Babylonian influence, became the language of the administration of the empire with the rise of Assyrian imperial ambition after the first half of the second millennium BC, but to an extent always remained a slightly parochial dialect, even if the great Assyrian cities of Assur, Nimrud and Nineveh were centres of learning where literary texts, frequently from Babylonia, were collected and studied.

It is not clear whether there was a genre of love poetry as such in Akkadian or whether other generic categories had priority within which songs to do with love can be isolated as a particular sub-category that may or may not have meant anything in ancient times.[23] A Middle Assyrian tablet dating from the late second millennium BC excavated at Assur (modern Qalat Šerqat) in northern Iraq preserves a list of the first lines (incipits) of numerous songs or poetic compositions (some 152 preserved) in the Akkadian language, some of which, but by no means all, are associated with love themes.[24] This tablet has subscripts classifying groups of these song titles under certain categories and is thus of fundamental importance for research into the native understanding of poetic genre.[25] One section, containing fifty-five titles, deals according to its subscript with so-called Breast(-song)s, Akkadian *irātu* (plural of *irtu* 'breast, chest'), which are again divided into further subsections according to criteria which clearly have to do with their musical accompaniment or performance, with both string and reed instruments being mentioned.[26] Could *irtu* have been an ancient genre term for love poetry?[27] The term is currently restricted to the second millennium, seemingly having dropped out of use in the first millennium BC, and its usage, summarized later, does not seem to indicate that it would have encompassed all types of poetry that we might associate with love.

These *incipits* listed on the tablet from Assur give a good overview of the types of themes, language and lexicon that characterize Akkadian love poetry, even if they are all that remain of the poems. Typical topics are the laughter of lover or beloved, a garden (of desire), night-time, play, lovemaking, the wilderness; typical poetic figures include the comparison of love to precious metals, stones, honey or aromatics, the comparison of genitalia to fruits; typical lexical items beyond those associated with the above topics and figures include voluptuousness, lustiness, shining and blooming.[28] The mention of a king and deities in some of the first lines may or may not indicate a more formal or ceremonial setting for some of the songs (see below on the 'Divine Love Lyrics'), but on the whole it is difficult to imagine what the context for these songs was supposed to have been, whether courtly, cultic or popular, as it is also difficult to fathom the function of the larger list of song titles preserved in the tablet.[29]

Other songs listed on the same tablet by first line, but not called *irtu*, are also connected with love. The whole poem of one of them appears on a Middle Babylonian (ca. 1500–1100 BC) tablet in the British Museum, which is probably from southern Iraq and has a colophon indicating the name of the series of which the song formed a part and a catchline indicating the next song in the series.[30] This series is called *mārumma rā'imni* 'the boy who loves me (lit. us)'. The two songs belonging to it appear in the same order on the catalogue of song titles from Assur, and all have to do with the love between the goddess Ištar and the shepherd Dumuzi.[31] These are given the generic category *zamārū* 'songs' on the tablet from Assur rather than being any particular type of song such as an *irtu*.[32] It would thus seem that the *irtu* is not necessarily just a category denoting love poetry according to content, as these songs are also love songs, but are not called *irtu*.

The term *irtum*, with final -m, is further used on another list of five poem *incipits* on another tablet written in Middle Babylonian (ca. 1500–1100 BC) script kept in the British Museum, one of which at least must date from or before the reign of the Late Old Babylonian king Ammiṣaduqa (1646–26 BC) due to his being mentioned.[33] B. Groneberg thinks that the subscript '5 *ir-túm*' on this tablet means that this is one *irtum*-song of five lines, however, rather than what might seem a more natural interpretation that the tablet contains five *irtum*-songs.[34] The following two lines, which are also concerned with love, have the subscript *meḥrum*, 'antiphony, (choral) response', which may refer to a refrain to the lines that went before. This might support Groneberg's interpretation that this tablet contains one extended song but does not have to, and it seems a stronger contention that the *meḥrum* is the antiphony to all the songs listed previously on the tablet by their first lines.[35] In this case the particular *irtum*-song, which specifically mentions Ištar and an Old Babylonian king, may have had a ceremonial context within the wider field of the so-called sacred marriage, although it is entirely unclear what that entailed (see below on Cultic Love Songs).

A further four-columned tablet from the late Old Babylonian period, now held in Geneva, also contains a colophon at the end of the tablet mentioning '4 *irātum* of the series "where has my beloved (gone)? He is precious"'.[36] The first line of the first poem on column one is identical to the name of the 'series' mentioned in the colophon, *êš rāmī šūqur*. The tablet is badly broken, but one can tell that the individual *irātum* are likely to have consisted of more than one stanza each. The first column contains five stanzas over twenty-six preserved lines, although the tablet is likely to have contained a few more lines in each column. The tablet's first editor, B. Groneberg, makes the caveat that the term *irātum* might only apply to the poems on the obverse, but it would be usual for the colophon to refer to all the text on the tablet.[37] The preserved text is spoken by a woman and mentions a location in the wilderness, the land beyond human civilization, where the lover has been made to go out to, enveloping the beloved in laughter and catching a dove, apparently a figure for sexual relations. Preserved on the reverse is a dedication to the king Ammiditana (1683–40 BC), with a prayer to Ištar to grant him life and an interesting address to a presumed audience finishes the last poem, if not the whole collection:

limdā limdā šitālā	Learn! learn! Ask each other
mā šurrâssu inḫē uya	'Are sighs of woe its beginning
u ṣeḥer râmī	And is my loving small?'[38]

The plural imperatives may but do not have to suggest a context of public performance.[39] A subscript immediately after this and before the main colophon uses a Sumerian technical term (ĝeš-gi₄-ĝál-bi) which is usually interpreted as meaning 'its antiphon', as in the Akkadian *meḥrum* we saw earlier, probably referring to a refrain possibly even spoken by a chorus.[40] Groneberg wonders whether it might be a feature of this type of song that it contains some kind of dialogue, in which case a number of other Old Babylonian love poems could belong to this category.[41] It may well be that it is simply the primary topic of love that qualifies a song as an *irtum*, although it is suggestive that both of these Old Babylonian examples contain mention of the king and of the goddess Ištar. A solely cultic or ceremonial application of songs called *irtum* cannot be ruled out, but even in this case, the king and the goddess or the goddess and her divine lover may serve as models or archetypes for human love generally.[42]

D. Shehata has argued that the label *irtum* may have something to do with the manner of performance.[43] The various sub-categories of *irtum* referred to on the tablet from Assur certainly seem to denote different musical instruments, so it is possible that *irtum* in fact refers to the manner of singing or accompaniment by particular wind or string-instruments.[44] This is an attractive idea but does not necessarily negate the premise that the *irtum* was a category particularly associated with love poetry, as all of the songs known so far which are given the title *irtum* appear to be love poems.

As we shall see, the topics and words of love seem to be consistent across different sub-types of, and across, Akkadian literature in general when love is the theme. In this case it may be legitimate to bracket various types of poetry under the term *irtum*, but we should bear in mind that this is a terminology that we do not understand and which may be related to musical aspects of the performance context that we are not usually informed about. Content, structure, musical accompaniment and performative situation may all have played a role in defining the applicability of the term.

Looking at those poems which are primarily concerned with love from a modern analytical perspective, rather than trying to understand the ancient terminology on its own terms, it seems useful to distinguish three basic types, according to the alleged purpose for which the poem was written, thus in the sense of the primary word used to describe a poem's genre in Arabic literary theory, the assumed ġaraḍ, 'aim, intention' of its poet: (1) poetic spells of love magic, which are designed to have an effect on a beloved as an object of desire; (2) cultic poems, belonging to the type of so-called divine love lyrics which appear to be articulated by divine beings or their human representatives as part of state ritual; (3) personal or so-called 'secular' love poetry, which appears to have none of the above magical or divine aspects and is thus a negatively defined category.[45] In the following we shall look at some of the poems from these categories to see if it makes any sense to maintain them, and whether they are bound together by any super-ordinate features of language or context. We will try to explore the extent to which the modern notion of role play within social power relationships, whether they be gender or politically based, can be of use in understanding the ancient social institutions in which these compositions had functional roles. Thus, we will ask what characters, or stereotypes, are to be found in poems associated with love in Akkadian literature and what are our expectations of them.

Love magic

The earliest poem related to love in the Akkadian language is an incantation from Kiš (modern Tell Uhaimir), about 18 kilometres to the north-east of Babylon dating to the twenty-third/twenty-second centuries BC. This almost completely preserved clay tablet was excavated in 1930 by a British archaeological expedition and is now kept in the Ashmolean Museum in Oxford. Due to a lack of precision in excavation technique and recording methods, the archaeological context in which the tablet was excavated is not known sufficiently well to be able to make any inferences about its function. Considerations based partially on the allegedly poor quality of the script have suggested to some scholars that it might be an exercise tablet for someone learning to write.[46] The function of the text, rather than the tablet on which it was found, is almost certainly as a spell designed to attract the amorous attention of a beloved. In parts it even appears to involve the verbalization of a ritual designed for that effect. The ritual may have been performed and the incantation uttered by a third party, depending on one's interpretation of the speaker's perspective.

There have been numerous editions and translations of this poem, which has some claim to being the oldest attested love poem in the world.[47] It is, however, an incantation or spell connected with love and should be grouped under that rubric. The most recent version, excluding that contained in Lambert 2013 which was completed in the 1980s, is the online edition by N. Wasserman for the project 'Sources of Early Akkadian Literature', which has now appeared in print.[48] The text is presented here in transliteration (sign by sign) and transcription, in which an attempt is made to indicate the grammatical forms, which are very much a matter of interpretation.[49] References to some of the main differences in previous renditions are given in footnotes:

1	^{d}EN.KI *ir-e-ma-am*	(1)	*Ḫayya ir'emam yira''am*
2	*è-ra-[?]-am*		*ir'emum mara' Aθtar*
3	*ir-e-mu-um* DUMU ^{d}INANA		*in sāqēsa yuθθab*
4	*in za-ge-[sa? u?-ša?-a]b*		
5	*in ru-úḫ-t[i ga-na]-ak-tim*	(2)	*in ruġti kanaktim*
6	*ú-da-ra wa-a[r-d]a-da*		*yūtarrā wardatā*
7	*da-me-iq-da tu-úḫ-da-na-ma*		*damiqtā tuḫtannamā*
8	*ki-rí-súm tu-ur₄-da*	(3)	*kirīsum turdā*
9	*tu-ur₄-da-ma a-na* ^{giš}KIRI₆		*turdāma ana kirîm*
10	*ru-úḫ-ti ga-na-ak-tim*		*ruġti kanaktim tiptatqā*
11	*ti-ip-da-ad-ga*		
12	*a-ḫu-uz₇*(EŠ) *ba-ki ša ru-ga-tim*	(4)	*āḫuz pâki θa ruġātim*
13	*a-ḫu-uz₇ bu-ra-ma-ti*		*āḫuz burramāti 'ēnīki*
14	*e-ni-ki*		*āḫuz ūrki θa θīnātim*
15	*a-ḫu-uz₇ ur₄-ki*		*ashit kirîs Su'en*
16	*ša ši-na-tim*		*abtuq ṣarbātam yūmissa*
17	*a-ás-ḫi-iṭ ki-rí-ís*		
18	^{d}EN.ZU		
19	*ab-tùq* ^{giš}ÁSAL		

Rev.
20	*u-me-ís-sa*		
21	*du-ri-ni i-da-as-ga-ri-ni*	(5)	*dūrinni ittaskarinnī*
22	*ki* SIPA *i-du-ru ṣa-nam*		*kī rā'ium idurru ṣānam*
23	ÙZ *ga-lu-ma-sa* U₈ SILA₄*-[za]*		*enzum kalūmazza*
24	*a-da-núm mu-ra-as*		*laḫrum puḫāzza*
			atānum mūras
25	*se-er-gu-a i-da-su*		
26	Ì *ù ti-bu-ut-tum*	(6)	*sergu'ā idāsu*
27	*sa-ap-da-su*		*samnum u tibuttum saptāsu*
28	*a-za-am* Ì *in ga-ti-su*		*azzam samnim in qātīsu*
29	*a-za-am i-ri-nim in bu-ti-su*		*azzam erēnim in būdīsu*

30	ir-e-mu ú-da-bi-bu-si-ma	(7)	ir'emū yudabbibūsīma
31	ù ís-ku-nu-si a-na mu-ḫu-tim		u yiskunūsi ana muḫḫûtim
32	a-ḫu-uz₇ ba-ki ša da-ti		āḫuz pâki ša dādī
33	ᵈINANA ù ᵈiš-ḫa-ra	(8)	Aθtar u Isḫara utammēki
34	ù-dam-me-ki		adi ṣawārsu u ṣawārki
35	a-ti ṣa-wa-ar-su		lā 'etamdā lā tapaθθaḫīni
36	ù ṣa-wa-ar-ki		
37	la e-dam-da		
38	la da-ba-ša-ḫi-ni		

(1) Ea Loves the Ir'emu
     The Ir'emu, son of Ištar
     Sits? between her? thighs[50]

(2) *In/by means of* the sap (lit. 'spit') of the *kanaktum*-tree
     The two girls *are being woken up*[51]
     'Beautiful (girls),[52] you are both blooming

(3) To the garden you both descended
     You both descended to the garden'
     They both *drank* the sap (lit. 'spit') of the *kanaktum*-tree[53]

(4) I (hereby) grasp your mouth of spit[54]
     I (hereby) grasp your speckled eyes
     I (hereby) grasp your vulva of urine[55]
     I (hereby) jump into the garden of Sîn (the moon-god)
     I (hereby) cut down the poplar at its time[56]

(5) *Encircle* me among the boxwood trees[57]
     Like the shepherd *encircles* the flock
     Like the goat her kid
     Like the ewe her lamb
     Like the donkey mare her foal

(6) *Bejewelled* are his arms[58]
     Oil and a harp are his lips
     A cruse of oil is in his hand
     A cruse of cedar(-oil) is on his shoulder

(7) The Ir'emus have been talking to her
     They have made her go wild
     I (hereby) grasp your mouth (full) of caresses

(8) (By) Ištar and Isḫara I conjure you
     As long as his neck and your neck
     Are not entwined, you will not rest.

The literary structure of this poem has been well analysed by B. Groneberg, so remarks here will be kept to a minimum. The verse structure of the poem is fairly consistent, with short lines of verse, which largely do not correspond to the lines on the tablet, using two or three stress beats and a weak caesura in the middle of each. The grouping of the lines into stanzas varies according to the section of the poem. As divided here the poem starts with three three-line stanzas (verses 1–3), which appear to set the scene with a mythological introduction mentioning the god Ea (Ḫayya), the Ir'emu (sometimes translated as 'love-charm' or 'cupid'), two women and a garden, presumably spoken by a ritualist; two five-line stanzas in which an incantation is recited possibly over a substitute, maybe a doll or even a dog,[59] and an address is made directly to the woman, possibly spoken by the ritual client and evoking the garden along with floral and faunal imagery (verses 4–5); one four-line stanza setting out the beauty of the ritual client, possibly spoken by the ritualist (6); and it returns at the end to two three-line stanzas (7–8), in which the ritualist addresses the woman directly, observes the effect of the Ir' emu mentioned earlier, reprises the words of the incantation turning the mouth of spit into a mouth of caresses, invokes the two love-goddesses Ištar (Aθtar) and Išḫara, who may also be the two women mentioned earlier on, and possibly manipulates figurines of the lovers-to-be, entwining their necks. Despite falling into sections possibly spoken by different actors but certainly projected from differently focalized perspectives, the composition shows a remarkable degree of poetic unity.

A specific framework of associations is evoked by beginning the poem with the god Ea. Ea is, at least in later incantation literature, specifically the god who finds solutions. This is the realm of problems that need to be solved. There is some debate as to the precise nature of the next figure to be introduced, the Ir'emum, who, as part of a group of such entities, is going to play a role in solving the problem at hand, namely that the attentions of a woman need to be won by a man. The Ir'emu-beings, the word is a proper noun derived from the Semitic root *r'm 'to love', are attested in other love incantations, and the contexts have been reviewed by B. Groneberg. She comes to the conclusion that they are jewels special to Ištar, goddess of sex and war, which have magic qualities as love-charms.[60] Other interpretations focus more on the agency attributed to these beings, seeing them as cupids or personifications of sexual attraction.[61] The two interpretations do not need to be mutually exclusive, with the Cupid sometimes appearing as or lending its allure to the objects associated with the goddess of love.

Although designed as a spell to assert control over another, to subject that person to the will of the suitor, the poem contains a number of features that recur in Akkadian love poetry: the dripping liquids of oil, sap and spit, the garden with the fragrances and aromas of its trees.[62] Indeed, it might well be asked how much other types of Akkadian poetry concerned with love were also designed to serve the functional context of domination. Furthermore, this is a theme or subtext to love poetry more generally, thinking, for example, of the struggle not to objectify the other in words, as expressed by Adrienne Rich's poem we cited earlier. From objectification it is only a small step to control and under the wrong circumstances to abuse. The darker shades of common cultural discourses of love are all too easy to identify. The perspective of the suitor seeking possession of his beloved woman in this earliest of love poems is quite clearly male, given that the pronouns used in Akkadian for the person who is object of the actions of the ritualist or the ritual client are consistently female. The ritual client is described as emanating attractiveness. He is not acted upon by another in the poem. The language used is specifically dominating.[63] However, some subsequent Akkadian love incantations are projected specifically from a female perspective, in fact using language that appears to be asymmetrically reciprocal with the language used here.

A tablet with a series of incantations, some of which are related to love, was excavated at Isin (modern Išan Baḥrīyat in southern Iraq) in 1984, probably to be dated to the reign of the Old Babylonian king Samsuiluna (1750–12 BC), some 400 years later than the tablet from Kiš we have just looked at.[64] It was found broken in half in a closed vessel filled with sand, built into the wall of the house of a professional lamentation-singer (gala-maḫ). This immediate archaeological context strongly suggests that there was something special about the tablet. Consideration of the contents, a series of incantations designed to gain power over other individuals sometimes by winning their love, suggests that the tablet had been disposed of in this way either in order to disarm its magic in some way or to hide evidence for the use of aggressive magic.[65] The first Akkadian language incantation of the group appears to be addressed by a woman to a man and contains language that is strikingly similar to that of the love incantation from Kiš.

IB 1554, 9-22

elliʾat kalbim ṣūmi . . . emṣūtim	The spittle of the dog, of thirst?, hunger
miḫiṣ pānim šipir tūrti īnim	A blow in the face, the work of turning the eye
amtaḫaṣ muḫḫaka uštanni ṭēmka	I struck your head, I changed your mind
šuknam ṭēmka ana ṭēmīya	Add your mind to my mind
šuknam milikka ana milkīya	Add your thought to my thought
akallāka kīma Ištar iklû Dumuzi	I am restraining you like Ištar restrained Dumuzi
Siraš ukassû šātîša	(Like) Siraš (beer-deity) binds her drinkers
uktassīka ina pīya ša šarātim	I have bound you with my hairy? mouth[66]
ina ūrīya ša šīnātim	With my vulva of urine
ina pīya ša ruʾātim	With my mouth of spit
ina ūrīya ša šīnātim	With my vulva of urine
āy illik nakratum ina ṣērīka	May a female enemy not approach you
rabiṣ kalbum rabiṣ šaḫium	The dog is lying down, the pig is lying down
atta ritabbiṣ ina ḫallīya	You (too), keep lying down in my thighs!

Despite being punctuated by minimal ritual instructions, the incantation continues until it reaches a subscript in line 37, which identifies the foregoing lines as a love incantation, and thus most likely a single unified composition. Here, there are no mythological niceties in the manner of trips to the garden or aromatic incense-trees; this is a straightforward spell as part of a ritual to gain power over a beloved. The same images are used in lines 17–20 to demonstrate this taking of possession as are used in lines 12–16 of the Old Akkadian incantation from Kiš, but in this poem they are directed from woman to man. The usage is not symmetrically reciprocal, however: the woman uses her vulva to take hold of the man; she does not bind him by taking hold of his genitals, as the man 'took hold' of the woman's genitals in the love incantation from Kiš. We may ask if this is the voice of a lusty, self-confident woman using magic, particularly the power residing in her genitalia, to gain the attention of a man.[67] This may be, but the final four lines before the subscript are clearly addressed to a woman, as identified by the gender of the enclitic pronoun, presumably by a man, possibly even the specific man who is directly addressed by name in line 30.[68]

IB 1554, 30-36

lū ālikā purīdāka Erra-bāni	let your (m.) legs get walking, Erra-bani,
qablāka limmušā	let your (m.) hips move
lū rēdû šerḫānūka	let your (m.) sinews follow on
liḫdû libbūki	may your (f.) insides rejoice
liḫšuša kabtattaki	may your (f.) liver be joyful
lūbi kīma kalbim	'may I swell up like a dog
kīma šumunnim ḫubbušāki ē tatbukīm	like a halter-rope (are) your (f.) two humps, don't waste (them), please.'[69]

It is uncertain whether we should imagine some sort of dialogue going on with male and female actors within the framework of the ritual. Another possibility is that the speaker of the last few lines is in fact the same as that of the rest of the incantation, a man who uses male projections of female sexuality to imagine his female beloved trying to conjure him into sex? The change in gender would then be a change in focalization, of the perspective from which the words are spoken, in this case the man taking on the role of the woman saying what he wants to hear.[70] In reverse, the final lines could of course also be an impersonation of the male performed from the perspective of the female, in order to ensure his potency. Either way, we are in the realm of love poetry as a form of control, and the context is securely magical.[71] The desired end seems to be achieved by imagining the response of the beloved as part of the utterance of the spell.

There are not a great many more of this type of composition attested in Akkadian. One tablet held in Yale begins with an address to the ir'emu, whom we encountered earlier, and attempts to attract the attention of a beloved woman who has not yet noticed the lover.[72] It contains some verbal overlap with the love incantations from Isin and shares further phrases with an incantation on a tablet from the Schøyen collection which contains a *historiola* explaining that love originated when the daughters of the sky-god (visualized as stars or sunbeams, literally, 'lights of the sky') were cleaning the highest heavens.[73] The knowledge of this primordial genesis of love is used by the speaker to conjure a similar love in the recalcitrant female object of his desires.

A number of shorter spells are found on tablets collecting various examples of magical utterances. One poetic example directed by a young woman at a man is edited in this volume by A. R. George. It was found on a tablet with other incantations in Sumerian. A Sumerian incantation with an accompanying Akkadian ritual indicating that its purpose was to attract an estranged wife, also on a tablet collecting several compositions, is found on a late Old Babylonian tablet currently in the British Museum.[74] Another tablet with collected spells held in Yale has one in which a woman describes her desired effect on the man as being like that of beer and casts a spell of vertigo on him.[75] A short Old Babylonian incantation on a single small tablet currently held in Berlin attempts to attract the attention of a beloved but hostile woman by conjuring with the ingredients of make-up, according to a recent interpretation by N. Wasserman.[76] A subscript describes it as an 'incantation for the fire of the heart'.[77]

A further short incantation associated with a detailed ritual description designed to cure sexual impotence is preserved on a fourteenth- to thirteenth-century BC tablet from the royal archives on the citadel at the Hittite capital of Hattusa (modern Boğazköy/Boğazkale in Turkey).[78] As a ritual against sexual impotence, it thus has much in common with the series of so-called šà-zi-ga incantations and rituals from the first millennium BC, which have the same goal.[79] The incantation addresses the love-goddess Nanaya, here equated with another love-goddess Kilili, and expresses the desire of the speaker to have sex with the goddess.[80] This kind of impersonation of the lover of a love-goddess is found in some Akkadian texts associated with the cult of the so-called sacred marriage rite, where the king is projected as her lover. The very unusual use of this motif in the ritual tablet from Boğazköy may show its application to more everyday amorous situations, although the tablet was found in a royal archive.[81] There is, to my knowledge, no further evidence for such a literary *topos* in the texts from Boğazköy, although Hittite goddesses did have mortal lovers in Hittite mythology.

We should remember that the words of these incantations are unlikely to be associated with one single person's yearning for another, although they may possibly have originated in that form. They are the words that ritualists put into their clients' mouths while performing rites that would help them achieve their goals. They, thus, represent types of lover, roles that a particular client might have been supposed to be inhabiting and are likely to have been tailored or chosen according to the individual circumstances of the particular lovesick individual.

Cultic love poetry: Inana-Dumuzi songs and the 'Divine Love Lyrics'.

Sumerian has a particular genre of love songs specifically related to the cult of the goddess Inana (Akkadian Ištar), the deity responsible for sex and war, and her lover, the shepherd Dumuzi. A Sumerian narrative poem and a much later one in Akkadian tell how she allowed him to be sent down to the underworld for half the year as a substitute for herself, after she had been trapped there by her sister, the queen of the underworld.[82] The same rich fertility imagery of this story of the 'Descent of Inana' is not apparent in the highly erotic love songs, although these too have their own fertility themes. The love songs may have been composed sometime near the end of the third and beginning of the second millennium BC, more likely the latter. Certainly the clay tablets on which they are written date from the first half of the second millennium, the so-called Old Babylonian period. They are supposed to be connected with a controversial type of ritual commonly but vaguely referred to by modern scholars as the 'sacred marriage' ceremony, a union between king and goddess to which one has references particularly in a Hymn of Šulgi king of Ur (2094–47 BC) and in one to Iddin-Dagan (1910–1890 BC) third king of the dynasty of Isin.[83]

What modern scholars have understood by 'sacred marriage', a term which is not translated from any Akkadian or Sumerian phrase but which is transferred wholesale from Classical Studies, has varied from a ritual copulation between a king and a priestess as manifestations of Inana and Dumuzi to a metaphorical discourse concerning the role of the king as a link to the world of the divine.[84] A ritual from Mari on the Syrian Middle Euphrates (early eighteenth century BC) has also been called a 'sacred marriage', as it is related to the New Year's festival, similarly to the hymn to Iddin-Dagan, and seems to involve a union of the king with the goddess Ištar, also citing *incipit*s of Sumerian songs.[85] Further evidence for a 'sacred marriage' rite of some kind, this time associated with Akkadian poems regarding the gods Nabû with his wife Tašmetu and Marduk with his wife Zarpanitum, is to be found in the first millennium BC, this time also in non-literary contexts such as letters.[86] On the evidence of the letters the rites clearly involve the manipulation of statues of gods. There are also two fragmentary first millennium tablets of ritual instructions associated with 'Love Lyrics' detailing a rite extending over three days in Babylon involving the city-god Marduk, his wife Zarpanitum and Ištar of Babylon.[87]

It is unlikely that we will ever know precisely what was going on in these rites in the early second millennium BC in southern Iraq, but it does appear that the preserved Sumerian love songs were directly connected with them and thus largely to be understood in a cultic context.[88] Apart from these there is little other Sumerian love poetry, other than that which occurs incidentally in narrative poems or hymns, which occasionally contain highly erotic language. To what extent the 'divine' cultic love songs of Inana and Dumuzi were supposed to be modelled on the discourse of contemporary love, or even the other way round served as archetypes for 'secular' love experience, is a very difficult question, the evidence for which can ultimately only be assessed subjectively.[89] However, the reference to restraining the beloved like Ištar restrained Dumuzi (IB 1554, 14), cited above in connection with the love incantations from Isin, is suggestive in this regard, as is the evidence from the incantation preserved at Boğazköy, where the sufferer from impotence declares his intention to have sex with the love-goddess Nanaya.[90] As W. G. Lambert pointed out, it is possible that every pair of lovers saw themselves as Inana and Dumuzi, that is, as re-enacting a central myth of divine courtship and love, possibly without countenancing the concomitant unpleasant results for the male partner in the relationship.[91] However, there are many other lovers in the divine world, if models are needed by which one could psychologically or socially validate one's emotional activities. It is also unclear whether the Sumerian divine love lyrics served as models for those that appear in Akkadian or were themselves rather the creation of the same or a similar social and historical context that saw the genesis of the Akkadian ones. Notes in Akkadian on some of the tablets of the Sumerian poems indicate that these were transmitted by Akkadian-speaking scribes.[92]

Although not strictly an example of 'divine love lyrics', the poem on the Middle Babylonian tablet in the British Museum published by J. A. Black, which is also cited on the Middle Assyrian song-catalogue from Assur (see above, on genre), should be mentioned again here.[93] It presents a poem of a very similar type to the Dumuzi-Inana poems in Sumerian. This includes an invitation to the shepherd to enter the goddess's house and meet her parents, who are mentioned frequently in the Sumerian Dumuzi-Inana poems, followed by a visit to the shepherd's sheepfold. J. A. Black characterized its genre as a 'ballad' in order to capture its popular character, brisk narrative and lyrical moments.[94] It is unclear how far one can apply the constructed modern distinctions between content that was appropriate for popular, cultic or courtly contexts to the performance of the Inana-Dumuzi poems, as the ancients seem not to have insisted on them. Its presence in a 'series' of songs collected on a catalogue tablet at Assur, a series which is also referred to in the tablet's own colophon, indicates its participation in a formalized poetic repertoire, whatever the function of that repertoire might have been. The specific tablet collection to which it belonged was also according to the colophon that of an official of a temple of Ištar.[95] A cultic context may thus be difficult to exclude for this composition, despite the fact that its style is very different from that of the so-called divine love lyrics.[96]

Another tablet from Assur contains a poem with an Akkadian version of content related to the theme of Ištar and the shepherd.[97] Ištar searches for the shepherd, who is out in the steppe. She meets him in a hut and invites him to come to a meadow rich in juniper trees bestowed by Assur, the supreme god of Assyria. The text is then broken off, and when it resumes on the reverse of the tablet, if it is the same poem, there is mention of food, wine and beer along with a general benediction. The poem ends with the lines:

| rev. 6' | *ša Šalmānu-ašarēd nīš qātātīšu imtaḫar* |
| 7' | *iddina ša ērišu zamāru ša attūya mimma nizzamur* |

          she accepted the hand-liftings (= prayers) of Shalmaneser
          she gave (him) what he asked for. We have sung whatever song
                                                                                                                                  is mine

The preceding text, if it is all one poem, is thus part of a prayer offered by king Shalmaneser I (1265–35 BC) for well-being. It is questionable whether a poem with this ending can be labelled a love poem, despite its explicit mythological content involving Ištar and the shepherd, which is comparable to the theme of Ištar and Dumuzi. However, there are further examples of love poems offered as prayers.[98]

The earliest 'divine love-lyric' attested in Akkadian is that from the reign of Rim-Sin (1822–1763 BC) of Larsa (modern Tell as-Senkereh).[99] The tablet containing it allegedly forms part of a group of texts from the temple of Enki/Ea excavated at Larsa and is now held in the Yale Babylonian Collection.[100] The abrupt break-off in the poem at the end of the text and the doodles and dislocated signs on the blank part of the reverse indicate that this might have been a practice tablet. The poem is difficult, with an irregular verse division. It has been suggested that the poem is itself not a coherent whole but another list of incipits, a caveat which should certainly be kept in mind when reading it.[101] However, irregular verse division is on the whole a feature of Akkadian love poetry in the third and second millennia BC. M. Sigrist and J. G. Westenholz divide the words between a chorus, the love-goddess Nanaya and King Rim-Sin.[102] Frequently, the person, as indicated by the gender of the pronouns, verbs and adjectives, changes in the middle of a line. The goddess explains to the chorus her love for the king, who we later learn is Rim-Sin. Her love is expressed as joyous laughter rising like a prayer (i 4). The context appears to be the New Year (i 18). When Rim-Sin appears, he addresses the goddess asking her to be his 'one and only' (i 7a), and she replies that he must have heard her prayers (i 7b-8).

A number of parallels between the language of prayer and that of love in Akkadian have been noted by W. G. Lambert and more recently by A. Cavigneaux, who points to the essential semantic overlap between verbs of praying and verbs of seducing, which is to be explained in terms of the intention to overpower either a god, in order to obtain one's desires, or a beloved.[103] In the case of the 'divine love lyric' from Larsa, it is the goddess who has been offering her prayers to the king as if to a god. The poem continues with an explicit invitation to the king on the part of the goddess to a night of love-making (l. 20-25a). Towards its end (ii. 6) the goddess addresses the king's offering a prayer to her, although there are numerous problems with the exact interpretation.[104]

A tablet from the reign of king Abiešuḫ (1712–1684 BC) excavated in Babylon and now kept in Berlin offers a variation on the theme.[105] The 'divine lovers', in this case Nanaya and Muati, a divine partner of Nanaya who later became merged with the god Nabû, engage in a lover's dialogue that is punctuated by narrative sections in the third person. Instead of the king being projected into the role of the divine lover, here it appears that a third person promises to intercede with Muati on behalf of Abi-ešuḫ, for whom eternal shepherding of his people (obv. 5–6) and long life (obv. 14) are requested. These wishes appear to be granted in rev. 6, where Nanaya looks kindly on Babylon and causes Abi-ešuh to dwell 'in a dwelling of peace'.[106] Later, it is clear that Abi-ešuḫ is at least being compared to Muati, for just as Nanaya has caused Abi-ešuh 'to dwell in a dwelling of peace' (*tušūšibšu*), so too she has seated Muati (*tušēšibšu*), and the 'love-charm (*Ir'emu*) is raining down (on him) like dew' (rev. 11).[107]

Although it is possible to see an identification of the king and the god as the direct lover of the goddess, in my view the text remains here at the level of a comparison rather than identification. It may be possible to use this notion, comparing the king to the divine lover rather than assuming that he is the divine lover, to understand the prayer of Shalmaneser I from Assur that was referred to earlier. The poetic understanding of the king in the role of the divine lover acts as a motif of prayer in order to obtain health and well-being for the land. Of course, it would not be legitimate to infer back from this interpretation of the Late Old Babylonian and the Middle Assyrian poems an identical literary function for the idea of the king's sexual union with the goddess in the so-called 'sacred marriage' rite from the earlier Old Babylonian period, but such a metaphorical interpretation of the literary evidence should not be excluded. The king is figured in a role that is recognized in a genre of love poetry where his union with the goddess was an expected element. To celebrate his playing that role was one way of celebrating him.

Non-cultic dialogues: Man versus woman

In their review of Akkadian love poetry published in 2008, J. Klein and Y. Sefati decided that there was only one work in the whole of Akkadian literature that could possibly be understood as a 'secular' love poem.[108] This is the text now known as the *Dialogue of the Faithful Lover*, which has been translated and edited many times.[109] The situation has now changed somewhat given the 2009 publication by A. R. George of a number of love poems from a private collection in Norway (Schøyen). It will be useful briefly to reconsider the *Dialogue of the Faithful Lover* in the light of these new additions to the corpus of Babylonian poetry. Two of the new poems, especially, appear to belong to a similar genre and show a close connection with each other in terms of phraseology, while at the same time showing strong thematic and structural similarities to the individual monologues contained in the dialogue. It will therefore be useful to present parts of all three poems both in sequential and parallel comparisons.

The *Dialogue of the Faithful Lover* poem is contained on a tablet that was excavated at Sippar (modern Tell Abu Habbah) in the early twentieth century and is now held in Istanbul. It contains eighteen verses of varying length in pairs of identical length. Each verse spoken by a male persona is answered by a verse of identical length spoken by a female persona. The word 'answered' is perhaps too strong to illustrate the connection between all the verses of the male and female interlocutors, as they rarely seem to address the same topic, although they are frequently linked by phraseological echoes and puns, as B. Groneberg has demonstrated.[110] The poem thus falls into the well-known ancient Iraqi genre-category of the dialogue or dispute poem, in which two characters, usually personifications of animals, trees or agricultural implements, argue about which of them has the more virtue.[111] The difference here is that the content of the argument is more psychologically nuanced, the two opponents in the dialogue being a man and a woman figured as lovers, possibly even lovers who have reached a somewhat advanced and jaded stage in their relationship.

The gender characterization is very clear.[112] The male participant presents himself as an arrogant misogynist, not interested in what the woman has to say, and speaking in general terms about his opinion of the way women are and the way men should behave towards them. The woman appears at first sight to be meek, presenting her devotion to his love ('being true, respectful, enticing' i 13) in the face of his callousness, but at the same time affirming that her supporters are the love-goddesses Ištar and Nanaya. She prays to these goddesses to obtain his favour, and the effect of that prayer is expressed by 'grasping' or 'taking hold' of him (*uṣabbatka* i 22), precisely the language of control that we encountered in the love incantations reviewed earlier. The first four stanzas are reproduced here below in transcription and translation:

Man

i(1)	[ḫ]urbī?[113] turki ezbī	Hurry up and stop your answering back[114]
i(2)	lā magal dabābum	(isn't there) too much chatter?
i(3)	qabê qabûmma	I have not changed what I say
i(4)	ul ēni'akkim	for you through talking.
i(5)	atwâm mali ṣabtāku	as far as I think about the matter[115]
i(6)	ša ana sinništim ipparaqqadu	he who lies flat for a woman
i(7)	samān dūrim	(is) a weevil of the city-wall
i(8)	šumma lā itqud	if he is not worried (about that)
i(8)	ul awīlum miḫiršu	he is not a man of any kind

Woman

i(9)	lizziz kittī	My truth shall stand
i(10)	ina maḫar Ištar šarratim	before Ishtar the queen,
i(11)	liḫbit râmī libâš	my love shall triumph,
i(12)	karrištī	my detractor shall be ashamed.
i(13)	k[ân]am palāḫam kuzzubam	As for *being true*,[116] respectful, enticing
i(14)	itašḫur mārim	fussing around (my) darling,
i(15)	ina qabê Nanaya bēlam dāriš	by the command of Nanaya *ruling* forever[117]
i(16)	ali meḫertī	where (is) a woman of my kind?[118]

Man

i(17)	elīki ḫassāku	I am wiser than you
i(18)	ana šibqīki ša panānum	as for your previous tricks
i(19)	mugrī atalkī	kindly get lost,
i(20)	ana māliktīki šunnî	tell your lady counselor (i.e. Nanaya?)
i(21)	kīma ērēnu	that we are wide awake.

Woman

i(22)	uṣabbatka ūmam	I shall take hold of you by day
i(23)	râmka u râmī uštamaggar	I shall reconcile your love and my love
i(24)	ussenellīma ana ᵈNanaya	I shall keep praying to Nanaya
i(25)	salīmka bēlī dāri'am eleqqe	I will receive your eternal goodwill, my lord,
i(26)	nadnam	as a gift.

As we have noted, A. Cavigneaux has pointed to the semantics of verbs used for praying in Akkadian that are also used for seduction.[119] The attitude of prayer constitutes an attempt to exert influence over the deity that seems to belong to a similar semantic nexus as the act of seduction by using words. By the time we reach the fourth and final column of the composition, at least after a break on the tablet, the male character's intransigence does not seem to have softened at all at first sight:

Woman:

iv(5)	lūšib lūteqqi šumma ša girrīya	I shall sit and wait in case he comes across my path

Man:

iv(6)	atmākim ᵈNanaya u Ḫammurapi šarram	I swear to you by Nanaya and Hammurapi the king
iv(7)	ša kīnātīya lū aqabbīkim	Let me tell you my truths
iv(8)	râmki eli diliptim	(I swear) your love is no more
iv(9)	u ašuštim lā watru ina ṣērīya	for me than trouble and depression

However, 'trouble (diliptum) and depression (ašuštum)' are specifically the effects of love that one might expect to feel as a result of erotic bewitchment or successful seduction. Compare the short three-line incantation addressed to a woman from the same Isin collection as cited earlier (under Love Magic):

(38)	dilpī mušītam	be disturbed (f.) through the night
(39)	urrī ē taṣlalī	do not sleep (f.) by day
(40)	mušī ē tušbī	do not sit (still) (f.) by night
(41)	ka-inim-ma ša ki-áĝ-kam	it is an incantation of the lover[120]

Could this be a hint that the woman's repeated protestations of submission combined with her supplications to the love-goddesses are having an effect, whatever the male participant might say or indeed want to the contrary? Unfortunately, the final stanza, spoken by the man, is not only quite damaged but also uses obscure phraseology, so it is difficult to see whether there has been a development in his attitude throughout the poem. He appears, at any rate, to have had the last word. His very last words (*maḫar Ištar* iv 24) echo the first words of the woman in i 9-10 (*lizziz kittī maḫar Ištar šarratim*). Throughout the poem he appropriates the supports that the woman appeals to, the goddesses Nanaya and Ištar and the notion of 'my truth' *kittī* (cf. i 31, iv 7').

The most recent literary assessment of the use-context for this poem considers it a kind of competitive performance poetry based on the use of puns made by playing on words used by the opponent in the competition.[121] The fact that the man swears by Nanaya and by Hammurapi the king may mean that we might envisage a court context for the performance of this piece, possibly after Hammurapi had died, but it could doubtless also have been performed in non-court circles.[122]

A tablet from the Schøyen collection in Norway, with no known provenance but dated on the basis of script, language and format to the Old Babylonian period, has now been published, which contains a poem using two of the stanzas from the *Faithful Lover* (stanza I = IX, II = I) alongside a number of its own, which are all spoken by a male figure.[123] There is, in this poem, no mention of the king nor of any goddess. This is an extremely bitter poem, interpreted by A. R. George as a poem of love's demise.[124] It begins with the stanza that occurs as no. IX in the *Dialogue of the Faithful Lover*, where the man is at the height of his arrogance, and continues with stanza no. I of the *Dialogue of the Faithful Lover* as its second, which we already cited earlier.

The two stanzas known from the *Faithful Lover*, largely the same but slightly altered, are not bound into the same series of puns and verbal echoes that B. Groneberg has identified for the *Faithful Lover* composition. Rather than saying that the *Faithful Lover* is in any sense the 'original' poem and that the Schøyen tablet (MS 3285) has borrowed from it, it is more accurate to say that Akkadian and Sumerian poetry sometimes used stock phrases or indeed whole sections of verse for particular topics. In a culture where the vast majority of literary productions did not have an author, this is not surprising. However, the use of a passage would belong to a particular poetic register, just as the choice of a particular word might belong to a linguistic register, which either introduces, as in this case, or jars against the tone and possibly the genre of the poem. Despite there only being one speaker in this poem, it is quite possible that the text was meant to play a role in just such a dramatic performance context as the *Dialogue of the Faithful Lover*, using some of the same building blocks. It merely records the male persona's contributions to that exchange. In order to gain an idea of just how bitter each of them sounds as a monologue, let us compare the male part of the *Dialogue* with the text of the tablet in Norway in translation.

A Field Full of Salt	Dialogue of the Faithful Lover The male part
I obv. 1-8	I obv. i 1-8 (cf. *Field Full of Salt* II)
[I] spurn the girl who will not seduce me I don't desire the girl who does not flirt I will not give her my love-charm I will rise above her Talking in order to disagree,	Hurry up and stop answering back (isn't there) too much chatter? I have not changed what I say for you through talking. as far as I think about the matter

why does that exist?[125]
[I shall] give my love to the midst of darkness
No one shall gain control of [it]

II obv. 9-16 (cf. *Faithful Lover* I)

Break off, leave, you have [made] me silent
Not so much chatter
What I say, through talking [. . .]
I have not changed [for you]
He who [lies prostrate] for a woman
[he] is a weevil of the city-wall
If he is not [worried (abo ut that)]
He is not a man of [any kind]

III obv. 17-25

[You were] born the daughter of a substitute
With [no] dowry.
You have a mole [on the] forehead
As long as you show disrespect, you [are] shameful?

Let me tell you [your] place[128]
You do not listen to me
As you please
You ride clouds
You chase every boyfriend away

IV obv. 26 – rev. 34

You go [too] far! Why are you rebellious?
Ask the previous women
Like a field of salt (you are?)

Should I take pleasure in all of (it)?
[I took] pleasure in the fruit
[Should I take] pleasure in all of (it)?
and(?) [. . .]
mouth [. . .]
lover [. . .]

V rev. 35-39

You must not [put . . .] . . .
To your canal no one will approach
You lord? is your task

he who lies prostrate for a woman
(is) a weevil of the city-wall
if he is not worried (about that)
he is not a man of any kind

III i 17-21

I am wiser than you
as for your previous tricks
get lost,
tell your counselor (i.e. Nanaya?)
that we are wide awake.

V i 27-31

I shall lay siege to you
I shall gather my clouds[126]
May your supporter (f., ie. Nanaya) take
A boyfriend, end your unjust words[127]
Accept the truth

VII ii 1-5

. . . .

Does not exist
nothing in my heart . . .
. . . is/will be paid out to her
(she?) is/will be deprived of my [love]

IX ii 10-19 (cf. *Field Full of Salt* I)

[I] spurn the girl who will not seduce me
I don't desire the girl who does not flirt
I will not give her [my love-charm]
Talking in order to [disagree],
Why [does that exist]?
I shall have [my?] slanderers stopped
I shall not listen . . . .
into the middle [of the darkness?]
I have cast my love
why do you (f. pl.) try to control me?

Do not place me? in the salt
Your field is well explored?

VI rev. 40-45

You who have not brought forth for me
    from your womb
Like the people's flesh you have become
    (too) hot for me.[129]
Must I swallow a potsherd?
Shall I let the bitch go?
He who swallows a potsherd in letting
    you go
When could he have his say?

VII 46-50

Actually, when someone approached you
Like the goddess Belili you were
    staggering about
Dancing around in the early hours (meant)
    for sleeping
You are producing your own suffering.

XIII? iii 6'-10'

As for the women who keep telling you
    'you [are] not the only one'
Stop! I have taken away my love, not . . .
I removed (it) from your body
I *sent* my fruits a thousand miles away

XV? iii 16'-19'

I repeat and I repeat a third [time]
I'll not let 'pleasant' [enter] my mouth
Take your place at the . . . of the window
Come on! Catch my love!

XIX iv 6'-9'

I swear to you by Nanaya and
                      Hammurapi the king
I am really telling you my truths
Your love is no more (important)
For me than trouble and depression.

XXI iv 17-24

My only one, weren't your previous
Features ugly?
[Would I/did I] stand by you?
They (f.) call you the mistress of
                      counsel.
You have leaned . . .
Insolence is your name.
May the [. . .] be our evil,
in the presence of Ištar.[130]

Formally speaking, the two monologues are quite different with regard to the length of the stanzas employed. The *Dialogue of the Faithful Lover* employs more variation in the number of lines per stanza. The topic also seems to be slightly different in each. *A Field Full of Salt* appears to concern a wounded male ego lashing out at a lover who refuses to submit to his view of how a relationship should be. He begins with pompous observations on the relationship between men and women and proceeds along the route of personal insults until he reaches the conclusion that he does not want to give up the object of his desire. In fact, it is possible that his remarks at the end of the poem imply that he has been emotionally 'stewing' at home with jealousy, while the woman he is talking to has been out late at night, which reading of the situation suddenly allows much of the apparent misogyny of his previous utterances to appear in a different light, one that is negative for him. He appears pathetic and impotent and his insults petulant.[131] The man in the 'Dialogue of the Faithful Lover' is fed up with his lover and has little but insults for her depending on one's view of the final stanza. They appear to have been in a relationship for some time. He blusters but, as Groneberg observes, does not withdraw entirely, while the woman both stands up to him at the same time as acting in an outwardly meek and humble manner.[132] The tone of the male voice in both poems, however, is very similar, and both poems seem to deal with relationships that have gone wrong in some way.

A further poem from the Schøyen collection (MS 5111 – *I Shall Be a Slave to You*) seems to represent what may be the female *partie*, if not to MS 3285 (*A Field Full of Salt*), then at least to a poem very much like it. Aspects of language and verse structure make it clear that these are essentially different compositions. As the tablets are both unprovenanced, it is difficult to make any firm conclusions about their use-context. However, by far the majority of literary tablets found in Iraq in secure archaeological contexts dating to the second millennium BC are school tablets, so one might assume that these were exercises for trainee scribes based on compositions they had heard. Both tablets show southern orthographic conventions. Their formats, while sharing a general shape and size, are slightly different when it comes to the distribution of the writing over the tablets, so it is unlikely that they formed a direct pair produced on one occasion and meant to correspond to one another. The divisions into stanzas that are made by the dividing lines on the tablets do not correspond to each other, the poem on MS 3285 having eight stanzas over fifty lines (stanza length 8–9 lines), MS 5111 having nine stanzas over a minimum of thirty-six lines (stanza length 4–5 lines). Even if we disregard the dividing lines written on the tablet as a mistake in the case of MS 5111 and re-construe the text as a group of four stanzas with six to eight lines each, a satisfactory correspondence is not produced. The content of the texts on the two tablets, however, is related one to the other in a manner parallel to the male and female parties in the 'Dialogue of the Faithful Lover' from Sippar: *A Field Full of Salt* is related to *I Shall Be a Slave to You* just as the male voice from the *Dialogue of the Faithful Lover* is related to the female one.

B. Groneberg convincingly demonstrated that at least some stanzas in the *Dialogue of the Faithful Lover* are knitted together by a series of verbal echoes and responses. While it is not easy to see such a chain of verbal echoes running through either of the newly discovered poems individually, it may be the case that such a chain can be reconstructed for the relationship between MS 5111 and MS 3285, in as far as the verbal echoes are not simply those that belong to Akkadian love poetry generally. Perhaps the most sensible conclusion is that these two poems consist of building blocks that could be knitted together if need be into a dialogue form, but as they stand, they do not represent the two parties of a single dialogue, rather standing alone as poems in their own right or collections of poetic units belonging to this type of poetry. For the moment, note the following correspondences, where part of the female monologue on one tablet appears to be an answer to part of the male one on the other, or otherwise echoes or anticipates it. The text is left in transliteration due to the uncertainty of interpretation and damage to the tablet in parts.

1. Power-Plays

MS 3285 'A Field Full of Salt'	MS 5111 'I Shall Be Slave to You'
(9) *ta-aš-t[a-ak-ni? q]ú-li* (10) *la ma-gal da-[ba-bu-um]*	(9) *ú-um-ta-aš-ši a-wa-ti-ia*
You have brought about my silence Isn't there enough talking?	I have forgotten my words
(17) *ma-[r]a?-[a]t pu-ḫi wa-a[l-da-ti]* (18) *i-na [la] ši-ri-[ik-tim]*	(25) *e-re-du-ku wa-aš-ra-ak* (26) *ù ši-ri-ik-ta-ka ra-mi-ma*
You were born the daughter of a substitute without a dowry	I will follow you, I shall be subservient And your dowry is my love
(25) *ru-ú-ḫa-am tu-uk-ta-na-aš-ša-di*	(24) *da-du-ú-a ú-ul ša ka-ša-di*
you drive every boyfriend away	my charms are not easily conquered
(27) *uṣ-ṣi-ṣi pa-ni-a-tim*	(11) *pa-ni-ti-ia–aḫ-sú-us₄-ma*
ask the previous women	I have thought of the previous woman
(30) *[a]ḫ!-du-ú in-ba-am* *[a-ḫ]a-d[u]-[ú] ka-la-[a-ma]*	(23) *in-bu-ú-a ú-ul ša mi-ši*
I enjoyed the fruit. Must I enjoy all (of it/you)?	My fruits are not forgettable
(43) *ka-al-ba-tam ú-uš-ša-ar* (44) *la-i-im ab-ni a-na wa-ša-ri-ki* (45) *ma-ti qá-ba-a-[š]u li-iš-ku-un*	(21) *na-as-qá-ku wa-aš-ra-tu ù a-ma-tu e-li-ka* (25) *e-re-du-ku wa-aš-ra-ak*
shall I let the bitch free? Swallowing a stone to let you go When would a man ever get his say?	I am chosen (as) the subservient one, and a slave for you I will follow you, I am subservient

The second to last stanza of the poem *A Field Full of Salt* on MS 3285 contains a wordplay on the verb *wuššurum* 'to let free': *uššar, ina wašāriki*. It is interesting that this appears to resemble the verb form *wašrāk* 'I am subservient' and the verbal adjective *wašratu* 'the subservient one', which form the defining characteristic of the woman pleading with her lover in MS 5111, *I Shall Be a Slave to You*.[133] Even if the poem on MS 5111 is not directly responding to the words in the precise poem on MS 3285, it is responding to content of a type that is also found there.

One may also observe that the male speaker in *A Field Full of Salt* appears to bend his will in the penultimate stanza. He is not quite able to let his lover go, although he is clearly very angry with her for staying up dancing all night, as the final stanza suggests. Is it possible that he has been persuaded by a female interlocutor much like the one found in *I Shall Be a Slave to You*? This may be similar to the pattern we see in the *Dialogue of the Faithful Lover*. Taken together, such similarities indicate that these two poems from the Schøyen collection belong to the same world of convention as the *Dialogue*. I submit that they are to be considered as the male and female parts of just such dialogue poems, although it is unlikely to impossible that they belong to the same one in the form in which they are preserved.

A further tablet with a dialogue poem or poems relating to love, and presumably non-cultic, has recently been published, which does not seem at first sight to present such negative characteristics for either male or female interlocutors.[134] It is referred to as the *Moussaieff Love Song* on the basis of the private collection that the tablet belonged to when it was published. The text refers once to the man as 'shepherd', which may hint at a function in cult.[135] In my view, given that there are no other clear references to state cult or the Ištar-Dumuzi courtship themes, it is better to explain this reference as a reflection of the fact that imagery associated with the courtship of Ištar and Dumuzi could be called upon in non-cultic love poetry as well. The border between the two was thus entirely fluid. It is also possible, as noted earlier, that lovers saw themselves as enacting divine prototypes of love situations, in particular that between Ištar and Dumuzi.

The primary edition tentatively divides the text on the tablet up into various compositions, at least two, possibly more compositions, of which at least two have 'happy endings' for the lovers, that is they seem to culminate in intercourse.[136] There is a female voice, a male voice and what was interpreted in the first edition as a chorus of some kind, although the existence of this as a separate voice is not so apparent to this reader. The male and female voices are not divided over different stanzas but respond to each other in quick succession, with unequal and indeed hard to segment allocations of poetry. It is clear that the male and female voices are very keen on each other through most of the text, and the sexuality is explicit, possibly even containing a reference to the clitoris by the male voice.[137]

Contrary to the tentative division in the first edition of this poem, repeated mention of certain thematic or lexical elements in the different parts of the text may indicate that the different sections belong to one continuous composition, although this is extremely difficult to establish and by no means a secure conclusion.[138] It is not unusual for texts about love to talk about the same things, after all. My own subjective impression of the *Moussaieff* text is that it is one single poem that charts through extracts of dialogue in separate movements the growth of a relationship from passionate sexual infatuation mentioning primal emotions and wild mountain flowers through to a more organized emotional co-existence including gift giving, exchange and ostensibly set in the city and its agricultural environs, or at least using metaphors to do with these, and then to deterioration expressed with the word *šulummûm ikkir* (rev. 12) 'the well-being/greeting has turned hostile', which seems to echo the apparently positive use of *pî šulmi* 'word of well-being/greeting' earlier in the text (rev. 5). The text is too poorly understood to be sure one way or the other, but if correct this interpretation leads us once again into the area of a highly complex emotional development and negotiation of relationship roles as expressed through the medium of dialogue.

In three of these poems it is notable that not only certain themes but even whole passages appear to be adaptable building blocks migrating from one composition to another. Thus, even the psychologically nuanced profile of the male voice in the *Field Full of Salt* advocated here, or the subtle manipulating strategies of the female voice in the *Dialogue of the Faithful Lover* may correspond to wider stock characters using a variety of combinations of standard phraseology that is at home in this kind of poetry. The stock character need not be one-dimensional, but the role he or she plays is necessarily complex, whether in life or in poetry. In the *Moussaieff Love Song* similar tropes such as the agricultural sexual metaphors to do with ploughing the field are also employed as in the *Field Full of Salt*, although their use may have a different value judgement attached.[139] Stock characters playing type-roles and standard phrases associated with specific genres provide a yardstick by which to measure and evaluate difference from the expected and are thus a key means of manipulating audience reaction. They also further highlight the importance of love poetry of role play.

Insults against women as a literary form?

The theme of the rejection of love by a man has been addressed in two of the four poems we have just reviewed. Groneberg points out that addressing women in such a harsh and violent manner was unusual in Babylonian society, judging from the evidence of letters.[140] If this is the case, *A Field Full of Salt* is a poem that gives us a highly nuanced psychological profile of a single man and his selfish attitude to love. However, literature is often the place where the demons are exorcized that the polite society found in letter-writing usually does not like to countenance. It is thus ultimately unclear how acceptable such open hatred of women was in male-dominated Babylonian circles. In the case of the goddess of love herself, Ištar, it appears to have been perfectly legitimate to humiliate her in a literary context.

Groneberg has suggested that certain passages in the *Dialogue of the Faithful Lover* bear resemblance to a scene from the Standard Babylonian Epic of Gilgameš.[141] This work is preserved on tablets from the first millennium BC, mostly from the library of King Assurbanipal at Nineveh, but it was probably put together largely on the basis of earlier poetic segments sometime in the fourteenth to twelfth centuries BC or thereabouts.[142] In Tablet Six of the Standard Babylonian Epic, Gilgameš and his companion Enkidu return from their more or less heroic quest to slay the guardian of the cedar forest, Humbaba. Gilgameš changes his clothes and, in doing so, is spied by the goddess Ištar, who promptly propositions him, inverting the traditional Babylonian marriage formula to put the female voice first.[143] The hero's response is to compare her to a list of useless and destructive creatures and objects, after which he proceeds to list her previous lovers and the dreadful consequences they suffered after enjoying her embrace.[144] The list ranges from Dumuzi, 'the love of your youth, to whom you allotted perpetual weeping',[145] the speckled *allallu*-bird (hoopoe) whose wing she broke, the lion, whom she caused to be trapped in pits, the horse to whom she gave the whip, muddy water to drink and also perpetual weeping, through to Išullanu the gardener, whose poorly understood fate (he was possibly turned into a dwarf) is presented in the form of a *historiola* (little story) which has the additional function of allowing us to better understand the larger narrative.[146]

None of the previous stories are known in anything other than allusive detail, but that of Išullanu appears in a Sumerian work from the Old Babylonian period, the *Tale* of *Inana and Šukaletuda*, although with somewhat different details.¹⁴⁷ After a lengthy but obscure introduction associating the raven or crow with the invention of the *shadoof*, Šukaletuda the gardener sees Inana asleep under a tree and rapes her.¹⁴⁸ What she does precisely to Šukaletuda is unknown, because the end of the poem is broken, but it is clear that he will remain a subject of song, which does not necessarily have to be a positive thing.¹⁴⁹ This narrative is precisely the opposite of the way Ištar and Išullanu interact in the Epic of Gilgameš.¹⁵⁰ Here Išullanu the gardener is approached by Ištar who makes a proposition to him much as she does to Gilgameš, although with a far more direct eroticism.¹⁵¹ Išullanu's response is to refuse her in a series of indignant questions. The divine reaction is to turn him into something that we do not understand entirely (*ana dallali*). Gilgameš then asks, 'And you would love me and [*change* me] as (you did) them?'¹⁵² This is of interest, because Išullanu did not love Ištar and was still transformed. Rejected by Gilgameš, the goddess Ištar then seeks from her father Anu, the sky-god, the help of the Bull of Heaven, the constellation Taurus, in killing the man who has just rebuffed her advances. However, the hero and his friend kill the bull and Ištar is sent scuttling off to the city-wall, with Enkidu throwing a haunch of the dead bull after her. The narrative of Išullanu serves to demonstrate that Gilgameš is such a superior hero that he can reject the goddess of love and not suffer any consequences, by contrast to Išullanu who did something similar and was punished.¹⁵³

Of course, the consequences of killing the Bull of Heaven are keenly felt in the Epic of Gilgameš, in that the gods decide to kill Enkidu as a result. There are still no consequences for insulting and rejecting Ištar, however.¹⁵⁴ It is possible that the male part of the *Dialogue of the Faithful Lover* and the Schøyen tablet with the poem *A Field Full of Salt* form part of a tradition or mini-genre of anti-woman poems, one to which the scene of Gilgameš insulting Ištar was closely related as a literary type. The observations on the man who lashes out verbally after his lover does not conform to his thinking on relationship politics may well be psychologically astute in the poem on the Schøyen tablet. He was, however, behaving in one of the ways he was expected to behave by denigrating and insulting a woman in a literary context. The female voice in the *Dialogue of the Faithful Lover*, and possibly also that of *I Shall Be a Slave*, is not bowed by this monolithic male aggression but subtly works against it, turning tenderness as a form of strength back on its simplistic and bombastic brutality.

Further non-cultic love poetry?

One tablet from the Schøyen collection contains a poem that is addressed by a man to a woman and is not a misogynistic tirade but, instead, a sensitive love poem charting in few lines the uncertainty of the lover with regard to the object of his affections and the accompanying mood-swings generated by his train of thought.¹⁵⁵ Initially entitled *Oh Girl, Whoopee . . .* by its first editor, A. R. George, being an attempted translation of its first two words, the poem has now been re-edited by N. Wasserman, who thinks it is addressed to the 'daughter of an exile', which is also a suggested translation of those first two words and thus concerns the worries of an insecure lover who is separated from his beloved. Neither suggestion for the interpretation of the first line is particularly convincing.¹⁵⁶ The poem contains the unforgettable image of the love that 'infests', which Wasserman parallels with imagery from the Hebrew Bible.¹⁵⁷ At the end of the poem it emerges that the lover, who is a dreamer of dreams, has in fact been dreaming for real and wakes up writhing around on his bed to the sound of the song of the swallow.[158] While this is perhaps the composition most like a modern love poem among those we have reviewed, it cannot be excluded that it belongs to the category of love-magic incantations, like the highly poetic piece published by A. R. George in this volume. There is no evidence that would either prove or disprove this hypothesis.

Two other compositions are spoken from the perspective of a woman directed at a male lover and may belong to the Ištar-Dumuzi material. The poem on the tablet kept in Geneva, which is explicitly referred to as an *irtum*(-song) and was discussed above in that context, appears to address the issue of separation, because the lover is sent out into the steppe, while the woman fantasizes about his embrace.[159] The poem is rich with the typical language of love poetry, as its initial editor has demonstrated.[160] The poem ends with a prayer to Ištar and dedication to king Ammiditana and thus most probably has a cultic background, although it does not show the repetition typical of cultic poetry.[161] It may nevertheless be that the woman is imagining herself in the role of Ištar, possibly even with the king being Dumuzi.[162] Perhaps all we need to assume is that the prayer and dedication are made to Ištar and the king as the ultimate lovers. Whether 'cultic', 'royal' or none of the above, we have seen that the performance context of this poem was likely to have been public.

One final Old Babylonian fragment from Kiš was given the label 'secular' by J. G. Westenholz.[163] Its explicit sexual content is voiced in a monologue by a woman entreating a man to make love to her and shares one striking parallel with the language used by Ištar to seduce Išullanu in the Epic of Gilgamesh.[164] It is unclear how it can be excluded that this poem belongs to the Ištar-Dumuzi group, thus with the possibility of a cultic use, but it is also uncertain how far belonging to this group excludes that the song might have had a 'secular' use as well. Westenholz considers use as a wedding song, adducing a number of parallels from Palestinian folk songs in her commentary, although the immediate use-context of the text on this particular tablet is likely to have been as a scribal exercise.[165] The description of the bed contains reference to the 'incense-tree' (*kanaktum*), which can be found in love incantations.[166] The poem contains several examples of the so-called plural of ecstasy, where body parts particularly are referred to as if they were the shared property of the lovers.[167]

Concluding reflections

A frequent phenomenon to be observed within the poems is their fluctuating verse structure, as well as irregular lines and stanza length. They are not to be compared with the more regular metric arrangements of Akkadian epic poetry, usually into couplets of bipartite lines of verse. Such formal characteristics might be seen as a genre characteristic suitable to the subject matter in that the short sentences and wandering focus of passionate discourse might be said to be iconically reproduced in the construction of the stanza.[168] This hypothesis is only very tentative.

Unsurprisingly, the love-magic incantation is designed to gain possession (*ṣabātum*) or control of the beloved object by magical means combining the utterance of the spell and the performance of a usually analogical ritual. In a similar way to the analogical magic contained in the ritual, the use of the language of love in the spell is designed to bring about the desired effect. But is not this attempt to enchant or spellbind the beloved partially the conceit, and the risk, involved in writing love poetry in the first place? The language of the other poems associated with love frequently uses similar forms and imagery to that of the incantations. The image of the garden of desire is found as a locus of erotic activity in the love-magic incantations, as well as in love poetry (whether divine love lyrics or not); the metaphor of 'fruits' and sexual activity or genitalia is also found throughout; specific items such as the 'incense-tree' (*kanaktu*) are also found in both love-magic incantations and love poetry, as are the love-charms/cupids known as the *Ir'emus*. On the other hand, the sexually arousing 'laughter' of the beloved occurs twenty times in the thirty-four love poems collected by N. Wasserman, but only one dubious attestation occurs in a clearly identifiable love-magic incantation.[169] It is unclear whether any reason should be sought for this, given that the corpus is so small.

The type of lover portrayed in the incantations is frequently not sympathetic, and the violence involved in using magic to sway affections comes out in the imagery used: grab, strike, bind, make dizzy with vertigo. There seems to be little difference if the protagonists are male or female, although we did note that whereas the man 'grabs' the vulva of the woman in the third millennium BC love incantation from Kiš, the woman uses her vulva to 'bind' the man in an Old Babylonian incantation from Isin, which uses similar language. The use of violence is thus or can be asymmetrical.

The three poems that we grouped together as examples of or elements of dialogue or competition poems between men and women in section (5) appear to demonstrate a homogeneity of theme and language that is to an extent different to the other poetry associated with love and should quite possibly be given a sub-grouping of their own. Here the language of the poetry is usually less lyrical than in the other love poetry, more prosaic and the topics of conversation more every day. Certainly, we observed implied allusions to the effects of love magic on the male participant in the *Dialogue of the Faithful Lover*, possibly indicating a subtext to the narrative of domination and resistant adaptation that develops throughout that poem. The three poems are, however, not lyrical in the sense of using high poetic language to emphasize heightened emotion. This contrasts with the recently published *Moussaieff Love Song*, which seems to use poetic language in a fluidly structured dialogue format to suggest emotional peaks and troughs.

The emphasis on role play, whether that be the stereotyped gender-positions which are occupied by the participants in the *Dialogue of the Faithful Lover* or the figuring of the lover as a token or manifestation of the type represented on the divine level by Ištar or Dumuzi, a role which the lover performs, appears to be a central part of these types of love poetry. In the *Dialogue of the Faithful Lover* and the two poems that conceivably also belong to one or the other side of similar dialogues (*Field Full of Salt*, *I Shall Be a Slave to You*), the positions taken by the male or alternatively the female figures are variously so similar that one might almost talk of their appearing in such characters as being one of the rules of the genre. This is something that could easily be understood in terms of the modern gender theoretical notion of 'performativity'. This conception, outlined by Judith Butler over a quarter of a century ago, argues that gender is a complex and ambiguous category, which we force into a monolithic, black and white, either/or polar scheme of male versus female appearances by repeatedly performing social gender roles that have been learnt as prototypes for social behaviour.[170] Although Butler was clearly talking about gender as a social category, the application of this theoretical framework to drama, where characters appear in roles by definition, and from there to literature more generally, is of course readily comprehensible. A good deal of analytical mileage could be gained from seeing the form of poetry found in these three poems, which were very likely performed in public, as a forum for the enactment and negotiation of power within and between gender roles.[171] The focus for expressing this enactment and negotiation of roles is the love relationship expressed in dialogue in a poetic love drama.

W. G. Lambert commented, despite the small sample that we have of this type of literature, on the apparent absence in Babylonian love poetry of the typical image of the male lover enslaved by the female beloved as is known from Roman elegiac and much later love poetry.[172] Rather, in the poem from the Schøyen collection *I Will Be a Slave to You*, spoken by a woman to a man, sentiments of self-abasement in the service of love seem at first sight to be female in gender. However, recent readings of the *Dialogue of the Faithful Lover*, supported by the understanding of its parallel monologue *A Field Full of Salt* promoted here, show that the female participant, who appears as a partial parallel to the voice of *I Shall Be a Slave to You*, is in no way passive or enslaved.[173] Instead, she presents a complex and adaptable strategy of response and indeed manipulation. The negotiation between the two is multifaceted on the social level and multi-layered on the literary one.

What we do find occasionally, as we saw earlier, is the enslavement ('binding') of the man by the female sexual organ where the male drive to possess (*lulappit ḫurdatki* 'let me touch your vulva') is co-opted by the female into a means of taking control over him (*luppitma ḫurdatni* 'touch our vulva').[174] Here one cannot avoid the question of whether all these texts were ultimately written by men, projecting gender-hierarchical fantasies and an ideology of how women should be in a sexual relationship as the social norm, but for the moment I feel this question is not answerable within the framework of this chapter. What we have is what the texts say, and that shows a surprisingly nuanced approach to the distribution of power between gender roles.

The comparison of the king to the divine lover of the love-goddess, in whose role he appears in some of the 'divine love lyrics', allows the apex of the social order to be figured in intimate and reciprocal relations with the divine. The cultic context of the 'divine love lyrics' of Abi-ešuḫ, probably also of others too, is clear from their content, whatever that cult may actually have consisted of. However, it remains very difficult to find any Akkadian love poetry that can certainly be regarded as manifestly non-cultic. The three poems reviewed in section (7) cannot be safely assumed not to have had either a cultic or a magical use-context. Conversely, that which had a cultic use in celebrating the (metaphorical?) marriage of the king with the goddess of love may well also have had a more popular use in providing an archetype to which all lovers could appeal.

At the one end of the spectrum of use of the Dumuzi-Ištar material, we thus have the clearly cultic context of the Divine Love Lyrics. At the other, we have the personal use of much the same material, as possibly exemplified by the *Moussaieff Love Song*. The declaration of the speaker of a potency-incantation found at Boğazköy to the effect that he too will sleep with the goddess of love can be seen as evidence of this type of attitude. It can only be verified in the rarest of circumstances that the poems were thus used, as this is a layer of data to which we can have little or no access. The preservation of certain songs as the fruits of scribal exercises, pieces known by heart, which might have been written down by trainee scribes precisely because they were popular, indicates that these were not originally compositions associated with anything like secret knowledge or the halls of learning.[175]

The performance of typical love poetry including Dumuzi-Ištar motifs may thus have linked the top of society with the life experience of the rest of the population, although this remains a crude and uncertain theoretical assessment at present. Even in ancient Iraq of many thousands of years ago love poetry in the forms outlined may have the potential to tell us a great deal about the values, hierarchies and ideological institutions which characterized society. It was part of the living social fabric, even though the documentary evidence has preserved so little of it. However, it is important to understand the voices and characters that speak through ancient Iraqi love poetry from a literary perspective, first of all, as literary types particular to certain genres. The images of love relationships that are to be gained from other genres of texts, such as law-codes, legal or economic documents, medical texts, rituals and royal inscriptions, are themselves also likely to be varied according to the habitual forms and expectations of the genre concerned.

Notes

* I am grateful to Andrew George and Martin Worthington for comments on a draft of this manuscript, which was initially completed in 2014, then revised in 2017. Any errors or infelicities of interpretation remain my responsibility. Abbreviations used are as follows: AHw.: W. von Soden, *Akkadisches Handwörterbuch* (Wiesbaden: Harrassowitz, 1959–81); CAD, *Assyrian Dictionary of the University of Chicago* (Chicago: University of Chicago Press, 1956–2011); ETCSL: Electronic Text Corpus of Sumerian Literature. http://etcsl.orinst.ox.ac.uk/, last accessed 27 September 2014; CDLI: Cuneiform Digital Library Initiative, http://cdli.ucla.edu/, last accessed 12 May 2015; SEAL: M. P. Streck and N. Wasserman, *Sources of Early Akkadian Literature*, http://www.seal.uni-leipzig.de/, last accessed 27 September 2014.

1 A. Rich, *The Dream of a Common Language* (New York: W. W. Norton & Co., 1978), 28 (Poem VII). I am grateful to my friend Noah Cohen for alerting me to this wonderful piece of poetry many years ago.
2 R. Barthes, *A Lover's Discourse* (New York: Hill and Wang, 1978), 3.
3 Ibid., 9.
4 R. Barthes, 'The Death of the Author', (first published 1968), in *Image, Music, Text*, trans. S. Heath (London: Fontana, 1977), 142–8. D. Kennedy, *The Arts of Love, Five Studies in the Discourse of Roman Love Elegy* (Cambridge: Cambridge University Press, 1993), 80.
5 J. Butler, *Gender Trouble: Feminism and the Subversion of Identity*, 2nd edn (1st edn 1990) (New York: Routledge, 2006).
6 L. Berlant, 'Love, A Queer Feeling', in *Homosexuality and Psychoanalysis*, ed. T. Dean and C. Lane (Chicago: University of Chicago Press, 2001), 432–52.
7 For example, M. Sanchez, *Erotic Subjects: The Sexuality of Politics in Early Modern English Literature* (Oxford: Oxford University Press, 2011).
8 J. Griffin, *Latin Poets and Roman Life* (London: Duckworth, 1985); M. Wyke, 'Mistress and Metaphor in Augustan Elegy', *Helios* 16 (1989), 25–47.

D. F. Kennedy, *The Arts of Love, Five Studies in the Discourse of Roman Love Elegy* (Cambridge: CUP, 2012), 1–12; K. Ormand, *Controlling Desires: Sexuality in Ancient Greece and Rome* (Westport, CT: Praeger, 2009).

9   J. A. Black, 'Babylonian Ballads: A New Genre', *Journal of the American Oriental Society* 103, no. 1 (1983): 25–34. B. Groneberg, '"The Faithful Lover" Reconsidered: Towards Establishing A New Genre', in *Sex and Gender in the Ancient Near East, Proceedings of the XLVIIe Rencontre Assyriologique Internationale*, ed. S. Parpola and R. M. Whiting (Helsinki: The Neo-Assyrian Text-Corpus Project, 2002), 165–83.

10 J. Frow, *Genre. The New Critical Idiom* (London and New York: Routledge, 2006), 26–7.

11 W. Ch. Ouyang, 'Genre, Ideologies, Genre Ideologies and Narrative Transformation', *Middle Eastern Literatures* 7, no. 2 (2004): 128.

12 For the term 'super-genre', see G. Hutchinson, 'Genre and Super-Genre', in *Generic Interfaces in Latin Literature: Encounters, Interactions and Transformations*, ed. Th. D Papanghelis, S. J. Harrison and S. Frangoulidis (Berlin: De Gruyter, 2013), 19–34.

13 For discussion relating to the world of Roman poetry, see S. J. Harrison, *Generic Enrichment in Vergil and Horace* (Oxford: Oxford University Press, 2007), 10–18.

14 For paradigmatic examples of the varying reception of Homer depending on time and place, see the works reviewed in J. Burgess, 'Recent Reception of Homer: A Review Article', *Phoenix* 62 (2008): 184–95.

15 For early Arabic literary theory, see W.-Ch. Ouyang, *Literary Criticism in Medieval Arabic-Islamic Culture: The Making of a Tradition* (Edinburgh: Edinburgh University Press, 1997).

16 Ovid, *Amores*, ed. and trans. J. Booth (Oxford: Oxford University Press, 1973), 1.1, 1–4; Harrison, *Generic Enrichment in Vergil and Horace*, 7.

17 K. Eksell, 'Genre in Early Arabic Poetry', in *Literary History: Towards a Global Perspective, Volume 2: Literary Genres: An Intercultural Approach*, ed. G. Lindberg-Wada, S. Helgesson, A. Pettersson and M. Pettersson (Berlin: De Gruyter, 2006), 163.

18 Ibid., 165. Although this is not the only Arabic concept she discusses in this context, Eksell further comments (ibid., 166) that the focus on the *ġaraḍ* 'aim, intention' of the poet, keeps the medieval Arabic notion of genre firmly in the realm of the concrete, contextually based speech act, as opposed to the term 'genre' itself, which is regarded by her as being 'neutral' in this regard. One should note that this dynamic approach seems superficially different from the critical standpoint which tries to minimize the role of the author's intention, which can never really be known, in the reading process. For texts which typically have no explicit authors, as is the case with the vast majority of Akkadian literature, this is not such a paradox.

19 Theoretical works of hermeneutics begin to appear in the first millennium BC in the form of commentaries, mainly on omen texts. See E. Frahm, *Babylonian Text Commentaries: Origins of Interpretation*, Guides to the Mesopotamian Textual Record 5 (Münster: Ugarit-Verlag, 2011). It is likely that these existed in oral form earlier. The second millennium BC clearly also had a tradition of scholarly hermeneutics based around experimentation with Sumerian poetry as evidenced in productions such as the *Scholars of Uruk* (*Babylonian Literary Texts in the Schøyen Collection*), Cornell University Studies in Assyriology and Sumerology 10 (Bethesda: CDL Press, 2009), 78–112 and parts of the lexical series *Erimḫuš* which may itself have its origins in commentaries on obscure Sumerian literature (N. Veldhuis, 'Intellectual History and Assyriology', *Journal of Ancient Near Eastern History* 1, no. 1 (2014): 27).

20 J. Hackl, 'Language Death and Dying Reconsidered: The Rôle of Late Babylonian as a Vernacular Language', Version 01, in *Imperium and Officium Working Papers*, 2011, http://iowp.univie.ac.at/node/206, last accessed 11 August 2014.

21 For a brief history of the Akkadian language, see A. R. George, 'Babylonian and Assyrian: A History of Akkadian', in *Languages of Iraq, Ancient and Modern*, ed. J. N. Postgate (London: British School of Archaeology in Iraq, 2007), 31–71. For Aramaic, see H.

Gzella, *A Cultural History of Aramaic. From the Beginnings to the Advent of Islam*, in Handbuch der Orientalistik 1/111 (Leiden: Brill, 2015).

22   For the linguistic affinities of third millennium BC Akkadian, see M. Hilgert, *Akkadisch in der Ur III-Zeit*, Imgula 5 (Münster: Rhema, 2002); R. Hasslebach, 'The Affiliation of Sargonic Akkadian with Babylonian and Assyrian: New Insights Concerning the Internal Sub-Grouping of Akkadian', *Journal of Semitic Studies* 52, no. 1 (2007): 21–43.

23   General overviews of Akkadian love poetry can be found at J. G. Westenholz, 'Love lyrics from the ancient Near East', in *Civilizations of the Ancient Near East*, ed. J. M. Sasson (New York: Scribner, 1995); B. Musche, *Die Liebe in der altorientalischen Dichtung*, Studies in the History and Culture of the Ancient Near East 15 (Leiden: Brill, 1999); J. Klein and Y. Sefati, '"Secular" Love Songs in Mesopotamian Literature', in *Birkat Shalom. Studies in the Bible, Ancient Near Eastern Literature, and Postbiblical Judaism Presented to Shalom M. Paul on the Occasion of His Seventieth Birthday*, ed. Ch. Cohen, V. A., Hurowitz, A. Hurvitz, Y. Muffs, B. J. Schwartz and J. H. Tigay (Winona Lake: Eisenbrauns, 2008), 613–26. Recent editions of Akkadian love poems can be found on the website SEAL ('Sources of Early Akkadian Literature') maintained by M. P. Streck (Leipzig) and N. Wasserman (Jerusalem). See now N. Wasserman, *Akkadian Love Literature of the Third and Second Millennia BCE*, Leipziger Altorientalische Studien 4 (Wiesbaden: Harrassowitz, 2016), for an accessible monograph collecting, editing and translating thirty-four Akkadian love poems from the third and second millennia BC.

24   E. Ebeling, *Keilschrifttexte aus Assur religiösen Inhaltes Bd. I* (Leipzig: Hinrichs, 1919), 269–76, no. 158 (German translation: 'Ich zähle die Lieder', in *Hymnen, Klagelieder und Gebete*, Texte aus der Umwelt des alten Testaments, Neue Folge 7, ed. B. Janowski and D. Schwemer (2013), 54–63, reference to translation courtesy M. Worthington; Wasserman, *Akkadian Love Literature of the Third and Second Millennia BCE*, 195–234). The reason for compiling this list is unknown. It might be a library register, although there is a strong emphasis on the musical accompaniment of the poems. B. Groneberg supposes it might even have been a list of songs to be performed in a ritual, B. Groneberg, '"Brust" (irtum)–Gesänge', in *Munuscula Mesopotamica, Festschrift für Johannes Renger*, ed. B. Böck, E. Cancik-Kirschbaum and Th. Richter, AOAT 267 (Münster: Ugarit-Verlag, 1999), 58. Wasserman, *Akkadian Love Literature of the Third and Second Millennia BCE*, 21) sees a public compositional and perhaps performative context for many of the poems catalogued but also characterizes the list as in some sense belonging to the official sphere as opposed to more popular compositions that have survived but are not listed in this catalogue, as well as by comparison to other catalogues of first lines which have a more 'private' character (Ibid., 205). See further H. Limet, 'Le texte, *KAR 158*', in *Collectanea Orientalia: Histoire, Arts de l'espace et industrie de la terre: Etudes offertes en homage à Agnès Spycket*, Civilizations du Proche-Orient, Series 1, Archéologie et Environment 3, ed. H. Gasche and B. Hrouda (Neuchâtel: Recherches et publications, 1996), 151–8.

25   D. Shehata, *Musiker und ihr vokales Repertoire, Untersuchungen zu Inhalt und Organisation von Musikerberufen und Liedgattungen in altbabylonischer Zeit*, Göttinger Beiträge zum alten Orient Band 3 (Göttingen: Universitätsverlag, 2009), 10 and 308.

26   Ibid., 328–30.

27   Thus the central contention of Groneberg, '"Brust" (irtum)–Gesänge', although other Akkadian terms are preserved that are used to characterize love-related compositions (Wasserman, *Akkadian Love Literature of the Third and Second Millennia BCE*, 20).

28   B. Groneberg, 'Searching for Akkadian Lyrics: From Old Babylonian to the "Liederkatalog"', *KAR 158*', *Journal of Cuneiform Studies* 55 (2003): 68–9.

29   The tablet containing this list was allegedly excavated in a secondary layer (Neo-Assyrian, first millennium BC) in the south-west court of the Assur temple along with a number of other tablets according to Groneberg ('Searching for Akkadian Lyrics', 58 with fn. 45). For this archive, see Q. Pedersén, *Archives and Libraries in the City of Assur. A Survey of the Material from the German Excavations, Part I*, Acta Universitatis Upsaliensis (Uppsala:

Studia Semitica Upsaliensia 6, 1985), 31–42. However, note the cautious comments of J. A. Black, 'Babylonian Ballads', 25 fn. 3 regarding the tablet's missing excavation number. The notion of a 'Library of Tiglath-Pileser I' (1114-1076 BC) referred to in Black, 'Babylonian Ballads', and Groneberg, 'Searching for Akkadian Lyrics', has now been given up as an illusion of modern scholarship (see H. Freydank, *Beiträge zur mittelassyrischen Chronologie und Geschichte*, Schriften zur Geschichte und Kultur des alten Orients 21 (Berlin, 1991), 94–7).

30 Black, 'Babylonian Ballads'; Wasserman, *Akkadian Love Literature of the Third and Second Millennia BCE*, 110–14, dated to the Late Old Babylonian period ibid., 110.

31 The tablet is numbered BM 47507 (Black, 'Babylonian Ballads'). The poem's title is on obv. 1 *erbamma rē'û [ḫarmi Ištarma]* 'come in to me shepherd, lover of Ištar' (= Ebeling, *Keilschrifttexte aus Assur religiösen Inhaltes Bd. I*, no. 158 i 6); the catchline indicating the next song in the series is found ibid. rev. 40: *uršānam rē'â azammurma* 'I will sing of the brave shepherd' (= Ebeling, *Keilschrifttexte aus Assur religiösen Inhaltes Bd. I*, no. 158 i 7); series title *mārumma rā'imni* 'the boy who loves me' ibid. rev. 42 (Ebeling, *Keilschrifttexte aus Assur religiösen Inhaltes Bd. I*, no. 158 i 43). See Black, 'Babylonian Ballads', 28. E. Frahm, *Historische und historisch-literarische Texte*, Keilschrifttexte aus Assur literarischen Inhalts 3 (Wiesbaden: Harrassowitz, 2009), 144 has cautiously suggested a further fragmentary poem on a Middle Assyrian tablet from Assur as a candidate for a whole song corresponding to a song title from this catalogue. The poem seems to be a duet between a king and a woman and is characterized by floral imagery.

32 Ebeling, *Keilschrifttexte aus Assur religiösen Inhaltes Bd. I*, no. 158 ii 43.

33 I. L. Finkel, 'A Fragmentary Catalogue of Lovesongs', *Acta Sumerologica Japan* 10 (1988): 17–18.

34 Groneberg, 'Searching for Akkadian Lyrics', 66.

35 Shehata, *Musiker und ihr vokales Repertoire*, 329.

36 iv 16': 4 *irātum* (17') *iškar êš rāmī* (18') *šūqur*. Groneberg, '"Brust" (irtum)–Gesänge', 181. Shehata, *Musiker und ihr vokales Repertoire*, 328. Wasserman, *Akkadian Love Literature of the Third and Second Millennia BCE*, 104–9 with further literature.

37 Groneberg, '"Brust" (irtum)–Gesänge', 177.

38 As M. Worthington points out to me, these lines do not formally have to be translated as questions. I would find it unusual if *ṣeher râmī* 'my loving is small' were not a rhetorical question to be answered in the negative. Possibly understand: 'my sighs are its beginning, but is my loving small?' (Wasserman, *Akkadian Love Literature of the Third and Second Millennia BCE*, 107) translates '(*though*) its beginning is sighs of woe, *still* young is my love'.

39 Groneberg, '"Brust" (irtum)–Gesänge', 90; Wasserman, *Akkadian Love Literature of the Third and Second Millennia BCE*, 109 (more cautiously).

40 For discussion of this term, see Shehata, *Musiker und ihr vokales Repertoire*, 344–7.

41 Groneberg, '"Brust" (irtum)–Gesänge', 190, mentioning the texts in M. Held, 'A Faithful Lover in an Old Babylonian Dialogue', *Journal of Cuneiform Studies* 15 (1961): 1–26; W. G. Lambert, 'Divine Love Lyrics from the Reign of Abi-ešuḫ', *Mitteilungen des Instituts für Orientforschung* 12 (1966-67): 41–56; M. Sigrist and J. G. Westenholz, 'The Love Poem of Rīm-Sîn and Nanaya', in *Birkat Shalom: Studies in the Bible, Ancient Near Eastern Literature, and Postbiblical Judaism Presented to Shalom M. Paul on the Occasion of His Seventieth Birthday*, vol. 2, ed. Ch. Cohen, V. A. Hurowitz, A. Hurvitz, Y. Muffs, B. J. Schwartz and J. H. Tigay (Winona Lake: Eisenbrauns, 2008), 667–704. However, the love lyrics of Abi-ešuḫ and Rim-Sin seem to belong more to a state oriented cult than does the *Dialogue of the Faithful Lover*.

42 Groneberg, 'Searching for Akkadian Lyrics', 69.

43 Shehata, *Musiker und ihr vokales Repertoire*, 237–8.

44 Ibid., 344–7.

45 Compare the typology of Sigrist and Westenholz, 'The Love Poem of Rim-Sîn and Nanaya', 667–8, '(1) poems with deities personifying the role of lovers, (2) poems with kings acting as lovers of the goddess Inana, or less frequently their consorts, (3) poems with ordinary mortals performing the roles of lovers'. This grouping pays less attention to the use-context of the poems, more attention to the identities of the participants in the discourse, and may ignore or group elsewhere the category of love-magic incantations. For further comments on genre, particularly the difficulties of sustaining generic boundaries across Akkadian literature and distinguishing between 'secular' and 'religious' contexts, see Wasserman, *Akkadian Love Literature of the Third and Second Millennia BCE*, 20–1.

46 A. Westenholz and J. G. Westenholz, 'Help for Rejected Suitors: The Old Akkadian Love Incantation MAD V 8', *Orientalia Neue Serie* 46 (1977): 198–216, 198–9, where the presence of a small vertical wedge after certain signs is also held to be indicative of a school tablet, on the basis of a *comparandum* from Ešnuna. The poor writing on its own may just as well be an indication of a writer who does not write very often, but it is difficult to say. Contrast the remarks of Wasserman, *Akkadian Love Literature of the Third and Second Millennia BCE*, 242.

47 I. J. Gelb, *Sargonic Texts in the Ashmolean Museum*, MAD 5 (Oxford, 1970), 7–12; Westenholz and Westenholz, 'Help for Rejected Suitors', 198–219; B. Groneberg, 'Die Liebesbeschwörung MAD V 8 und ihr literarischer Kontext', *Révue d' Assyriologie et d'archéologie orientale* 95, no. 2 (2001): 103–5; W. G. Lambert, *Babylonian Creation Myths*, Mesopotamian Civilizations 16 (Winona Lake: Eisenbrauns, 2013), 31–2.

48 Wasserman, *Akkadian Love Literature of the Third and Second Millennia BCE*, 242–6, no. 22. See also CDLI P285640 (credit Englund, Wagensonner, Brumfield, CDLI Staff).

49 Assyriologists may note that this transliteration attempts to represent the tripartite phonology of the sibilants in Old Akkadian and does not use the convention which deploys [ś] for a sibilant represented by signs using S which corresponds to a later Old Babylonian /š/. This is both transliterated and normalized as /s/. The transliteration and normalization [z] = phonetic /tˢ/ is used where the signs using Z are deployed, even when they correspond to a later /s/, and the transliteration [š] is used when Š-signs are used to write the interdental affricate /ṯ/ (= θ). Logographically written words containing sibilants are reconstructed etymologically where possible. On the other hand, no attempt has been made at a fully phonetic representation of the approximate sounds, for example, of probably glottalized sibilants such as /tˢ'/, corresponding to the usual transliteration [ṣ] written with signs using Z. See R. Hasselbach, *Sargonic Akkadian. A Historical and Comparative Study of the Syllabic Texts* (Wiesbaden: Harrassowitz, 2005), 95–7.

50 'Her' is restored, as is most of the verb. Groneberg, 'Die Liebesbeschwörung MAD V 8 und ihr literarischer Kontext', 103, restores the verb as *uṭāb*, 'makes pleasant, happy', and the prepositional phrase as *in sagīsa* 'in her shrine', giving the translation: 'erfreut in ihrem Heiligtum'. One might have expected *uṭābši* 'makes her happy' in that case. *sagû* 'shrine' is attested at least once in Old Babylonian (CAD S 27). *sāqu* 'thigh' is not attested so early, except in this instance (CAD S 169). The choice of image obviously makes a difference to the tenor of the poem.

51 Understanding *ú-da-ra* as third dual present Dt-stem of **êrum* 'to be awake' (*yūtarrā*). Admittedly, the Dt-stem is not attested for this verb, although the D-stem may be (AHw 247; CAD E 326, Groneberg, 'Die Liebesbeschwörung MAD V 8 und ihr literarischer Kontext', 104 fn. 41) understands the verb to be from *turrum* 'turn (transitive)', but translates as a passive 'ist geleitet', with the subject being the Ir'emu, which is an unusual sense for the D-stem of this verb, in addition to the fact that the verb would have to be ventive (*yutarram*), whereas final -*m* is mostly signalled in this text. The D-stems of *warû* 'lead' *tarû* 'to fetch, lead away' are not attested. Wasserman similarly (*Akkadian Love Literature of the Third and Second Millennia BCE*, 244) has 'turning', but again apparently intransitively with a ventive. Derivation from *watārum* 'to increase' has also

been proposed (W. G. Lambert, 'The Language of ARET V, 6 and 7', *Quaderni Semitici* 18 (1992): 53). A secure solution is not in sight.

52 Groneberg, ('Die Liebesbeschwörung MAD V 8 und ihr literarischer Kontext', 104 fn. 42) interprets *damiqtā* as a P3f stative 'they are beautiful', usually *damqā*. Here the form is understood as vocative, with (Wasserman, *Akkadian Love Literature of the Third and Second Millennia BCE*, 244 and CDLI).

53 Verb highly suspect, here understood as third f. dual perf. Gt stem of *patāqu* B 'to drink' (with CDLI 'you are drinking', Wasserman 'you *have drunk*(?)', although understood as second dual), which is only otherwise attested in the first millennium BC, albeit in two literary texts (CAD P 275) where it could conceivably belong to an archaic linguistic register. The third (or second?) dual verbal prefix *ti-* is possibly archaic here. Other translations have used *batāqu* 'to chop off', or *patāqu* A 'to cast, to mould'. Wasserman, *Akkadian Love Literature of the Third and Second Millennia BCE*, 243 and CDLI translate the previous verb 'descend' as an imperative addressed to the two women.

54 This and the following verbs are perhaps to be understood as performative preterites (suggestion A. R. George, also Wasserman, *Akkadian Love Literature of the Third and Second Millennia BCE*, 245), which would support the notion that the speaker is manipulating a figurine of some kind representing the beloved. Westenholz and Westenholz, 'Help for Rejected Suitors', 208 understand *ša rūqātim* 'which is far away'. To be understood as a writing of the old Semitic phoneme */ġ/* before a back-vowel, later amalgamated with /ḫ/ and /ʾ/ (thus from *ruʾtu* 'spit'). For the fate of */ġ/* in Akkadian see L. E. Kogan, '*ġ* in Akkadian', *Ugaritforschungen* 33 (2001): 263–98; Additions and Corrections to '*ġ* in Akkadian', *Ugaritforschungen* 34 (2002): 315–17.

55 There is no reason to think this phrase represents a 'change of sentiment' with W. G. Lambert, 'Devotion: The Languages of Religion and Love', in *Figurative Language in the Ancient Near East*, ed. M. Mindlin, M. J. Geller and J. E. Wansbrough (London: School of Oriental and African Studies, 1987), 34, as the urine is simply mentioned as something that characterizes the vulva.

56 For the suggestion of this understanding of *yūmissa* see Groneberg, 'Die Liebesbeschwörung MAD V 8 und ihr literarischer Kontext', 104 fn. 47. Westenholz and Westenholz, 'Help for Rejected Suitors', 209, followed by Wasserman, *Akkadian Love Literature of the Third and Second Millennia BCE*, 245, suggest 'for her day', that is, the lover's day, which is attested in one other love poem. The poplar tree is something the lover wants to reach in the Sumerian Dumuzi-Inana poem R (A) 24, (C) 12' (Y. Sefati, *Love Songs in Sumerian Literature* (Ramat Gan: Bar-Ilan University Press, 1998), 237), which was written down some 400 years later than this poem.

57 Understanding this and *i-du-ru* in line 22 as a form of an otherwise unattested verb *dwr 'to go around, encircle, protect', the root of which is preserved in *dūru* 'wall' (Westenholz and Westenholz, 'Help for Rejected Suitors', 208; Wasserman, *Akkadian Love Literature of the Third and Second Millennia BCE*, 245–6 with further literature). Alternatively to be understood as *tūrinni* from *tʾr 'to turn (intransitive)'. However, the intransitive sense 'turn to me' is difficult to match with the transitive meaning needed for *iturru* in the next clause, which must be the same verb, but would in this case be formally intransitive. See Lambert, 'Devotion', 35. *i-da-az-ga-ri-ni* has also been interpreted as a verbal form, S2f Ntn-stem of *zkr, meaning 'keep talking to me' (Groneberg, 'Die Liebesbeschwörung MAD V 8 und ihr literarischer Kontext', 105 fn. 49; Wasserman, *Akkadian Love Literature of the Third and Second Millennia BCE*, 246).

58 B. R. Foster, *Before the Muses: An Anthology of Akkadian Literature*, 3rd edn (Bethesda: CDL Press, 2005), 68, translates as 'his arms are two round bundles of fruit', using *šerkum* 'clump of fruit', although it is difficult to understand the origin of the weak consonantal ending in this case. The word *serg/kû* is only attested here in Akkadian, and its meaning 'adorned' is reconstructed etymologically from Ethiopic *tasargawa* 'to be adorned' (AHw.

1216a, CAD Š/3, 102b). This is not the most secure method for elucidating meaning, it must be admitted.

59   Groneberg, 'Die Liebesbeschwörung MAD V 8 und ihr literarischer Kontext', *Révue d' Assyriologie et d'archéologie orientale* 95, no. 2 (2001): 101.

60   Groneberg, 'Die Liebesbeschwörung MAD V 8 und ihr literarischer Kontext', *Révue d' Assyriologie et d'archéologie orientale* 95, no. 2 (2001): 110–12. For jewellery as a metaphor for sexual organs in ancient Near Eastern literature more generally see J. G. Westenholz, 'Metaphorical Language in the Poetry of Love in the Ancient Near East'. In D. Charpin and F. Joannès (eds) *La circulation des biens, des personnes et des idées dans le proche-orient ancien*. Actes de la XXXVIIIe Rencontre Assyriologique Internationale (Paris, 8–10 Juillet 1991), 383–6.

61   Lambert, *Babylonian Creation Myths*, 32; A. R. George, *Babylonian Literary Texts in the Schøyen Collection*. Manuscripts in the Schøyen Collection, Cuneiform Texts 4. Cornell University Studies in Assyriology and Sumerology 10 (Bethesda, MD, 2009), 53.

62   Westenholz 'Metaphorical Language in the Poetry of Love', 382–3.

63   Wasserman, *Akkadian Love Literature of the Third and Second Millennia BCE*, 52 comments that the scene 'is not far from rape'.

64   IB 1554, C. Wilcke, 'Liebesbeschwörungen aus Isin', *Zeitschrift für Assyriologie* 75 (1985): 188–209. Wasserman, *Akkadian Love Literature of the Third and Second Millennia BCE*, 257–60.

65   See the analysis of J. A. Scurlock, 'Was there a "Love-Hungry" Ēntu-priestess Named Eṭirtum', *Archiv für Orientforschung* 36, no. 37 (1989-90): 107–12, who sees the tablet as a collection of different incantations. B. Groneberg, 'Liebes-und Hundesbeschwörungen im Kontext', in *Studies Presented to R.D. Biggs, June 4, 2004*, ed. M. T. Roth, W. Farber, M. W. Stolper and P. von Bechtolsheim (Chicago: Oriental Institute, 2007), 100–6, sees all of the nine incantations with subscripts on the tablet as combining to form a single larger ritual procedure designed to ward off the magic of a love-rival and at the same time assure oneself of the potency of the beloved. However, the characterization of the whole group in the final colophon as 'incantation(s) of a potsherd at the crossroads' (Wilcke, 'Liebesbeschwörungen aus Isin', 191, 204, 205, l. 124) might indicate the sort of use-context that the spells of this collection might have had: short (aggressive love-)magic spells for practical purposes.

66   Lambert, 'Devotion', 35 prefers it to be a 'mouth of winds', using a rare fem. Pl. of *šāru* 'wind'. However, this is in my view the vulva, again.

67   Groneberg, 'Liebes-und Hundesbeschwörungen im Kontext', 110) thinks that this passage is to be understood in the context of incantations against dog-bites, which sometimes show a similar language and imagery to parts of this text. The addressee would be a substitute for the man, which she tentatively assumes to be a fish referred to in a ritual interjection (l. 23, Groneberg, 'Liebes-und Hundesbeschwörungen im Kontext', 107 fn. 55). The speaker would be speaking through the medium of a dog (Groneberg, 'Liebes-und Hundesbeschwörungen im Kontext', 101), using the imagery of the dog's vulva to bewitch the object of her desire. The potency of intercourse between dog and bitch is, according to Groneberg, a central analogy of love-magic, and the image of the male dog's penis being held fast by the bitch's vulva does indeed recur in cultic love poetry from the first millennium BC ('divine love lyrics' Lambert, 'The Problem of the Love-Lyrics', in *Unity and Diversity. Essays in the History, Literature, and Religion of the Ancient Near East*, ed. H. Goedicke and J. J. M. Roberts (Baltimore and London: Johns Hopkins University Press, 1975), 104, iii 7; Groneberg, 'Liebes-und Hundesbeschwörungen im Kontext', 91) and in potency incantations (R. D. Biggs, *ŠÀ.ZI.GA: Ancient Mesopotamian Potency Incantations* (Locust Valley: J.J. Augustin, 1967), 33).

68   It is possible that each of the sections punctuated by the ritual instructions is a self-contained incantation, as interpreted by Scurlock, but even this analysis does not obviate the problem of the switch in gender between the speakers in lines 30–6.

69   ḫu-bu-ú-ša-ki = ḫubbušāki (nom. Dual), with unexplained plene-spelling in the second syllable: Wilcke ('Liebesbeschwörungen aus Isin', 201, 207) 'Wölbungen'; Wasserman,

Akkadian Love Literature of the Third and Second Millennia BCE, 260 'your two curves' from an otherwise unattested word *ḫubūšu. The form *ḫubbušā* would be substantivized a D-stem verbal adjective in the dual, allegedly meaning 'swollen up'. The root is otherwise attested as a description of a still-born foetus, of a man, of a horse and as a male and female personal name. AHw, 351; CAD Ḫ 214–215. Scurlock ('Was there a "Love-Hungry" Ēntu-priestess Named Eṭirtum', 111 fn. 38) thinks the line refers to the man's fear that a discharge of fluids (*tabāku* lit. 'pour out') on the part of the woman during intercourse will bring a premature end to the sexual act. She leaves the noun spelled *ḫu*-BU-*ú-ša-ki* untranslated. Groneberg, 'Liebes-und Hundesbeschwörungen im Kontext', 107 fn. 68) has the form as a verb (S3 masculine stative + dative feminine pron., *ḫubbušakki*) referring to the man's penis: 'wie ein Halteseil ist es stark geschwollen für dich, verschütte es mir nicht'. One would expect *—kim* for the dative of the S2f. pronoun on *ḫubbušāki* in this case. 'Please' in my translation is an attempt to reproduce the sense of the S1 dative pronoun on *ē tatbukīm*.

70 The literary device of 'focalization', which identifies the character through whose perspective a narrative has been filtered, is discussed at M. Worthington, 'On Names and Artistic Unity in the Standard Version of the Babylonian Gilgamesh Epic', *Journal of the Royal Asiatic Society Series 3* 21, no. 4 (2011): 407–9 with regard to the Epic of Gilgameš.

71 On Mesopotamian magic ('an unavoidable misnomer') in general, see D. Schwemer, 'Magic Rituals: Conceptualization and Performance', in *Oxford Handbook of Cuneiform Culture*, ed. K. Radner and E. Robson (Oxford: Oxford University Press, 2011), 418–42.

72 A. Goetze, M. I. Hussey and J. van Dijk, *Early Mesopotamian Incantations and Rituals*, Yale Oriental Series 11 (New Haven: Yale University Press, 1985), no. 87; Wasserman, *Akkadian Love Literature of the Third and Second Millennia BCE*, 252–6, no. 26.

73 MS 2920; George, *Babylonian Literary Texts in the Schøyen Collection*, 67–70; Wasserman, *Akkadian Love Literature of the Third and Second Millennia BCE*, 236–8.

74 BM 79022; Wasserman, 'From the Notebook of a Professional Exorcist', in *Von Göttern und Menschen, Beiträge zu Literatur und Geschichte des alten Orients, Festschrift für Brigitte Groneberg*, Cuneiform Monographs 41, ed. D. Shehata and Z. Weiershäuser (Leiden and Boston: Brill, 2010), 329–49.

75 Goetze, Hussey and van Dijk, *Early Mesopotamian Incantations and Rituals*, no. 21c; Wilcke, 'Liebesbeschwörungen aus Isin', 209. Wasserman, *Akkadian Love Literature of the Third and Second Millennia BCE*, 250–1, no. 25.

76 VAT 8354; J. van Dijk, *Nicht-kanonische Beschwörungen und sonstige literarische Texte*. Vorderasiatische Schriftdenkmäler der Staatlichen Museen zu Berlin 17 (Berlin: Akademie, 1971), no. 23. N. Wasserman, 'Piercing the Eyes: An Old Babylonian Love Incantation and the Preparation of Kohl', *Bibliotheca Orientalis* 72 (2015): 601–12; *Akkadian Love Literature of the Third and Second Millennia BCE*, 249–50, no. 24.

77 Dijck, *Nicht-kanonische Beschwörungen und sonstige literarische Texte*, no. 23, l. 8; interpreted specifically as jealousy at Wasserman, 'Piercing the Eyes', 607–8.

78 D. Schwemer, 'Ein akkadischer Liebeszauber aus Hattusa', *Zeitschrift für Assyriologie* 94, no. 1 (2004): 59–79.

79 Biggs, ŠÀ.ZI.GA. George, *Babylonian Literary Texts in the Schøyen Collection*, 67.

80 KBo 36.27 obv. 15'-20'; Schwemer, 'Ein akkadischer Liebeszauber aus Hattusa', 62–4. This sentiment is very unusual, but the interpretation is unavoidable from the formulation. Wasserman, *Akkadian Love Literature of the Third and Second Millennia BCE*, 240.

81 The fact that this tablet was found in a royal archive is to be explained by its status as carrier of a learned text in the context of the archives at Hattusa, on the very outskirts of the cuneiform world, where Akkadian was a language of scholarship. It is unclear what the tablet's use-value might have been at Hattusa beyond research and learning.

82 Descent of Inana (Sumerian): ETCSL t.1.4.1 (W. R. Sladek, *Inanna's descent to the netherworld. Inanna's Descent to the Netherworld* (Baltimore: Johns Hopkins University, 1974); Descent of Ištar (Akkadian): P. Lapinkivi, *Ištar's Descent and Resurrection. Introduction, Cuneiform Text and Transliteration with a Translation, Glossary and*

Extensive Commentary, State Archives of Assyria Cuneiform Texts 6 (Helsinki: Neo-Assyrian Text Corpus Project, 2010). Sumerian Love Songs: B. Alster, 'Marriage and Love in the Sumerian Love Songs', in *The Tablet and the Scroll: Near Eastern Studies in Honor of William W. Hallo*, ed. M. E. Cohen, et al. (Bethesda, 1993), 15–27; Sefati, *Love Songs in Sumerian Literature*.

83 Šulgi X, 14-35 (ETCSL t.2.4.2.24; J. Klein, *Three Šulgi Hymns. Sumerian Royal Hymns Glorifying King Šulgi of Ur* (Ramat-Gan: Bar Ilan University Press, 1981), 124–66; Iddin-Dagan A., 187–94 (ETCSL c.2.5.3.1; D. Reisman, 'Iddin-Dagan's Sacred Marriage Hymn', *Journal of Cuneiform Studies* 25 (1973): 185–202).

84 For a synopsis of views taken on this rite in modern scholarship, see, for example, J. S. Cooper, 'Sacred Marriage and Popular Cult in Early Mesopotamia', in *Official Cult and Popular Religion in the Ancient Near East*, Papers of the First Colloquium on the Ancient Near East – The City and its Life held at the Middle Eastern Cultural Centre in Japan (Mitaka, Tokyo), Mar 20–22, 1992, ed. E. Matsushima (Heidelberg: Winter, 1993), 81–96; Sefati, *Love Songs in Sumerian Literature*, 30–48; P. Lapinkivi, *The Sumerian Sacred Marriage in the Light of Comparative Evidence*, State Archives of Assyria Studies 15 (Helsinki: Neo-Assyrian Text Corpus Project, 2004), 2–13; B. Pongratz-Leisten, 'Sacred Marriage and the Transfer of Divine Knowledge: Alliances between the Gods and the king in Ancient Mesopotamia', in *Sacred Marriages. The Divine Human Sexual Metaphor from Sumer to Early Christianity*, ed. M. Nissinnen and R. Uro (Winona Lake: Eisenbrauns, 2008), 47–58; J. S. Cooper, 'Sex and the Temple', in *Tempel im alten Orient. 7. Internationales Colloquium der Deutschen Orient-Gesellschaft 11.-13, Oktober 2009, München*, Colloquien der Deutschen Orient-Gesellschaft 7, ed. K. Kaniuth, A. Löhnert, J. L. Miller, A. Otto, M. Roaf and W. Sallaberger (Wiesbaden: Harrassowitz, 2013), 49–58. While it is clear that the king may be representing Dumuzi in the rite, it is entirely unclear who, if anyone, is supposed to be representing Inana. F. R. Kraus's proposal that the copulation scenes of Šulgi X and Iddin-Dagan A are a literary fiction, rather than a concrete ritual enactment, needs to be taken more seriously in my view than allowed for at Cooper, 'Sacred Marriage and Popular Cult in Early Mesopotamia', 88–9, even if one does not agree with all the details (F. R. Kraus, 'Das altbabylonische Königtum', in *Le palais et la royauté*, ed. P. Garelli (Paris: Geuthner, 1974), 249–50; Lapinkivi, *The Sumerian Sacred Marriage in the Light of Comparative Evidence*, 243, now Cooper, 'Sex and the Temple', 55).

85 J. M. Durand and M. Guichard, 'Les Rituels de Mari', *Florilegium Marianum III* (1997): 52–8, no. 2; Sigrist and Westenholz, 'The love poem of Rim-Sîn and Nanaya', 670.

86 M. Nissinen, 'Love Lyrics of Nabû and Tašmetu: An Assyrian Song of Songs?', in *'Und Mose schrieb dieses Lied auf': Studien zum Alten Testament und zum Alten Orient, Festschrift für Oswald Loretz zur Vollendung seines 70. Lebensjahres mit Beiträgen von Freunden, Schülern und Kollegen*, Alter Orient und Altes Testament 250, ed. M. Dietrich and I. Kottsieper (Münster: Ugarit-Verlag, 1998), 592–7.

87 W. G. Lambert, 'Divine Love Lyrics from Babylon', *Journal of Semitic Studies* 4 (1959): 1–15; 'The Problem of the Love-Lyrics', in *Unity and Diversity. Essays in the History, Literature, and Religion of the Ancient Near East*, ed. H. Goedicke and J. J. M. Roberts (Baltimore and London: Johns Hopkins University Press, 1975), 98–134; D. O. Edzard, 'Zur Ritualtafel der sog. "Love Lyrics"', in *Language, Literature and History: Philological and Historical Studies Presented to Erica Reiner*, American Oriental Series 67, ed. F. Rochberg-Halton (New Haven, 1987), 57–69; A. R. George, 'Four Temple Rituals from Babylon', in *Wisdom, Gods and Literature. Studies in Assyriology in Honour of W.G. Lambert*, ed. A. R. George and I. L. Finkel (Winona Lake: Eisenbrauns, 2000), 260, fn. 6.

88 Three love songs associated with the late third millennium BC king Šu-Sin may present an exception to what is perceived to be the regular cultic context of Sumerian love poetry by being regular wedding songs depicting the king's union with a mortal woman. See Klein and Sefati, '"Secular" Love Songs in Mesopotamian Literature', 615–16; Sefati, *Love*

Songs in Sumerian Literature, 344–64. It is not clear that a distinction between 'cultic', in the sense of performed in a temple context, and 'secular', as in performed in a palace or domestic context, would have been comprehensible to contemporary scribes, who gave these songs the same subscripts as other love poems of the Dumuzi-Inana type.

89 See particularly Lambert, 'Devotion'; Klein and Sefati, '"Secular" Love Songs in Mesopotamian Literature', 614–18.
90 Schwemer, 'Ein akkadischer Liebeszauber aus Hattusa'.
91 Lambert, 'Devotion', 22. See also the notion 'archetypal lover' at Sigrist and Westenholz, 'The love poem of Rim-Sîn and Nanaya', 668.
92 DI A ms. B l. 8 (Sefati, *Love Songs in Sumerian Literature*, 121); DI H passim (Sefati, *Love Songs in Sumerian Literature*, 184–93).
93 Black, 'Babylonian Ballads'.
94 Ibid., 29, with fn. 10.
95 Black, 'Babylonian Ballads', 3, l. 43.
96 Klein and Sefati ('"Secular" Love Songs in Mesopotamian Literature', 620) prefer to keep this 'ballad' within the frame of reference of the 'cultic-mythological' poem until more clearly popular and 'secular' poems from the Assur song-catalogue are identified.
97 E. Ebeling, *Literarische Keilschrifttexte aus Assur* (Berlin: Akademie-Verlag, 1953), no. 15; W. Meinhold, *Ištar in Aššur – Untersuchung eines Lokalkultes von ca. 2500 bis 614 v. Chr.* Alter Orient und Altes Testament 367 (Münster: Ugarit-Verlag, 2009), 301–12; Wasserman, Akkadian Lover Literature of the Third and Second Millennia BCE, 2016, 119–123.
98 The poem presented in Groneberg, '"Brust" (irtum)–Gesänge', for example, referred to in section (3) and section (7).
99 Goetze, Hussey and van Dijk, *Early Mesopotamian Incantations and Rituals*, no. 24. Sigrist and Westenholz, 'The love poem of Rim-Sîn and Nanaya'. Wasserman, *Akkadian Love Literature of the Third and Second Millennia BCE*, 169–74, no. 15.
100 Sigrist and Westenholz, 'The love poem of Rim-Sîn and Nanaya', 672, referring to the unpublished dissertation Dyckhoff, Chr., *Das Haushaltbuch des Balamunamhe*, Inaugural-Dissertation zur Erlangung des Doktorgrades der Philosophie an der (München: Ludwig-Maximilians-Universität, 1999).
101 A. Westenholz *apud* Sigrist and Westenholz, 'The love poem of Rim-Sîn and Nanaya', 671 fn. 12. See also the difficulties in assessing the status of the list-like collection of typical phrases or lines from love poetry found on a tablet published at George, *Babylonian Literary Texts in the Schøyen Collection*, 71–5 (MS 3391).
102 Sigrist and Westenholz, 'The love poem of Rim-Sîn and Nanaya'.
103 Lambert, 'Devotion'. A. Cavigneaux, 'Prier et séduire', in *Dans le laboratoire de l' historien des religions. Mélanges offerts à Philippe Borgeaud*, Religions en Perspective 24, ed. F. Prescendi and Y. Volokhine (Geneva: Labor et Fides, 2011), 496–503.
104 Goetze, Hussey and van Dijk, *Early Mesopotamian Incantations and Rituals*, no. 24, ii 6: *tu-ša' iṣ-ṣe-ri-ia sú-up-pa-am te-le-eˀ* (text IA), 'perhaps you could pray in my presence' Sigrist and Westenholz, 'The love poem of Rim-Sîn and Nanaya', 679, 683. Wasserman (Akkadian Love Literature of the Third and Second Millennia BCE, 172) translates ii 5–6: '(You fought against an opponent for . . .) // assuming (wrongly) that you could pray in my presence'. Possibly the form is to be understood as present *teleyyi < tele ʾ i*, in which case no mistake in the cuneiform need be assumed (suggestion courtesy A. R. George). This would give us: 'Will you be able to pray in my presence?' If the first word is *tuša*, this may be a rhetorical question expecting a negative answer.
105 W. G. Lambert, 'Divine Love Lyrics from the Reign of Abi-ešuḫ', *Mitteilungen des Instituts für Orientforschung* 12 (1966–67): 41–56; Wasserman, *Akkadian Love Literature of the Third and Second Millennia BCE*, 124–9.
106 obv. 7 *ātawwu rāʾimišša* 'I will speak to her lover'. Lambert, 'Divine Love Lyrics from the Reign of Abi-ešuḫ', 42; Wasserman, *Akkadian Love Literature of the Third and Second Millennia BCE*, 127. Possibly *rāʾimišša* is supposed to be adverbial 'in the manner of her lover'.

107 Rev. 7: *tušūšibšu ina šubat nēḫti* 'she made him dwell in a dwelling of peace'. Both the causative form *tušūšib* (cf. regular *tušēšib* in rev. 10) and the spelling *šu-pa-at* for *šubat* are archaizing elements of language and spelling that were used in highly literary contexts and omens.

108 Klein and Sefati, '"Secular" Love Songs in Mesopotamian Literature', 623. The use of the term 'secular' is quite problematic for the ancient world, where it is difficult to conceive of any activities not having a religious dimension. See Wasserman, *Akkadian Love Literature of the Third and Second Millennia BCE*, 20–1.

109 W. Von Soden, 'Ein Zwiegespräch Ḫammurabis mit einer Frau (Altbabylonische Dialektdichtungen Nr. 2)', *Zeitschrift für Assyriologie* 49 (1950): 151–94; M. Held, 'A Faithful Lover in an Old Babylonian Dialogue', *Journal of Cuneiform Studies* 15 (1961): 1–26; K. Hecker, 'Akkadische Hymnen und Gebete. A. Texte der altbabylonischen Zeit', in *Lieder und Gebete* I (= Texte aus der Umwelt des alten Testaments II/5), ed. O. Kaiser, 1989, 743–7; S. Ponchia, *La palma e il tamarisco e altri dialoghi mesopotamici* (Venice: Marsilio Editori, 1996), 115–19; Groneberg, '"The Faithful Lover" Reconsidered'; Foster, *Before the Muses*, 155–9; Wasserman, *Akkadian Love Literature of the Third and Second Millennia BCE*, 175–85, no. 16.

110 Groneberg, '"The Faithful Lover" Reconsidered', 174–5. See particularly the male assertion in iii 9-10: *uttessi ina zumrīki // kīma šar bīrī inbīya urtīq* 'I have removed (my love) from your body // I have placed my fruits as far away as thousands of miles'. To which the woman replies in iii 11-12: *asaḫḫur inbī[ka] // bēlī ṣummâku râmka* 'I am prowling around [your] fruits // My lord, I thirst for your love'. 'Fruits' are a common image for genitalia, apparently both male and female (Lambert, 'Devotion', 23–7), so their mention is to be expected in love contexts. The contradiction between the male voice's assertion that he has removed the fruits and the response of the female voice, which seem to exclude each other, is to be explained through the psychological tension that characterizes this piece, with both voices presenting highly complex and even contradictory personality traits. The male overstates the case aggressively, while the female presents a more self-controlled rhetorical strategy.

111 An apparent subscript to the whole composition is contained at col. iv lower edge. It is mostly broken but contains at least the verbal form [x]-x [*t*]*a-ap-pa-al* 'you shall answer', which may refer in some way to the responsive structure of the piece. Von Soden ('Ein Zwiegespräch Ḫammurabis mit einer Frau (Altbabylonische Dialektdichtungen Nr. 2)', 172) and Held ('A Faithful Lover in an Old Babylonian Dialogue', 2 fn. 17) saw two lines of erasure followed by {. . .}–bi-im, which presumably refers to the number of lines spoken by each speaker. Held thought [*lā*] *tappal* 'don't answer', with a restoration of the negative, might have been the first line of a previous tablet. It could also be the catchline of a next one, or a general name for the composition, not corresponding to the first line on the Sippar tablet.

112 Groneberg, '"The Faithful Lover" Reconsidered', 174.

113 Proposals for reading the first word: [*k*]*u-úr-bi* Held, 'A Faithful Lover in an Old Babylonian Dialogue', 6, a greeting or farewell ibid., 9; Groneberg, '"The Faithful Lover" Reconsidered', 168 ('bend down'). [*ṣ*]*ú-úr-pí* K. Hecker, 'Akkadische Hymnen und Gebete. A. Texte der altbabylonischen Zeit', in *Lieder und Gebete* I (= Texte aus der Umwelt des alten Testaments II/5), ed. O. Kaiser, 1989, 743, 1a; 'lamentati', Ponchia, *La palma e il tamarisco e altri dialoghi mesopotamici*, 89; Wasserman, *Akkadian Love Literature of the Third and Second Millennia BCE*, 178, 'yell'. The partially parallel text at George, *Babylonian Literary Texts in the Schøyen Collection*, 62 no. 10, 9 has *ḫu-uṣ-bi* 'break off' in the corresponding line. [*ḫ*]*urbī*, cautiously suggested here, from *ḫarābu* 'to do something early', fits the traces of the first sign drawn at M. Held, 'A Faithful Lover in an Old Babylonian Dialogue: Addenda et Corrigenda', *Journal of Cuneiform Studies* 16 (1962): 37, but the verb is not otherwise attested in precisely this usage (CAD Ḫ 87).

114 Held, 'A Faithful Lover in an Old Babylonian Dialogue', 6; CAD T 272; Groneberg *tūrki* = 'your restriction'. 'Dein Zieren' von Soden, 'Ein Zwiegespräch Ḫammurabis mit einer Frau (Altbabylonische Dialektdichtungen Nr. 2)', 172; AHw 278, s.v. *ezēbum* 7a. 'Zurückweichen' AHw 1373.

115 Cf. the usage of *ṣabtāku* for 'I think' noted at CAD Ṣ 22 (von Soden, 'Ein Zwiegespräch Ḫammurabis mit einer Frau (Altbabylonische Dialektdichtungen Nr. 2)', 172). George, *Babylonian Literary Texts in the Schøyen Collection*, 64 'whatever words I own'.

116 Held, 'A Faithful Lover in an Old Babylonian Dialogue': *k[a-a-a]m* without translation; Groneberg, '"The Faithful Lover" Reconsidered', 169 *ka[nâ]m* 'preening', presumably following one example of G-stem of *kunnû* 'treat kindly, honour' cited at AHw. 440 (cf. CAD K 159, 452 s.v. *kunnû*), a verb which is otherwise always D-stem. SEAL 4.1.2.1 (Wasserman, *Akkadian Love Literature of the Third and Second Millennia BCE*, 182). *k[a-t]i* (?) 'you', suggested by Wilcke ('Liebesbeschwörungen aus Isin', 195) does not fit the traces drawn at Held 1962, 37.

117 *i-na qá-bé-e* ᵈ*na-na-a-a be²-lam da-ri-iš*. Groneberg's ('"The Faithful Lover" Reconsidered',169) *bêlam* 'to rule' fits the traces but does not fit the context unless it introduces a subversive twist. SEAL 4.1.2.1 (Wasserman, *Akkadian Love Literature of the Third and Second Millennia BCE*, 182) reads *ub!-lam!* translating 'I have always (taken upon me) ... to take care of (my) baby!' which does not fit the traces on the photo so well but makes good sense and fits the grammar.

118 Note the lexical and echo and response in i (8) *ul awīlum miḫiršu* and i (16) *ali meḫertī*.

119 Cavigneaux, 'Prier et séduire'.

120 IB 1554 obv. 38–40 (Wilcke, 'Liebesbeschwörungen aus Isin', 200–1); Wasserman, *Akkadian Love Literature of the Third and Second Millennia BCE*, 261.

121 Groneberg, '"The Faithful Lover" Reconsidered'.

122 Cf. Klein and Sefati, '"Secular" Love Songs in Mesopotamian Literature', 623–4. M. Worthington points out to me that the composition is unlikely to have mentioned Hammurapi by name while he was king.

123 MS 3285 'A Field Full of Salt'. George, *Babylonian Literary Texts in the Schøyen Collection*, 60–6; Wasserman 2006, 95–100.

124 George, *Babylonian Literary Texts in the Schøyen Collection*, 60.

125 Translation from Wasserman, *Akkadian Love Literature of the Third and Second Millennia BCE*, 96.

126 A phrase used in hostile circumstances, with Wasserman, *Akkadian Love Literature of the Third and Second Millennia BCE*, 182.

127 'boyfriend' reading *ru-ʾà-am* as in MS 3285 obv. 25.

128 Translation after Wasserman, *Akkadian Love Literature of the Third and Second Millennia BCE*, 97.

129 As noted by George (*Babylonian Literary Texts in the Schøyen Collection*, 65–6) *šīr nišī* is a good Babylonian phrase connected with the people's well-being, although he is unable to make sense of it here. It is also unclear precisely what it means in this translation, possibly an expression for sensual human feelings that are accessible to anyone. The reading *tēmam* 'you have become hot for me' obviates the need for a restoration. The point is perhaps that the woman has, in the man's view, developed an entirely sexual passion for him, one that is not on the surface connected to producing children.

130 iii 17 [*e*]*t-ti la ma-ás-ku* (18) [*š*]*a pa-na zi-mu-ki* (19) [*lu-/li-/az-*]*zi-iz-ki-im-ma* (20) [xx] x-*di te-te-en-di-i*? (21) [*ma-g*]*i²-ir-tum šum-ki* (22) [*be-l*]*e-et mi-il-ki-i na-ba-ki* (23) [x-n]*i-tum*(-)*mi lu li*(-)*mu-ut-ta-ni* (24) [*ma-*]*ḫa-ar* ᵈ*ištar*. Sense obscure: *ittī* is read as 'my omen' by Groneberg ('"The Faithful Lover" Reconsidered', 178, see fn. 28 for further suggestions); other translators do not consider (18)-(19) to be a question, which is possible because of the use of the negative *lā* rather than *ul*. Other interpreters have read it as a negated attributive adjective 'your not ugly features'; (21) *magirtum*, if it is the correct reading of the traces, can mean 'insolence' or 'favour' (CAD M/1 44 s.v. *magirtu*, 46–7 s.v. *magrītu*,

magru). The allocation of signs to words in line (23) is entirely insecure. The subject of the final sentence (23) is important and could be restored *šanītum* 'the other woman', *tanittum* 'praise', but also *panītum* 'the previous woman'. For a translation with an altogether more positive assessment of the man's attitude at the end, see Held ('A Faithful Lover in an Old Babylonian Dialogue', 9); Klein and Sefati, '"Secular" Love Songs in Mesopotamian Literature', 623; Wasserman, *Akkadian Love Literature of the Third and Second Millennia BCE*, 181.

131 I prefer this interpretation, but it should be remembered that it is reading extra information into the text. The reader may wish to leave their understanding of the meaning of the text with the fact that the man is criticizing the woman for staying up late, which is all the text explicitly says.

132 Groneberg, '"The Faithful Lover" Reconsidered', 174.

133 (*w*)*uššurum* (D-stem only?) means 'release' (CAD U/W 310-325). The G-stem verb *ašāru* B 'to be humble' posited at CAD A/2 422 is only attested in lexical texts, where it appears explaining the same Sumerian word as also explained by (*w*)*uššurum*. It is to be expected that it existed on the basis of the verbal adjective (*w*)*ašrum* A 'humble' (CAD A/2 454-55), from which the feminine form *wašratu* and the S1 Stative *wašrāk* are derived. It is currently unclear whether *ašāru* B can be construed as a G-stem 'be loosened, sent down, dejected' to the D-stem factitive (*w*)*uššuru* 'release', as per AHw. 1484, or whether it should remain a separate lexeme. If the examples here of *wašratu*, *wašrāk* are in any sense answering a *wuššurum* in a male speech, then this would be good evidence for (*w*)*uššuru* and *ašāru* B being the same verb. Of course, this is in no way demonstrated here.

134 Wasserman, *Akkadian Love Literature of the Third and Second Millennia BCE*, 130–45 (no. 11). I owe an important part of my interpretation of this poem to ideas developed with regard to another love poem by SOAS student David Wilson.

135 Wasserman, *Akkadian Love Literature of the Third and Second Millennia BCE*, 135, l. 13.

136 Wasserman, *Akkadian Love Literature of the Third and Second Millennia BCE*, 132–3.

137 Obv. l. 2: *appi lalêki* 'your (f.) nose/tip of desire', suggestion of M. P. Streck *apud* Wasserman, *Akkadian Love Literature of the Third and Second Millennia BCE*, 136. See also an apparent reference to male erection (*tīb . . . tīb* 'rise . . . rise') in obv. l. 11, although spelling difficulties make the interpretation insecure. Also a reference to the vulva in rev. 8: *ša tarammu ūrī nadīkum bābum? rapšum šuddulum* 'that which you love, my vulva, is laid down for you, a wide, spacious gate?', where the word for gate is largely restored due to damage on the tablet. Translation after Wasserman, *Akkadian Love Literature of the Third and Second Millennia BCE*, 140.

138 The more striking echoes between obverse and reverse of the tablet are the following: Obv. 1 *nawartum* 'light', rev. 7 *nawār kabattim* 'happy mood (lit. light of liver)'; obv. l. 10 *kabattī imḫi* 'my mood has become stormy', rev. 7 *nawār kabattim* (as above), rev. 10 *libbī ittawir* 'my hear rejoiced (lit. became light)'; obv. 2 *appi lalêki* 'tip of desire (clitoris?)', rev. 6 *tāmarātu . . . lalêki* 'gifts . . . (that are) your desire'; obv. l. 4 *bītam adūl* 'I pace round the house', rev. l. 7 *ina bītim lumaḫḫirka nawār kabattim* 'let me present you with happy mood in the house'; obv. l. 6 *pīya anaṣṣar* 'I watch my words', obv. l. 7 *pī ūṣi* 'my speech came out', rev. l. 5 *pī? šulmi* 'word of greeting', rev. 12 *šulummûm ikkir* 'the greeting turned hostile'; obv. l. 9 *anāku erdēši* 'I followed her' rev. l. 10 *eredde ūmī* 'I will follow my day'; obv. l. 9 *alalû paspasim* 'duck cries (of joy)', rev. l. 5 *ba-AZ-ki paspasī* 'duck squawks/laments?' (See Wasserman, *Akkadian Love Literature of the Third and Second Millennia BCE*).

139 *Moussaieff Love Song* rev. l. 9: *ugārum eriški tīdî maniātīšu* 'the field is ploughed for you, you know its measurements', Wasserman, *Akkadian Love Literature of the Third and Second Millennia BCE*, 136. According to my interpretation of the poem, it is unclear whether this is actually to be read positively or negatively at this stage in the development of the relationship, where a far less passionate and more matter of fact tone has set in with language and metaphors for love relating to economic relations and agricultural

production rather than wild mountain flowers (obv. l. 13) and taking a plunge (into love, cf. obv. l. 15). Might the use of this phrase even not sound a little passive-aggressive?

140   Groneberg, '"The Faithful Lover" Reconsidered', 166.
141   Groneberg, '"The Faithful Lover" Reconsidered', 174. The subsequent characterization of the male voice as Gilgameš to the female's Ištar advocated by Groneberg is stretching the comparison too far in my view.
142   A. R. George, *The Babylonian Gilgamesh Epic. Introduction, Critical Edition and Cuneiform Texts* (Oxford: Oxford University Press, 2003), 618–31. There is also a Middle Babylonian fragment of this episode from Emar (George, *The Babylonian Gilgamesh Epic*, 326–39).
143   SB Gilg. VI 7 (George, *The Babylonian Gilgamesh Epic*, 618–19).
144   SB Gilg. VI 22-29 (George, *The Babylonian Gilgamesh Epic*, 618–23).
145   SB Gilg. VI 46-47 (George, *The Babylonian Gilgamesh Epic*, 620–1).
146   See the most recent analysis of this episode in B. Currie, *Homer's Allusive Art* (Oxford: Oxford University Press, 2016), 169–73.
147   SB Gilg. VI 64-79 (George, *The Babylonian Gilgamesh Epic*, 622–3); K. Volk, *Inanna und Šukaletuda: zur historisch-politischen Deutung eines sumerischen Literaturwerkes*, SANTAG 3 (Wiesbaden: Harrassowitz, 1995).
148   Inana and Šukaletuda, ll. 123-4.
149   Inana and Šukaletuda, ll. 297-300.
150   Currie, *Homer's Allusive Art*, 171-2.
151   SB Gilg. VI 68 *išullanīya kiššūtaki ī nīkul* (69) *u qātka šūṣâmma luput ḫurdatni* 'Oh my Išullanu, let us taste your power, (69) stretch out your hand to me and touch our vulva!' (after George, *The Babylonian Gilgamesh Epic*, 622–3). A similar phrase appears in an incantation-like Old Babylonian love poem from Kiš, again addressed by a female voice to a male (i 13' *bilamma šumēlek luppitma ḫurdatni*, 'bring (m.) your left hand to me, stroke (m.) our vulva', Wasserman, 151-2), and the other way round in a so-called *pārum*-hymn to Ištar which praises her for her inexhaustible sexual appetite: Wasserman Akkadian Love Literature of the Third and Second Millennia BCE, no. 12 obv. 11 *alkī lulappit ḫurdatki* 'come (f.), let me stroke your (f.) vulva'.
152   SB Gilg. VI 79 (George, *The Babylonian Gilgamesh Epic*, 622–3).
153   It is unclear how far Šukaletuda's fate is to be considered inglorious after raping Inana in the Sumerian poem, as he is to remain a subject of song. For exploration of possible political explanations for this paradoxical ending, see Volk, *Inanna und Šukaletuda*, 37–8.
154   We should emphasize that it is the rejection of Ištar's advances, not necessarily the litany of apparent insults directed at her by Gilgameš, which enrages the goddess. Compare the hymn (more specifically called a *pārum*-song) in her honour (fn. 151) which celebrates her ability to exhaust countless male lovers, edited at W. von Soden and J. Oelsner, 'Ein spat-altbabylonisches pārum-Preislied für Ištar', *Orientalia* Neue Serie 60, (with plate CVI) (1991): 340; Wasserman, *Akkadian Love Literature of the Third and Second Millennia BCE*, 146-9, no. 12.
155   George, *Babylonian Literary Texts in the Schøyen Collection*, 50-3, no. 8.
156   The spelling *ma-ar-ti a-la-ni* of the *mārti alānê* needed for Wasserman's initially quite attractive interpretation (Wasserman, Akkadian Love Literature of the Third and Second Millennia BCE, 87) is not convincing, but this poem contains a number of unusual spellings. The word *alānû* 'exile' is also rather infrequently attested (CAD A/1 334) but is no less unusual than the spelling *a-la-lí* suggested for reading these signs as an exclamation or interjection (George, *Babylonian Literary Texts in the Schøyen Collection*, 52). The same objection is valid for a reading as *allallī* 'my hoopoe', with bird imagery standing in for the beloved (compare 'my restless girl takes herself off like a hoopoe', George, *Babylonian Literary Texts in the Schøyen Collection*, 72-3, l. 4). A reading (*mārtī*) *allānī* '(my darling) my hazelnut/acorn' is also worth considering (suggestion courtesy A. R. George).

157 Wasserman, *Akkadian Love Literature of the Third and Second Millennia BCE*, 88.
158 George, *Babylonian Literary Texts in the Schøyen Collection*, 51, no. 8, 20–1.
159 Groneberg, '"Brust" (irtum)–Gesänge'.
160 Ibid, 181–90.
161 Ibid, 174–5.
162 Ibid, 176, 190.
163 Westenholz, 'A Forgotten Love Song', 417.
164 See fn. 151 above.
165 Westenholz, 'A Forgotten Love Song', 420, 425.
166 Westenholz, 'A Forgotten Love Song', 422, 8'.
167 Westenholz, 'A Forgotten Love Song', 417. L. 9' *rēšīni* 'of our head', *uznīni* 'of our ears', 10' *budīni* 'of our shoulders', *irtīni* 'of our chest', 11' *qātīni* 'of our hands', 12' *qablīni* 'of our waist', 13' *ḫurdatni* 'our vulva (acc.)', 14' *tulêni* (spelled *tu-li-i-ni*) 'of our breasts'. Sigrist and Westenholz, 'The love poem of Rim-Sîn and Nanaya'.
168 For a similar observation, see George, *Babylonian Literary Texts in the Schøyen Collection*, 54 on *I Shall Be a Slave to You*, due to its short lines of two to three prosodic units, reproducing a sense of 'breathless excitability'. See also Lambert, *Babylonian Creation Myths*, 32.
169 Wasserman, *Akkadian Love Literature of the Third and Second Millennia BCE*, 54, ibid., no. 26 word mostly restored in line 27. As discussed in section (7), the poem 'Oh Girl, Whoopee . . .' may or may not have been a magical incantation, and also contains this image in line 1 (George, *Babylonian Literary Texts in the Schøyen Collection*, 50–3; Wasserman 2006 no. 2).
170 Butler, *Gender Trouble*, 189–93.
171 See Groneberg, '"The Faithful Lover" Reconsidered', 174.
172 Lambert, 'Devotion', 33. Lambert saw this as a matter of courtship strategy based on allegedly different gender hierarchies in the respective societies where the literary motifs occur.
173 Groneberg, '"The Faithful Lover" Reconsidered',174.
174 See fn. 151.
175 It is possible that the situation regarding the degree of learning involved in their composition was different for the Dialogues, but this would require a separate investigation.

Chapter 2

'BE MY BABY' IN BABYLONIA

AN AKKADIAN POEM OF ADOLESCENT LONGING

Andrew George

I'll make you happy, baby, just wait and see,
For every kiss you give me, I'll give you three
Oh, since the day I saw you, I have been waiting for you,
You know I will adore you 'til eternity!
So won't you, please, be my, be my baby,
Be my little baby, my one and only baby![1]

'Be My Baby' was the title of the Ronettes' first hit, in the autumn of 1963. It was sung in fine adenoidal-teen style by Veronica (Ronnie) Bennett, over Phil Spector's densely layered and echoed backing music. For one commentator it numbered among the 'purest, most aching and idyllic of all teen ballads'.[2] The keywords here, important for the present study, are 'aching' and 'teen'. The revolutionary musical arrangement deployed by Spector was inspired by a desire to bring a Wagnerian style to popular music and became known as the Wall of Sound. The lyrics of 'Be My Baby', though, were not revolutionary. They fall into a well-populated genre of love song in which a young person, usually female and innocent, expresses aloud her ardour for someone who has just caught her eye and looks forward excitedly to a blissful future of perpetual love. There have been many other examples of the genre in modern popular music. Some, like the Teddy Bears' 'To Know Him Is To Love Him',[3] and the Crystals' 'Da Doo Ron Ro',[4] were also produced by Phil Spector, who had a fascination for adolescent emotion. Others from the same era, like Doris Day's 'Secret Love',[5] Helen Shapiro's 'You Don't Know'[6] and Marcie Blaine's 'Bobby's Girl',[7] are equally fine examples and attest to the genre's widespread appeal.

It is not the purpose here to chart the history of this kind of love song in modern popular music but, instead, to add to the corpus a very ancient relative, a Babylonian 'Be My Baby'. Only a little love poetry has reached us from ancient Mesopotamia.[8] It employs two languages: Sumerian, the oldest written language, and Akkadian, the oldest known Semitic language. These are the languages of the world's earliest literatures. The recovery of the long-lost literatures in Sumerian and Akkadian by a small band of international specialists known as Assyriologists is one of the most remarkable – but least advertised – achievements of the human intellect in the twentieth century, and the work continues today.

Love poems in Sumerian are mostly contextualized in the archetypal love affair of the goddess Inanna and the shepherd god Dumuzi in mythical time. The two deities play the roles of bride and bridegroom in poems that speak excitedly of their courtship, the preparations for their wedding and the consummation of their marriage. Many of the poems were intended to be sung and some of them may have been performed as part of a sacred marriage rite.[9] A smaller body of love poems survives in Akkadian, mainly addressed by women to men.[10] Poems in both languages are often erotic and sometimes lewd. Their social and performative contexts (if any) are not known.

A related genre is the love charm, an incantation or spell designed to incite love for the speaker in the object of his or her desire. Few survive in Sumerian,[11] and Akkadian examples are hardly numerous.[12] These incantations often express desire in the same erotic language as the love poetry and are only identifiable as incantations because they are followed by a short rubric explicitly stating so. The poem that is the object of this study has no such rubric but is written on a clay tablet that bears two other texts. The first is Sumerian and bears the rubric 'bone' and is thus a spell to help heal a broken limb. The third text is certainly another Sumerian incantation but less intelligible. Accordingly, the short Akkadian text that falls between these two Sumerian incantations is securely identifiable as having a magic purpose.

The clay tablet on which this poem is written is now in a Norwegian collection (Figure 1). Its exact provenance is unknown, but it certainly comes from somewhere in southern Babylonia. The date of the tablet is determined from the script as Old Babylonian, roughly 1800 BC. The following is a sign-by-sign transliteration of the cuneiform text and a literal translation, set out line by line:[13]

7	*a-sú-uḫ ba-aš-ta-am*	I uprooted the *baštum*-thorn.[14]
8	*a-za-ru-ú ka-ra-na-am*	I am sowing a grapevine.
9	*a-na i-ša-tim*	On to fierce
10	*e-ze-tim me-e*	fire, water
11	*aš-pu-[u]k*	I poured.
12	*ki-ma pu-⟨ḫa⟩-di-ka*	Like your (masc. sing.) lambs(!)[15]
13	*ra-ma-an-ˈniˈ*	love me.
14	*ki-ma ṣe-e-ˈnimˈ*	Like a flock
15	*na-as-ḫi-ra-am-ma*	seek me out and
16	*am-ra-an-ni*	find me.

The composition is identifiable as poetry through its prosody and formal structure. It exhibits the non-prose word order and stress on the penultimate syllable of clause-final words that are prosodic features typical of all Babylonian poetry. Various conventional structural devices – syntactic parallelism and semantic opposition, vowel patterns and repetition of simile – organize the text's short units of sense into a carefully balanced sequence, leading to a final one-word climax.

The poem can be arranged in lines of poetry (verses) to show the organization more clearly, transcribed into romanized Akkadian with stressed syllables in bold:

1   [7] **assuḫ baštam** || [8] **azarru karānam**
2   [9] **ana išātim** [10] **ezzetim** || **mê** [11] **ašpuk**
3   [12] **kīma puḫādīka** [13] **rāmanni**

4   ¹⁴ *kīma ṣēnim* ¹⁵ *nasḫiramma*
5   ¹⁶ *amranni*

The first two verses (ll. 7–11 on the tablet), which focus on the speaker, are both lines of four stressed lexical units, each divisible by a caesura (indicated by ||) into two half-verses (or cola) of equal weight. The four cola each have a syntactic integrity, making a sequence of two whole clauses, an adverbial noun phrase and a predicate. In the first two cola the pattern of vowels formed by the stressed syllables is repeated (a-a || a-a). In the latter pair the pattern recurs in mirror image (a-e || e-a). The next two verses (ll. 12–15) turn attention to the addressee. They have three stresses each and are not divisible into equal halves. Each is a full clause on the same pattern of syntax (simile + imperative) and almost the same pattern of stressed vowels (i-i-a, i-e-a). The change

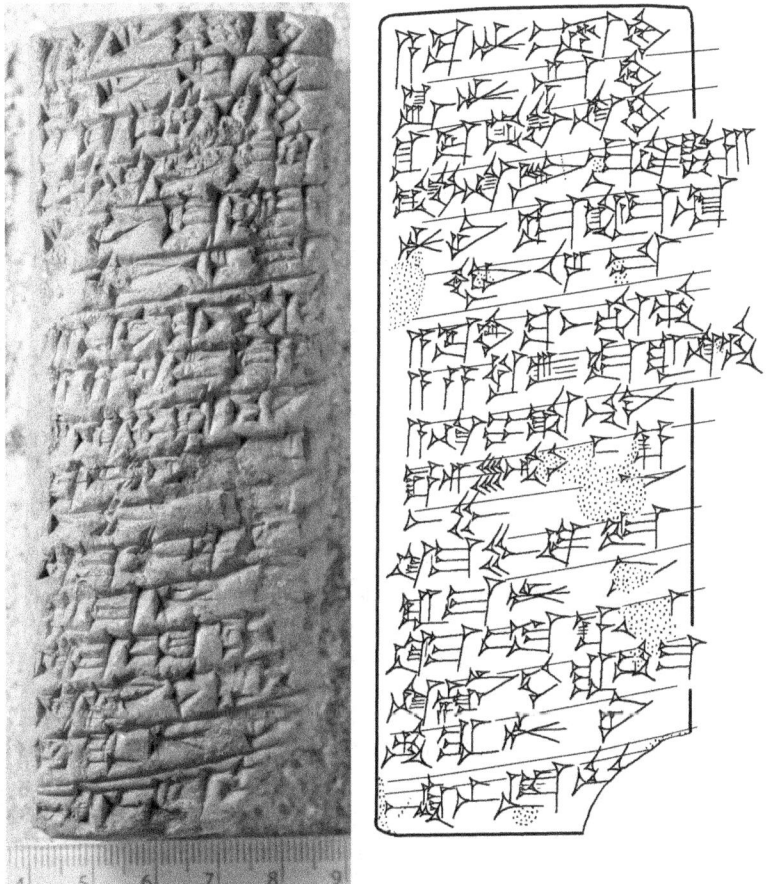

Figure 1 Cuneiform tablet MS 3062. The Schøyen Collection, Oslo and London. Photograph and line drawing by the writer.

from four-stress verses to three-stress verses gives the impression that excitement yields to calm. The last verse is made up of a single word (l. 16), a very rare device.

Other divisions of the text into units are possible, for our understanding of Babylonian prosody is to some extent subjective, but probably all arrangements will terminate with this orphaned *amranni*, the third of three consecutive imperatives. The poem thus ends with an abrupt truncation of normal versification that I have elsewhere called a 'shocking void'.[16] This is surely deliberate, for the last imperative bears the essential message of the entire composition: 'find me!'

A less mechanical translation replaces the alien flora with a familiar counterpart and modernizes the idiom. What emerges is a bucolic lyric that is markedly innocent of the explicit sensuality of much ancient Mesopotamian love poetry:

1   I'm through with pulling thistles, I'm going to sow a vineyard!
2   The raging fire I've doused with water.
3   Love me as you love your lambs,
4   Look for me as you look for the flock!
5   Find me!

Akkadian is an inflected language, and by this means we learn that poem is addressed to someone masculine and singular. Babylonian love poetry is conventionally heterosexual, so a love poem addressed to a man will presume a female voice. The content of the poem confirms this, for it holds clues within it about the voice's background and identity.

The first verse places the poem's voice in agricultural settings. It consists of two simple statements, syntactically parallel but containing three contrasting ideas: (a) past versus present future, (b) uprooting versus planting and (c) prickly weed versus fruit-bearing vine. In the last pair there is also an implicit sensory contrast, in that the first-mentioned plant is a source of pain, the second a source of pleasure. The business of clearing weeds from the arable land was unskilled labour in ancient Mesopotamia, and thus a chore in which youngsters, perhaps especially girls, could participate. All who toiled in a Babylonian field would know how unpleasant it was to pull the prickly weeds called *baštum*, but few would have experience of growing grapevines, for they did not grow easily in lowland Mesopotamia and were expensive to cultivate.[17] Wine was a luxury commodity, imported down the river Euphrates from higher and cooler places, and few would have tasted it. What grapes were grown in the south were turned into raisins and grape syrup. These were surely known to many, and the sweetness of grape syrup was already proverbial. The hackneyed phrase that became the title of the Weavers' song 'Kisses Sweeter than Wine',[18] a hit for Jimmie Rodgers and Frankie Vaughan in 1957, has a literary ancestry stretching back at least to a Babylonian love poem that describes a girl, more originally, as 'like grape-syrup fresh of fruit'.[19].

The deployment of the grapevine is an especially clever device. The woman who voices the poem has had enough of the painful and miserable business of clearing weeds in the fields. She imagines a different kind of work that would bring a harvest of sweetness. Because she knows what grapes and grape syrup are, that they bring sweet pleasure, sowing grapes is what fills her mind. But that expression reveals her naivety. She knows nothing of grapevines and their propagation. The single word *azarru* ('I shall sow') captures her ignorance perfectly, for it is used to describe planting seed corn in furrows. Of course, that is all she knows of cultivation; it is a matter beyond her experience that domesticated vines were surely not sown like barley but propagated by cutting and rooting or by grafting.[20]

The prickly weed and the grapevine are metaphors for the woman's life. The weed represents her past experience of drudgery and pain. The grapevine stands for her future, which she imagines as bringing the sweet pleasure she longs for. The deliberate misapplication of the verb *azarru* (work she knows) with the noun *karānam* (a plant she does not) signifies that she yearns for something that she has never encountered and does not really understand. Nevertheless, she knows this new experience is just around the corner. It is proposed here that this female voice is an adolescent girl who is in the state of mind described by a modern singer-songwriter, Taylor Swift, in 'Am I Ready for Love?', a song written in her early teenage years:[21]

> I know I'm not a little girl any more,
> 'Cause I'm feeling things I've never felt before:
> Sweet sensations and anticipations,
> Calling commotion to my emotions.

The next three lines of the Babylonian poem are a single clause. The verb is past, but the scene has shifted from the fields to a domestic environment. The girl says that she has put out a fierce fire, so we think of her at home, indoors with her father and mother. Looking after the hearth, where cooking took place, was no doubt women's work in Babylonia. Lighting, tending and dousing the fire were part of their domestic duties. In this poem, fire has a twofold function: as well as indicating the scene shift to a new location, it also serves as a metaphor. Today fire is a common metaphor for passion, especially sexual desire. For Jim Morrison, who sang, 'Come on Baby, Light My Fire' in 1966,[22] dousing the fire would definitely have been a move in the wrong direction. In ancient Mesopotamia fire is more commonly a metaphor for anger and fever. When the voice of our poem declares that she has put a fire out, she does not imply that she has quenched the passion rising in her heart. Quite the opposite: in making the decision articulated in the two opening statements, she has put behind her all her apprehension. In choosing the grapevine over the thistle, the unknown future over the familiar present, she is consigning to the past her life as a child in her father's house and embracing her destiny as a woman. She has been standing on the brink of this great transformation, physical, social and sexual, and has now committed herself to it. The fire that she has doused is an adolescent fever: the anxiety of growing up. For a girl, then as now, adolescence brings special worries. In a traditional society, a teenage girl must reflect with mixed feelings on the end of childhood. Looming large are marriage, leaving home, joining a new family, and rites of passage of defloration and, above all, childbirth. Before modern obstetric care reduced the risk of death in giving birth, hopes of happiness were offset by the fear of death.

There is another, more concrete reason for the girl's new resolve: a boy. The poem announces his presence by closing with her cry to him. Perhaps she had seen him when going to fetch water from the well or glimpsed him loitering in the street to watch the girls dance on a holiday. She has fallen for him, maybe feeling as Darlene Love sang, 'Today I met the boy I'm gonna marry, the boy whose life and dream and love I wanna share'.²³ A Babylonian poem that might express the same idea is known only by its first line, quoted in an ancient catalogue;²⁴ it is pregnant with promise: *eṭlu ištu āmurūka* ('Lad, since I saw you'). In our poem the boy is the key to the girl's state of mind. In committing to him, she makes a mental break with her life as a girl labouring in the fields and doing chores at home and imagines her future with him. Henceforth, all will be sweet pleasure, if only he would notice her. But, clearly, he has not seen her, for she positively yells at him, thrice demanding his attention in words full of aching longing, an ancient analogue of the Ronettes' 'Be My Baby'.

Again, figurative language is used with full intent and carries a hidden semantic load. The girl desires the boy to search for her as for his flock and love her like one of his lambs. Thus, she identifies him as a shepherd. She, however, is a cultivator. A tension is thereby created, not unlike that between the lovers Curly and Laurey in the musical *Oklahoma!*,²⁵ in which the song 'The Farmer and the Cowman' expresses the historical conflict of interests between farmers and cattle-ranchers on the American prairies in the early twentieth century. In ancient Mesopotamia there was also a division between farmers and breeders of livestock. The economy rested on two main areas of production: the cultivation of cereal crops, especially barley, and the herding of livestock, especially sheep and goats. Flocks had to be kept off the arable land for most of the year and were often grazed in upland pastures very far removed from the irrigated plain below Baghdad. In the Old Babylonian period there seems to have been a festival to mark the departure of the pastoralists from the plains to the uplands, at which was sung a poem that described this transhumance in mythological terms: the Song of Bazi.²⁶ The working life of many people was determined by this dichotomy: some grew crops, others grazed sheep, and for much of the year they led very separate lives.

The social division between farmers and shepherds was common in the pre-modern Near East and finds expression in Genesis, where Adam's sons Cain and Abel are respectively 'tiller of the ground' and 'keeper of sheep'. Their story of archetypal violence articulates the stereotypical (not universal) hostility of settled agriculturalists for nomadic pastoralists. The dichotomy gave rise to the English phrase 'the desert and the sown', memorably deployed in the title of a book in which the British adventurer Gertrude Bell described her extraordinary journeys across the Middle East before the First World War.²⁷ The phrase derives from Edward Fitzgerald's influential nineteenth-century versions of the *Rubáiyát of Omar Khayyám*, where a liminal place in which to forget the cares of the world, including work, is 'some Strip of Herbage strown that just divides the desert from the sown'.²⁸ There is thus a social gulf between the voice of our poem and the boy she desires, but it is a gulf which can be occupied in the romantic imagination.

It is no accident that the girl of our poem has fallen for a shepherd. There is an obvious allusion to the old tradition of the courtship of the young goddess Inanna and the shepherd Dumuzi.²⁹ Much love poetry survives in Sumerian that transmits this tradition of girl and shepherd; there was also much in Akkadian, though only a little is extant.³⁰ But there is a deeper signification. What is at hand, if the girl and her boy pair off, is a symbolic unification of the desert and the sown. The idealistic notion that love can mend and unite the world is an old idea. It was particularly influential on popular music during the late 1960s, in America especially as a reaction to the escalation of the war in Vietnam and the struggle for civil rights. Typical expressions of it were voiced by the Beatles, who proclaimed, 'With our love, we could save the world',[31] and by Marvin Gaye, when he sang, 'Only love can conquer hate'.[32]

It is readily apparent that, in expressing the longing of an adolescent girl, this short Babylonian poem shares much common ground with modern popular song. Because of this, we recognize the girl and know her story. It would not be difficult to find other versions of the same girl in the song, poetry and literature of other cultures, but another matter calls. In introducing the poem, attention was drawn to the ancient function of the poem as rooted in magic. Before concluding, it is necessary to situate the poem more exactly in its context as a spell.

The poem's presence on a tablet of incantations leaves no doubt that its purpose was to enlist magic forces to help a woman win the love of a man. The persona of the girl yearning to be noticed by the shepherd lad could be adopted by any lovesick woman seeking to attract a man's attention. In this function the text is a companion piece to many of the incantations or spells inscribed on an Old Babylonian tablet excavated at Isin in central Babylonia.[33] These could be recited during the course of a magic ritual whose aim was to gain control over an uncooperative person, especially someone who does not reciprocate love.[34] Some of the incantations bear the simple rubric 'spell for love', but others have more functional rubrics: '[spell] for salving with oil', 'spell for the lump of salt', 'spell for soapwort' and 'spell for a potsherd from the crossroads'. These latter rubrics all cite actions and materials typical of magic rituals and give an intimation of the *agenda* that accompanied the *dicenda*. It is very likely that the short poem discussed earlier was also believed to be more effective when accompanied by ritual actions. But Old Babylonian incantations are seldom accompanied by prescriptions of ritual, probably because the rituals were generic and easily mastered, while the spells were specific and perhaps difficult to memorize. Consequently, we lack all knowledge of any *agenda* that may have been attached to our poem.

Much later, in the first millennium BC, texts were compiled that had related functions, but from the male perspective: incantations to induce a woman to have sexual intercourse and spells to ensure sexual potency.[35] These included detailed prescriptions for the magic rituals that went with the spoken words. One example instructs the would-be lover, 'You recite the spell three times to an apple or a pomegranate, then you give (the fruit) to the woman and let her suck its juice. That woman will come to you and you will make love to her.' This is magic by contagion: the spell is absorbed by the fruit and ingested by the woman, on whom it then works its power. Other rituals prescribe making a figurine of the woman, subjecting it to magic influence and thus bringing her under control. These or other techniques of contagious and sympathetic magic might have been used with our Old Babylonian poem, to gain a man's love, but this is speculation.

In ignorance of how a lovesick woman may have embellished with magic actions the spell discussed here, it has been the purpose of this chapter instead to concentrate on it as a work of literary creativity. It should be clear that the poem's voice is a girl giving a first, aching expression to the adolescent longing that was preparing her for the next stage in her life. In this she is a very ancient example of an archetypal character that today populates popular song but is perhaps found universally in human culture.

Notes

1. P. Spector, J. Barry and E. Greenwich, *Be My Baby* (Los Angeles: Philles Records, 1963).
2. N. Cohn, 'Phil Spector', in *The Rolling Stone Illustrated History of Rock & Roll*, ed. J. Miller (London: Picador, 1981), 148–59.
3. P. Spector, *To Know Him Is to Love Him* (Los Angeles: Doré Records, 1958).
4. Spector et al., *Da Doo Ron Ron* (Los Angeles: Philles Records, 1963).
5. S. Fain and P. F. Webster, *Secret Love* (New York: Columbia Records, 1953).
6. J. Schroeder and M. Hawker, *You Don't Know* (New York: Columbia Records, 1961).
7. G. Klein and H. Hoffman, *Bobby's Girl* (New York: Seville Records, 1962).
8. See generally J. G. Westenholz, 'Love Lyrics from the Ancient Near East', in *Civilizations of the Ancient Near East*, 4 vols, ed. J. M. Sasson (New York: Scribner's Sons, 1995), 2471–84.
9. Y. Sefati, *Love Songs in Sumerian Literature. Critical Edition of the Dumuzi-Inanna Songs*, (Ramat-Gan, Israel: Bar-Ilan University Press, 1998).
10. N. Wasserman, *Akkadian Love Literature of the Third and Second Millennium BCE*. Leipziger altorientalische Studien 4 (Wiesbaden: Harrassowitz, 2016).
11. M. J. Geller, 'Mesopotamian Love Magic: Discourse or Intercourse?', in *Sex and Gender in the Ancient Near East: Proceedings of the 47th Rencontre Assyriologique Internationale, Helsinki, July 2–6, 2001*, 2 vols, ed. S. Parpola and R. M. Whiting (Helsinki: Neo-Assyrian Text Corpus Project, 2002), 129–39.
12. A. R. George, *Babylonian Literary Texts in the Schøyen Collection*. Manuscripts in the Schøyen Collection, Cuneiform Texts 4. Cornell University Studies in Assyriology and Sumerology 10 (Bethesda, MD: CDL Press, 2009), 67.
13. A philological edition of the text appears in A. R. George, *Mesopotamian Incantations and Related Texts in the Schøyen Collection*. Manuscripts in the Schøyen Collection, Cuneiform Texts 8. Cornell University Studies in Assyriology and Sumerology 32 (Bethesda, MD: CDL Press, 2016), 147–8.
14. *baštum*, better known as *baltum*, is a prickly weed, perhaps the camel thorn *Alhagi maurorum*.
15. In l. 12 the signs *pu-di-ka* could yield *būdīka* ('your shoulders'), but the text is certainly better emended to read *puḫādīka* ('your lambs') to match the simile in l. 14.
16. A. R. George, 'The Assyrian Elegy: Form and Meaning', in *Opening the Tablet Box: Near Eastern Studies in Honor of Benjamin R. Foster*, ed. S. C. Melville and A. L. Slotsky (Leiden: Brill, 2010): 203–16.
17. M. Powell, 'Wine and the Vine in Ancient Mesopotamia: The Cuneiform Evidence', in *The Origins and Ancient History of Wine*, ed. P. E. McGovern, S. J. Fleming and S. H. Katz (London: Routledge, 1996), 97–122.
18. L. Hays and P. Seeger, *Kisses Sweeter Than Wine* (New York: Decca Records, 1951).
19. George, *Babylonian Literary Texts in the Schøyen Collection*, 51 l. 9.
20. D. Zohary, 'Domestication of the Grapevine *vitis vinifera* L. in the Near East', in *The Origins and Ancient History of Wine*, ed. P. E. McGovern, S. J. Fleming and S. H. Katz (London: Routledge), 23–30.
21. T. Swift, no date. Am I Ready For Love? http://www.azlyrics.com/lyrics/taylorswift/amireadyforlove.html, last accessed June 2014.
22. Doors, The, *Light My Fire* (Los Angeles: Elektra Records, 1967).
23. E. Greenwich, T. Powers and P. Spector, *Today I Met the Boy I'm Gonna Marry* (Los Angeles: Philles Records, 1963).
24. E. Ebeling, *Keilschrifttexte aus Assur religiösen Inhalts*, 2 vols (Leipzig: J. C. Hinrichs, 1919–23), 158 rev. iii 26; see B. Groneberg, 'Searching for Akkadian Lyrics: From Old Babylonian to the "Liederkatalog" KAR 158', Journal of Cuneiform Studies 55 (2003): 55–74.
25. R. Rodgers and O. Hammerstein II, *Oklahoma!* (1943).
26. George, *Babylonian Literary Texts in the Schøyen Collection*, 1–15.

27   G. Bell, *Syria: The Desert and the Sown* (London: Heinemann, 1907).
28   *Rubáiyát of Omar Khayyám Rendered into English Verse by Edward Fitzgerald*, ed. George F. Maine (London: Collins, 1954), 57, 98, 156.
29   Sefati, *Love Songs in Sumerian Literature*.
30   J. A. Black, 'Babylonian Ballads: A New Genre', *Journal of the American Oriental Society* 103 (1983): 25–34, republished in *Studies in Literature from the Ancient Near East by Members of the American Oriental Society Dedicated to Samuel Noah Kramer*, ed. J. M. Sasson. American Oriental Series 65 (New Haven: AOS, 1984); K. Hecker, 'Akkadische Hymnen und Gebete', in *Texte aus der Umwelt des Alten Testaments* NF 7. *Hymnen, Klagelieder und Gebete*, ed. B. Jankowski and D. Schwemer (Gütersloh: Gütersloher Verlagshaus, 2013), 51–98.
31   G. Harrison, *Within You Without You* (London: Parlophone Records, 1967).
32   A. Cleveland, R. Benson and M. Gaye, *What's Going On* (Los Angeles: Tamla Records, 1970).
33   C. Wilcke, 'Liebesbeschwörungen aus Isin', *Zeitschrift für Assyriologie* 75 (1985): 189–209.
34   J. A. Scurlock, 'Was there a "love-hungry" *ēntu*-priestess named Eṭirtum?', *Archiv für Orientforschung* 36–37 (1989–90): 107–12; J. S. Cooper, 'Magic and m(is)use: Poetic Promiscuity in Mesopotamian Ritual', in *Mesopotamian Poetic Language: Sumerian and Akkadian*. Cuneiform Monographs 6, ed. M. E. Vogelzang and H. L. J. Vanstiphout (Groningen: Styx, 1996), 47–57; B. Groneberg, 'Liebes- und Hundebeschwörungen im Kontext', in *Studies Presented to Robert D. Biggs, June 4, 2004*, ed. M. T. Roth et al. (Chicago: Oriental Institute, 2007), 91–107.
35   R. D. Biggs, *Šà.zi.ga: Ancient Mesopotamian Potency Incantations*. Texts from Cuneiform Sources 2 (Locust Valley, NY: J.J. Augustin, 1967).

Chapter 3

ANCIENT EGYPTIAN LOVE POETRY

Robert Anderson

The various groups of ancient Egyptian love poems all date from the New Kingdom (ca.1550–1070 BC). It may be that such precious survivals from what may have been an extensive literature were designed for musical performance in contexts similar to those wonderfully depicted as funerary banquets in the private tombs of Western Thebes. The players shown there are nearly all female, and they form part of small chamber groups with such instruments as a double pipe, harp, lute, lyre and frame-drum. Occasionally, a lead player's mouth seems shaped as if for the utterance of words that were the original inspiration for the music, even if more often than not the text is missing. No one has tried more successfully to give meaning to that silent music than John Keats in his *Ode on a Grecian Urn*: 'Heard melodies are sweet, but those unheard / Are sweeter.'[1] A musical scene from a Theban tomb now in the British Museum depicts six female performers. Two are dancing, one plays a double pipe and the rest clap their approval. The text above them was probably sung by one of the group. It celebrates the benefits of the inundation, with mention of the gods most closely concerned.

Though there is no such poetry from earlier times, expressions of love are ubiquitous. They occur in the remarkable series of texts inscribed on pyramid walls from the Fifth and Sixth Dynasties, based on ideas probably current from very ancient times, to ease the passage of the dead king to the abode of the gods in the heavens above. Known simply as the *Pyramid Texts*, they are carved in hieroglyphs of remarkable beauty and precision, though containing some very primitive conceptions. Throughout ancient Egyptian history, the word for 'to love' is expressed by means of three basic signs, a wooden hand-held plough, the human mouth and a papyrus roll. As such, the signs have no direct significance for the word; it is their sound value, derived over time in a variety of ways, that has produced the ultimate meaning. Perhaps the most telling use of the word, not only important in itself but relevant to so many inscriptions on temple walls throughout the long history of ancient Egypt, occurs in Utterance 269 of the *Pyramid Texts*. This is essentially a prayer for the proper censing of the dead king, couched in terms that express a common interest between the gods and their mortal representative, himself considered divine:

> May I live with you, you gods;
> May you live with me, you gods.
> I love you, you gods;
> May you love me, you gods.[2]

This close relationship lies behind those scenes in the Valley of the Kings at Luxor where the king is shown hand in hand with a series of different gods, on the same scale as his divine companions and in easy relationship with them. While on earth the king was equated with the hawk-god Horus. After death he was thought of as Osiris, the father of Horus. Utterance 20 makes clear that the earthly bond with the king still has resonance: 'I have come in search of you, for I am Horus.' An important mythical event is commemorated in 303, where it is described how Horus and Osiris were able to ferry through the heavenly spaces their appointed place among the gods within the firmament. The king must follow the same route and be challenged concerning his credentials: 'Are you Horus, son of Osiris? Are you the god, the eldest one, the son of Hathor?' The mention of Hathor is significant. Her name can be written by means of the Horus-hawk depicted within a small rectangular shrine, so that she can be equated with the Mansion of Horus. The *Pyramid Texts* utter a stern warning on behalf of the king and his burial place in Utterance 534: 'As for anyone who shall lay a finger on this pyramid and this temple which belong to me and to my double, he will have laid his finger on the Mansion of Horus in the firmament, he will have offended the Lady of the Mansion.'

It is psychologically apt that the nature of Hathor should be ambivalent. On the one hand, she is the goddess of love, delighting in music and all manner of festivities; on the other, she was entrusted with the destruction of mankind when the sun-god Re was wearied with our wrongdoing, and she returned daily to the heavens sated with an abundance of human blood until Re repented of his wrath and supervised the production of an enticing mixture of potent beer tinted with red ochre. Hathor was enchanted with her reflection in this unusual brew and proceeded to imbibe it so plentifully that she became drunk and could only totter back to the sky without having noticed a single human being. The Egyptians knew what they were doing when they represented Hathor as a cow, the most kindly and useful of the domestic animals reared in the countryside. Nor did the Greeks have any problem in equating her with their Aphrodite, who emerged as a goddess of surpassing beauty from the foam of the surging waves around Cyprus. Yet she too was ultimately responsible for the Trojan War, causing Prince Paris to make off with the wondrous Helen from her marriage-bed in the Peloponnese to the Ionian shore. The only other god mentioned in the poems is Amun, whose origin may have been in the theology of Hermopolis, but who eventually became the imperial state god of Egypt.

Hathor's main temple in Egypt is at Dendera, not far north of Luxor, where the ancient name preserves a close link with Re's base at Heliopolis. In the Bible, Heliopolis becomes 'On', whereas Dendera, which does not appear, should have the feminine equivalent of 'Onet'. Hathor's musical sympathies are dramatically enshrined in the temple architecture, where the columns of the hypostyle hall have been designed as monumental versions of the sistrum, the apotropaic rattle sacred to the goddess and used to ward off evil influence. Even a brief inspection of the temple reveals much of interest. There are some miniature musical scenes around the bases of these columns. The Roman emperor Augustus is shown on a roof carving and wielding the two types of temple sistrum, as if converted to a religion he could only despise. On the back wall of the building, and nowhere else, are representations of Cleopatra VII and Caesarion, her son by Julius Caesar, making offering to the local gods and presenting evidence of what was perhaps more than a satisfactory political love affair, since Cleopatra was actually resident in Rome when Caesar was murdered. Facing them is a small shrine to Isis, constructed in the name of that same Augustus who had destroyed both the Egyptian queen, her children, and the Antony who was to be the last of her lovers.

And in the centre of the wall are the features of Hathor herself turned south towards the temple of Edfu, main centre for the worship of Horus, with whom her links were so close, and where her statue was to make solemn annual pilgrimage. The walls of the massive Dendera temple are covered with inscriptions, but certainly there is no love poetry among them.

The private tombs of Egypt abound with terms of affection, but they show no sign of taking shape as poetry. A typical example, not so well known because it is off the beaten track, is the tomb of Pepiankh the Middle at Meir. It is the burial place of a notable *grandee* and his wife, both holding important posts in the ancient town of Cusae, long since obliterated by later building but familiar to the Roman rhetorician Aelian (X.27): 'There is a district in Egypt called Cusae (it is reckoned as belonging to the province of Hermopolis, and though small in extent it possesses charm), and there they worship Aphrodite under the title of Urania (heavenly). They also pay homage to a cow.'[3] This makes abundantly clear that the most important deity of this district, south of Asyut and north of Mellawi, was Hathor. The necropolis in the western hills contains much evidence of the close connection between the local rulers and the cult of Hathor. Pepiankh's father was a 'Superintendent of the Prophets of Hathor', while his mother was a musician-priestess and a prophetess of Hathor. Among the forty-odd titles borne by Pepiankh himself was one having the same link to the goddess as that of his father. His wife Hutiah carries on the tradition, as do certain members of his entourage. It is Hutiah who rightly has first claim on her husband's affection. She is constantly referred to as 'his wife, his beloved'. Similar endearments are bestowed on three of his six sons, as also on his two daughters. It is a particular enchantment of the tomb scenes that the two daughters, one named Pekhernofret after her grandmother and the other Meretit, are both shown playing the harp in company with a noble and accomplished flautist called Imysheth. It seems the two young ladies take it in turn to sing in honour of Horus, the first to the effect that 'The falcon of gold shines splendidly in the great gateway of heaven', the other that 'Your crown is lofty, says Horus'. How the two songs would have continued nobody can guess.

The love poetry of the New Kingdom dates apparently from the beginning of the Nineteenth Dynasty to the end of the Twentieth, and all sources originate from ancient Thebes. One of the papyri, known as Harris 500 and now located in the British Museum, was found in the ruins of the Ramesseum, the extensive mortuary temple of Ramesses II celebrated by Shelley as Ozymandias. Of two other papyri, one belongs to the Chester Beatty collection in New York; another is in the Turin Museum, while further fragments have been assembled from a broken vase belonging to the Egyptian Museum, Cairo.[4] All three of these sources stem from the workmen's village at Deir el-Medina, home to those trudging daily over the western mountain to toil on the royal tombs in the Valley of the Kings. At first sight it seems odd that poetry of such wondrous imagination should have been found among the humble and crowded dwellings purposely so placed as to allow minimal contact with the outside world. Yet there were accomplished scribes in the village, primarily concerned with negotiations about conditions and progress in the royal necropolis, but more than able to take an informed interest in literary matters beyond their immediate surroundings.

The earliest set of poems is probably that on the Harris papyrus, which may date from the reign of Seti I, a ruler determined to establish the legitimacy of the new Nineteenth Dynasty in the multiple shrines of his temple at Abydos, with its corridor listing in detail both the numerous gods and kings of Egypt. The lovers in these poems are usually referred to as brother and sister, who address each other alternately. Initially it is the girl who speaks:

> Unless I am with you, where will your heart turn?
> Unless you embrace me, where will you be?
> If you experience good fortune, still you will be discontented.
> But if once you touch my thigh and breast,
> Then you will be content.
>
> If you feel hungry, would you then depart?
> Is it only your stomach you consult?
> Are you more concerned with the cut of your clothes,
> Leaving me only with their materials?
>
> If hunger or thirst seem more pressing,
> Then take my breast with its bountiful gifts.
> One day in your arms is preferable to 100,000 elsewhere.
>
> My love for you pervades my whole body,
> Like salt dissolved in water,
> Like medicine to which sweetness is added,
> Like water transformed by milk.
>
> So hasten to behold your beloved,
> Like a racehorse on its track,
> Like a falcon diving to the marshes.
> Love of her is sent from heaven,
> As fire consumes the stubble.

But now the young man takes over:

> My work in the fields distracts me,
> For the mouth of my beloved is as a lotus bud,
> Her breasts resemble ripe apples,
> Her arms are delicate as the vine shoot,
> Her eye has the brightness of a berry,
> Her hair is like a snare set among the reeds,
> And I am the wild bird to be trapped.

The girl resumes:

> My heart does not yet enjoy your love,
> So leave inhibition as if intoxicated.
>
> But I will not abandon my love, unless
> Sticks dispatch me to the Delta swamps,

Cudgels drive me north towards Syria,
Blows of the palm branch send me to Nubia,
A fugitive to both desert and marshes.

I will pay no attention to any argument
That bids me renounce my need of you.

Hitherto both young people have expressed their longing for the security of their own homes. But now the man heads north to Memphis and makes reference to the power of the local divine triad, Ptah as the creator god of thought, word and deed, Sekhmet as lioness goddess ranging the desert highlands and Nefertum as lord of the lotus. Iadet is otherwise unknown:

I sail north in the ferry
On the strength of the current,
A bundle of reeds on my shoulder.
I shall reach Memphis as Life of the Two Lands
And bid Ptah, the lord of truth,
Grant me my beloved this very night.

The river is generous as wine,
Ptah is manifest in its reeds,
Sekhmet lurks in the rushes,
Iadet tends the young buds,
And Nefertum guards the lotus flower.

Hathor the golden rejoices,
As the land grows bright with her beauty,
For Memphis is a draft of fine wine
Offered to the fair countenance of Ptah.

At home the young lover pretends to be unwell so that he can enjoy the sympathy of his friends and neighbours, in the hope that his beloved will be among them:

I shall lie prostrate at home,
Feigning some sickness.
The neighbours will pay me a visit,
Among whom the loved one must come.
The doctors will hardly be needed,
For she alone comprehends my pain.

He then imagines the door of her house left open in error, and her tantrum of indignation. It occurs to him he would rather like to be her doorkeeper, however cross she might be:

Back at the dwelling of my beloved,
The door at the centre of the house

Is slightly ajar by mistake,
As the latch has been lifted.
My loved one is outraged.
Why am I not her doorkeeper,
So that I could have her fly at me?
Then at least I could hear her angry voice
And play the part of a fearful child.

The girl has heard enough, and it is now her turn to make a mythical journey and share its delights with her young man:

I sail north on the Prince's canal
And continue to the canal of Re,
For I must make ready the stands
On the hillside above the locks.

I sail at speed, halting nowhere,
My heart mindful always of Re,
Anxious for my lover's arrival,
As he heads for our park.

I'll await you at the lock gate,
That my heart may join you at Heliopolis,
Where Re will guide us to the trees
That give their shade to the park.

I will cut some twigs the park
To prepare the outline of a fan,
Careful to fashion it rightly
As I seek the shelter of shade.

My arms are laden with Persea,
Fine perfume has covered my tresses;
I am now the royal sovereign of Egypt,
With a happiness no one can rival.

The next group of poems, all to be uttered by the young girl and much concerned with bird-life, some from the incense-bearing land of Punt, has a separate heading in the original Egyptian:
Beginning of the songs of delightful enjoyment, composed for your beloved sister, as she returns from the fields:

My brother, my loved one,
My heart pursues your love
And all that pertains to you.
I will now relate a vision of the future.

When I return from chasing birds,
I hold the traps in one of my hands,
While the other grasps a cage
And the throw-stick to attack them.

All birds from the land of Punt
Reach Egypt drenched in myrrh.
The first one to arrive
Falls captive to my bait.

He is redolent of Punt,
With perfume on his talons.
My heart is yours, so let him go,
And may the solitude be ours alone.

But yet you heard my sadness
For the incense that he brought me.
And you were at my side
When I set my trap again.

Beloved as I am, need I regret
My pleasure in the open fields?

* * *

The cry of the wild goose
Betrays its capture.
But love of you restrains me,
A bond I cannot loose.

I shall abandon my nets,
But how explain to my mother,
To whom I return daily
Proud of my catch?

I set no traps today,
So completely have you ensnared me.

* * *

The wild goose soars and dives,
It alights in the farmyard pool.
Many birds are circling aloft,
And I should take action.

But I cannot escape my love of you
In my loneliness.

My heart goes out to yours,
And your beauty holds me.

        *   *   *

Now must I leave this brother
[Who has so entranced me].
And as I pine for your love,
My heart cries out within me.

When I behold sweetmeats,
They seem no different from salt
The wine of pomegranate is bitter,
More than the droppings of birds.

But your arms around me
Alone revive my heart.
May Amun the god grant for ever
What I have once discovered.

        *   *   *

Most handsome boy of creation,
Let me keep house at your dwelling,
As we stand arm in arm,
And your love encircles me.

I pray to my heart within
That my lover is absent tonight,
It is as if I am already dead.
Are you not indeed my strength and life?

Joy is mine through your strength,
And my heart yearns for you.

        *   *   *

The voice of the dove gives warning:
It's day-break, but where are you?
Please don't scold me, my bird;
I found my lover on his bed.
And my heart overflowed.

Both said: I will never leave you
While my hand is in yours,
And I can wander with you
In all our choice places.

For him I am foremost of women,
And he brings balm to my heart.

* * *

I set my mind on the garden gate,
For my brother should come to me,
Watching the road with ears alert
Lest he neglect my waiting.

My only concern is this brother's love,
Nor will my heart be silent.
It sends me a hot-foot messenger
With word he has wronged me.

It seems he has deceived me,
And another has dazzled his eye;
But no such intrigues
Should cause me vexation.

* * *

I bethought my love for you
When half my hair was plaited;
I rushed on my way to find you,
And thought no more of my hair.
But let me finish the task,
And I'll be ready at once.

The love poems of the Harris Papyrus are here interrupted by the so-called Song of the Harper, which invokes the wisdom of such traditional sages as Imhotep of the Third Dynasty and Hordedef, son of Khufu, builder of the Great Pyramid, only to dismiss them and recommend instead enjoyment of the fleeting moment. This is followed by more poems to be recited by the young girl, each verse starting with a pun on the name of a flower and the following verb. To such subtlety English cannot hope to do justice. This section is entitled

Beginning of the songs of delight:

As a flower inclines to the warmth,
So does my heart lean towards you;
I shall perform its bidding,
Once I am in your arms.

I must adorn my eyes
So that they are bright for you.
Then I shall look close and see your love,
Dearest of men, who rules my heart.

This little hour is so pleasurable,
May it endure for ever.
Since I lay beside you,
My heart has floated on high.

In sadness or joy,
Never abandon me.

* * *

As dense grow the flowers,
So is the love of your sister.
I am best friend to you,
Faithful as the earth you tread,
Which I sowed for your delight
With sweet-scented herbs.

Water flows through it,
Channelled by your own hand,
Refreshed by the north wind
And apt for our wandering
With hands clasped together.

My body exults, my heart rejoices
As together we stroll.
Hearing your voice is finest wine,
For I live only to listen.
Every look you bestow on me
Is more than any food or drink.

* * *

Where flowers are abundant,
I'll make wreaths for you.
Should wine bring you home
To recover in sleep,
I'll massage your slumber,
While children in the garden
Stand guard at the gate.

The first of the Chester Beatty papyri has three sets of love poems. The initial set has seven stanzas, with the relevant number clearly indicated in each of the first lines. Translation can do scant justice to such a scheme and can only limp behind at a considerable distance. The boy and girl address each other alternately. Again there is a formal heading.

Beginning of the sayings of great happiness:

One above all, the sister with no equal,
Loveliest beyond her peers.
She resembles the rising of the morning star
At the opening of an auspicious year.
Bright her eye, and fair her complexion,
As she gazes upon me.
Sweet are the words of her lips,
Nor does she multiply speech.
She stand well poised, with ample breast;
Her hair seems lapis lazuli.
No gold can match her arms,
Her fingers resemble the lotus bud.
Her thigh is ample, the waist slender,
While legs proclaim her beauty.
Delicately she treads the ground;
Her grace has captured my heart.
Men turn their head to observe her,
With eye entranced by such elegance.
Joyous is the man she embraces;
He is then the first among men.
When she wanders abroad,
She is unique, like the sun in the sky.

* * *

Every second my brother torments me,
His voice stirs the longing of madness.
His house is next to my mother's,
Yet I cannot approach him.
Mother's wisdom holds him at bay,
Urging him to give me up.
The thought of him brings suffering;
I consumed by my love.
I know well enough his folly,
For I too am foolish.
He knows not my desire to embrace,
Or he would inform my mother.
Hathor the golden has ordained
That I should be yours, my brother.
Come, handsome boy; let me see you;
Both father and mother must rejoice.
My people as one will salute you
With affectionate greeting, my brother.

* * *

Every third wish is to behold her beauty,
While seated within her house.
On my way I saw Mehy in his chariot
Accompanied by a group of young friends.
I wondered how I could avoid him,
Even hastening along to pass by.
But streams were either side of the road,
And there was no chance of escape.
I upbraided my heart for its folly;
Why should I bother with Mehy?
If I must encounter him,
I will explain my plan.
I shall say I'm at his service.
Then he will cry out my name
And assign me a prominent place
Amid his entourage.

* * *

Four times my heart missed a beat
As it considered my love for you.
It prevents any sensible action,
And wanders erratically.
It will not allow me to dress properly,
Nor permit a scarf on my head.
I cannot be bothered with make-up,
Nor to adorn myself suitably.
'Just go there', it says to me,
Whenever he enters my thoughts.
My heart is behaving stupidly;
I must try to check its foolishness.
Be still, for the brother will come to you,
Followed by the prying of many eyes.
I must not let them say concerning me
'She is a woman betrayed by love.'
I must try to assess him steadily
And bid my heart be calm.

* * *

This fifth day I praise Hathor the golden,
The majestic lady of heaven.
Adoration is due to the goddess,
And worship for the mistress of joy.
I called, and she heard my plea,
Sending my beloved here.
Alone she came just to see me,
A wonder beyond understanding.
I was joyous in exultation,

When they announced her very presence.
The young men respected her entry,
Themselves just a little in love.
Hathor deserves my devotion
For this gift of a wondrous sister.
Three days have I prayed to her name,
And now it is five days since she left.

* * *

Just six minutes to the front of his house,
Where I found the door slightly open;
I saw my lover in talk with his mother,
His brothers in respectful attendance.
Love of him has subdued my heart,
As of all who approach him.
Young man without any equal,
Outstanding in all virtues.
He glanced at me as I passed on,
At which I could only rejoice.
My heart was exultantly happy
As I briefly observed you, my brother.
If only his mother understood my heart,
By now she should welcome me.
Goddess of gold, just convince her;
Then I can hasten towards him.
I would kiss him before all his friends,
Not a tear would I shed in their presence.
I would exult in their understanding
That I might now join their circle.
My goddess shall not be forgotten,
As my heart longs for a meeting.
Just let me see my brother tonight,
As foreseen by a sixth sense.

* * *

Seven days since I last saw her,
And already I feel unwell.
Weariness pervades my limbs,
And my body is a stranger to me.
When the doctors appear before me,
Their remedies provide no comfort.
Those purveying patent cures
Could not avail my sickness.
All I needed were the words 'She's here'.
Her name alone would revive me.
Some visit from her messenger

Would stir my heart to feeling.
My love is preferable to all prescriptions;
Only she understands the medicine.
My only hope is her presence,
For the sight of her restores me.
Her tender glance revives my body,
Her words alone can strengthen me.
Her embrace dispels all maladies,
But now the seventh day has gone.

The Chester Beatty papyrus contains also a cycle of three poems in which the girl implores her young man to speed his presence like that of a king's messenger, a champion royal horse or a gazelle fleeing a pack of hounds. This is more nearly poetry of the court, though there is not the slightest reason why it should not have been pleasurable also to those working in the Valley of the Kings.

Please make speed to your lady love
With the swiftness of a royal messenger,
Whose master is anxious for the tidings
Contained in an urgent despatch.
All stables on the route are ready,
Horses are harnessed in succession,
Chariots await his arrival.
There is no tarrying on the way,
But when he reaches the house of his lady,
His heart is exultant.

* * *

Please make speed to your lady love
Like a champion royal horse,
Chosen from among many thousands,
The pick of the king's stables.
Its fodder is specially prepared,
Its paces are known to its lord.
When it hears the crack of a whip,
It can in no way be restrained.
No charioteer of experience
Could make headway against it.
His lady knows well enough
He cannot be far from her.

* * *

Please make speed to your lady love
Like a leaping gazelle in the wild;
With wounded foot and exhausted limbs,
It senses the fear of the chase.

The hounds of the huntsman pursue,
But dust obscures their vision.
A refuge may not be secure,
The river may offer escape.
May you find her hiding-place
Before kissing your hand four times.
As you give chase to your lady love,
The golden goddess declares her yours, my friend.

The next group of Papyrus Harris poems is very different. It is apparently the work of a necropolis scribe called Nakht-Sobek, though whether as author or copyist is uncertain. Again there are seven stanzas, but the subject matter is more down-to-earth than in the other collections, with touches of irony. Indeed, it would seem there are no holds barred in this particular sexual tussle. How far the young man succeeds in getting his way is anybody's guess, but for the most part he is the protagonist, fully realizing he is engaged in a dangerous game. The original title is more elaborate than in previous examples.

Beginning of the pleasant sayings found in a scroll written by Nakht-Sobek, scribe of the necropolis:

If you bring poems to the house of the beloved
And convey them into her secret chamber,
It will cause havoc,
For the owner of the house will slay her.
Ensure that she has song and dance,
Wine and beer are what she likes.
Intoxicate her resistance,
And possess her tonight.
She will certainly ask you
To place her in your arms;
When daylight comes,
It is time for another turn.

* * *

It you bring them to the beloved's window,
By yourself and with no one else,
You can achieve your desire with the shutters,
Even though the noise might disturb,
And the heavens decide on a storm
 Which they refuse to hold back.
Yet also they'll bring for your senses
That exhalation as water covers the land
And delights all who watch.
Hathor the golden will donate her to you,
That you may achieve all you wish.

* * *

Like the farmer she can cast a lasso,
But is careful to avoid paying tax.
With her hair she would entrap me,
With her eye she captivates me,
With her necklace she entangles me,
With her seal ring she brands me.

* * *

Why converse with your heart?
To embrace her is my ardent wish.
As Amun lives, I shall come,
With my jacket over my arm.

* * *

I found my lover at the ford
With his feet at the edge of the water.
He prepares a table for a feast,
And embellishes it with beer.
As I watch him I blush,
He is so tall and slender.

* * *

My beloved has played me false;
I will not keep quiet about it.
She left me standing at the door of her house
While she disappeared inside.
There was no saying 'Come in, young man',
She was as if deaf to me tonight.

* * *

I passed by her house in the dark;
I knocked, but received no response.
A good night for the doorkeeper.
Open, you bolts of the door;
That door is fatal to me.
Once in, I will slaughter you an ox.
Door, stop exerting your strength.
The bolt will receive a long-horned bull,
The lock a short-horn,
A wild bird for the threshold,
And its grease for the key.
But the best cuts of our ox
Shall be saved for the carpenter's lad,
To produce a door made of grass,

And a bolt formed from reeds.
So any time the lover appears,
He'll find her house open,
Beds ready with fine linen sheets,
And a wondrous girl within them.
This is all she will say to me:
'You have mistaken the mayor's son's home.'

The Turin love poems are perhaps the most imaginative. The countryside of Egypt now takes control, with its landscape of trees bending slightly towards the south under pressure from the prevailing north wind. Each of the three stanzas is uttered by a typical garden tree, gracefully complicit in whatever the young people may attempt, but naturally silent when it is more discreet to be so, even if it is not always clear on which side of the moral fence the tree would prefer to be. They are indeed songs of the orchard, and it is as well to remember that the sycamore was sacred to Hathor. A note on the papyrus suggests that the original owner was a man responsible for handing out copper to the necropolis workmen.

Speech of the pomegranate:
My seeds are like her teeth,
My fruit like her breasts;
I am best in the orchard,
Since I am ready at all seasons.
The sister and brother rejoice
To rest beneath my outstretched branches
When drunk from the vine and my own fruit,
Their bodies glistening with unguent.

Other trees all fade away,
Except me, alone in the orchard
Enduring for twelve full months,
Waiting whatever may come.
Should a flower fall from me,
Another bud will replace it.
I am the first of all trees,
Nor brook to be thought of as second.

If they attempt it again,
I cannot be silent
Or longer conceal her,
That her lie remain hidden.
Then the beloved must learn
Not to squander her pollen
Of white and blue lotus
In the splendour of feasting.

The lover has found satisfaction
In many kinds of beer.

You can pass the day joyously
In a reed hut's seclusion.
See, she has really emerged;
We must now urge her on.
Let her pass the whole day
Shaded by the tree which hides him.

* * *

The fig starts a speech
With outspread foliage.
How pleasant to be tended
For the delight of my mistress.
She is as noble as I,
And should she lack servants,
I'll play the slave from distant Syria,
Brought to please the beloved.

She had me planted in her garden,
But forgot to provide drink
On days of festivity,
Let alone water for the good of my trunk.
Some think it ridiculous
That I now drink so little.
By my soul, dearest lady,
I'll have you in court.

* * *

The little sycamore,
Planted by her own hand,
Now wishes to speak.

The flowers on its twigs
Are like profusion of honey.
Its beautiful branches seem
More verdant than a lawn.
The ripeness of notched figs
Flames brighter than carnelian.
Turquoise are its leaves,
While the bark resembles glass.

Its wood is green feldspar,
The sap like an opiate.
It attracts those not under it,
For its shade cools the breeze.
The head gardener's daughter

Receives a message to take
With speed to the lady love:
'Spend time with the maidens.'

The country is festive;
There is an arbour beneath me.
The gardeners rejoice
Like children at your presence.
Send your servants ahead
With pots for the cooking.
I am lightheaded with haste,
Though I've not drunk a drop.

Let those servants of yours
Bring all supplies for a feast,
Beer of every variety,
With dough to make loaves,
Flowers of yesterday and today,
And much fruit for refreshment.
Spend this day and two more,
While I shade your enjoyment.

The young man on her right
Is quickly made drunk,
Though she heeds what he says.
The feast is disordered by wine,
But she remains with her lover.
There is room underneath me,
As she attends to her guests.
She knows my discretion,
That I'll repeat nothing I heard.

There was a further collection of love poems on a reconstructed tall vase now in the Egyptian Museum, Cairo. In 1897 three fragments were found and were originally assumed to be ostraca. It was only some fifty years later that further excavation in the village of Deir el-Medina produced another twenty-eight pieces, and it was realized they all formed part of a vase. Though some gaps in the original texts were filled, much is still missing after more than another half-century has passed. Only the first poem expresses the thoughts of the young girl, the rest are concerned with the lover.

My god, my lover,
It is pleasant to go to the lake
And bathe in your presence,
So that you may see my beauty
In my fine garment of royal linen
When it clings to my body.
I'll enter the water when you wish,
And emerge later with a red fish,

Lying content upon my fingers.
So come to observe me.

My sister's love on the other bank
Leaves the river between us,
And a crocodile lurks on the sandbank.
Yet I'll enter the water and brave the current;
My heart is strong in the flood.
To me the crocodile looks like a mouse,
The waters resemble dry land.
Her love gives me strength,
Casts a spell over all opposition.
I gaze at my only beloved,
As she stands awaiting me.

My sister has come, my heart rejoices,
With my arms outspread to embrace her.
My heart leaps within me,
Like the red fish in its pool.
This night must endure for ever,
Since my lady has come to me.

I embrace, and her arms spread wide,
As if incense from Punt overwhelmed me.
I kiss her opened lips,
And am drunk without beer.

How should her bed be prepared?
I instruct fine linen above and below,
Not royal sheets, or dazzlingly white,
But sprinkled with costly perfume.

Would I were a Nubian servant,
To follow her every movement.
Then should I readily know
The texture of her every limb.

Oh to be her laundryman,
If only for one single month.
Then would I have the enchantment
Of washing out the precious oils
That pervade her clothing.

Might I be the signet ring
That protects her finger,
Wondering what message to send
To the youth who adores her.

Perhaps such Egyptian poetry can be regarded as a modest precursor to the biblical *Song of Songs*. Since the ancient language did not indicate vowel sounds, it is impossible to tell how sensuous these verses may have seemed. It can safely be said that the Hebrew poems outdo them in range of thought and vocabulary, to say nothing of the version in the King James Bible, which drew so successfully on the wealth of Elizabethan and Jacobean English. Ancient Egyptian literature prefers simplicity of structure and directness of thought, even if its visual impression, when written in hieroglyphs, produces a richness all its own, conjuring in such detail the environmental phenomena of that astonishing land. These ancient authors set out their lines by means of verse points and indication of paragraphs, playing with words now and then but showing for the most part the simple strength that informed their idea of love between boy and girl.

Notes

1. J. Keats, *Ode on a Grecian Urn*, in *Annals of the Fine Arts*, nr.15, 1820.
2. All the translations of the *Pyramid Texts* reported in this chapter are Anderson's.
3. A. F. Scholfield (trans.), *Aelian on the Characteristics of Animals* (London: William Heinemann and Massachusetts, Harvard University Press, 1958).
4. The Chester Beatty papyri have been collected and published by Frederic G. Kenyon (ed.), *The Chester Beatty Biblical Papyri: Descriptions and Texts of Twelve Manuscripts on Papyrus of the Greek Bible* (London: Emery Walker, 1933–58).

Chapter 4

THE LOVE OF JACOB AND RACHEL IN
MODERN HEBREW POETRY

Tamar S. Drukker

The earliest surviving and most famous love poem in Hebrew is no doubt the biblical *Song of Songs*. The poem, attributed to King Solomon, is set in a garden and tells of an explicit sexual desire, both male and female, and its consummation. Set in a garden and alternating between the male and female speakers, it offers models of how to write in Hebrew about different aspects of love and desire. As one of the books in the Hebrew Bible, this erotic love poem has received numerous religious allegorical interpretations throughout the ages, most commonly read as a metaphor for the relation between God and its people. Nonetheless, it has remained an obvious source of inspiration for love poets.[1] The model for describing the beloved, both female and male, as set by the *Song of Songs*, and the erotic language, has been used by Hebrew poets in the Middle Ages and in the time of revival. However, by the twentieth century and following the revival of Hebrew and its use by Zionists as the language of the emerging Hebrew nation, the language of the *Song of Songs* has become a cliché, and many poets actively refrain from echoing it. Instead, the earlier books of the Bible, along with the histories in Judges and Kings, have become a source of inspiration and identification. The book of Genesis, with its family dramas told in a language that almost requires further investigation, offers the modern poets (and prose writers) an opportunity to identify with and comment on the lives of these proto-figures.[2]

This chapter will focus on the very first love story narrated in the Hebrew Bible and examines its echoes and influence on love poetry in Hebrew written in Israel in the course of the twentieth century. The Bible follows the patriarch Jacob on his quest to find a wife:

> And it came to pass, when Jacob saw Rachel the daughter of Laban his mother's brother, and the sheep of Laban his mother's brother, that Jacob went near, and rolled the stone from the well's mouth, and watered the flock of Laban his mother's brother. And Jacob kissed Rachel, and lifted up his voice, and wept. And Jacob told Rachel that he was her father's brother, and that he was Rebekah's son; and she ran and told her father. And it came to pass, when Laban heard the tidings of Jacob his sister's son, that he ran to meet him, and embraced him, and kissed him, and brought him to his house. And he told Laban all these things. And Laban said to him: 'Surely thou art my bone and my flesh.' And he abode with him the space of a month. And Laban said unto Jacob: 'Because thou art my brother, shouldest thou therefore serve me for

nought? tell me, what shall thy wages be?' Now Laban had two daughters: the name of the elder was Leah, and the name of the younger was Rachel. And Leah's eyes were weak; but Rachel was of beautiful form and fair to look upon. And Jacob loved Rachel; and he said: 'I will serve thee seven years for Rachel thy younger daughter.' And Laban said: 'It is better that I give her to thee, than that I should give her to another man; abide with me.' And Jacob served seven years for Rachel; and they seemed unto him but a few days, for the love he had to her. And Jacob said unto Laban: 'Give me my wife, for my days are filled, that I may go in unto her.' And Laban gathered together all the men of the place, and made a feast. And it came to pass in the evening, that he took Leah his daughter, and brought her to him; and he went in unto her. And Laban gave Zilpah his handmaid unto his daughter Leah for a handmaid. And it came to pass in the morning that, behold, it was Leah; and he said to Laban: 'What is this thou hast done unto me? did not I serve with thee for Rachel? wherefore then hast thou beguiled me?' And Laban said: 'It is not so done in our place, to give the younger before the first-born. Fulfil the week of this one, and we will give thee the other also for the service which thou shalt serve with me yet seven other years.' And Jacob did so, and fulfilled her week; and he gave him Rachel his daughter to wife. And Laban gave to Rachel his daughter Bilhah his handmaid to be her handmaid. And he went in also unto Rachel, and he loved Rachel more than Leah, and served with him yet seven other years. And the Lord saw that Leah was hated, and he opened her womb; but Rachel was barren. (Gen. 29.10-31)[3]

In sparse words the biblical narrator offers us the very first Hebrew love story, a tale of love at first sight, which results in an extended period of longing and devotion. Jacob, the patriarch, is here presented as a passionate man – the very first biblical character known to publicly, and emotionally, kiss a woman, and one whose actions result from his love to her. In Genesis 29, in Jacob and Rachel's love story, the Bible demonstrates the meaning of conjugal union, as predicted already in the story of the creation: 'Therefore shall a man leave his father and his mother, and shall cleave unto his wife, and they shall be one flesh' (Gen. 2.24). Here we witness the power of love to change a person and to change the course of one's life, and thus of history. Nonetheless, this very essentially human story is told in few words, with many narrative gaps and unanswered questions. The surprising richness in detail, yet the minimalistic description, has resulted in endless attempts by Hebrew readers of this passage to explain, expand and understand this unique and moving love affair: from the very first encounter by the well, to Rachel's death during childbirth. Following on a long tradition of *midrash*,[4] as well as rabbinic exegesis, which retells and interprets this story, modern Hebrew poets too turn to this unique love story, with each new version revealing something about the biblical narrative but much more about the poet's own passions.[5] Interestingly, while the *midrash* tries to expand on the original text and look for those untold elements that belong to it, many poets use the source to create an independent and original composition.[6]

The early-twentieth-century modern Hebrew poet Rahel Bluwstein (1890, Saratov Russia–1931, Tel Aviv) used her first name as her pen name and until today is known simply as Rahel, or Rahel the Poetess. For her, the very first Rachel, the biblical matriarch, was an obvious model and source of inspiration. Raised in an affluent, traditional Jewish home, she received both traditional and modern education and aspired to become an artist. While living in Odessa she befriended other Jewish young people and together they travelled to visit Palestine in 1909. Rahel decided to stay, not to return to art school and to adopt Hebrew as her new and only language. This was a conscious choice, and required year-long dedicated study, to give her initial command of the language. To fully engage with the Zionist culture and state-building project, Rahel moved to Kinneret, to study agronomy, to work in agriculture and to experience life in a Zionist commune. After the First World War, which she spent in Europe, she returned to Palestine and joined Kibbutz Degania. It was there that Rahel published her first poem and gradually established herself as a Jewish pioneer and found the language and words to express this new self.[7] In several poems, Rahel describes her own life as a reflection of the life of the biblical Rachel, wishing to be reborn in her image, as a native of the land and one at the heart of national history. The most obvious example is her poem *Rachel* from 1926:

> For her blood runs in mine,
> And her voice sings in me,
> Rachel who shepherds Laban's sheep
> Rachel – the Mother of mothers.
>
> And therefore I find the house narrow
> And the city strange.
> For her veil would flutter
> In the desert winds;
>
> And therefore I hold on to my path
> Assured,
> For my feet remember
> From thence, from thence.[8]

In the poem, the modern Rahel longs to emulate the agrarian life of the biblical figure, wishing to return to the fields of Kibbutz Degania, where she felt most at home in her life but had to leave due to poor health.[9] The poet does not retell Rahel's biography but, rather, focuses on her antiquity, presenting herself as a direct descendant, continuing her lineage.[10] Nothing here hints to that fateful encounter by the well, as Rachel was shepherding her father's flock, nor is that love found in another poem, *Barren*,[11] where Rahel equates herself with the biblical Rachel in her desperate wish for a child. But in these poems, for the first time in modern Hebrew poetry, is the biblical Rachel presented as a young woman, not as the matriarch, as has been the tradition. Throughout the ages, and in the nineteenth-century Hebrew poetry of the *Haskala*, Rachel is usually portrayed as the prototype older mother lamenting the fate of her children, echoing Jer. 31.14: 'A voice is heard in Ramah, lamentation, and bitter weeping, Rachel weeping for her children; she refuseth to be comforted for her children, because they are not.'[12] In this earlier tradition, Rachel is not the young woman who cannot marry the man who loves her until her older sister marries first and is then denied her wish to bear children – a right that is given to her sister Leah, to compensate for her loveless marriage to Jacob. On the contrary, the barren Rachel, who eventually becomes a mother and dies in childbirth, is, in this tradition, the most maternal of all four matriarchs.[13]

The poet Rahel Blawstein never married and did not have children. She does not share with her biblical namesake a love story which finds a very public and long-lasting devotion. Nonetheless, the modern poet finds in her life experience parallels to the love story of Jacob and Rachel. Interestingly, in the poem *Here upon This Earth*, also from 1926, the mother is not the biblical matriarch, but mother earth:

> Here upon this earth – and not in the clouds above –
> Upon the earth so near, the mother:
> To be sad in her sadness and rejoice in her meagre joy
> Which knows so well how to comfort.[14]

Mother earth is the source of comfort but also a reminder of the need to live each day to the fullest, or in Rahel's own words: 'to drink this short, single day to the full / this day here upon our earth' (lines 7–8). But the poet is aware that sometimes one needs a superhuman force to be able to seize the day, and in the final couplet of this poem, she conjures the image of the shepherds of Haran all putting their strength together to roll the stone from the well, at the scene where Jacob first meets Rachel.

> Before night approaches – come, come all!
> A united effort, stubborn and wakeful
> Of a thousand arms. Will it not be possible
> To roll the stone from the well's mouth? (lines 9–12)

Interestingly, there is no mention here of the singular feat of the love-struck Jacob who has done just this: roll the stone off the mouth of the well and thus make that day the most memorable day of *his* life. But perhaps, this is what Rahel finds lacking in the biblical story, that it is Jacob's story and not Rachel's.

Here, as in her other poems, Rahel does not depend on biblical lexis or syntax and feels no need to remain faithful to her source. The poet has no doubt that her Hebrew readers identify the scene evoked in this final stanza and can assume her readers' familiarity with the biblical text. And thus, in the only obvious love poem where Rahel echoes her biblical namesake, once again the biblical model is found only in the final line.

> *A melancholy melody*
> Will you hear my voice, my distant one
> Will you hear my voice wherever you are –
> A voice calling with force, a voice crying with tears
> And above time, commands a blessing.
>
> This universe is vast, and has many paths,
> Which meet fleetingly, and depart forever.
> Man seeks, but his feet fail him,
> He cannot find that which is lost.
>
> My last day may be approaching,
> The day for tearful farewell is near,

I shall wait for you till my life fades out,
As Rachel waited for her beloved.[15]

Interestingly, Jacob is not mentioned by name, as the loving partner in this relationship here is the woman, not the man. Instead of his name, the poet uses the term for the beloved male figure – *dod* – which does not appear in Genesis but in the *Song of Songs*.

Waiting – seven years of service to Laban, only to have to wait even longer to marry the woman he loves – is one of the central predicaments of Jacob's love life. But, although there is no mention of it in the original story, Rachel, too, is left waiting – from the very first meeting by the well, years pass before she is united with the man who yearns for her. The female poet Rahel is interested in understanding the experience of the woman's many long years of lonely anticipation. However, Jacob's love for Rachel helps him endure the long wait, so that, as the biblical narrator suggests, those long years 'seemed unto him but a few days' (Gen. 29.20). Here again we see the metaphysical power of love: it can change one's destiny, as it can change the meaning and sense of time. In these few words, the Bible beautifully alludes to the sincerity of Jacob's feelings and the power of his emotions, passionate love that may be characterized by this unnatural sense of time.[16] David Grossman notes that it was not Laban, Rachel's father, who demanded the seven-year's servitude and the long awaiting, but Jacob himself. When coming to ask the father for his daughter's hand, it was Jacob who proposed to work for Laban until he was found worthy or ready to have his daughter. For Grossman, this seems to suggest that although one cannot doubt Jacob's love to Rachel, as it is repeatedly emphasized in the biblical narrative, Jacob also loves the anticipation, the wait. And thus Jacob loves to love Rachel, to long for her, and he loves the promise of a love in future time.[17]

But the untold, silent waiting of the woman, of Rachel, receives no mention, and Rachel is not commended for her patience. This is the theme of another poem by a Hebrew female poet, Leah Goldberg (1911, Köningsberg, Prussia–1970, Jerusalem). The poem, from 1937, is set in modern-day Tel Aviv, and in a playful yet bitter voice the female poet retells the biblical story, with a reversal.

Jacob and Rachel

At night boats sing to the moon
And bodies sail to the end of heat
And I am sitting in the café
Counting the movements of the light in the street –

Twenty-nine. Thirty-two . . .
The flame licks black glass pane.
– Oh Lord! You have spread the sky
Over a land of an ancient eastern tale.

Here was the desert where the sheep grazed,
The lambs fell asleep in the women's lap.
And at night, the sands turn black, like a Ka'aba
From the kisses of robbers' lips.

And the shepherd's son walked to the beach
To scoop from the sea a star that fell
And he heard a voice: 'Jacob, Jacob,
Angels are building ladders in Beit El.'

But at this place a little café was built
(six tables inside, and four out here).
And then Jacob said to the daughter of Laban:
Wait for me, Rachel, seven years.

And she sat and smoked. Fatigue. Stagnation –
The pendulum dictates: to wait to wait . . .
Chasing after the hands of the clock
Rachel's eyes are also weak . . .

'Jacob, Jacob, to you I'm engaged,
But time is changing, I fear,
For in my love for you – one night
Was to me like seven years!'[18]

There is little in the situation described in this love poem that resembles that biblical love story between Jacob and Rachel. The marked modernist setting of the urban cafe and the lone smoking woman do not evoke in the reader the well-known biblical narrative. Nor is the sentiment expressed, that of a woman whose date does not show up, and she is left on her own waiting, similar to the long silent years that Rachel lives alongside but without her loving and devoted Jacob. Why, then, does the speaker in the poem turn back to this canonical story and conjures up the shepherd boy Jacob and his beloved Rachel? The location is the trigger, the modern Hebrew city of Tel Aviv, on the shore of the Mediterranean. This is the same land that holds the imagination of the European poets in its oriental magic, the desert sands, the robbers and heroes of the *Arabian Nights*. The same skies and the same summer heat feature in all these tales; where in the Bible the well is used to quench the thirst of the flock, in the modern poem, the cafe is the well, where one's need for drink is answered and where strangers and lovers meet. But it is not simply the biblical landscape that the speaker, with the imaginary power of the poet, can see behind and beyond the concrete and steel of the modern urban street. With the same imaginative power, the 'I' from the first stanza can see herself as 'she' (stanza 6), as the biblical Rachel, who despite the long years of loneliness can be sure of Jacob's love for her. There is added irony here in the fact that the poet's name is Leah, and yet the persona in the poem presents herself in the image of Rachel. The female figure in the cafe wills to be like Rachel: to insist on the fact that her lover is missing is no sign of a problem in the relationship, on the contrary. And from this empowered position of assurance, she can then play with the biblical narrative and its suggestion of the power of love to change the essence of time.[19] Goldberg does not need to echo the language of the biblical story, as she wishes to insist on the exterior differences, of time, culture, personas. She manages to mix the ancient narrative with the personal, for example, in her depiction of the passage of time counting '[t]wenty-nine. Thirty-two' (l. 5); as Wendy Zierler shows, these are significant dates in Goldberg's biography, her movement from Berlin to Bern and eventually in 1935 to Tel Aviv. These are also the chapters in Genesis where Rachel's biography is given, from her first meeting with Jacob to her early death.[20]

Almog Behar (b. 1978, Netanya), a young Israeli male poet, returns to this original love story to give voice to the female experience of Rachel and to her frustrated long years of waiting. Lacking Goldberg's sarcasm, the poem is dedicated to Rachel and reverses the biblical suggestion of the magic of love to hasten time. Putting the female protagonist in the centre, the poem is entitled 'A Poem for Rachel':

> Rachel on the eve of Jacob's betrothal to Leah
> Was crying shepherds' songs
> And in the morning she lingered on sleeping so as not to think
> And suddenly a few days
> Seemed unto her like long years, for the love she had to him.[21]

What Rachel tries to avoid by sleeping, and what the poet avoids by keeping silent, is confronting Rachel's own feelings towards the deception that Laban played on Jacob. In Genesis we are told of Jacob's enraged reaction, but nothing is revealed of the feelings of the two women, Rachel and Leah. By echoing the original text, Behar suggests that Rachel's moment of trial was that fateful wedding night: by choosing to echo the language of the Bible, he gives his poetry an aura of authority and tradition, turning this personal love story back into an epic.

Time is again the central theme in the song 'I Shall Wait', lyrics by Eli Mohar (1948–2006) and music by Miki Gavrielov (b. 1949, Tel Aviv).[22] This piece is a product of three male artists, Mohar, Gavrielov and the singer Arik Einstein (1939–2013), all working together to give expression to Jacob's years of lonely devotion.

> I shall wait
> All night long
> I shall wait
> And by day I will water
> The flock
> And I shall wait.
>
> Time will wash
> And a year like a day
> Shall pass
> And my heart will not cease
> To love
> Thee, Rachel.
>
> Strength –
> Give me strength to forgive,
> The lie to forget
> Only to remember that
> The stone was not heavy, then,
> In the field
> When I met you

Oh Rachel –
I shall wait for you
And will anticipate
And my voice will trail[23] at night
After Rachel

I shall wait –
All night long
I shall wait
And by day I will water
The flock
And I shall wait for Rachel.

Using simple and everyday Hebrew, the poem includes direct usages of the biblical passage. These ('water the flock', 'a year like a day shall pass') sit easily in the rhyme scheme, and rather than elevating the language of the poem, they bring the original biblical story into everyday contemporary Israel. This poem is about waiting but also recalls the deception played upon Jacob. In the middle of the song, in line 15, the speaker wishes to forget the lie and forgive, alluding to Jacob's matrimony. After seven years of anticipation, Jacob prepares to marry his beloved Rachel, only to find out, after his wedding night, that the bride at his side is no other than her sister, Leah. And once again, the biblical narrator hides a human drama in just a few words: 'and it came to pass in the morning that, behold, it was Leah' (Gen. 29.25).[24] What happened during that night? Was Jacob totally unaware of the identity of his bride? And how did the sisters feel about this? The Bible leaves all these questions unanswered, provoking generations of readers to speculate and attempt to understand.

It seems that Eli Mohar, in this poem, is reluctant to try and imagine the details of that fateful wedding, yet he knows that it cannot be forgotten nor removed from this love story. The repetition at the end of the poem seems to suggest that despite the painful discovery of deceit, Jacob remains unchanged: unchanged in his devotion to Rachel and in his patience, a man defined by his waiting and his loyalty, not by the lack of it displayed by others. Traditional Jewish commentaries on this passage point to the symmetry between the swap of siblings here with the deceit that Jacob played on his father Isaac, when pretending to be his first-born son Esau (see Genesis 27).[25]

Beeri Zimmerman (1951, Kibbutz Givat Haim-Ihud) tries to re-imagine that night and its meaning. His poem 'And He Went out' opens with Jacob's wedding night:

If the night would have continued
Jacob would not have noticed at all –
It is astonishing how insensitive was
our patriarch's soul.

For seven years was Jacob
A knight of love renowned.
For seven years, in her tent,
Rachel waited for her beloved.

In simple and casual language, moving away from the biblical lexis, Zimmerman reduces the patriarch to an ordinary human. Despite the allusion of grandeur and chivalry, an image created by those – almost magical – seven years of devoted labour, his actions on a single night reveal to us his true nature.

> And the morning came, with first light,
> The bare truth was found:
> The great lover cannot distinguish
> Between Rachel's sweetness and Leah's charms.
>
> Pitiful is Laban's deception
> But Jacob is more pitiful still –
> For Laban deceived Jacob,
> And Jacob betrayed his own will.[26]

Whereas the Bible differentiates between Rachel, who was beautiful, and Leah, whose eyes were weak, Zimmerman suggests that both sisters were equal in their sweetness and charm (l. 12), or at least so it seemed to Jacob. The repetition of pitiful (lines 13-14) and the concluding line which suggests that Jacob is guilty of self-deception, which is worse than lie and deceit, present a Jacob far-removed from the image of the ideal lover. The poet unabashedly accuses Jacob of insensitivity and portrays him as unromantic to the core. Such a critical attitude and a cynical use of a biblical character in modern Hebrew writing should not surprise us. The tradition of re-reading and reinterpreting Scripture resulted in an application of the Bible to many uses and changing meanings. With the rise of secularism also among Jews in eighteenth-century Europe, and the national Zionist renewed interest in the Bible as a national epic, the Hebrew Bible was no longer read as a sacred text. Honoured as the Book of Books, an authoritative and canonical compilation, it was still widely read, studied and used. But in modern Israeli society and culture, a less revered approach to the text and its narratives results in poems such as Zimmerman's and Amichai's quatrain later.[27]

Yehuda Amichai (1924 Würzburg–2000, Jerusalem) also tries to understand the meaning of Jacob's first night as a married man, but rather than condemning the man Jacob, he keeps to the traditional Jewish reading of Genesis as a story of humankind, and Jacob, the patriarch, teaches us all the nature of love and marriage. In four short lines, Amichai, like Zimmerman, removes the romance from the story of Rachel and Jacob:

> It is morning now and behold thy art Leah, you were Rachel only yesterday,
> It was not Laban who deceived me in the dark of night.
> This is the way of the world, and thus it will stay:
> Today you are Leah,[28] and Rachel only yesterday.[29]

The blame is not with Laban, nor with Jacob. A straightforward reading seems to suggest that the fault is with the women, and particularly with Rachel. Being unattainable is the source of her attraction, and thus when love is achieved and consummated, the idealized, remote and perfect object of love must change. Amichai claims that this is true of 'you' (l.1 and 4) and it is true of all of us, but in doing so he offers an unorthodox reading of the biblical passage to suggest that the two women are different aspects of the same one. Rachel and Leah are not two distinct and inherently different women, but they are one and can be found in all women. Thus Rachel can be both the exemplary barren woman and a symbol of devout maternal affection; she is both beautiful and plain, both submissive and demanding, both loved and betrayed.

Does Jacob betray Rachel in marrying her sister? Does he betray Leah? Or, as Zimmerman seems to suggest, does he betray himself? Once again, the Bible leaves these questions unanswered, though it stresses Jacob's love and devotion to Rachel also after marriage. She remains, throughout her life, his favourite wife, his beloved. However, it is at her death that Jacob acts against her will, and, as she dies, he betrays her. The Bible tells us of Rachel's dying hours:

> And they journeyed from Beth-el; and there was still some way to come to Ephrath; and Rachel travailed, and she had hard labour. And it came to pass, when she was in hard labour, that the mid-wife said unto her: 'Fear not; for this also is a son for thee.'[30] And it came to pass, as her soul was in departing – for she died – that she called his name Ben-oni; but his father called him Benjamin. And Rachel died, and was buried in the way to Ephrath-the same is Beth-lehem. (Gen. 35.16-19)

Many scholars have pondered the meanings of these two names and the reasons for Jacob's decision to change his son's name. 'Ben Oni' is usually read as 'the son of my strength', the one who has taken to himself his mother's vitality. Benjamin, 'the son of the right side', is a name that denotes justice and moral strength. But for many poets, this passage can be read as an insight into the characters of this baby's parents. Rachel's last act was to name her son, but Jacob renames him, thus refusing Rachel her last wish, her will.[31] Rachel's death, in mid-labour, at the prime of her life and en route, is forever a life cut short and incomplete. Her lonely tomb, by the road to Bethlehem, stands as a relic to the fact that, despite Jacob's lifelong love and devotion, she has spent most of her life, as in death, alone. And yet, the Israeli poet Dalia Rabikovitch (1936, Ramat Gan–2005, Tel Aviv) finds poetic justice in Rachel's final moments and voices a request:

To die like Rachel

When the soul shaking like a bird
Trying to escape.
Behind the tent stood Jacob and Joseph fearful,
Speaking of her, trembling.
All the days of her life move inside her.
As a baby willing to be born.

How difficult.
Jacob's love consumed her
Hungrily
Now as the soul departs
She does not want all that.

Rabikovitch sees Rachel as the victim of Jacob's love, with its weight too hard to bare, and thus her dying moments are those of liberation. The 'alone' that she has experienced in her life and will experience to the end of days is what she can live and enjoy to the full at this very moment, with her husband and son not by her side and the newborn baby still inside her, Rachel is herself, defined by motherhood, and remembered as such, rather than solely as the beloved woman. Rachel's new self comes here to life, at the moment when her son emerges into the world, and she resigns to death,

> Suddenly the baby cried
> And Jacob came to the tent
> But Rachel does not feel
> Tenderness pours over her face
> And head.
>
> A great repose fell upon her.
> Her breath will no longer shake a feather.
> They placed her among the mountain rocks
> Without lament.
> To die like Rachel
> Is what I want.[32]

The poem focuses on Rachel and is faithful to the biblical narrative, but in the final line Rabikovitch makes it clear that she uses the biblical story to tell her own.

And as for love? As we have seen, very few of the modern Hebrew poets turn to the biblical stories as a model for expressing their feelings to their loved one, sexual desire or to celebrate love. While there are some examples of enamoured poets whose Hebrew verse can be read as a hymn to their beloved and to the experience of love as one of nature's gifts, their number is small. Perhaps one of the greatest and first exponents of modern Hebrew poetry is to blame for this lack of purely romantic poetry. Haim Nahman Bialik (1873 Radi Volhynia–1934 Vienna), one of the pioneers of modern Hebrew poetry and considered until today to be Israel's national poet, sets a sceptical tone towards love in his lyrical poetry. One of his most celebrated poems, first published in 1905, is 'Take Me under Thy Wing.'[33] It opens with what promises to be a romantic situation, a situation of intimacy between the male speaker and his beloved, but this is used to express deep distrust of the possible existence of love, as the love complains in the middle stanza,

> And I shall reveal to you one more secret
> My soul burnt in flame;
> They say, there is love in the world
> What is love?

Returning at the end of the poem to the opening stanza, the poet asks to be taken under the wing of his beloved and to rest his head upon her breast, to be comforted, but not free of his tormented search for youth, love and a dream.

Very few Hebrew poets can answer Bialik with a confident belief in love. Instead, they can only look back at the first Hebrew book and to its many stories of human relations. The ancient model is sought but also questioned and subverted. Ruth Kartun-Blum has noticed that when Israeli writers are asked about their source of inspiration, the Bible is the most common textual source cited.[34] For Israeli writers of Hebrew, it is almost impossible to escape biblical echoes in their writing, as the language used shares so much with the ancient language of the Scripture. Israel is also the locale of many biblical narratives, and its culture is linked to and derives from the Bible.[35] And thus, a tradition of poetry and popular song that echoes and derives from the Bible continues in Israel till today. The biblical origin, however, does not dictate the tone, the subject matter or the language employed by the poets who freely use it as a trigger to create a world, and a love relationship, unique, each time anew.

Notes

1. See Ariel and Chana Bloch's translation *The Song of Songs: A New Translation, Introduction and Commentary* (New York: Modern Library Classic, 2006), for the English version of the poem and a reflection of its place in Western culture.
2. This can be clearly seen from the sheer volume of poems relating to figures from Genesis and from the historical books of the Bible found in Malka Shaked's anthology *I'll Play You Forever: The Bible in Modern Hebrew Poetry*, vol. II (Tel Aviv: Miskal, 2005) (Hebrew). For a brief view of the themes from and uses of the Bible in modern Hebrew culture, see chapter 17 'The Golden Age of Biblical Culture', in *The Hebrew Bible Reborn: From Holy Scripture to the Book of Books*, ed. Yaacov Shavit Yaacov and Mordechai Eran (Berlin, 2007), 503–11.
3. All citations from the Hebrew Bible are based on the JPS 1917 English edition, published by Mechon-Mamre at www.mechon-mamre.org, last accessed 23 August 2014.
4. For an overview in English of traditional Jewish interpretations of the story of Rachel, see Shera Aranoff Tuchman and Sandra E. Rapoport, *The Passions of the Matriachs* (Jersy City, NJ: Ktav, 2004), part 3, and Judith Reesa Baskin, *Midrashic Women: Formations of the Feminine in Rabbinic Literature* (Hanover, NH: Brandeis University Press, 2002), chapter five.
5. Rachel Ofer, 'Biblical Women in Modern Hebrew Literature – Rachel and Leah as a Test Case', *Research Proposal* (2010), http://www.herzog.ac.il/files/raheli%282%29.pdf, last accessed 14 April 2014 (in Hebrew).
6. On the difference between the method of *midrash* and of poetry, see Uriel Simon, 'The Status of the Bible in Israeli Society: From National Midrash to Existential Exegeses', in *Yeri'ot: Essays and Papers in the Jewish Studies Bearing on the Humanities and the Social Sciences*, ed. Elhanan Reiner, Israel Ta-Shma and Gideon Ofrat (Jerusalem: Hes, 1999) (in Hebrew).
7. For a brief biography of Rahel and her importance as a Hebrew poet, see Dana Olmert, 'Rahel Bluwstein', in *Jewish Women: A Comprehensive Historical Encyclopedia*, 1 March 2009. Jewish Women's Archive. http://jwa.org/encyclopedia/article/rahel-bluwstein, last accessed 7 September 2017.
8. Rahel, *Shirat Rahel* (Tel Aviv: Davar, 1972), 59 (in Hebrew). All translations are my own, unless otherwise stated. An alternative translation of this poem can be found in the bilingual edition of selected poems by Rahel entitled *Flowers of Perhaps*, trans. Robert Friend with Shimon Sandbank (New Milford, CT and London: Toby Press, 2008), 37.
9. Rachel Ofer notes that here the poet highlights an aspect of the biblical character that is almost insignificant in the original, biblical text, her role as a shepherdess, and makes it the centre of the poem. Ofer, 'Biblical Women in Modern Hebrew Literature'; Ofer also

offers a comprehensive list of modern Hebrew poems that touch upon the love triangle of Rachel-Jacob-Leah.

10 Yael Zerubavel describes in detail the new periodization of Jewish history by early Zionists, harking back to heroic Biblical times, thus emphasizing a link between the Jewish people and the biblical national narrative of the people in Israel, allowing a link between the land, the people and the narrative. See Yael Zerubavel, *Recovered Roots: Collective Memory and the Making of Israeli National Tradition* (Chicago: University of Chicago Press, 1995). Especially chapter 2, 'The Zionist Reconstruction of the Past'.

11 See Malka Shaked, *I'll Play You Forever*, 82 (Hebrew anthology) and in Robert Friend's (trans.), *Flowers of Perhaps*, 61.

12 See, for example, the poems *In the Cornfields of Bethlehem* and *Rachel's Tomb* by Konstantin Abba Shapiro (1839, Grodno–1900, St Petersburg), and *Rachel's Tomb* by Shimon Ginzburg (1890 Poland–1944, New York).

13 It is interesting to note that after 1967, among the popular victory songs written and composed in Israel, there is also a return to the image of the weeping Rachel, lamenting the loss of her children. Most notable among these songs is Shmulik Rosen's 'We Shall Not Go Again' (known as 'Behold, Rachel, behold'). This can partly be explained by the fact that what is traditionally considered to be Rachel's tomb, on the way to Bethlehem, was now in Israeli hands, and the military victory which allowed it cost the lives of many Israeli soldiers. On the changing image of Rachel in Hebrew songs and lyrics, see Nathan Shachar, 'Women in the Bible and in Hebrew Song', *Beit Mikra* 49, no. 3 (2004): 97–115 (in Hebrew).

14 Rahel, *Shirat Rahel*, 62, lines 1–4.

15 Ibid., 42. This poem is one of Rahel's better-known love poems, partially due to the fact that it was set to music by Yosef Mustaki and again by Schmulik Kraus and performed by well-known singers.

16 The Israeli novelist Meir Shalev (born 1948) named his third novel *As a Few Days* (1994), a reference recognized by his contemporary Hebrew readers, but English language editions are entitled *Four Meals* or *The Loves of Judith*. In this novel, the biblical story is subverted to tell the story of the female protagonist who enjoys the love and devotion of three different men in her life.

17 David Grossman, '"The Days of the Years of My Life": The Story of Jacob, Rachel and Leah', in *Stories of Our Beginnings: Conversations about Human Relations, a Dialogue with the Book of Genesis*, ed. Tanya Zion (Tel Aviv: Lamiskal, 2002), 391–8 (in Hebrew).

18 Leah Goldberg, *Poems*, ed. Tuvia Rinber (Bnei Brak: Sifriat Poalim, 1986), vol. 1, 163–4 (in Hebrew).

19 For a reading of this poem as a modernist ironic female take on the biblical story, see Wendy Zierler, *And Rachel Stole the Idols: The Emergence of Modern Hebrew Women's Writing* (Detroit, MI: Wayne State University Press, 2004), chapter 2. On the cafe in Goldberg's poem as a bourgeois alternative to the socialist Zionist labour movement, see Shachar Pinsker, 'A Modern (Jewish) Woman in a Café: Leah Goldberg and the Poetic Space of the Coffeehouse', *Jewish Social studies: History, Culture, Society* 21, no. 1 (Fall 2015): 1–48.

20 Zierler, *And Rachel Stole the Idols*, 89.

21 From Behar's first collection *Wells' Thirst* [tzim'on be'erot] (Tel Aviv: Am Oved, 2008), 49 (in Hebrew). The poem, with an English translation, is also found on Behar's website https://almogbehar.wordpress.com/english/, last accessed 17 September 2014.

22 The song 'I Will Wait' is the last song in Arik Einstein's album *Ohev lehiyot babayit* (I like to be at home) from 1986. The track can be found on YouTube at this link https://www.youtube.com/watch?v=X61zra9iPDU, last accessed 1 July 2014. Interestingly, it was Arik Einstein, with the trio 'The high windows' (*hakhalonot hagvohim*) who made Rahel's *Melancholy melody* popular, including it in their 1967 album.

23 The Hebrew here uses the future tense of the verb 'to follow', from which the name 'Jacob' derives, *Ya'akov* as the second twin who followed his brother at birth, holding on to his heel, *'akev*.
24 The original Hebrew text is more concise, made up of only five words.
25 For a selection of *midrashim* and other commentaries, as well as modern Hebrew poems about Jacob, Rachel and Leah, see Israel Zmora's invaluable anthology *Women of the Bible: Legends, Poems, Stories, Essays and Concordance* (Tel Aviv: Davar, 1964) (in Hebrew).
26 The poem in Hebrew can be found in Zion, *Stories of Our Beginnings*, 425.
27 Ofer, 'Biblical Women in Modern Hebrew Literature', 8.
28 The name Leah can also be read in Hebrew as an adjective to mean 'tired' or 'weary'. On this poem and on the use of Biblical Hebrew names, see David Fishelov, 'Biblical Women in World and Hebrew Literature', *Jewish Women: a Comprehensive Historical Encyclopaedia*, Jewish Women's Archive. http://jwa.org/encyclopedia/artical/biblical-women-in-world-and-hebrew-literature, last accessed 23 May 2014.
29 In Zion, *Stories of Our Beginnings*, 425.
30 Rachel has already given birth to her first son, Joseph, before she and the entire family embark on this journey.
31 See Grossman, '"The Days of the Years of My Life"', 398.
32 Dalia Rabikovitch, *Like Rachel* from her collection *Deep Calleth unto Deep* (1976), in *The Complete Poems so far* (Tel Aviv: Hakibbutz Hameuchad, 1995), 190–1 (in Hebrew). An English translation by Chana Bloch and Chana Kronfeld appears in *Hovering at a Low Altitude: The Collected Poems of Dahlia Ravikovitch* (New York and London: Norton, 2009), 156–7; and in David C. Jacobson, *Does David Still Play Before you? Israeli Poetry and the Bible* (Detroit, MI: Wayne State University Press, 1997), 191–3.
33 H. N. Bialik, *Poems: With Introductions, Notes and Supplements*, ed. Avner Holtzman (Or Yehuda: Kinnert, Zmora-Bitan, Dvir, 2004), 307 (in Hebrew). There are several existing English translations of this poem, see, for example, Ruth Nevo's translation in *Chaim Nachman Bialik: Selected Poems* (Tel Aviv: Dvir, 1981). The poem has been sung to a traditional tune and also set to music at different times by Shmuel Halman, by Nurit Hirsch and in 1981 by Miki Gavrielov and sung by Arik Einstein. Many of the poem's musical versions can be found here http://www.zemereshet.co.il/song.asp?id=1088, last accessed 29 August 2014.
34 Ruth Kartun-Blum, ed., *Writers and Poets on Sources of Inspiration* (Tel Aviv: Yediot Aharonot, 2002), 9–14 (in Hebrew).
35 On the Bible in Israeli culture, see Jacobson's introduction to his *Does David Still Play*, 17–38.

Chapter 5

AN ARAB AND ISLAMIC VIEW OF LOVE

THE POETRY OF THE 'UDHRĪ S

Atef Alshaer[1]

> The ethical and rhetorical approaches are incompatible with a conception in which reality is a development of forces.
>
> Eric Auberbach[2]

Pre-Islamic poetry abounds with images of heartbroken lovers, giving way to an important and enduring genre of poetry called the ghazal, love poetry.[3] These images constitute loss, trauma and travel, raḥīl. The poet uses language in its metaphorical sense to his utmost visual capacity to express the human emotions, memories and aspirations that the experience of love and separation caused. While recounting and lamenting his fate, the poet realizes that he has to re-integrate into a community from which he had become seperated due to his individualistic passion. This constitutes the first stage of seperation and recovery. Even passion at its most unruly nature had to be brought back into the fold of tribal norms. This process, known in the literary and anthropological literature as separation, liminality and re-aggregation,[4] defines the majority of pre-Islamic poems: it demonstrates the ever-present tension between individual impulses and social norms and conventions with the norm being that the latter often prevails over the former.

With the emergence of Islam in the seventh century, the order of things changed once and for all. But like any new grand order, and despite the remarkable speed of its spread, Islam took time to establish roots and for it to become further nuanced, expansive and responsive to new issues and contradictions as it inculcated itself amidst societies riven with their own tribal customs and set in their ways. During the life of Prophet Mohammad and his Companions, religious, cultural and political struggles took place in order to win recruits for the cause of Islam, the new budding faith that propagated and reinforced values such as modesty. Love, in its romantic and relational sense, does not appear to be at the forefront of this struggle or that paramount in its poetic or prosaic discourse. It is the relationship of the individual with God, through particular religious practices and societal commitments underpinned by religious unity and solidarity, that defines the individual and society, whereas the nature of such relations, as embedded within and emanating from psychical realities and dynamics, is not emphasized or given prominence. There is an underlying assumption here that if an ideological order from above has succeeded to trickle down and settle, that higher authority and its commandments would override everything else, including the emotional and sexual aspects of human beings. To this end, there are no extensive narratives about the effects of love on particular individuals or communities in such a way as can be noticed from the second phase of Islamic expansion, namely the Umayyad period (661–750), onwards.

Even though poetry was marginalized in the process of the creation of the Islamic faith in favour of affective and effective forms of prosaic communication, it remained still part of the Islamic milieu in a way that made its manifest resurgence later, instructive in so far as its relationship to Islam and its spiritual and epistemological discourses. Though poetry cannot be viewed through watertight definitions, it is more often than not conversant with its time, whichever form it takes to do so. This makes poetry a source of knowledge and insight. This is particularly true in the context at hand, as poetry expands in its styles and purposes during the Umayyad and Abbasid periods, mirroring a complex life layered with a new creed, inherited sentiments and emergent philosophies underpinned by an unprecedented mélange of peoples and cultures. Poetry flourishes as an unrivalled artistic form of expression, which affects all levels of intellectual, aesthetic and existential life, and therefore becomes an indispensable source of cultural history.[5]

By then, Islam becomes increasingly city-centred and the previous, mostly nomadic, ways of the pre-Islamic period are perceived as of a bygone era. Traits, such as decorum, piety, unity, brotherhood and faithful austerity of some kind, are the hallmarks of the early phase of Islam, particularly as the faith consolidated its existence, established its order as a cultural and political entity. The topic and issue of love were treated accidentally and sporadically without devoted discourses or philosophical concerns that settle and account for its nature and meanings. Islamic doctrine abounds with references to human relations, including that between men and women. Yet, these do not amount to a full-fledged discourse that covers every aspect and eventuality of love. This is despite the richness and illustrative nature of some of the early Islamic discourses as alluded to in the Qur'an and the tradition of the Prophet, as will be later explained. To this end, it is with the Umayyad period where a new phenomenon of poets totally devoted to love tropes in their poetry emerges, and similar and other trends of love poetry continue in the culturally versatile Abbasid period (750–1258).

As will be argued in this chapter, those poets gave rise to a stream of issues that such love reveals about Islam itself, the pre-Islamic society and the organization of human relations in general. In particular, the phenomenon of the 'Udhrī poets,[6] named after the famous Arab tribe of Banū 'Udhra whose many sons and daughters tended to die in the cause of love, continued to inspire and resonate with generations of Arab poets and the Arab public in general. This continued popularity of the 'Udhrīs suggests similar conditions with regard to lack of freedom in love and stultifying separation between men and women in the Arab world, with the latter being subject to the hegemonic patriarchal practices of the former. The emergence of such epic stories communicated through poetry such as that of the Majnūn Layla, Jamīl Buthaina and others, with their evocative and ringing verses of love, sets the cultural scene for centuries of similar dramas and transformations.[7] These shed light on the sociopolitical and existential dimensions and changes which Islam transpired and that the experience of love arguably enlarged and nuanced. To this end, Islam functioned as a marker of monumental change for the Arab and Muslim people in general. It changed them in more than one way, particularly with regard to the relation of the individual to his society and the tension this relation engendered and vice versa.

This chapter aims to shed light on the poetry of love in thematic terms in order to expand and explore the points introduced earlier. It will show how love as a natural force developed as a theme in Arabic poetry, and how Islam marked and influenced this development. Yet, it would also argue that though Islam influences Arabic love poetry, Islam also was itself informed and enlarged by the poetry of love. In this context, Islam is treated as a textual and spiritual experience, shaped and enlarged through people from diverse cultural and political backgrounds and experiences. To this end, the chapter explores the differences between pre-Islamic poetry and poetry in the period afterwards and the continuities and changes therein.

Changes and implications

Psychological studies of the individuals, particularly in relation to their affiliation with their societies, attest to the fact that all lives are marked by degrees of tension.[8] The tension is often accommodated and allayed in various ways, but no society or individual for that matter is immune from it. If in pre-Islamic poetry this tension was somehow resolved and settled with the *qasīda* form, where the society ultimately triumphs over the individual through the protective power of belonging, in Islam the individual is tied to an existing order that defines love and provides solution for passion, and in effect, contains it. Therefore, the tension moves from being between the individual and the tribe to one between the individual and God/religion. In pre-Islamic society, the tribe with its moral code of honour and pride was the arbiter of good and evil. Eloping with more than one woman in the pagan society of the pre-Islamic community was not an issue in the strict sense, whereas in Islamic society and according to Islam, it is. This engendered major consequences in terms of the social and existential dimensions for the individuals involved, causing a shift in the way relations between men and women were conceived and treated. In Islam, the individual was furnished and constituted with virtues and values where he was answerable for his own deeds first and foremost. Here, God is not an extraneous force but also an internal one that sets the norms of good and evil. When the individual transgressed in pre-Islamic society in terms of breaching the mores of the tribe or alienating himself from it, he, more often than not, returned to the society, the tribe, because it functioned as the supreme protector of his existential possibility. With Islam, the individual observed and interiorized his limits in relation to God, more so than to society. This change, at least at the manifest level, gave way to individuals observant of the religious order to the extent that they could leave their tribe for it. This was a fundamental change that touched every sphere of life, including the way people related to each other and in return to God, from the most mundane to the most intimate and particular aspect.

Pointedly, this change affected the poetry of love and the nature of poetic expression. It took it towards metaphysical terrains and new symbols that pre-Islamic poetry did not manifestly recognize. Islam did so in a collective and virtue-laden manner that transcended and subdued the discourse of physical passion, a common theme in pre-Islamic poetry. Islam emphasized and gave new meanings to values such as *'al-'iffah wa-t.ahaarah* (decorum and purity). It offered definitions of love and manners that nuance the nature of love poetry. To this end, Islam ultimately contained its sexual and exhibitive aspects, yet without being the only force operating in the poetry of love. With time, the poetry and references to love in general take subversive elements, conflating human and divine life in the most intimate ways. Yet, there is a turn here from passion unalloyed to virtue observed. Passion unalloyed can be most seen in the most versatile of the famous pre-Islamic *Mu'allaqah* poems, the suspended poems, namely of Imru' al-Qays.[9] There, the women whose disappearance from his life he laments are recalled with physical passionate intensity – passion writs large over the prologue of the poem:

(19) O Fātimah, do not try me with your teasing
[or] if you have resolved to cut me off
then do it gently.
(20) Are you deluded about me because
your love is my slayer
And whatever you command my heart does . . .
(42) [Grown] men find consolation from
The follies of their youth
But my heart refuses solace for
Its love for you . . . .

(29) Then, when we had crossed
The clan's closure
And made our way to a sandy hollow
surrounding by long-winding dunes,
(30) I drew her temples toward me, and she
leaned over me
with hollow wait, but plump the place
that anklets ring.
(31) Slender-waisted, white,
not flabby,
her collarbone shone like
a polished mirror . . .
(36) A waist delicate, like
a twisted bowstring, trim,
a lower leg like the papyrus reed,
well-watered, tender.
(37) In the forenoon crumbs of musk
still deck her bed,
and she, late morning sleeper, still is clad
in sleeping gown, ungirded . . .[10]

While the poet Imru' al-Qays laments the disappearance of his beloved, Fātimah, (among others) from his life in an emotional and nostalgic manner, it is the physical experience that he had with those women that gain such prominence in the Qasīda. Spiritually, it is rather an inconsequential remembrance: the poem moves in a journey-like manner towards exploring the inner-self of the poet against the natural landscapes with which he interacts, foregrounding the beloved but not dwelling on her till the end, as the case of the *'Udhrī* poets. At one point, she ceases to be the subject of the poem and appears as an underlying symptom and symbol of the poet's alienation and trauma. Whereas for the *'Udhrī* poet, the beloved woman is the very subject and aim of his world. While she might latently stand for something else and other issues, she is a cause in and of herself. For the poet Imru' al-Qays, the physical aspects of passion with their details and sexual consequences on the poet prevail over the spiritual and divine-like encounter with the beloved that the 'Udhrī poets elevated. Suzanne Stetkevych illustrates the relevant opening section in the poem and explains with telling concision what it stands for and what it violates, and how it differs from Islam and the norms of virtue it sets in motion.

> The eroticism of Imru' al-Qays' *nasīb* which is dangerous, frivolous, nonproductive, stands diametrically opposed to the sanctioned sexuality of marriage, which is safeguarded, serious, and productive. The erotic section breaks down into five episodes, all of which . . . express the concept of illicit liminal sexuality.[11]

It was Islam, after all, that reinforced marriage as the legitimate umbrella under which all intimate relations were to be organized; and thus, it limited the extreme masculine tendencies rife in pre-Islamic society of foraying beyond their marital nests and treating women as mere objects. Marriage guaranteed safety of some sort for both the women and the men. To this end, Islam with its extensive repertoire of engagement in human conditions – professedly comprehensive – attempts to protect the individual from loss and alienation, aspects associated with unfulfilled love, evidently clear in Imru' al-Qays's poem. It is concerned with human happiness, yet the dialectical contradiction remains that human happiness does not subscribe to set formulas; and the soul can never be disciplined enough when it comes to love. Love is associated with tension and concurrence, whereas faith, such as Islam, is premised on basic certainty, suggesting that unfulfilled love and its consequences cannot be resolved through religious observances and practices, even though this is what Islam insists on by way of treating all unfulfilled passions and instinctive desires.

As such, the 'Udhrī Arab poets, who entrenched themselves in singular love affections and images, such as the most famous poet-lover Qays Ibn al-Mulawwah of the seventh century, known as Majnūn Layla, and Jamīl Buthaina of the eight century, subscribed to what amounted to a creed of love, as they experienced it. Their stories are fundamentally similar. They chanced upon a young woman within an emotionally charged yet innocent natural setting like a well of water (the Majnūn)[12] or a valley where animals graze (Jamīl Buthaina),[13] and through eye-contact and small talk, they felt an irreversible passionate closeness and affinity to those women. It is perhaps a translation of earlier latent passions harking back to a childhood where they did not have contact with women and where time was spent performing religious and cultural observances. These romantic encounters developed to be passionate involvement on the part of the poets-lovers, who lost their beloved to other men from their own tribe. Love became the sole cause of their life.

Though Islam cut through the tribal fault lines, honour was still entrenched in Arab life, sometimes even at the expense of Islamic solidarity and unity, which, as a relational category of belonging, should override all conceptually. Thus, the 'Udhrīs' love is premised on an unfulfilled star-crossed love that induces inner euphoria, tension and tragedy. This tension between Islam and the tribe, the individual and society, the openness and closure defines the poetry in question and highlights the fluidity of the human subject beyond its fixed, and largely imposed, frames of reference. This state leads to an overflow of emotions and thoughts which predate any set mature forms of reasoning or feelings. The poets lament their fate and compare and describe conditions with extraneous states and aspects that Islam naturally sanctioned. When Majnūn Layla says, 'she left me envying two wild beasts for their love . . .', in effect, he is stating what his nature at its primal state is provoking within himself, breaching or bypassing such an unseemly state of envy to animals, which does not set well with Islamic mannerisms and indeed faith. The Quranic verse stating God's preference for human beings over other creatures is quite clear:

ولقد كرمنا بني آدم وحملناهم في البرّ والبحر ورزقناهم من الطيّبات وفضّلناهم على كثيرٍ مِمَّن خلقنا تفضيلاً[14]

And We have certainly honored the children of Adam and carried them on the land and sea and provided for them of the good things and preferred them over much of what We have created, with [definite] preference.

Furthermore, it is telling that when the Majnūn's father, egged on by his relatives and neighbours, takes the lover to pilgrimage, to Mecca, the Majnūn yields to his father's wish. However, the outcome is not what society or his father expected. The Majnūn ends up evoking Layla rather than God. The Majnūn recounts what he experienced:

وَدَاعٍ دعا إذْ نحن بالخيفِ من مِنَى فهيَّجَ أطرابَ الفؤادِ وما يدري
دعا بِاسْمِ ليلى غيرها فكأنَّما أطَارَ بليلى طائرًا كان في صَدْري

Somebody called out while we were by Mina
Unbeknown to him, he stirred the depths of the soul
He called at another in the name of Layla
And then as if a bird flew out from my bosom

The story as narrated in the tradition continues as follows:

> When the Majnūn and his father reached the Ka'ba (the holiest site in Islam), his father asked him to cling to its hangings and appeal to God in order to heal him from the love of Layla. He did so, and clung to the hangings of the Ka'ba, but instead said: 'God increase me in my love of Layla, bring me close to her, and never make me forget to remember her.'[15]

At the very site where the cradle of Islam and the Islamic spirit is consecrated, the Majnūn succumbs to the imperatives of his instinct, and the balance between his faith in God and his devotion to Layla tilts decisively towards Layla. This is a glaring example of how human psychology can override the imperatives of abstract metaphysical beliefs. This begs the question if human life is possible without uncertainty and tension, to which the conditions of unfulfilled love give rise.[16] Among the various artistic genres, love is also premised on openness and tension. To this end, love appears as an existential experience par excellence. While ideology might mark its expression in a particular way, it cannot obliterate its psychical dimensions, which are psychological and deeply personal. Therefore, it is possible to find shared psychical and spiritual poetic manifestations that cut across all the ages and traditions pertaining to unfortunate lovers facing the same predicament of rejection and alienation, attesting to the apt observation of Stefan Sperl: 'We are here faced with the fundamental unity of the human psyche which surfaces more clearly in the confrontation with extreme events and the reactions they engender.'[17] Society wants the Majnūn to cease remembering Layla and stop loving her, as if the manners of his love were an ongoing 'sin', but her love is so integral to his soul that he cannot repent from loving her:

يقولون تبْ عن ذِكرِ لَيلى وحُبِّها وما خَلَدي عَنْ حبِّ لَيْلى بتائبِ

They say abstain from remembering Layla and cease loving her
But my soul cannot repent over loving Layla.[18]

The Majnūn goes further, asserting the demanding resonance of his psyche:

وإن حارَبَتْ ليلى نُحاربْ وإن تَدِنْ نَدِنْ دِينَها لا عَيْبَ للمُتَوَدِّدِ

If Layla fights, we (people) fight, and if she believes
We believe in her religion, for the lover should have no shame to do this.[19]

All the terms used here, namely *tub* (repent, abstain), *dhikr* (remembrance), *khaladī* (my soul, inner-self) and *tā'ib* (repentant), are normally reserved to evoking man's relation to God; they are religious terms in the strict sense. Yet, Layla displaces God by having such a hold over the Majnūn's inner world that she effectively becomes his ascertained reference of blind belief. In the second line, he says as much: he sees Layla as a potential God that should be followed, whatever that 'God' decides, violating clear Quranic junctions against assigning divine attributes and entitlements to mere mortals. But the dilemma here is that the Majnūn, who to all intents and purposes professes Islam, resorts to subverting Islamic teachings and rituals in a manner that reflects the contradiction between his faith and his experience as a lover, thus even subjecting God and taking advantage of the Islamic understanding and obligation towards the divine. The Islamic tradition, as primarily represented in the Qur'an and the sayings (*Ahādīth*) of Prophet Mohammad, intended to foreground and inspire Muslims' lives,[20] is used here as a wellspring of linguistic and literary ingenuity to describe the Majnūn's feelings for his beloved and to authenticate his sentiments. Among his many subversions is the purpose of prayer, which should be intended for God, in accordance with the monotheistic creed of Islam. Instead, the Majnūn is directing his prayer towards Layla. He admits in the process that the immensity of his love for her sickens even the one who could possibly treat him:

أراني إذا صَلَّيْتُ يَممتُ نحوها بِوَجهي وَإن كانَ المُصَلَّى وَرائيا
وَما يَ إشراكٌ وَلَكنْ حُبُّها وَعُظْمَ الجَوى أَهيا الطَّبيبَ المُداويا

If I am praying, I catch myself being directed towards her
even when the direction of prayer is left behind me
I have had not abandoned Islam, but her love
and its depth in my soul had ailed the curing doctor[21]

Whether the character of the Majnūn is fictional or not,[22] the poetic materials at hand, including that of the epic lover Jamīl Buthaina, are riddled with terms and sentiments of the type highlighted earlier. These manifest the contradiction between faith and its purportedly certain and fixed frames of reference and the human experience at the psychical levels and its fluid and tension-riddled nature. This arresting and irreconcilable contradiction is vividly expressed in the second line. It juxtaposes the two aspects that tear apart the Majnūn: on the one hand, he is keen to assert that he is still a Muslim. He underscores the fact that he does not subscribe to apostasy (*Ishrāk*), treated grievously in Islam as the highest form of disbelief, punishable by death. And, on the other, he describes the extent of his affliction. Here, he is aware that he is incapable of performing Islamic practices to the letter, as if he were literally sick, giving credence to Ibn Hazm's observation: 'Love . . . is in truth a baffling ailment, and its remedy is in strict accord with the degree to which it is treated; it is a delightful malady, a most desirable sickness.'[23] The contradiction in the description of the inner state of the Majnūn, pitting his mind against his heart, is not resolved. Yet, his poetry, though stemming from a love object, is of a meditative nature and encompasses the various layers of his own reality. Among other things, it treats his feelings towards Layla, his relation to God and Islam, his view of the society, his understanding of the world and his vision of the past, the present and the future. It does so in a conversation-like manner – it is conversational, it *poetically* reasons with the primary sources of the Islamic traditions, mainly the Qur'an and the Prophet's sayings, with his conditions and his experience in mind.

Therefore, it is notably different from what can be found in pre-Islamic society in the famous story of 'Antara Bin Shaddād, the protagonist of another great love tale in Arabia of the sixth century. His unfulfilled love for 'Abla is compensated for through heroic battles in which the lover is serially engaged, asserting his masculinity in accordance with the tribal order in which he functions and where he was raised. 'Antara is doggedly assertive in his pursuit of the enemies from within his tribe of Banū 'Abs: they denied him the right to love and marry his cousin 'Abla, discriminating against him because the dark colour of his skin, inherited from his Ethiopian slave mother, did not befit 'Abla, daughter of Mālik, who is depicted as fair and of noble origins. Yet, his assertiveness takes masochistic masculine traits, as he boasts about his prowess and rebellion. And 'Abla, the initial provocateur of his passion, is submerged in the vagaries of his battles and heroic forays:[24]

> I have encountered heroes in every war, and I have defeated
> Men in every valley bottom . . .
> I conquered the kings in both the east and west and I
> Destroyed courageous equals in the day of rout.[25]

On the contrary, the Majnūn does not strike as a masculine figure at all, but his *idée fixe* stands for a particular type of love that challenges the tribal order and engages the Islam of his society in an extraordinary conversation. The great German philologist Eric Auberbach explains similar instances in European literature, especially Medieval Spanish literature, to the Majnūn and the *'Udhrī* lovers: 'the will working for an ideal must accord with an existing reality at least to such an extent that it meets it, so that the two interlock and a real conflict arises.'[26] The conflict is conducted through varying strategies, including factual statements and rebuttals, arguments and counterarguments and digressions. It exhausts all the conversational possibilities provoked in the lover by his state in relation to his beloved, society and ideology where love is embedded. And though the expression of love and conflict is circular and repetitive, the poetic discourse in which it is couched seems always new and expansive.

In addition, passion-ridden as it is, the poetry is permeated with psychical rationality, it can be argued. I mean by psychical rationality as consciousness centred on the belief that the psyche is entitled to defend its own subject of attraction so long as it is in harmony with consciousness as a content of rational (and even ethical) exploration and explanation, which in return is a defence of nature, including one's own, against unreasonable societal repressions and assaults. I have already given a few examples earlier where the verb *qul* and other related derivatives from it, such as *yaqulūn,* are prominent in the two diwans in question. Such verbs serve conversational purposes, suggesting that the poetry itself is in conversation with various forces, including social conventions, religious texts and interpreters of them, etc. The use of these active verbs draws on earlier Islamic styles of narration and expression as exemplified in the Qur'an and the tradition of Prophet Mohammad. In particular, the use of the verb stem *qala* (to say) and its various derivations, which is central to foreground and authenticate the prophetic message and action of the Prophet,[27] is also employed repeatedly in the 'Udhrī poetry for such effects as dialogic authentication.

Therefore, it bears arguing that the poetry of the 'Udhrīs serves as a significant layer of elaboration to the Islamic discourse, not necessarily an antithesis or a challenge to it, as has been argued by Tāher Labīb in his important book, *The Sociology of Love among the Arabs: The Case of 'Udhrī Poetry.*[28] Labīb contends that the poetry in question is essentially a Bedouin response and defence of a tribal order which had lost its power and privileges to Islam, with the subordination of the tribe to religion in the name of Islamic unity. As such, Labīb's reading is an indictment of the tribal and collective structure, which the 'Udhrīs are viewed as its wounded adherents. They have been marginalized to the point where the power of their tribe, whatever its former glories, has been lost to Islam – it is not love that they defend but their tribal privileges.

Interesting as it may be in showing the force of the tribal norms, which persist and linger on after Islam, this reading ignores what the poetry itself says about 'the Islamic norms'. In effect, it makes light of the actual acceptance of Islam by the poets and the consequences thereof. Moreover, Labīb's reading does not consider the text, what it communicates and means, in the Islamic context in which it was produced. It is also focused on the group, rather than the individual who produced the poetry. Through a close textual reading of the poetry itself and concurrent texts, I proceed differently in order to demonstrate the meanings of the texts in question within their own contexts. I emphasize the force of love afflicting the poets, and the social, religious and existential implications of their poetry within the context of Islamic precepts and practices.[29]

The poetry commences right after the end of the golden age of Islam, led originally by Prophet Mohammad (AD 570–632) through revelation and insight, and later by the four guided caliphs who experienced the prophecy of Prophet Mohammad and abided and expanded its sociopolitical and religious base and scope. This poetry is enriched with the freshness of a new expression pertaining to the faith. It is a conversation with the premises of Islam, a conversation conducted through poetry, not prose and discourse, the way the Islamic identity in its theological sense communicated. Here, poetry gives further scope for subversion, freedom and interior rationality in congruence with the premises and tendencies of the human psyche in its natural swings and sways. This is particularly so in such a context where religion, in its prosaic discourse, attempts to seal itself behind a discourse of conviction and fate and reward and punishment in order to protect its hermetic and authoritative construction. In this sense, it is a poetry that reconnects with pre-Islamic poetry. Islam disrupted or at least marginalized poetry the moment the discourse shifted to the message of the Prophet; this message, in the conventional sense, was not central to poetry. This reconnection with the old pre-Islamic poetry and its varied purposes (*aghrād*) adds and elaborates on what existed before, but it does so in light of the new reality of Islam and its expansion, not in contradiction or against it. Thus, it builds the foundations for the elaboration of a love discourse that never ceased to engage, which subverts and reveals the hidden forces animating the human conditions.

Therefore, with poetry being a subversive form of expression, that in some ways stirs waves of rebellion within language itself, the socio-religious norms do not apply to it the same way they do to prose and religious texts. In this sense, it is interesting to further juxtapose the religious with the worldly and existential in the Arabic tradition that shows how Islam conceptualized love and subjected it to its teachings and norms, and how, in return, the experiences of love subverted and enlarged the scope of Islamic edifice in its interpretational sense. Indeed, as will be further explained, the Islamic tradition abounds with discourses that are not as dogmatic as not to take account of the uncertain aspects of human nature. While on the face of it, Islam seems to create a conceptual caesura between pre-Islamic and post-Islam poetry of love, it in effect maintains and in some ways accommodates this unresolved tension, but still in a radically different way to that of the pre-Islamic society of Arabia.

Islam and love

There are a number of sayings and insights that the Qur'an and Prophet Mohammad articulated with regard to love. The procreative dimension of love foregrounds the Islamic discourses: what is at stake here is the continuity, perpetuation and indeed the well-being of humankind. These sayings serve as guiding thoughts and indeed principles on the way love is comprehended and practised. There is hardly any Arabic book on love in the classical sources of the medieval age (seventh to thirteenth century) that does not include references and commentaries on these sayings.[30] Yet, while the Quranic verse is evoked in contexts where love is fulfilled and its virtues and benefits are recounted and celebrated, the saying by Prophet Mohammad concerns love at a spiritual and psychical level: it defines love without seemingly intending to do so by describing its initial sources. The two quotes in question are due before further commentary is made. The Quranic verse says:

وهو الذي جعلَ لكم من أنفسكم أزواجاً لتسكنوا إليها، وجعلَ بينكم مؤدةٌ ورحمة إنّهُ هو الغفورُ الرحيم

He who has created among yourselves wives and husbands to inhabit and dwell in each other. And he created amongst you love and mercy and He is the most forgiving and merciful.[31]

The Prophet is reported to have said:

الأرواحُ جنودٌ مجندةٌ، منها ما تآلف فآتلف، ومنها ما تخالف فأختلف

> Spirits are regimented battalions: those which know one another incline to each other, while those which do not know one another remain at variance (effectively separate).[32]

What these two sayings share is their concentration on the *nafs* and *rūḥ*: both mean the spirit and the soul at the same time. They highlight the existence of something transcendent and indefinable in human life yet so abiding as to influence life's. This is a world in which the mind is subsumed, and it is not even mentioned – the mind is 'overpowered', 'won over' as the lover-poet Jamīl Buthaina describes his own condition vis-à-vis Buthaina, ويالكِ خلَّةً ظَفَرَتْ بعقلي 'what a beloved companion who had seized my mind'.[33] In this regard, the soul operates as the epicentre of existence, one that emits *mawaddah* (affection, love) and (*raḥmah*) mercy on the one hand, and antipathy and disgust, on the other. The suggestion in these sayings is far-reaching: they not only treat human love in its pristine and unaffected sense but also shed light on sameness and conflict, with which humanity in all its senses is ridden. In effect, the Quranic verse speaks at two levels. On the one hand, it connotes that God fashioned the world in such a way that all souls are meant to inhabit other souls; every soul will be touched by another soul– foreshadowing the modernist idea that identity, any identity, is premised on alterity, on an Other that shapes and perhaps sustains it.[34] On the other, the sayings imply that souls differ from each other: those that have sameness between them associate and unite in the name of their higher spirits, even though they might not be aware or able to communicate as to what makes that extraordinary unity of spirits. Yet, those souls that do not suit each other, their spirits, the atoms of the soul, do not cluster as the letters of a word merge to make a word: they remain at variance, apart from each other. Unless there is that prior higher unity of *nafs* and *rūḥ*, love remains illusively beyond reach. In the case of the Quranic verse, if one's soul has not been inhabited by another in that romantic-spiritual and fulfilled way, then the soul is effectively homeless, searching for a home, and it still is on the road, so as to say. The chosen word in the verse (*li-taskunū*, from the root *sakana*, to live, to inhabit, to dwell) is intentionally loaded with that idea of homelessness until love is found. In that sense, love is the ultimate home of every soul. But *sakana*, as an active verb, has two senses: one emphasizes the dual living and inhabiting that love engenders; the second concerns human engagement and construction of intimacy and affection. Thus, love requires both: the naturalness of spirits and their concurrence, and the human attention and labour required to construct and sustain it.

However, it happens that souls sometimes collide; they clash and do not inhabit each other. Then, they, as the saying of the Prophet suggests, remain at variance. What is striking in the saying of the Prophet is the chosen imagery. The imagery of war, *regimented battalions*, is evoked to show that souls are mobilized in the battlefield of love: they are furnished with alertness as to what makes the bond, as one might say. Effectively, some win it and others lose it – and it is beyond language. The story of Jamīl in his love to Buthaina is borne amidst a conflict that evolves into dialogue and reconciliation before plunging into a war-like situation where the two lovers are deprived of each other by their respective tribes:

وأَوَّلُ ما قادَ المَوَدَّةَ بيننا بوادي بغيضٍ، يا بُثَيْنَ سِبَابُ
وَقُلنا لها قولًا، فجاءتْ بمثلِهِ لكلِ كَلامٍ، يا بُثَيْنَ جوابُ

What first triggered love between us in a spiteful valley,[35] O Buthaina,
were insults that we threw at each other
(I) said something to her and she responded in alike manner
O Buthaina, each discourse has its counterpart.[36]

The image of conflict and war deepens as the lovers are separated, each beholden to their tribe's norms.[37] Jamīl shows the effects of tormented souls in constant movement, like armies in war, to secure their release from unbearable emotional shackles:

أمشي، وتمشي في البلادِ، كأنّنا أسيرانِ للأعداءِ مُرتهنانِ

I walk in the land and so does she as if we were
Captives in the hands of enemies . . .[38]

In Jamīl's case, the lovers are not at war with each other, yet they are implicated in the tribal order that prevents their love. It is peace that Jamīl holds out for Buthaina:

فإن تكُ حربٌ بين قومي وقومها فإنّي لها في كلِّ نائبةٍ سَلم

If there is a war between my people and hers
I carry peace for her in every speck of existence[39]

Yet, war between tribes or nations for that matter instils sentiments and thoughts of war in individuals; and this is acutely felt when love is involved. It is this intense emotion of alienation that the lover wishes to be saved from, which makes up the war-like persona who gives birth to such images of conflict. The conflict is an original translation of individuals and indeed nations' psyche as tension-ridden and as made in relation to an Other. Thus, there is the constant image of humanity in harmony and divided at the same time, free and besieged as well. The epic love tale of Majnūn Layla evokes exactly this imagery of the soul being engulfed by war:

غزتني جنودُ الحبِّ من كلِّ جانبٍ إذا حانَ من جُندٍ قفولٌ أتى جُندُ

The soldiers of love invaded me from every side
if I overcome one solider, another comes[40]

In the Majnūn's case, the beloved is not virtually available, but he is surrounded by her spirit and he is bound by its commanding effect; her physical absence is compensated for by her spiritual presence. The lover is not physically besieged; but it is his soul that experiences and laments the invasion of unfulfilled love: it is an image of psychological war in the full sense of the word. But while echoing and confirming the veracity of the Prophet's description with regard to love, the Majnūn has become so utterly incapable of controlling his desires that his freewill has no influence on their poetic manifestation. His cultural world, as that of the ʿUdhrī lovers in general, is one of observing Islamic norms and expressing regret that their conditions are such they cannot adhere to Islam to the letter – the familiar Islam of his society and culture. Their language shows them as individuals who have lost the capacity to be willed enough to perform religious duties. Therefore, there is a paradox between culture and nature, all embodied in the characters of those unfulfilled lovers-poets; and this paradox between nature and culture, that they are not brought in harmony together, is what gives their poetry its epic character, while showing the limits of ideology in the process.

The poetry facilitates the proposition that there is an entrenched mythic element to human life which, while seemingly transcendental, remains deeply earthy. It is a by-product of the human soul and its yearnings and the psyche and its accumulations. Such accumulations are beyond ideological seizure and definite claim. Ideology tends to be transcendental without being earthily, while myths become transcendental through latent earthiness lodged in the bursting emanations of the afflicted human soul. Ideology does not want the soul to explore its options and run its natural courses during psychical arrests. It wants to obliterate the soul by prescribing ways of recovery outside the human body and being: a recovery set to be achieved not in the present, but in the future – in the case of monotheistic religions, with salvation.[41] The normative Arabic tradition gave the certain and the complete an edge over the problematic and the unsolved.[42] In this respect, Edward Said writes, 'whereas the former (Islamic) literary tradition views reality as plentiful, complete, and divinely directed, the latter (European) sees reality as radically incomplete, authorizing innovation, and problematic.'[43] Meanwhile, as true as this is at a normative level, it is yet to take account of the experiences and underlying discourses that rendered the Arabic and indeed Islamic tradition in general open to further answers and innovations, and it questions its stable references in line with evolving human contexts and experiences.

Acknowledging the depth and indeed inevitability of such love through the *hadith* tradition, Islam resorts to the discourse of punishment and rewards. In this sense, the Prophet seizes on this extraordinary dilemma by apportioning transcendental rewards for those who not only endure such love but also keep silent about it:

من عشق فعفَّ فكتم فمات فهو شهيد

That who loved passionately, and embraced decorum and took refuge in silence, and then died, he is a martyr.[44]

Whatever a Muslim cannot attain in life because of his observance and sacrifice for his faith, he would obtain increasingly in the hereafter. Accordingly, the hereafter is unknown, yet so full of rewards that 'no eye has seen nor ear heard of', according to the Prophet's expression of God's promise.[45] The Prophet resorts to assigning an ultimate reward for such an austere lover, who conceals their love and perishes for it. In the Islamic tradition, the martyrs have the rewards and status of the prophets; they sacrifice their souls, if need be, for their faith. However, the hadith is clear in one sense but is not so in another. In that, the hadith does not mention at all those lovers who cannot conceal their love and who manifest and express it. Despite the disciplinary facade through which Islam is often presented, Islam is endowed with windows of openness towards those who cannot do what they have been religiously exhorted to do, particularly when their inability is tied to natural, physical and psychical limits. Lovers cannot forgo their love if it is that spiritually intense and psychically abiding.[46]

Yet, the normative interpreters do not refrain from castigating obsessive lovers for their immersion in passions that seem to replace their love and devotion to the divine.

The Islamic thinker of the eighth century Ibn al-Qiyam al-Jawziyya highlighted the severity of the paradox between the world of the *'Udhrī* poets-lovers and that of Islam. In this respect, he sanctioned against this type of love, *'ishq'* (passion, unbridled attachment), because 'it is feared that who follows this love will be derailed from attending to faith, and will become unconscious of its obligations', and because

> monotheism and the pursuit of love are contradictory. Love is an idol, and each human being has an idol inside his heart that concurs with his streak of love. Whereas God sent his messengers to obliterate the idols (break them down) so that people can devote themselves to worshiping him alone, without any associates. God does not intend to break the constructed idols, and to leave those that are in the heart, but he intends to break them in the heart first.[47]

The contradiction pertaining to the *'Udhrī* love as a state of *'ishq* is that it is alluded to – acknowledged in Islam. There are attempts to limit and undermine, if not eliminate, it altogether in favour of decorum, purity and devotion to God above any other mortals. Yet, there are tacit hints that this tension and paradox, explained earlier, between the world of faith and that of nature is at its most visceral state, which suggests that this tension is left unresolved. Monotheism, as much as it is strict in its emphasis on the obligations of the faith, ultimately accommodates human forces – including psychical and metaphysical ones – that are beyond human beings' capacity to strictly contain. Therefore, religion is endowed with elliptical statements and discourses that leave open avenues of exploration and interpretations of psychical, social and philosophical realities, the organization of societies and the needs of individuals. To this end, religion can become an interpretive and creative conversation. And it is in the nature of such a conversation that it can undergo change – an unhesitant change that makes religion an integral part of the human experience and its instinctive and practical imperatives.[48]

Thus, equally, if the Sunna tradition of the Prophet and the Islamic tradition itself is to some extent open to interpretation regarding the abiding turns of the heart and soul, then the world of the *'Udhrī* poets totters between attending to the Islamic faith in its strict and decorous sense, and between bowing down to the force of their emotions in such a way that clearly subverts the manifest sanctions of the Islamic creed against transgressions where the beloved becomes the unrivalled *prime force* of the poet's universe, eclipsing God in the process. In this respect, the Islamic discourse and the intense lovers balance each out. Both, Islam and the subversive poets themselves, are the manifestation and the agents of love and change in their own ways.

The archetypical paradox of love is that it happens between souls, and it morphs into several contradictions that operate at the natural and constructed levels and reveal itself in almost all the manifestations of love.[49] In this respect, love and its dynamics stand for the drama that human history, conditions and indeed human nature is. In other words, love is love and conflict at the same time. To this end, the illustrious Arab thinker Ibn Hazm al-Andalusi's definition of love, arguably foregrounded in the sayings quoted earlier, is inclusive of the natural and the constructed aspects of love and their consequences:

> For my part I consider love as a conjunction between scattered parts of souls that have become divided in this physical universe, a union affected within the substance of their original sublime element... every form always cries out for its corresponding form; like is ever at rest with like.[50]

There is something primordially accurate about Ibn Hazm's definition of love.[51] A close reading suggests that the human soul is originally united, being conceived in the unity of the human beings that regenerates each other – in the seed. The separation of the child from the mother is the first instance where the soul becomes scattered as it starts searching for an other. Thus, what Ibn Hazm refers to as the 'sublime element' is indeed one of significant importance as it takes love back to its root consequence and manifestation, the infant, even if the infant was not born with love in its social–literal sense.

Since separation embodies loss, the journey to reclaim unity starts earnestly at birth. The child suckles at his mother's nipples affirming attachment, compensating for the primordial separation from once being inside her, surviving and growing in the process.[52] At a certain age, depending on the culture, the child grows out of that phase, transcending the phase of birth. Then comes independence and the search for an identity. Psychical love of the type explored here is one of the most vivid aspects that upset one's identity and reveal the human capacity and limits of the soul. Everything is laid bare at once, not only in relation to others but also within the person whose highs and lows will reach the peak of their manifestation.

The epic response and the dialectical conversation

The two love stories taken into question often invoke an innocent childhood, unaware of that 'primordial separation', but burdened with feelings of loss. There is always a moment, an incident, that disturbs the norm, ushering in a never-ending drama of remembrance and invocations. In the Majnūn, the landscape of his childhood is filled with Layla, his love that was taken away from him and entrusted to another person. In a searing and nostalgic manner, the Majnūn laments and implies that his attachment to Layla is psychical and spiritual, before being physical:

تَعلقْتُ لَيْلى وهي ذاتُ ذؤَابةٍ ولم يَبْدُ للأتراب من ثَدْيها حجمُ
صغيرَين نرعى البَهْمَ يا ليتَ أنّنا إلى اليوم لم نَكبرْ ولم تكبُرِ البَهَمُ[53]

I fell in love with Layla when she was a heedless child
When no sign of her bosom had yet appeared to playmates
Two children guarding the flocks, would that we never
Had grown up, nor had the flocks grown old.[54]

The lines are shot with the spirit of return, return to a state that is no longer available. It teems with impossibility. Introducing the above lines, Khairallah As'ad summarizes the tropes of loss:

> We have already seen that whether in the Arabic, in the Islamic, or in the general context, alienation might begin by being a divorce between man and his social

environment, but it often reaches the dimensions of a psychological and metaphysical rupture which is impossible to heal.[55]

The second layer of alienation that disturbs the balance of the soul and carries metaphysical reverberations is that which pertains to its deep effect on the soul, the *rūh*. The soul, which in the Islamic tradition is prior to the body, is mysterious and entrusted to God for his all-knowing attributes become almost known-felt to the lover when he is in this state of metaphysical love. This state opens to him avenues of self-understanding that he would not have accessed otherwise. But it also endows him with a sense of discovery and reunites him with the 'missing' elements of his soul that had eluded him since birth. Ibn Hazm elaborates on the role of the soul in a way that echoes other sources and thinkers in the Arabic tradition, such as Ibn Sina, who also conceives the power of love as residing in the soul and its link to visual-perceptual and sensual forces that signal the concurrence with other spirits–souls:[56]

> As for what causes love in most cases to choose a beautiful form to light upon, it is evident that the soul itself being beautiful, it is affected by all beautiful things, and has a yearning for perfect symmetrical images; whenever it sees any such image, it fixes itself upon it; then, it discerns behind that image something of its own kind, it becomes united and true love is established. If however the soul does not discover anything of its own kind behind the image, its affection goes no further than the form, and remains mere carnal desire. Indeed, physical forms have a wonderful faculty of drawing together the scattered parts of men's soul.[57]

In effect, the soul that carries such light which perceives its resemblance in another becomes pregnant with the other person's light. The latter's light has the effect of conjuring all the potential sources and origins of this attachment and love to the beloved in ways that blur the lines between reality and delusion, making reality in its inclusive sense subject to procreative perceptual magnets. The poet stumbles upon a dangerous realization, albeit a delusional one in the conventional sense, that his love to the beloved predates its actual physical occurrence, harking all the way back to when he was a mere seed in his mother's womb. That seed carried his and his beloved's soul. The Majnūn and Jamīl Buthaina relay the same sentiment and idea, even though each of them is aware of a particular moment and incident when their beloved deserted their innocent conformed life:

The Majnūn:

تعلَّقَ روحي روحَها قَبلَ خَلْقِنا ومن بعدِ أن كنَّا نطافاً وفي المهدِ
أيا ربِّ إنْ لم تَقْسِمِ الحُبَّ بيننا سَواءين فأجعلني على حُبِّها جَلْداً[58]

> My soul clung to hers before we were born
> And after we became a clot and in the cradle
> O God, if you do not make love between us possible
> Then make me patient to endure her love

Jamīl Buthaina:

أبى القلبُ إلا حبُّ بثنةَ لم يرد سواها، وحبُّ القلبِ بثنةً لا يجدي
تَعَلَّقَ روحي رُوحَها قبلَ خَلْقِنا، ومن بعدِ ما كُنَّا نطافاً وفي المَهْدِ
فزادَ كما زِدْنا، فأصبحَ نامياً، ولَيْسَ إذ مُتْنا بِمُنتقضِ العَهْدِ
ولكنهُ باقٍ على كلِّ حالةٍ، وزائرُنا في ظُلمةِ القبرِ واللَّحْدِ

The heart persists absolutely in loving Buthaina:
O Buthaina, the love of the heart is in vain
My soul clung to hers before we were born
And after we became a clot and in the cradle
It grew as we became older, and matured
The covenant of love won't be broken when we die
It will all remain as it is
Our visitor in the dark space of the grave.[59]

Like the belief in one God and Islam that the two poets subscribe to, they both emphasize in an ascertained fashion that their love is predestined and eternal; it is monotheistic, to one person as their belief in one God – time is synthetically frozen: the past is where love began, the present where it is intensely felt but unrealized, and the future where love seals and yet confirms the predestined journey of love and reunion again. The lovers-poets demonstrate what Ibn Hazm refers to in his seminal book on love, *The Dove's Necklace*, as the impossibility of healing. The beloved has had a hold on his life from the very moment of conception and will have it until death. On this type of love, Ibn Hazm inflicts his observations and analysis with the absoluteness of the predicament that the conditions of the beloved engender:

> The only true passion, which has the mastery of the soul: this is the love which passes not away save with death. You will find a man far advanced in years, who swears that he has forgotten love entirely. . . . In none of the other sorts of love does anything like this happen: that mental preoccupation, that derangement of the reason, that melancholia, that transformation of settled temperaments, and alternation of natural dispositions, that moodiness, that sighing, and all the other symptoms of profound agitation which accompany passionate love.[60]

By emphasizing on predestination and on the transformative power of passionate love, Ibn Hazm puts the poets at the centre, without ever eschewing their Islamic culture. Jamīl Buthaina still resorts to God to grant him patience, so that he can tolerate the trauma of separation from his beloved. In that, the poets adopt the language of devotion to God in parallel with their devotion to the beloved. The use of religious language in the discourse of lovers indicates that those lovers expand the existential grounds of the Islamic faith. They are aware of the cultural limits and prohibitions of their societies. Therefore, they address them in such a way as to suggest that they are upholders of particular truths that Islam in its essence is open to accommodating and that they are not intentionally blasphemous or wayward individuals who do not have a conscience and disregard religious authorities. As if in their afflicted understanding of love, they understand Islam from a unique position of inner revelation and closeness to the divine that qualifies them to reinterpret, re-imagine and expand their conception of the divine. This experience allows them to converse with Islam as a living and fluid tradition, not as a fixed template beyond discussion and spiritual expansion. Accordingly, it becomes possible to consider God as an earthly manifestation that, as much as it (its collective soul, it can be said) dwells in a higher heavenly realm of some sort, it is also present among humans and reveals himself in all his attributes, the rewarding, the forgiving and the punishing ones, in their relations. This concurs with what Khairallah As'ad wrote regarding the inseparability of the lover experience from his faith in God:

> Love does not become necessary only because of eternal predestination. It is the essence and meaning of man's relation to God, and, hence, a defining characteristic of Magnun's archetypal existence.
>
> Love is life itself. This is a central point in the Diwan, as well as in the tradition which it represents . . . remoteness from the beloved becomes equivalent to separation from one's soul.[61]

The quest for the beloved is latently grounded in search for unity with the divine as well. Yet, though the 'Udhrī lovers' interpretation may be subjective, they still live within societies conforming to the Islamic creed and are not, in general, tolerant of manifest transgressions, particularly ones populated with vivid praise and devotion to the beloved woman, and seemingly at the expense of devotion to God. Therefore, for the Majnūn to function and write poetry as he did within the Arab-Islamic society where his epic emerged, he had to be Majnūn, a 'madman', with the original meaning of the word being 'to be possessed by a jin'. Therefore, he is exempted from the rules of religion. But the Majnūn commands an ordered language that conveys consciousness (or the unconscious for that matter) and imagination, confirming that madness is a trope for subversion of the Islamic order as much as it is a manifestation of unfulfilled love in the first place. In this sense, because love involves instinctive dimensions beyond all social and religious confinements, it is subverted through poetry, an art that escapes the constraints of the norm. Meanwhile, through his self-professed madness, the Majnūn acts as an intellectual alongside being a lover and poet. He understands and articulates his own very nature as part of the natural order of things, not as society conceives of it, a state of unproductive and futile madness. As'ad explains the issue at hand as follows:

> If sanity is generally equated with conformity to established norms, then we can see how madness becomes one of the best literary symbols of the universal rebel against any established order that stands between his free self and reality, whether this reality be the inner introspective or the outer physical world. The madman will represent the rebellion against the stifling laws of reasonable society and its common sense. His imagination is his reason, and where 'sane' people hesitate in front of social and intellectual norms, he simply asserts his mode of vision with the same innocence and force of prophetic utterance. This purity of vision, and the courage of expressing it make the madmen an almost poetic ideal.[62]

Many of the terms and discourses associated with such lovers spring from the physical and natural world, be this of the human beings themselves or the external nature. The poets become enabling voices of a nature that has stumbled upon its own psychical limits. The metaphysical sickness of unfulfilled love afflicts the heart, the liver, the soul, the eyes and the body. All these attract darkness that weakens, strikes and renders the human subject alienated from himself and everything around him. In this respect, Buthaina expresses his inner state more than once:

لها في سوادِ القلبِ بالحبِّ منعةٌ هي الموت، أو كادت على الموت تُشرفُ
وما ذكرتكِ النفسُ، يا بثّ، مرةً من الدهر، إلّا كادت النفسُ تتلفْ[63]

She is ensconced in the dark essence of the heart
She is the death, or almost that
The spirit had not evoked you even one time, o Buthaina,
Without almost fading away.

But the mind, another active force in the creation of poetry, is also rooted and is interactive with social and cultural memories and habits that become very much part of the humanity – it is the force that absorbs, facilitates and concentrates remembrance. To this end, the poets are the brainchildren of their own linguistic, cognitive and emotional dispositions, subjective contexts and their surroundings. These various levels of belonging compel the poets to attend to nature and to culture, particularly in such an expanding Islamic community, where the manifest belonging of the individual to tradition ensures cultural cohesion, security and togetherness. All the ʿUdhrī poets, and indeed all poets, oscillate in their poetry between attending to nature and to social norms along the lines explained earlier. There are manifest and hidden realities to their poetry which bear witness to their very subject formation as embodied people.

Nature and culture

Most of the accounts of love, in poetry or prose, confirm the dynamics of natural-instinctive and spiritual forces at play that transcend the boundaries and norms of religion in terms of its sanctions and prohibitions,[64] and indeed any societal norms for that matter.[65] Language becomes a self-fulfilling tool of expression that allows the poet to be free. Therefore, the breaching of the rules extends the gamut of the individual himself, who becomes his own object and stares in at his own turbulent transformations, as well as that of society, an ordered system of communication, subject to social and historical conventions. Hence, the lovers-poets tackle the two overriding aspects surrounding their lives: their pressured nature and the norms of their society.

To this end, the Majnūn challenges his father to make his union with Layla possible; then he would be a sound member of the society, respecting the responsibilities and obligations of the societal norms:

فيا أبتي إنْ كنتَ حقّاً تريدني وترجو حياتي بينكن أقيمُ
فجُدْ لي بليلى واصطنعني بقربها أصيرُ لها زوجاً وأنتَ سليمُ...
وتُنهشُني من حبِّ ليلى نواهشٌ لهنَّ حريقٌ في الفؤادِ عظيمُ

O my father if you genuinely want me
And wish for me a life amongst you
Then, find Layla and bring her close to me
I will become a husband for her and you will approve of this . . .
I am devoured from the love of Layla by voracious forces
With such great burning effects on the soul.[66]

Given the fact that the father could not help him fulfil his wishes, the Majnūn has become estranged from himself, has lost control of his very essence and indicates his abandonment of society. He is asking his father for the impossible, trying to elicit an existential sympathy of some sort by stressing how it is all beyond his control: he is devoured by mysterious forces that set his soul on fire. This also applies to Jamīl Buthaina. Both find the social norms stifling and unbearable, and think that their urge for love would not be fulfilled in their societies; as they were ostracized and spied upon in order to prevent from seeing each other. The poets-lovers would not be understood. Therefore, the Majnūn is scathing about society altogether, affiliating himself with nature in its seemingly innocent and harmless sense and shunning the society to extremes. Nature becomes such an exalted refuge, with the poet wishing to be one of its objects because its laws and dynamics cannot be subject to people's judgement:

ألا ليتنا كنّا غزالين نرتعي رياضاً من الحوذان في بلدٍ قفر
ألا ليتنا كنّا حمامي مفازةٍ نطيرُ ونأوي بالعشيّ إلى وَكرِ
ألا ليتنا حوتانِ في البحر نرتمي إذا نحن أمسينا نُلجَج في البحر
ويا ليتنا نحيا جميعاً وليتنا نصيرِ إذا متنا ضجيعينِ في قبرِ
ضجيعينِ في قبرٍ عن الناسِ مُعزَلٍ ونُقرَنُ يومَ البعثِ والحشر والنشر

I wish that we were two gazelles
grazing in a fertile ground in a deserted land
I wish that we were two free doves
flying and retiring to nests by the evening
I wish that we were two whales, playing about
once we take refuge in the depth of the sea
I wish that we could all live, and wish
if we die that we would lie next to each in the grave
Resting in an isolated grave away from people
and uniting in matrimony on the Day of Judgment.[67]

These are luminous images that indicate the utter alienation of the poet-lover from his society. The wish to an unbound sense of freedom as represented in the lives of animals, birds and sea-creatures, all attest to disenchantment with the society and its norms; these are creatures unbound by consciousness and language and therefore the dynamics and logic of their world is less burdensome and consequential – there is only nature in the world of such creatures, no rules-bound society in the conventional sense. Furthermore, death and love are natural associates in cases where love is unfulfilled – love is the force that reproduces and affirms life; without it, life is lifeless, inconsequential and burdensome to death. Death invokes a state of nature, untied to feelings, obligations, norms and trials. It is the end that ends all beginnings and all ends for that matter. It is an original seed of nothingness. However, the Majnūn knows that he is none of these creatures and suggests that if what is inside him was to afflict the natural world, the seas, animals, etc. they would cease to function in the way they do. He justifies his state of 'professed madness' to society:

فلو أنّ ما بي بالحصى فَلَقَ الحَصى وبالصَّخرةِ الصَّمَّاء لا نصدعَ الصخرُ
فلو أنّ ما بي بالوحوش لَمَا رعت ولا ساغها الماءُ النَّميرُ ولا الزَّهرُ
ولو أنّ ما بي بالبِحارِ لَمَا جرى بأمواجها بَحرٌ إذا زخرَ البَحرُ

Had stones been touched by what I bear, they would have split
And a deaf boulder torn asunder
Had wild beasts tasted my pain, they would not have grazed
Nor would they have desired the pure water or the flowers
Had the seas carried what is inside me, their waves would not have flowed
Nor a single sea emerges even if the sea was at its fullest.[68]

The Majnūn is certain that his state is compelling and incomparable in its utter naturalness but abnormal in his society, tribe and religion. Therefore, he dramatizes his condition in relation to nature and highlights how such strong and robust manifestations of nature would not function if they were in the same state as his. Nature is used for comparative purposes and a line of defence for his state of brokenness. But it is also a healing force that qualifies him to stand above it through his consciousness and language; he is stronger than them all. He is not mad because he chose madness, but because madness struck him. In the same vein, he is explaining to society and in fact tacitly to religious authorities and to his spiritual conscience that his state of madness affected him to such an extent that he could not fulfil social, religious and even existential obligations. Here he is drawing on the Qur'an, setting himself up as an instinctive force like Islam does: such love renders everything different to what it was. Thus, he should be respected for who he is, not watched, shunned and misunderstood by the society. He is justifying his own humanity, which is in an extreme condition and must be understood. His love is like the Qur'an in its effect on him. There are certain instinctive experiences that are beyond judgement or punishment. He wants to be embraced by the society as a lover, the way Islam was adopted by the Muslims, echoing the power of the Quranic verse that says:

لو أنزلنا هذا القرآن على جبلٍ لَرأيتَهُ خاشعاً مُتصدِّعاً مِّن خشية الله وتلك الأمثال نضربها للناسِ لعلَّهم يتفكرون.

If we had sent down this Qur'an upon a mountain, you would have seen it humbled and coming apart from fear of Allah. And these examples We give to people that perhaps they will give thought.[69]

Similarly, Jamīl Buthaina pleads to be believed that his love and what has befallen him is true:

أتقرحُ أكبادُ المحبيّنَ كالذي أرَى كبدي مِنْ حُبِّ بَثنةَ يَقرحُ
فواللهِ ثُمَّ اللهِ إنّي لصادِقٌ، لذكركِ في قَلبي ألذُّ وأملحُ

Do the livers of lovers darken and sicken
I see my liver darkening and sickening from the love of Buthaina
By God, by God, I am genuinely truthful
Remembering you fills my heart with sweetness and salt.[70]

Both poets present a dilemma to Islamic theology; but they offer themselves as truthful individuals with impeding instinctive experiences. Like Islam values truth, society should accept their truth, which is who they are as lovers. They are true to their nature but in conflict with their society and its norms. Indeed, the stories in question offer a lesson on how sensitive minorities, perhaps the marginalized,[71] should be embraced, how the society should be big, understanding and forgiving, for it is the absence of these values that deprived those lovers from their love in the first place. It is society that enervates the Majnūn and Buthaina more: lovers should be from the same tribe, and one should not write poetry that scandalizes the beloved and her tribe – all these restrictive and socially crippling constraints compel the Majnūn and Buthaina to affiliate more with nature than society. There is no solution to the Majnūn and Buthaina except through death; their love is uncompromised, their souls with all the wars they fought are dogged in their pursuit and invocation of the beloved, but ultimately, society is protective in its own right – even through intrusion in this case. To treat such maladies of love, it resorts to surveillance, methods of containing love, attempting to bring them back to the fold of religion, social norms, tribal structure and unquestioning tropes of existence. Ultimately, society is limited in its ability to accept diversity in comparison to an individual's capacity to experience private psychical afflictions that alienate him from his society, while opening avenues of understanding and introspection that offer profound lessons for the conformist society.

There are people watching and spying on the lovers, imposing norms and limits on their communication and togetherness. Jamīl Buthaina communicates these sentiments in a way that echoes the Majnūn. Both poets imply that they are not understood, that others regard their love as unproductive and dangerous:

وماذا عسى الواشونَ أن يتقوَّلوا سوى أنْ يقولوا إنني لكِ وامقُ؟
نعم صدقَ الواشونَ أنتِ حبيبةٌ إليَّ، وإنْ لم تصفْ منكِ الخلائقُ

What could the spies claim
That I follow and crave for you
Indeed, the spies are correct, you are my beloved
Even if other creatures could not understand you.[72]

Ultimately, nature is a more reliable source of solace than people. They survey and cajole people into submission to what they have deemed normal. Here the rebellion of the 'Udhrī lovers is in the open; and it ends with the death of the poets – seemingly the only natural course that could follow from the grip of natural passions. Culture is not equipped to accommodate lovers with such manifest opinions that subvert the familiar norms of marriage and togetherness that normative Islamic practices sanctify and promote.

To this end, the 'Udhrī lovers represent an interesting phenomenon within the context of the early development of Islamic identity. Yet, the lovers in question enriched and enlarged the scope of what can be described as Islamic existentialism[73] – a non-judgemental state where the spirit of Islam is expansive, mindful of people in their very natural dynamics and states as much as it is concerned with their sociopolitical organization and affiliations. The lovers benefited from the Islamic message through subversions and uses that nuance the meanings and values of Islam itself, placing love in all its senses at its heart as a psychical reality before anything else. One persistent value that emanates from their poetry is represented in its conversational, dialogic and interrelated styles: the poets converse with various aspects of their reality, with a plethora of transcendental coinages and references, in order to foreground their state in relation to their society with its present limits and its potential for growth in terms of human consciousness and relations. Clearly, such basis is anathema to the tribal order still prevalent and indeed responsible for the emergence of those poets-lovers. The conversation of the poets with the society and the Islamic tradition in general appears more than once;[74] and sometimes, it is directly educational, admirably humanist and touchingly free, as when the Majnūn describes how the society alleges that the mother of Layla is Christian, and therefore cannot effectively suit him as a Muslim. Most humanely, the Majnūn rebuts this, using psychical and existential corrections against narrow ideological conceptions entrenched in rigid frames of reference:

وقد قيل نصرانيةٌ أمُّ مالكٍ فقلتُ ذروني، كلُّ نفسٍ ودينها
فإن تكُ نصرانيةٌ أمُّ مالكٍ فقد صُوِّرَتْ في صورةٍ لا تشينها

It was said that Umm Mālik (Layla's other name) is a Christian
I said: spare me this; each spirit has its own religion
If Umm Mālik was portrayed as a Christian
This does not disrepute or incriminates her[75]

'It was *said*' and 'I *said*', the Majnūn drives his message in the passive form to converse and rebut the ideological frames of the society. It bears reiterating that the use of the verb 'to say' and the whole reasoning behind it is at the heart of the intricate and multidimensional conversation that the Majnūn conducts in his poetry. He explores and deconstructs himself, the society and its beliefs and norms, harnessing his experience of love towards universal lessons and implications. With the Quranic injunction that expresses sacred respect to people of other religions in mind, 'To you your religion, and to me mine',[76] the Majnūn expands and reminds people of the depth of the Quranic message that there is more to people than their religion or origin for that matter, suggesting that religion is not the sole criterion by which to judge or make relations with people. He resorts to a higher truth. It is the humanity of the other and the potential psychological and spiritual bonds that should drive and sustain the chemistry of love; and any social formation has to be constructed with notions of freedom, justice and love in mind. In one stroke, the Majnūn rebuts the tribal order and the narrow interpretation of Islamic sources, opening both to the possibility that fluidity and openness in understanding the human subject, and humanity in general, are productive and meaningful crucibles of human relations.

Conclusion

Poetry is not a medium that can control itself; it cannot replace a political discourse driven by intentionality and purpose. Poetry that relies on fluid emotional energy tends to manifest conscious and unconscious forces. In this sense, it can appear as the antithesis, or an unnecessary extra, of a reality saturated by normative habits and boundaries. However, it is precisely this mysterious and revelation-bent quality of poetry and art in general that makes it necessary, illuminating and ironically truthful vis-à-vis the unspoken and the marginalized that art makes central. In this instance, poetry reverses and conflates the order as to what is peripheral and what is central. It expands the meaning of the normative and the perception of the status quo in ways that challenge the political and cultural powers in question. This chapter considered how the case of a minority of Arab lovers-poets, the 'Udhrīs, belonging to the tribe of Banū 'Udhra can be understood in this light.

At some point, Islamic civilization and culture being sensitive and attentive to word and sound grounded themselves on prosaic narratives that marginalized poetry, treating poets as individuals with wayward tendencies, aimless in their pursuits. In this respect, the Quranic verse says, '*As for poets, the erring follow them. Did you not see how they stray in every valley, And how they say that which they do not do?*'[77] Given the predominance of poetry as the supreme artistic expression of pre-Islamic Arabia, the Quranic inclination is clear: it distances Prophet Mohammad from poets in order to elevate and confirm his message above any others that preceded it and to downplay the poets as the heroes and spokespersons of their tribes and community, as well as to emphasize the supreme matchlessness of Prophet Mohammad's power of revelation as established in the Quran. The Quran becomes the sacred reference point and the sphere of stylistic eloquence, accurate conduct and normativity; and Prophet Mohammad's sayings become the source of guidance, interpretation and wisdom. The political order that was established in Arabia and extended to far-flung areas forming the Islamic polity and empires preoccupied itself with interpreting and applying the word of God while complementing it with the sayings and deeds of Prophet Mohammad. It thus made poetry invisible, which was once the voice of the tribe and the manifest document of its presence and identity.

However, the preponderance of poetry and innovative language and its florescence during the Umayyad and the Abbasid period meant that poetry alongside prose occupied and restored its normativity as a linguistic medium for social, political and existential referencing and use.

More importantly, however, and this is the overarching argument of this chapter, is that poetry rooted in psychological dynamics and tension manifested truths and realities lurking behind the normative – decorous – discourses of the expanding Islamic societies in question. In this sense, the most important art of the Arabs then, poetry, interacted, enlarged and challenged the status quo and added to Islam as not only a theological reality emanating at a particular historical time but also a psychological one in conversation with intricate sociopolitical conditions. The poets represented their beloved in divine-like terms and used, where they did, the Islamic cannon of expression to their advantage, subjecting Islam to the revelation of their experiences of love and its holistic dimensions and truths, including social, political and psychological realities of universal qualities. In this vein, Islam appears as a mobile spirit, not an unimpeachable reference point, as ideologues make of it. By their very nature, spirits move, expand and even fade. The religion stems from human experiences, which is susceptible to change. It can undergo such changes that it can be left without being forgotten as an exemplary historical spirit that carried sea-changes forward.

The issue here is that the lovers-poets discussed in this chapter were not subjects who declared apostasy or abandoned any essential tenet of Islam, nor did they fight against the existing order in a grand and sweeping and reckless manner. They were ordinary individuals with evident talent for linguistic expression who experienced love at a significant stage in their life and were denied that love because of the conflicting tribal or familial order they belonged to. Through poetry, they deconstructed themselves as individuals and discussed emotions, thoughts of attachment and rebellion, often conflicting with the normative realms that Islam sanctified. This experience shaped their very characters to the point that their preoccupation with love, an unfulfilled one, has become the modus operandi of their lives, part of their indivisible and abiding psychological identity. The psychological grip of love induced an equally powerful outpouring of poetic energy concerned with the spectrum of issues and sentiments the poets experienced whether at bodily, mental or metaphysical levels. Therefore, while their poetry mirrors a reality circumscribed and normalized by rules and habits, it also gives voice to silent possibilities obscured by cultural practices justified by Islamic sources. Hence, their poetry is conversational at a profound level; and their conversation draws on Islamic manners and styles of conversation and reasoning. The conversation takes place with their beloved, their society, themselves and the world. By creating a dialogue with such diverse references, they appear as intellectuals, prophetic voices, questioning and worldly characters. Their poetry reveals their religion, as well as their society and their relationship to both as a by-product of profound human dynamics where they become objects of experience and agents of revelation at the same time. All, religion, the society and the poets function within this world, its hidden and not so hidden realties, thus creating potentials for worldliness rooted in the understanding of universal psychological truths.

Notes

1. All the translations in the text are the author's, unless indicated otherwise.
2. Erich Auerbach, *Memesis: The Representation of Reality in Western Literature* (Princeton, NJ: Princeton University Press, 2003 [1953]), 40.
3. In addition to the note about *ghazal* poetry mentioned in the Introduction to this book, it is worthwhile to refer to Bauer and Neuwirth's reference to it, as a prominent tradition within Middle Eastern poetry: 'The Ghazal is a text that intertextually refers to the tradition of independent love poems, as formed during the 7th, 8th, 9th centuries. For the fully developed ghazal of the 9th and 10th centuries, which can be regarded as the starting point for the entire ghazal tradition of the following millennium, it holds that nearly all its themes and motifs can be subsumed under five different categories, namely: 1) praise of the beloved's beauty; 2) a complaint made by the lover, who cannot or (or not yet, or no longer) attain a union with the beloved; 3) a declaration of passionate, unsurpassable and unavoidable love; 4) a reproach directed against the beloved who does not satisfy

the expectations of the lover in response to his expressions of unselfish love; and finally 5) a *portrayal* love, i.e. the description of successful or unsuccessful encounters with the beloved or the depiction of the beloved's individual traits, such as his/her religion, race, eye colour, social position, or his downy beard', in Thomas Bauer and Angelica Newwirth, 'Introduction', in *Ghazal as World Literature, Transformation of a Literary Genre: Why the Ghazal?* (Leiden: Verlago, 1996), 18.
4   See Suzanne, P. Stetkevych, *The Mute Immortals Speak: Pre-Islamic Poetry and the Poetics of Ritual* (Ithaca, NY: Cornell University Press, 1993).
5   See the interesting article of James E. Montgomery on the value of poetry as part of historiographical materials, reading the poet Abū Nuwās in that light: 'Abū Nuwās: The Justified Sinner?', in *Oriens*, 39 (Leiden: Brill, 2011), 75–164.
6   Parallel to the phenomenon of the *'Udhrīs*, there were also the *Ibaḥī* poets, those who exhibited sexual experiences, adventures and interests in their poetry, such as the famous Omar Ibn Rabī'ah, Abū Nawwas and al-Mu'tamad bin 'Abbas . All these poetic strands reflect the diversity of the Islamic societies regarding romantic and sexual norms.
7   The story of Majnūn Layla travelled wide and far with variations of it appearing in several traditions throughout the ages, including the Persian, Indian, English and French traditions. In modern Arabic poetry, there are several references to the story as an archetypal love story. The eminent Egyptian poet Ahmad Shawqi (1868–1932) was one of the first modern Arab poets to revive the story through his play *The [One] Mad about Layla*. The Egyptian poet Salah Abdul Sabur (1931–81) followed suit and wrote his play *Layla and the Mad Man*.
8   Margaret Iversen, *Beyond Pleasure: Freud, Lacan and Barthes* (Pennsylvania: Pennsylvania State University Press, 2007).
9   Stetkevych, *The Mute Immortals Speak*.
10 Ibid., 252–3.
11 Ibid., 261.
12 See Diwān Majnūn Layla, Qays Ibn al-Mulawwah (ed. by Adnan Zaki Darwish), Beirut, 'ālam al-Kutub, 1996.
13 See the introduction to the story of Jamīl Bouthina by Mahdī Muhammad Nāsir al-dīn, *Diwān Jamīl Bouthina* (Beirut: Dār al-kutub al-'ilmiyya, 2009), 5–10.
14 Qur'an, Isrā', v.70.
15 Diwān Majnūn Layla, 9.
16 In this context, Freud is interesting, as he considers tension an abiding aspect that life can't be exempt from. As he put it, 'pleasure, then, is nothing more than the elimination of unpleasure, or the sensation of discharge. Yet the complete reduction of tension would lead to a state of comparable death', 2.
17 Stefan Sperl, 'O City Set Up They Lament: Poetic Responses to the Trauma of War', in *Poetry and Warfare in Middle Eastern Literatures*, ed. H. Kennedy (London: I.B. Tauris, 2013).
18 Diwān Majnūn Layla, 47.
19 Ibid., 83.
20 Muhammad Zubayr Siddiqi, *Hadīth Literature: Its Origin, Development and Special Features*, ed. and rev. Abdal Hakim Murad (Cambridge: The Islamic Texts Society, 1993).
21 Diwān Majnūn Layla, 72.
22 It is not the intention here to dwell on the authenticity of poetry but to interpret the socio-psychological aspects of it, while taking the position that the doubt that the great Egyptian thinker Taha Hussain cast over the existence of the character Majnūn in the first place is not convincing. The Majnūn, originally Qays Ibn al-Mulawwaḥ, and his story are mentioned in one of the early and most authoritative books on Arabic literature concerned with the collection and transmission of literature and literary figures, namely the book of al-Aghānī by Abū Faraj al-Aṣfahānī. More concretely, the poetic materials are focused and thematically and organically linked, reflecting a rooted human experience in one person, time and setting. See Jihād Fādil,

hal wujida Qays haqqan am kana istūrrah (al-Rayya), http://www.raya.com/home/print/f6451603-4dff-4ca1-9c10-122741d17432/9c1d20e6-8118-42a8-93f9-d52a720a 2885, last accessed 15 September 2014.
23 Ibn Hazm, *The Ring of the Dove*, trans. A. J. Arberry, Litt. D. (London: Luzac & Company, Ltd., 1953), 31.
24 See Tāhir Labīb, *Susyulūjiyyā al-Ghazal al-'Arabī: al-sh'ir al-'Udhrī 'Udhrī namūdhajan* (Damascus: Dār at-Talī ah, 1981), 57–8.
25 See H. T. Norris, *The Adventures of Antar* (Surrey: Aris & Phillips, 1980), 54.
26 Auerbach, *Memesis*, 280.
27 See Stefan Sperl, 'Man's "Hollow Core": Ethics and Aesthetics in Hadith Literature and Classical Arabic adab', *Bulletin of the School of Oriental and African Studies* 70, no. 3 (2007): 459–86.
28 Labīb, *Susyulūjiyyā al-Ghazal al-'Arabī*.
29 It is worthwhile to refer to another important book on the *'Udhrīs*, which became popular among Arab intellectuals in particular, namely the Syrian thinker Sadiq Jalal al-'Azm's, *Fī al-Ḥubb wa al-Ḥubb al-'Udrī (On Love and the 'Udhrī Love)*, 2002, Dar al-Sada lil-Thaqafa wa-l-nashr. In short, aL-'Azm incriminates the lovers and sees them as masochists and narcissists who dwell on their pain rather than the realization of love per se. In this respect, the author offers a counter reading to that common in the Arab world where the *'Udhrī* lovers are seen as pure and innocent lovers. In my reading of this poetry, I do not subscribe to either of these views. I look at their poetry in terms of its context, its functions and the enduring lessons it teaches in terms of the relationship of the individual to society and vice versa. It is possible to argue that these two readings took place within a context of defeat in the Arab world, particularly after the 1967 Israeli war against several Arab countries, namely Egypt, Syria, Jordan and Palestine. In this case, the past and its often archaic reproduction were categorically seen in negative light, held responsible in and of itself for present ills and frustrations, most prominently by Sadiq Jalal al-'Azm himself in his book, *Self Criticism after the Defeat* (Dar al-Saqi, 2011). Accordingly, I argue that this is an irrational response inflicted with self-flagellation. It does not read this aspect of the past in its own right and context, conflating past and present histories without consideration to the merits and/or defects of each as such. It is a context of defeat that resulted in readings and interpretations wallowing in defeat.
30 See Ahmad al-Tuwayli, *Kutub al-Ḥubb 'inda al-'Arab* (Beirut: Riad El-Rayyes Books, 2001).
31 Qur'an, 39/53.
32 Hazm, *The Ring of the Dove*, 27.
33 *Diwān Jamīl Buthaina* (Beirut: Dār al-kutub al-'ilmiyya, 2009), 19.
34 See Yasir Suleiman, 'Constructing Languages, Constructing National Identities', in *Sociolinguistics of Identity*, ed. T. Omoniyi and G. White (London: Continuum, 2006), 50–71.
35 The reference to the 'spiteful valley' denotes the place where the lovers met. The poet was shepherding his animals in the valley when Buthaina passed with her neighbour, aiming to fetch water. She hit some of Jamīl's animals, at which point the latter cursed her, and she responded in kind. Then, they grew to know and love each other until they were forced to separate in response to the tribal order that deprived them of their love.
36 *Diwān Jamīl Buthaina*, 13.
37 The deadlock between the tribes finds vivid echoes in Shakespeare's sixteenth-century play Romeo and Juliet. Juliet confesses to the Nurse: 'My only love sprung from my only hate! / Too early seen unknown, and known too late! / Prodigious birth of love it is to me, / That I must love a loathed enemy.' William Shakespeare, *Romeo and Juliet*, Shakespeare Library Classics, 49.
38 *Diwān Jamīl Buthaina*, 83.
39 Ibid., 76.

40 Diwān Majnūn Layla, 68.
41 According to the Danish philosopher and critic, Søren Kierkegaard, Christian love is bound by a duty to God, which in turn is a duty towards other human beings, called neighbours. The dutifulness of love ensures security against an external world riddled with passionate relations based on despair, which Kierkegaard ascribes to passionate and erotic relations. Christian, love which entails suffering, also means salvation and redemption from an ever-tempting world of passions and desires. See Linell E. Cady, 'Alternative Interpretations of Love in Kierkegaard and Royce', *The Journal of Religious Ethics* 10, no. 2 (Fall 1982): 238–63.
42 See Adonis's great book on this, *An Introduction to Arabic Poetics* (London: Saqi Books, 2003). The book highlights how various orthodoxies within the Islamic world undermined thinking and creativity, thus freezing the inquisitive spirit that lies at the heart of the early Arab and Islamic tradition.
43 Edward Said, Introduction to Halim Barakat's novel, *Days of Dust* (Three Continents Press, 1998), 31.
44 See al-Tuwayli, *Kutub al-Hubb 'inda al-'Arab*, 103.
45 See http://fatwa.islamweb.net/fatwa/index.php?page=showfatwa&Option=FatwaId&Id=165593, last accessed 20 September 2015.
46 Perhaps one of the starkest sayings that shed light on the centrality of the human psyche and its unconscious dynamics is the saying of Imam Ali, the cousin of Prophet Mohammad, 'People are asleep. When they die, they wake up.' The saying extends to the loss of love; as when this happens, the lover is awakened to what was asleep inside him. The death of love inspires a grand sense of awakening as to the hidden forces within man.
47 In Labīb wa-Ṭāhir, *Sūsyūlogiā al-Ghazzal al-'Arabī (al-shi'ir al-'Araī namūdhajan)* (al-Dār al-Baydā: 'Uyūn, 1987), 103–4.
48 It is worth referring to Mohammed Arkoun's book, *Islam: To Reform or to Subvert?* The book reflects on the importance of plural contexts and human experiences in the organization of society. As he writes, 'the objective reality is always represented, experienced and expressed through the complex interactive contributions of reason, imagination, imaginary and individual and collective memories' (222). Also, Arkoun highlights how the extreme Islamist movements of today neglect context and experience in their discourses, thus reducing the vast edifice of Islamic interpretations and reasoning. See Mohammad Arkoun, *Islam: To Reform or To Subvert* (London: Saqi Essentials, 2002).
49 The Arab thinker Ibn Sīnā highlights the endowment of love in the divine and how this endowment is translated and transmitted in the creations of that divine: 'The most substantial point in the theory of Ibn Sināa regarding 'Ishq is that all creatures from their simplest to their most complex, from their highest to their lowest, and with whatever life, they all adhere to the motions of love. On the one hand, love is one of the most intimate traits of the divine; and on the other, it is one of the strongest instincts God bestowed upon creatures, and made them willing to accept His manifestation.' In al-Tuwayli, *Kutub al-Hubb 'inda al-'Arab*, 127.
50 Hazm, *The Ring of the Dove*; al-Tuwayli, *Kutub al-Hubb 'inda al-'Arab*, 117.
51 Ibn Hazm's definition of love is replicated in Shakespeare's play *Romeo and Juliet*. When Juliet is advised by her mother to love Paris instead of Romeo, Juliet diplomatically replies, 'I'll look to like, if looking liking move.' Shakespeare, *Romeo and Juliet*, 13.
52 In his explanation of the traces of love, Freud relates the suckling of babies to their mothers' breasts to hunger and sexual urges that signal psychosexual tendencies later reflected in adulthood. See Sigmund Freud, *The Psychology of Love* (London: Penguin Classics, 2006 [1905]). Several reflections in the Islamic traditions on love and poetic works can be interpreted as congruent with Freud's observations.
53 Diwān Majnūn Layla, 258.
54 Ibid., 76.

55 E. Khairallah As'ad, *Love, Madness and Poetry: An Interpretation of the Majnūn Legend* (Beirut and Wiesbaden: Orient-Institut der Deutschen Morgenländischen Gesellschaft, 1980), 76.
56 al-Tuwaylī, *Kutub al-Hubb 'inda al-'Arab*, 107–25.
57 Hazm, *The Ring of the Dove*, 28.
58 Diwān Majnūn Layla, 81.
59 Diwān Jamīl Buthaina, 30.
60 Hazm, *The Ring of the Dove*, 25–6.
61 Khairallah As'ad, *Love, Madness and Poetry*, 73.
62 Ibid., 20.
63 Diwān Jamīl Buthaina, 53.
64 Classical sources, as that of Ibn al-Qayam al-Jawziyya, highlighted two main perspectives on love among the Muslim scholars and thinkers of his day. One view suggested that love happens by choice *ikhtiārī*; and another one saw love as *iṭrarī*, obligatory, that it is outside one's control. In his book, *Imtizāj al-arwāḥ* (The Melange of Souls), the medieval scholar al-Tamīmī relays what one doctor said when he was asked about love: he said that 'falling in love is like any other ailment, and there is no difference between it and other ills' (in Qasid, *Textbook of Qasid Centre for the Teaching of Arabic, Part II* (Aman: Qasid Centre, 2015), 162). The Arabs then used to say that 'love is one type of torture, and no sane person chooses to torture himself.' The two sides, as outlined earlier, rely on several Quranic verses and sayings by the Prophet.
65 Perhaps one of the best references testifying to the statement in question is provided by Roland Barthes in his book *A Lover's Discourse*. Relying on perceptive sources, mainly European, the book paints a powerful panorama of expressions and scenes of unfulfilled love, exhibiting the manifestations of such love from various philosophical, literary and existential standpoints through iconic literary figures such as Werter and Charlotte in Geothe's *The Sorrows of Young Werther*. See Roland Barthes, *A Lover's Discourse: Fragments* (London: Vintage Classics, 2002).
66 Diwān Majnūn Layla, 189.
67 Ibid., 139.
68 Ibid., 95.
69 Qur'an, 59/21.
70 Diwān Jamīl Buthaina, 95.
71 The word 'minorities' is not meant to be ahistorical. Minorities in the modern period acquired particular meanings often associated with the nation state and how minorities are treated within it. In the case of Islamic societies, there have always been dissenters who challenged the status quo by a variety of means. In their challenge to the norms in the case at hand, the 'Udhrī poets represent an example of dissenters whose articulation of their predicament through poetry can be regarded as another lesson as to how minor voices speak to mainstream societies. In this sense, 'minorities', as a word, is to be understood in terms of the values, essentially those associated with freedom of choice in love, that the *'Udhrīs* (who happened to be a small group of people, a minority within the mainstream community where they lived) impart to modern societies.
72 Ibid., 140.
73 The use of the term 'existentialism' in the context at hand is to demonstrate how the experiences of the poets shaped their world perceptions and made them see Islam with existentialist lenses, to use a modern term. They choose to link Islam intimately to human experiences to which the believers respond within parameters of rationalism and practicality. In the case of Islam, or any other religion for that matter, this requires interpretations that adapt sacred texts and customs to changing human conditions, which, in return, are always open to discovery. The essence of existentialist life is freedom, which is what the poets seem to crave for in the case at hand.
74 See Diwān Jamīl Buthaina, 27, for a reference where Jamīl Buthaina is advised to go on Jihad, which is an Islamic obligation on those who are able to do it. Jamīl responds that

he does not require any other Jihad than that which would get him his beloved. Jamīl is drawing upon another prophetic tradition which values the personal quest for sincerity and love, considering this a greater form of Jihad.

75   Diwān Majnūn Layla, 209.
76   Qur'an, 109/6.
77   Qur'an, 26/224–226.

Chapter 6

A COMPARISON BETWEEN THE IDEAS OF LOVE FOUND IN AL-GHĀZĀLĪ'S *THE ALCHEMY OF HAPPINESS* AND THE FIRST VOLUME OF RUMI'S *MASAVI-YI MA'NAVI*

Huma Baig

Introduction

What is love? This question resembles Pilate's question, 'What is truth?'[1] One definition of love is, 'the heart's perfect focusing on the goal of union, implying that the lover has no awareness of anything else', according to the Historical Dictionaries of Religion.[2]

This research is focused on the love for God in the Islamic tradition, also referred to as Divine Love. In Islam, one attribute of God is the Most-Loving (*al-wudud*). It is a general belief among Muslims that He unconditionally loves humans first.[3] Reciprocating His love is proof of having belief in Him.[4] A personification of a God-loving human can be found in Prophet Muhammad and his *sunna*,[5] as many verses of the Quran suggest. However, these two elements are just a starting point: with the assistance of theology, philosophy and Sufism extensive theories on love were formulated.[6] Each theory of Divine Love is seen as a form of mysticism as it delineates a path to attain closeness to God.[7] For the purpose of this dissertation, the path to Divine Love through the eyes of al-Ghāzālī and Jalaluddin Rumi will be unfolded, as depicted in their corresponding texts: *The Alchemy of Happiness* (*Kaamiya'e Saadat*) and the first volume of *Masavi-yi Ma'navi*.[8]

Not only does this research compare the views of two giants within Islamic mysticism, but it compares what seems opposing forms of expression; it compares those ideas of Divine Love that pacified social chaos resulting in communal harmony. Both texts were written after a spiritual transformation of the author took place. As *The Alchemy* is not a highly studied text, other works of al-Ghāzālī will be used to understand the meanings better. But it is the best text to use for this research as it is referred to as the summary of *The Revival of Religious Sciences*, a very well-known and respected piece of work of the same author.

To commence, the project will analyse the texts as a whole to comprehend how the authors present their approach to love. Due to al-Ghāzālī's limited work on the topic, *The Book of Love (Kitaab al-Mahabba)* will be utilized to draw basic principles on Divine Love. *The Alchemy* will be analysed with the intention of tracing evidence of such principles, and other works by al-Ghāzālī will be explored to deepen understanding. To add direction to the research, these principles will then be used as a basis for comparison to the second text. Thereafter alternating between the views of Al-Ghāzālī and Rumi, the main attributes of love will be presented. To assist the understanding of the principles, the background of the writers and the texts will be summarized before delving into the main investigation. Additionally, for the same purpose, external influences and similar theories will be unfolded where necessary, but this will not be the main focus of the research. The writer will hypothesize that though on the surface the two approaches seem contrasting; there are more similarities between them than differences. As the texts under analysis are written in the Persian language, it is important to know the natural translation shortcomings that can be categorized as methodological limitations. This is because a word in Persian could have a variety of different meanings in English; and a word in English could have a variety of different meanings in Persian. When studying languages, direct and literal translations in many cases do not make sense in given sentences, and in other cases, they do not relay the same message. Such complexities cannot be overlooked.

For the purpose of this study, to limit the methodological issue, it seems that the most accessible translation of *The Alchemy* is Claud Field's one, published in 1909, and this will be used. Rumi's poems are often unconventional, ecstatic and abstract compared to the traditional Islamic dogma. Therefore, it is of utmost importance to utilize the translation of the *Mathnawi* that is most historically accepted, in order to understand the author's message. It appears that the translation by R. A. Nicholson fulfils this criterion. Another limitation is our distance from the historical contexts the texts were conceived. To accommodate this, the social context and its influence will be touched upon. Lastly, the limited research on the primary text of *The Alchemy* poses a further obstacle. This is not the case for Rumi's work, whose only difficulty is to analyse the extensive content of the *Mathnawi*. Thus, specific poems will be referred to in the main portion of this research.

Who was Ghāzālī?

Abu Hamid Muhammad ibn Muhammad Al-Ghāzālī (AH 449–504/AD 1058–1111) is described as a '*major* religious scholar and theorist, mystical and pastoral theologian as well as an author' in the Historical Dictionaries of Religion.[9] Born in the city of Tus, Persia, this dedicated student was raised by his father's Sufi friend.[10] He studied Shaf'i law, Ashari theology, medicine, philosophy *hadith*, logic, Arabic grammar and all the sciences at a local madrassa. In 1073 he travelled 350 miles for an in-depth study of Islamic law. Upon returning from his journey, a bandit mocked him and said his knowledge would be lost if he stole his notes. Ghāzālī decided to memorize all his notes. At the age of twenty he became a protégé of one of the most renowned scholars of the time, Imam al-Haramayn al-Juwayni (d.1085), at the Nizamiyyah Madrassa. Upon the death of his teacher Ghāzālī was presented with an opportunity to lead a group of travelling scholars from city to city. Inevitably, his qualities and uncanny passion for oratory and debate shined, and the famous Seljuk writer Nizam al-Mulk insisted he became the principal of the Nizamiyyah Madrassa.[11] He accepted the offer at the age of thirty-four and spearheaded Nizam's campaign to establish doctrinal orthodoxy, writing polemics against groups that held opposing views. Soon after, Ghāzālī became known as one of the most eminent scholars of the Muslim world and enjoyed a life of ease.[12]

Despite his political, financial and intellectual success, Ghāzālī felt hypocrisy in his life as the sincere desire to know and come to certainty was not fulfilled. This led to his search for the knowledge of certainty (*'ilm al-yaqin*) that lasted for four years and engaged with four intellectual groups who claimed to possess the whole absolute truth – the theologians (*mutakallimun*), the philosophers, the Imsa'ilis (*Batiniyyas*) and the mystics (*Sufis*).[13] Gazzali found a compromise between knowledge and practice within Sufism: he studied from the *Qut al-Qulub* of Abu Talib al-Makki (d.998), the works of al-Harith al-Muhasibi and fragments deriving from al-Junayd, al-Shibli, Abu Yazid al-Bastami and others.[14] Hence he highlighted the importance of direct experience or 'taste' to comprehend mystical knowledge.[15]

In 1095 his internal dissatisfaction escalated and became so burdensome that he was unable to speak. His experiential journey came to happen, and he abandoned his fame, teaching and wealth to embrace the life of a wandering Sufi ascetic. He travelled 500 miles away to Damascus by foot and took refuge in the Umayyad mosque.[16] In the two years he remained there, Ghāzālī concealed his identity, practised the methods of purification from vice he learnt from the Sufis in order to empty his heart of everything except God. During this time, he wrote his most famous pieces of work, *The Revival of the Religious Sciences* (*Iḥyā 'Ulūm ad-Dīn*), and by then Ghāzālī had found absolute certainty. The aim of this book was to help revive Islam through Sufism for all Muslims, the way it had done for Ghāzālī. Nevertheless, after he heard a professor in a Damascus college begin a lecture with the words, 'Ghāzālī said . . .', his pride swelled up again. Not wanting to strengthen his ego, Ghāzālī decided to leave the city to Jerusalem, Mecca and Medina in order to preserve his inner contentment. Ghāzālī returned to his homeland as a transformed man to address the concerns of his children. He wrote *The Alchemy* in 1105, just before resuming public teaching. He died at the age of fifty-three in his hometown of Tus.

An introduction to The Alchemy of Happiness

By analysing the writings of Ghāzālī it can be suggested that his primary concern after his spiritual crisis was attaining everlasting happiness. When the *Kaamiya'e Saadat* was written, Ghāzālī was settled in his approach to Islam: he had already compiled the *Revival of the Religious Sciences*, and *The Alchemy*, written in Persian, is considered a condensed version of the first book.[17] The first four chapters elaborate on the *hadith*, 'He who knows himself knows God', where Ghāzālī outlines imperative questions man must reflect upon. Ghāzālī then discusses aspects of music, the necessity for self-examination and matters regarding the observance of marriage. It is in the final chapter that Ghāzālī talks about the love and vision of God. He derives a basic blueprint to instruct man on how to fulfil the purpose of human existence by reaching its highest potential, to attain spiritual perfection, be in the presence of God and reciprocate His love.

The book was written under the rule of the Seljuk Empire when a rift between the traditional Islamic scholars and the mystics was taking place: the traditionalists claimed that the Sufis went against the fundamentals of Islam and lacked the fear of God. They used the case of Mansur al-Hallaj, who was executed after his ecstatic utterances of claiming to be God, as a prime example of heresy.[18] The mystics defended themselves by declaring that they were so in love with God that they did not need to fear him; and accused the traditionalists of being too harsh.

Ghāzālī's work forms a bridge between the two approaches by developing a rationalized form of mysticism. This resulted in cohesion between the two, a general more widespread acceptance of Sufism and orthodoxy.[19] In addition to the social chaos, the religious chaos caused by the spread of irreligious doctrines created a need for authoritative philosophy which was fulfilled by Ghāzālī.[20]

Who was Rumi?

Jalaluddin Mohammed Balkhi (603–671 AH/1207–1273 AD) was born in Balkh. His father was a scholar of theology and philosophy.[21] The family migrated to Samarqand, to Khorasan and settled in Konya, then known as Rum, in 1229, which became the basis for Rumi's name.[22] Thus, much of Rumi's childhood was spent travelling and the avenue for his education was through his father and the scholars his father encountered.[23] The rationale behind settling in Konya was to educate the populace according to Islamic doctrines.[24] Rumi's father passed away after teaching in Konya for two years and assigned Rumi as his heir.[25] Borhan al-Din (d. 1241) was his father's old friend and most devoted disciple, who was given the duty of Rumi's spiritual training. Borhan sent Rumi to Damascus to study Islamic history, the Quran, the *hadith* tradition, the Islamic canon and Arabic in 1233 in order to be scholarly qualified as his father's heir. As a student he excelled and was well known for his proposed solutions to historically unsolved issues. At the pinnacle of his training, after four to five years, he was recommended to fast for a week in seclusion. However, Rumi volunteered to fast in seclusion for forty days, and at the completion of this, Rumi was in deep meditation so Borhan returned after another forty days, only to find Rumi engrossed in prayer; he returned a third time another forty days later. This time he found Rumi smiling and Borhan pronounced the completion of Rumi's esoteric education. Rumi then returned to Konya and resumed public professorship. It has been suggested that Rumi as a jurisprudent had a following of 10,000 disciples before the arrival of Shams; and by the 1240s Rumi was teaching at 4 different respectable institutions.[26]

Shamsaddin, 'the Sun of Religion', from Tabriz was a charismatic and spiritually gifted wanderer.[27] He learnt from famous teachers as he travelled, hence became well versed in theology and philosophy. It has been narrated that he taught theology and the meaning of the Quran but abandoned this for the love of God.[28] Shams held the opinion that it was the charisma of the spiritual teacher that transformed the disciple's soul rather than the literature.[29] When he arrived at Konya, he was over the age of sixty, and it has been stated that Rumi and Shams exchanged long stares before Shams asked Rumi's opinion on the contradictory report of Bayazzid.[30] In 1244 Shams initiated a spiritual metamorphosis with Rumi, where mystical knowledge was transmitted from the heart of Shams to that of Rumi's, and Rumi felt the presence of God.[31] Shams encouraged Rumi to embody mysticism and practice the whirling dance (*Sama*).[32] After Rumi's encounter with Shams al-Din Tabrizi, he lost interest in books of formal material knowledge and became fully engrossed in his company. According to Shams,

Rumi had accomplished the second stage of spiritual development, which was the drunkenness of the soul, and this later became evident through his poetry.[33] He now became an intoxicated celebrant of Divine Love.[34] However, Shams departed from Konya after some time, and with this separation Rumi became a poet and compiled the *Divan-e Shams*, in which the poetry venerated his teacher.[35] Rumi's eldest son, Baha al-Din Muhammad-i Walad, requested him to return and heal Rumi's agony, and they were reunited. It has been narrated that Shams was murdered two years later in 1248, but by whom is not known. Rumi's restlessness and yearning increased when he was unable to *locate his teacher for two years*, but then he encountered Salahel-din Faridun Zerkab, to whom he referred as the reflection of Shams.[36] Zerkab acted as Rumi's assistant for ten years.[37] However, gradually Rumi understood that the presence of God was in his own heart as opposed to the heart of his teacher. Rumi became known as a master on the writings of divine love, and his followers formed the Mevlevi order.[38]

Background of the Mathnawi

The date the *Mathnawi* began to be compiled has been debated, with dates varying from 1263 to 1258.[39] Nevertheless, there are roughly 26,000 lines forming rhythmic rhyming melodies that stopped in 1273 after Rumi fell ill.[40] These form six Persian volumes, and a major theme is the love of God reflected through symbolism, metaphorical expressions and personifications. The language utilized is largely colloquial and didactic and aims to clear the individual's path to God by stirring emotions.[41] Excluding the first 18 verses of the first volume, composed of 4,563 verses, the couplets had to be recorded by his new assistant, Haussam-uddin Chelebi (d.1284), due to his own state of trance.[42] It has been suggested that Chelebi encouraged the compilation of the *Mathnawi* and was the reason it materialized; hence, the title 'the book of Haussam' (*Husamnama*) was also given.[43] The fifteenth-century mystical writer Jāmī labelled the *Mathnawi* 'the Quran in the Persian tongue'.

The era of Rumi's life was outlined as the darkest for the Muslim world. The Mongol invasion of Iran caused the destruction of Islamic art and the decline of literature and sciences. It is narrated that recipients disconnected from the social chaos and embraced the heart-warming works of Rumi. He spread love, contentment and satisfaction. As a result, harmony spread and united sects, religions and races.[44]

Ghāzālī's general approach to love

By analysing the text as a whole, it can be noted that the majority of the content focuses on the actual *path* to happiness. Ghāzālī uses worldly metaphors, visual imagery and practical examples to connect with the logical reasoning of the mind. Thereafter, this connection is utilized to portray the complexities of the subtle world. The term 'alchemy' relates to an investment of time, focus and a deep understanding to transform one's ordinary rusty life into an elevated 'golden' life. Therefore, it seems that the title itself encapsulates the content of the text. The aim is the love of God, otherwise referred to as happiness, which can be achieved following the process outlined in the book all the way to the final chapter. Ghāzālī describes love as an 'inclination to that which is pleasant'.⁴⁵ However, this vague definition creates the need to delve into the symptoms of love through the process of *tahqiq* (verification) to understand the different dynamics of the concept. Nevertheless, the topic of love is actually minimal in *The Alchemy* as in the *Iḥyā 'Ulūm ad-Dīn* it remains a mystery. This reflects Ghāzālī's opinion that the highest degree of love is a type of mystical knowledge that cannot be talked about, only directly experienced.⁴⁶ Therefore, it seems reasonable to suggest that Ghāzālī discusses the love of God as understood by the mind rather than experienced by the senses.

It is a reasonable conclusion to state that Ghāzālī's approach to love is systematic, rationalized and logically coherent. To achieve this, the method of syllogism has been utilized, and traces of this manner of argumentation can be found in al-Farabi's work as well as the Quran through the design argument.⁴⁷ Furthermore, this approach resembles one of the three Neoplatonic approaches to love as it is of a rational nature and is directed towards immortal objects.⁴⁸ Such consistencies can be understood as evidence for external influences on Ghāzālī s approach.

Rumi's general approach to love

For the Sufis, intimate experiences with God are described through poetry.⁴⁹ The *Mathnawi* is a compilation of Rumi's intimate experiences with God, and it aims to illustrate the mysteries of the spiritual realm utilizing the physical mortal world. This is reflected in the structure and the use of *segue*.⁵⁰ The irregular arrangement of tales, the lack of intercorrelation, the abrupt endings and lack of *telos* portray this text to be illogical, wayward and inconsistent.⁵¹ Therefore, researchers like Rene Wellek and Austin Warren preferred a restructured extrinsic format in order to understand the message.⁵² However, this has been seen as Rumi's unique weapon to adequately execute the didactic purpose with a homiletic method.⁵³ Similarly, Seyed Safavi suggests that the first volume of the *Mathnawi* as a whole text is tightly organized by utilizing the techniques of parallelism and chiasmus.⁵⁴ However, such literary features are not universally known and accepted.⁵⁵ Nonetheless, these factors reinstate Rumi's approach to love being of an ecstatic nature.

James Roy King outlines that the worldly story gives an outerworldly example that the reader can connect to; thereafter, Rumi's reflections enable the reader to use the example to travel to the inner spiritual realm and submit to its influence by utilizing ones' imagination. Such autonomous images are not graspable by the intellect but, rather, by the sixth inner sense of imaginative consciousness.⁵⁶ However, it can be argued that metaphors would create different images for individuals depending on their context, but outlining how successful Rumi is creating a spiritual uprising is beyond the scope of this research – in effect, reflecting his personal interpretation of the Quran by painting an exterior and interior meaning. In this sense, Rumi's *Mathnawi* is similar to Ghāzālī's text under speculation as both act as a guidebook to God. For Rumi, the initial literal meaning reflects the outer path (*shariyat*), the middle reflects the Sufi path (*tariqat*) and the deepest meaning reflects hidden realities of God (*Haqiqat*).⁵⁷ Rumi uses symbolism, allegory and anecdotes to escape from external chaotic necessitation, instils trust in God and invites the inner soul to experience God's organized overwhelming presence.⁵⁸ Therefore, he discusses love as experienced by the senses, though not always understood by limits of the mind, using the heart as an astrolabe for love.[59]

Love is preceded by knowledge

Ghāzālī's ideas concerning Divine Love occur in the *Book of Love* (*Kitab al-Mahabba*) in the compilation of the *Ihya*. He suggests that all spiritual stations such as repentance, asceticism and contentment are preliminary to the ultimate goal of love for God (*al-ghaya al-quswa min al- maqamat*).[60] He outlines three prerequisites for instilling the love of God: first that it is preceded by knowledge, second that it grants spiritual pleasure (*qurrat al-ayn*) and lastly that he loves Him beyond the hope of seeking benefit from it and this is the 'hidden affinity' in man (*munasaba khafiyya*).[61] For the purpose of this research, the first and third requirements will be utilized as the second point is intertwined in the two.

The centrality of knowledge is above all other ideas and concepts for Ghāzālī. This is also a consistent theme found within *The Alchemy*. It seems as though the rationale behind acquiring knowledge is so the transformation of the spiritual heart can take place and the love of God can be embodied. The cleaner the heart of man, the more sensitive and responsive he is to God's essence. Once the heart is transformed to a clean, golden and pure one, man is prepared to be subjected to the vision of God.[62] Supporting evidence is drawn from Abrahamov who puts forward the idea that intellectual knowledge of God's qualities and acts are most efficient in the path to God.[63] Ghāzālī states in his treatise 'The Balance of Action' ('Mizan al-'amal') that it is through the theoretical intellect that man can understand abstract concepts such as knowing God.[64] For Ghāzālī outlines over seventy types of happiness that man can feel, but only one of them is true happiness.[65] Such knowledge is the greatest happiness gifted to man, and the love of God is instilled within him.[66]

The importance of knowledge is reflected through the dedication of the first four chapters in the text to this notion. These are described as types of necessary knowledge and outlined as knowledge of the self, of God, of this world in its reality and of the afterlife in its reality. It can be recognized from this that one must understand their self, to understand God and to eventually love Him. The concept is derived from a *hadith* that states: 'He who knows himself knows God.' It seems as though each chapter removes a mystical barrier between man and God. God is described as the highest object of knowledge but the first step on this ladder to God is attaining knowledge of the self. Therefore, for Ghāzālī the person who knows can love; and the person who does not know cannot love.

Knowledge of the self is divided into two categories: knowledge of the body and knowledge of the soul. Ghazali outlines that the knowledge of the body grants a 'more intimate knowledge of God as he is a microcosm of the macrocosm (God)'.[67] The way the analysis of a great poem can lead to a better understanding of the author, the perfection of the body can be analysed to know more about the Creator. This design argument has been used in the Quran in order to illustrate the magnificence of God compared to the imperfections of man. Additionally, this links back to the initial concept that God loves humans first and is described as the third cause of 'arousing love for God'.[68] Ghāzālī adds that knowledge is independent of the body, and in a hierarchal sense, he places knowledge and love at the same level,[69] which escalates, highlights and purifies the status of knowledge. Furthermore, the body is perfectly synchronized and perfection is highlighted as the first cause of love.[70] In the same manner, God is the idea of complete perfection.[71] This contemplation utilizes the faculty of reason, which is why man is put on a pedestal compared to other animals. Also, this helps man to comprehend the masses of love God has bestowed upon him by creating him with such perfection.[72]

Similarly, an inscription above the temple of Apollo in Delphi, Greece, declares, 'Know Thyself', and Hellenism seeks God for the sake of man's happiness. This may be considered egocentric, but it is interesting that the text in consideration also denotes the path to happiness.[73] Ibn Sina was also known to have been influenced by the *hadith* mentioned.[74] It seems reasonable to conclude that similar ideas were generally prevalent in that era and expressed through different channels. The compilation of these avenues seems to have moulded Ghāzālī's view. Nevertheless, Ghāzālī argues that it is rather the knowledge of the soul, sometimes referred to as the he*art* in its spiritual entity rather than the physical organ, which is a more useful key to the knowledge of God.[75] This is the key to happiness and a more effective way to love God.[76] Quasem defines this as the negative aspect of happiness, as it is not happiness itself, but it is the logical discussion that comes before it.[77] He specifies that it is not only the philosophical knowledge of the soul that leads to an understanding of God but, rather, the practice of disciplining the soul, the strengthening of the angelic attributes, weakening the transitory devilish elements and controlling the similar animalistic traits.[78] He explains in the text that a mental strain is caused by vices of the soul, leading to the death of the mind.[79] Ghāzālī draws its basis on the Quranic verse: 'Those who strive in Our way, verily We will guide them to the right paths.'[80] He explains that the decision of how to use this soul is in man's control, it is his free will, but man uses the Quran to label this as a 'burden'. Furthermore, in *The Book of Knowledge*, he categorizes the knowledge of the states of the soul as obligatory knowledge (*fard 'ayn*) for all Muslims.[81] Ghāzālī urges man to discipline his morals in order to clean the heart from rust, diminish barriers to God, to then find underneath a mirror that reflects the light of God. Once man is absorbed in the essence of God, he is a lover of God.

The concept of man being a microcosm of the macrocosm is also applicable to the soul. Ghāzālī explains this *in the chapter of the knowledge of God*: the soul in man and the essence of God are both; 'invisible, indivisible, unconfined by space and time, and outside the categories of quantity and quality; nor can the ideas of shape, colour, or size attach to them'.[82] In this sense every man holds the potential of divinity due to its celestial origin; this is based on the Quranic verse, 'I breathed into man of My spirit.'[83] Ghāzālī uses the example that 'only a king can understand a king', and God has made all of mankind kings in miniature to explain that the role of the soul in the body is analogous to that God has in the world.[84] For a king (the soul) to be ruled by something inferior (the body) would be nonsensical. Though this approach can be problematic to the concept of *tawhid* (the oneness of God), exploring this is beyond the scope of this research.

Furthermore, the author uses examples of the body, nature and world through the text that are of such a universal nature so that everyone can relate to these. This reflects Ghāzālī's idea of *fitra* (disposition), a concept describing the soul's natural knowledge and affinity with God.[85] Similarly, Ghāzālī states in 'The Balance of Action' ('Mizan al-'amal') that one of the two types of acquiring such knowledge is by remembering what was already planted in the heart of man before existence.[86] It has been suggested that such an idea has been influenced by the Platonic theory of innate knowledge, which outlines what the soul experiences prior to its earthly existence.[87] However, distinction is made on the ground of knowledge. Ghāzālī outlines that 'God is one, but He will be seen in many different ways', with reference to how much knowledge of God one has.[88] A further distinction is made between the individual entities of the soul; so it is possible for two people of the same knowledge to be at different levels of mysticism.[89] This is the affinity of man towards God and is described as the fourth cause of love in *The Alchemy*.[90]

In terms of Ghāzālī's concept of *fitra*,[91] it is possible that this is a result of several influences. First of all, the Platonic theory of innate knowledge is a likely avenue due to its similarity. Furthermore, Ibn Sina held the view that each soul has innate love.[92] This could also be a source of influence. Ghāzālī outlines in his autobiography, *The Deliverance from Error (Al-Munqidh min al-Dalaala)*, that he did not view Plato or Aristotle's philosophy to be fruitful as it contained many defects and went against the Divine Law of Islam.

However, he takes into consideration those aspects of philosophy that do not go against the laws of Islam, in order to learn about one's self.[93] Furthermore, Abrahamov suggests that for Ghāzālī, a philosophical reasoning was most effective in attaining belief in God.[94] These similar traces could very well be the *fruits* of philosophy. Abu al-Qasim Muhammad al-Junayd was another Sufi who influenced Ghāzālī. He was of the view that man's soul is on a return journey to its primordial state, which is in the presence of God. The accomplishment of which is *fana*.[95] A common thread between all these theories is that the soul and the essence of God are interconnected, a point presented in *The Alchemy*.

Love is preceded by longing

Contrary to Ghāzālī's claim that the highest degree of love is experienced and not talked about, Rumi attempts to talk about this type of love through the *Mathnawi*, which reflects the general theme of 'to die before you die' based on the Quranic principle *of muutuu Qalban Muutuu*.[96] W. Chittick refers to this as the death, or annihilation of the self (*fana*), and the unification to the object of their love.[97] For Rumi, this object is in the highest realm of truth (*haqq*), though it can be manifested in the realm of the mind (*jabaruut*) and the tertiary realm of gross and subtle matter (*Amal-I Misal*). Rumi's aim through the *Mathnawi* is to reunite the spirit to the realm of Truth,[98] and this achievement is the sign of a true believer (*mu'min*).[99] While intellect only sees the worldly matter, love is the vision of the limitless realm.[100] The effect of such a wholesome love is the loss of reasoning, the recitation of poetry and the undertaking of the mystical whirling dance (*raqs*).[101] For such a love to materialize, one must feel the pangs of longing after being separated from the presence of the Beloved (God) in the primordial life in the realm of Truth.[102] To explain the sweetness of this pain, Rumi uses the example of a reed flute in the first poem of the *Mathnawi*, 'The Song of the Reed', whose first lines are reported below:[103]

> *Listen to the reed how it tells a tale, complaining of separations –*
> *Saying, 'Ever since I was parted from the reed – bed, my*
> *Lament hath caused man and woman to moan.*
> *I want a bosom torn by severance, that I may unfold (to such*
> *a one) the pain of love – desire.*

Safavi puts forward the idea that the first letter of the poem is the 'B' and the last is the 'M' which are also the first and last of *Bismillah* (in the name of Allah). The way the Bismillah is the essence of a Muslims' life; this poem is the essence of the six volumes of the Mathnawi.[104]

The reed flute played is representative of the longing felt after being separated from the primordial presence of God in His realm, *they cut my stalk away from the reed bed*, and aims to stir similar emotions in the listener's heart.[105] The reed plant forms the poets' pen and the musicians' flute.[106] Both are highly esteemed, and in Rumi's poetry the plant itself represents the people that are united with God. To acknowledge this separation is seen as the biggest veil between man and God.[107] In God's presence there was no acknowledgement of the individual self, and all spirits testified in the oneness of their Creator. The departure from within this realm leads to the pangs of homesickness.[108] Furthermore, it is only in this state of separation that man can feel the longing for God. This suggests that love is pre-eternal.[109] The way the reed cannot long for anything but its bed, the soul of man cannot long for anything but its Creator.[110] Rifai distinguishes in his commentary on the *Mathnawi* the two ways of returning to the origin Rumi discusses, death in its physical sense and death of the ego (*fana*).[111] Like Ghāzālī, Rumi claims that such a death leads to the vision of God and at this stage the mind (*aql*) and its mental restrictions are stupefied.[112] Therefore, this suggests that for Rumi there is no intellectual description of love, and neither is there an exit when love overtakes the heart.[113]

In the poem the reed is associated with burning in a fire. Schroeder highlights that fire is the substance that refines elements to bring out their purest form.[114] It seems as though the epitome of longing can bring man to embody the 'fire of love' for God, and in the process it diminishes all vices.[115] However, fire can also feel hot and scorching. It has been interpreted by Kenan Rifai that the one who is irresponsive and desensitized to the scorching and the harmful burning is the one who has annihilated the self, become free of material attachment and engulfed in love.[116] This is consistent with the example of the reed as it needs to be warmed and dried in the sun to become a flute and play the song of longing.[117] Furthermore, it appears that this bears similarities with Ghāzālī's process of purification; the latter purifies with the avenue of knowledge and Rumi purifies by the fire of annihilation.

On the other hand, it seems that Rumi's precondition of longing is indifferent to Ghāzālī's precondition of knowledge. The first is a mere extension of the second; and this idea was expressed in al-Hujwayri's *Kashf al-Mahjub*.[118] Mannani confirms that Rumi is of the view that in order to be successful in annihilating the self, one must purify the heart by defeating the ego and training the desires. This is consistent with the example of the reed as it also must be cleaned to produce harmonious melodies.[119] The doctrine of multiple consciousness denotes that as mental fields increase, the individual is subjected to a higher field of mental vision. Knowledge is related to normal perception and *fana* is related to the increase in mental vision,[120] and a higher mode of perceiving and responding. Thus this supports the claim that the mystical intoxication of *fana* is the peak, the embodiment and the completion of knowledge.

Contrastingly, it has been suggested that there is no room for rationality, intellect and logic when it comes down to matters of intoxicating love. This is because the intellect cannot embrace the flow of images that the imaginative mind can. Additionally, over-intellectualizing reflects an over-dependence on words; and as stated previously there is no intellectual description of love.[121] Evidence of the demolishment of the rational faculty in the song of the reed can be depicted through the symbolism of wine – *'tis the fervour of Love that is in the wine*.[122] This is used as a metaphor for the overpowering presence of God that erases boundaries built by the carnal senses and is said to be superior to the path of sobriety.[123] Rumi's embodiment of loving mysticism (*tasawuf-i ashiqanah*) requires the divorce of the intellect from the heart.[124] He argues that only love can comment about the state of being in love.[125] Schimmel explains this by clarifying that for Rumi, an intellectual explanation of love would be like an ass stuck in the mud; while if the pen was to describe love, it would break in two.[126] To love God one must trust God and jump into the unknown, and intellect, cleverness and pride hinder this from happening.[127] Furthermore, Corbin suggests that his use of images was intended to grasp the imaginative mind rather than the intellectual mind.[128] As a result, such evidence suggests Rumi's ecstatic approach to love and Ghāzālī's systematic approach to love need to be considered separately and are not interrelated. It seems that the first unfolds love as the fuel for the heart, whereas the latter unfolds love as the fuel for the mind.

Love is worship

Through *The Alchemy*, Ghāzālī emphasizes the empowerment of the soul through the channel of worship, and this results in the love of God.[129] Like knowledge, acts of worship take place in the extrinsic world but are embodied intrinsically within the character and are medicinal for the soul.[130] Knowledge and action are inseparable on the path of love.[131] Ghāzālī's book *Marvels of the Heart* can be used to further understand this. He illustrates that by submitting to the will of God, a greater awareness of God develops, which leads to invocations of Him; this in turn grants a sense of having achieved mystical knowledge.[132] *The Alchemy* talks about this higher knowledge in the chapter on the vision of God, and this is the mystic's aim agreed on by al-Muhasibi.[133] Ghāzālī states that this is the peak of mysticism and connects this kind of gnosticism with al-Bistami, al-Hallaj and al-Junayd.[134] Love is explained in *The Alchemy* by using the example of a seed; for this to blossom into happiness it must be watered with worship.[135] Love of God will only prevail when man is consistently aware of God's presence,[136] therefore minimizing any false claims to the love of God. Individual experiences and intuitions will differ but the goal of man is the same: annihilating the self so one can live in God and with God (*fana*).

In the second half of the text, *The Alchemy* talks about marriage and its maintenance, as well as utilizing dance and music to draw nearer to God; keeping nearness to God is the object of man's love.[137] These can be seen as double-edged swords: they can enhance the quality of worship or hinder the actualization of the heart's potential. Music and dance can only be useful in drawing nearer to God if the love of God is already present in man's heart, like attraction and desire in order to taste the sweetness of religion.[138] Abu Talib al-Makki, author of the Sufi text *Qut al-Qulub* (*The food of the Hearts*), also influenced Ghāzālī's ideology. Al-Makki held the view that it is better to worship God out of love for Him, than out of fear for him.[139] It seems that Ghāzālī combined both ideas to radiate Rabia al-Basri's (d. 801) doctrine of love. This states that one should worship for the sake of God, rather than to attain admittance to heaven or out of the fear of hell.[140] As a result, this will lead to an embodiment of love that is for the sake of genuine loving rather than for the expectance of reward.

On the other hand, marriage is referred to as a 'religious' institution in the text.[141] *The rights of the wife and children are similar to that of the process of self-purification.* Characteristics of patience, consideration and generosity are favoured.[142] Ghāzālī's book *On Disciplining the Soul* can be used to understand this: he highlights such ascetic practices as providing an opening to the spiritual world.[143] Ghāzālī outlines that when worship becomes easy, this is a sign that one has true love for God.[144]

Al-Harith ibn Asad al-Muhasibi (d.857) was a Sufi who influenced Ghāzālī's approach, too. He held the view that obedience to God is the beginning of love for Him, *awwal al-mahabba al-ta'a*.[145] It can be argued that the interchangeable meaning of 'love' and 'happiness' is a reflection of al-Muhasibi's view on Ghāzālī's approach. This is because he categorizes the vision of God, which is attained by sowing the seed of love, as the ultimate pleasure of paradise. This can be seen as the peak of happiness.[146] According to Ghāzālī's outline of the characteristics of real happiness, it must fulfil four conditions: it must be continual, be joyful without any sign of sorrow, be where knowledge is without signs of ignorance and be sufficient.[147] Being alive in the presence of God fulfils these four prerequisites for complete happiness and ultimately completes the approach to love and reaches the utopic destination of being filled with God's love.

Worship channelized through a perfected man is love

A similarity between Rumi and Ghāzālī's approach to worship is that it expresses the love of God as an external act but one which has internal effects.[148] It also radiates the doctrine of love by agreeing that acts of worship should be sincere expressions of love. However, while Ghāzālī suggests it is through worship that the soul is empowered and the love of God blossoms, Rumi proposes that a guide who has accomplished perfection is crucial in this process. This point becomes a dominant theme within the *Mathnawi*.[149] The importance of this is depicted through the poem about the diplomat who goes to meet Umar, the second caliph of the Islamic domain.

> *When the ambassador of Rum admitted these fresh (spiritual)*
> *words into his hearing (gave ear to them), he became more full*
> *of longing.*
> *He fixed his eye on seeking 'Umar, he let his baggage and*
> *horse be lost.*
> *He was going in every direction after that man of (great)*
> *accomplishment, inquiring madly for him,*
> *Saying, 'Can there be in the world such a man, and he be*
> *hid, like the spirit, from the world?'*

> *He sought him, that he might be as a slave to him: inevitably the seeker is a finder.*[150]

Rumi urges man to be careful and weary when associating himself with a guide. He should be able to distinguish between a false guide and a truly enlightened guide.[151] In the poem, the description of Umar has been given as that of a truly pious individual.

Rumi was of the view that God has to be initially found in the external world and then within the internal world of the self. At this point man is reconnected with God as he was in the primordial life, but as this is not a complete union, an emotion of sweet longing persists. This is a spiritual state known as self-disclosure.[152] An aura of light is created, and he is adorned with attributes of awe, love and longing, which can also be noted in the poem. As a result, man is qualified to be a spiritual guide and can awaken the idle soul within himself to channelize it to its origin.[153] For this to happen, God gives the guide knowledge of what man desires and what his affections are. These are seen as veils to the desire and affection for God as it is in the human predisposition to love God.[154] The guide will assist in eradicating the ego and the attachments of the world in order to reconnect with God.[155] However, Rumi highlights that man must entrust his guide as the reflection of God.[156] Rumi describes the diplomat's search as that of a '*madman*', and he aims to be the caliph's 'slave', which confirms such an idea. Furthermore, this portrays the idea that man must be fully absorbed in the path to annihilation in order to achieve it.

To use Ghāzālī's terminology, it seems that the guide is the alchemist who can transmute the rusty soul of man into one of gold.[157] It is evident in the poem that Rumi is portraying Umar's soul at the station of self-disclosure. Schimmel elaborates by highlighting that loving secondary causes like the guide, trusting him and obeying him are a means to the primary source, God.[158] It seems that this is the declaration of Divine unity, 'there is no god but God'. Therefore, this reflects Rumi's principle that love for anything is indirectly love for God.[159] When love is experienced, it engulfs man the way fingers hold a pen. The expressions thereafter are beyond man's awareness.[160] Also this procedure resonates with Rumi's own experience of encountering Shams, their separation and his eventual discovery of God's essence within himself. Additionally, this provides further evidence for Rumi's emphasis on being in the presence of a perfected man in order to eventually feel the presence of God and be able to love Him.

Albeit the importance of *sama* is evident through Rumi's life, the *Mathnawi* is the cultivation of his ideas and an expression of his thoughts. While Ghāzālī unfolds aspects of dance and music to draw nearer to God, on a parallel basis it is clear that *sama* is noted as the mode of transmission in the *Mathnawi*. Schimmel highlights that Rumi viewed everything through the lens of *sama*. Every created atom is circulating in its own orbit, with love at its core and testifying that nothing else truly exists. This is the ladder to heavenly visions.[161] For Rumi, this was a connection between the transcendent nature of God and the incarnation of man.[162] The further man 'travels in love', the greater happiness it finds; and as love is limitless, the happiness from experiencing love is infinite.[163] Therefore, for Rumi this was seen as the embodiment of the oneness of God and the cultivation of the Islamic creed, as there is no goal other than God. Moreover, after the advent of Shams, Rumi utilized such avenues in his congregational sermons.[164] Meditation with the sound of the flute and drums, while undertaking the mystical whirling dance, creates an emotional stir and allows the lover to be spiritually uplifted.[165] Hagiographical sources confirm that Rumi valued the effects of such avenues.[166] As a result, this attracted more people than did traditional forms of preaching and the practice developed into a ritual.[167] This was systemized by Rumi's son, Sultan Walad, and continued through the brotherhood of the Mevlevis.[168] This suggests that love is a joyous experience for each atom.[169]

Conclusion

The researcher initiated the task of defining love through the eyes of Ghāzālī and Rumi, by presenting a brief introduction to the writers and the texts in discussion. It was found that both writers underwent a spiritual transformation that changed their approach to professorship, and the evidence was reflected in the texts under speculation. Furthermore, it can be understood that both writers respond to the social atmosphere and address the needs of the society of the time. From an analysing of the scripts, it emerged that Ghāzālī's approach to love was specified to be systematic as it connects with the logical mind. On the other hand, Rumi's approach to love was seen as ecstatic and forming a connection with the imaginative mind. This equipped the writer with tools to undertake the task of unfolding a deeper understanding of each author's view.

To draw basic principles on love for Ghāzālī, the book of love was examined, from which it was concluded that Ghāzālī highlights aspects of knowledge and worship as prerequisites to the love of God. With such facets in mind the text was investigated to conclude that this was a consistent phenomenon in *The Alchemy*; and other texts by Ghāzālī were explored to gain a deeper understanding of his views. Ghāzālī accentuates the importance of gaining mystical knowledge of the body and the soul to attain love for God, with more emphasis on the latter component. The rationale behind this was that mystical knowledge cleanses the spiritual heart, so one can be responsive to the presence of God. Combining the rational approach and the use of the logical mind, Ghāzālī's approach resembled theories of Neoplatonism and some aspects of Greek philosophy.

Additionally, it was found that knowledge and worship are inseparable on the path of love. This is because worship was identified as the empowerment of the soul and the proof of claiming one's love for God. Marriage, music and dance are discussed in *The Alchemy* as ways of enhancing the quality of worship. Possible influences on this approach were al-Muhasibi and as al-Makki, while briefly discussing Rabia al-Basri's doctrine of love. Ghāzālī's ideas of *fitra* and a natural affinity to God are explored and are suggested to be a combination of the Platonic theory of innate knowledge and Avincenna's and al-Junayd's views on the matter. The common aim of man is still to accomplish *fana*; and this is true eternal happiness.

The love of God is the main theme within Rumi's work; therefore, there was no need to utilize other texts to gain a basic understanding of general principles. For Rumi, experiencing the love of God had to be preceded by the longing of God, felt by the acknowledgement of separation. Contrary to Ghāzālī's use of reason and logic, Rumi emphasizes the importance of an emotional connection with God reflecting love as a mystical experience. The *Song of the Reed* was used to illustrate this and highlight the inner meaning through the symbolism of the reed and of wine. This stage is referred to as 'the experiential stage' and understood to be superior to the stage of knowledge, as carnal senses hinder man from comprehending the mysteries of this realm.

Furthermore, Rumi outlines that being associated with a guide will act as a catalyst and this is crucial when undertaking the path to God. The poem about a diplomat meeting Umar the caliph was referred to with the aim of illustrating Rumi's view on the importance of being in the presence of a perfected human, in order to indirectly arouse love for God. Moreover, it was denoted that such importance resonated with Rumi's own experiences with Shams, the meditative environment of his sermons and the actual mode of transmission of the *Mathnawi*.

Considering the influences on Ghāzālī raises the question of whether Ghāzālī's ideas were authentically his own or a compilation of different theories. All discourses of theology, philosophy and Sufism were developed roughly in the same era. Albeit they may have external influences of culture, Greek philosophy, Neoplatonism and Hellenism, Abrahamov urges this doesn't diminish the worth of Ghāzālī's work.[170] Thus, such theories on love are considered authentic responses to the Quran and *Hadith* tradition.[171]

With reference to the researchers' initial hypothesis of assuming there would be more similarities between both definitions than differences, this can be seen in many ways. First of all, both writers share a similar experience of undergoing a spiritual transformation in their life. This affects their general approach to love, but in different manners. Ghāzālī formulates a text to connect with the logical mind to purify man's heart to contain God and experience love in the future tense. On the other hand, Rumi connects with the imaginative mind to describe the effects of sensing God's presence and experiencing the joys of his love in the present tense. Secondly knowledge and longing were put forward as similar attributes of love as they are a mere extension of one another. This idea was consistent with the views of al-Hujwayri, a scholar both writers had studied. Lastly, Ghāzālī outlined that knowledge without worship cannot lead to the love of God; therefore, worship is an attribute of love. This was indifferent to Rumi's approach as he also agrees worship must be sincere but extends this by utilizing a guide for the journey to God. Ghāzālī speaks little of a guide in *The Alchemy*; however, evidence could be found in the *Ihya* that taking a *sheikh* is an imperative for the path.[172]

Love of God can be seen through many avenues: through knowledge, through longing, through worship and through a perfected human. This is consistent with the initial definition of love found in the Historical Dictionaries of Religion as the focus is on the goal of union. The aim of all avenues is to diminish the ego and to accomplish *fana*. Conclusively, love can be many things, but it can never be one.

Notes

1 M. Smith, *Muslim Women Mystics: The Life and Work of Rabi'a and Other Women Mystics in Islam* (Oxford: Oneworld, 2001), 124.
2 The heart not as in the lump of flesh in the chest but the intangible essence of the human being; that is, the spiritual heart will be discussed throughout this chapter. John Renard, *Historical Dictionary of Sufism* (Lanham, MD: Scarecrow Press, 2005), 147.

3 'He loves them, and they love Him', Quran 5/54.
4 'What is belief? Belief means that God and His messenger are beloved by you more than anything else', B. Abrahamov, *Divine Love in Islamic Mysticism: The Teachings of Ghāzālī and Al-Dabbagh* (London: Routledge, 2003), 1–86.
5 When Muhammad practised seclusion in Mount Hira, a bedouin said, 'Muhammad is in love with his Lord!', in *Classical Islam: A Sourcebook of Religious Literature*, ed. Norman Calder, Jawad Mojaddedi and Andrew Rippin (London: Routledge, 2003), 231.
6 Abrahamov, *Divine Love in Islamic Mysticism*, 13–14.
7 Ibid., 25.
8 Henceforth, the spelling of 'Mathnawi' will be preferred as this is utilized in the translation by Reynold.
9 Henceforth, his name will be rendered to as Ghāzālī rather than al-Ghāzālī for a smooth read of the text. Renard, *Historical Dictionary of Sufism*, 94.
10 Edoardo Albert, *Imam Ghāzālī: A Concise Life* (United Kingdom: Kube Publishing, 2012), 19–21.
11 This was similar to being the head of Oxford, Cambridge or Harvard University in present day. Renard, *Historical Dictionary of Sufism*, 94.
12 Albert, *Imam Ghāzālī*, 35.
13 W. J. Skellie, 'The Religious Psychology of Al-Ghazzali', PhD thesis, 1938, xiv.
14 Norman Calder, Jawad Mojaddedi and Andrew Rippin, *Classical Islam: A Sourcebook of Religious Literature* (London: Routledge, 2003), 229.
15 Ibid., 228.
16 Albert, *Imam Ghāzālī*, 49–51.
17 Herbert L. Bodman Jr., 'Review of The Alchemy of Happiness', trans. Claud Feild and rev. Elton L. Daniel, *Journal of World History* (1993): 336–8.
18 'I am God' – Ana al-Haqq. Louis Massignon, *The Passion of Al-Hallaj: Mystic and Martyr of Islam*, trans. Herbert Mason (Princeton, NJ: Princeton University Press, 1994), 66.
19 Bodman, 'Review of The Alchemy of Happiness', 336–8.
20 C. Field (trans.), *The Alchemy of Happiness* (New York: Cosimo Classics, 2010), viii.
21 Franklin D. Lewis, *Rumi. Past and Present, East and West: The Life, Teachings and Poetry of Jalal al-Din Rumi* (Oxford: Oneworld Publications, 2000), 93.
22 M. G. Gupta, *Maulana Rum's Masnawi* (India: M.G. Publishers, 1990), 4–5.
23 Erkan Turkmen, *The Essence of Rumi's Masnevi Including his Life and Works* (Lahore: Jumhoori, 1999), 41.
24 Lewis, *Rumi. Past and Present, East and West*, 11.
25 Ibid., 115–16.
26 Ibid., 18.
27 Ibid., 135, 141.
28 Turkmen, *The Essence of Rumi's Masnevi Including his Life and Works*, 46.
29 Lewis, *Rumi. Past and Present, East and West*, 136.
30 Whether their first encounter was in Konya or not is debated, but for the purpose of this research, we will be following the mainstream theory. See Lewis, *Rumi. Past and Present, East and West*, 155–9.
31 See Annemarie Schimmel, 'Mystical Poetry in Islam: The Case of Maulana Jalaladdin Rumi', *Religion and Literature* 20, no. 1 (1988): 67–80; Turkmen, *The Essence of Rumi's Masnevi Including his Life and Works*, 44.
32 Lewis, *Rumi. Past and Present, East and West*, 163.
33 See Gupta, *Maulana Rum's Masnawi*, 44 and Lewis, *Rumi. Past and Present, East and West*, 166–8.
34 Manijeh Mannani, 'The Metaphysics of the Heart in the Sufi Poetry of Rumi', *Religion and Literature* 42, no. 3 (2010): 164.
35 Schimmel, 'Mystical Poetry in Islam', 71.
36 Turkmen, *The Essence of Rumi's Masnevi Including his Life and Works*, 51.

37 H. C. Paul, 'Rumi: His Life and Genius', in *The Maulavi Flute*, ed. S. H. Qasemi (India: New Age International Limited Publishers, 1997), 38.
38 W. Chittick, 'The Spiritual Path of Love of Ibn al-'Arabi and Rumi', *Mystics Quarterly*, 19 (1993): 5; Paul, 'Rumi: His Life and Genius', 30.
39 See Gupta, *Maulana Rum's Masnawi*, 5; Turkmen, *The Essence of Rumi's Masnevi Including His Life and Works*, 58.
40 See Lewis, *Rumi. Past and Present, East and West*, 314; Turkmen, *The Essence of Rumi's Masnevi Including His Life and Works*, 58.
41 Juliet Mabey, 'Introduction', in *Rumi: A Spiritual Journey* (Oxford: Oneworld Publications, 2000).
42 Turkmen, *The Essence of Rumi's Masnevi Including His Life and Works*, 65.
43 Paul, 'Rumi: His Life and Genius', 38.
44 Qasemi, *The Maulavi Flute*, viii.
45 Field, *The Alchemy of Happiness*, 73.
46 Ibid., 11.
47 Maha Elkaisy Friemuth, *God and Humans in Islamic Thought: Abd al-Jabbar, Ibn Sina and al-Ghāzālī* (London: Routledge, 2006).
48 Abrahamov, *Divine Love in Islamic Mysticism*, 4.
49 Farooq Hamid, 'Storytelling Techniques in the "Masnavi-yi Ma'navi" of Mowlana Jalal al-Din
    Rumi: Wayward Narrative of Logical Progession', *Iranian Studies* 32, no. 1 (1999): 28.
50 James Roy King, 'Narrative Disjunction and Conjunction in Rumi's "Mathnawi"', *The Journal of Narrative Techniques* 19, no. 3 (1989): 284.
51 See Hamid, 'Storytelling Techniques in the "Masnavi-yi Ma'navi" of Mowlana Jalal al-Din Rumi', 28; King, 'Narrative Disjunction and Conjunction in Rumi's "Mathnawi"', 282.
52 Hamid, 'Storytelling Techniques in the "Masnavi-yi Ma'navi" of Mowlana Jalal al-Din Rumi', 30.
53 Ibid., 28.
54 Seyed Ghahreman Safavi, *The Structure of Rumi's Mathnawi* (London: London Academy of Iranian Studies Press, 2005), 19.
55 Ibid., 22.
56 King, 'Narrative Disjunction and Conjunction in Rumi's "Mathnawi"', 280–3.
57 Safavi, *The Structure of Rumi's Mathnawi*, 23.
58 King, 'Narrative Disjunction and Conjunction in Rumi's "Mathnawi"', 277.
59 Schimmel, 'Mystical Poetry in Islam', 173.
60 Abrahamov, *Divine Love in Islamic Mysticism*, 42.
61 Ibid., 44–50.
62 Field, *The Alchemy of Happiness*, 78.
63 Binyamin Abrahamov, 'Al-Ghāzālī's Supreme Way to Know God', *Studia Islamica* 77 (1993): 141.
64 Friemuth, *God and Humans in Islamic Thought*, 78.
65 Muhammad Abul Quasem, 'Al-Ghāzālī's Conception of Happiness', *Arabica* 2 (1975): 156.
66 Ibid., 77.
67 Ibid., 10.
68 Ibid., 75.
69 Ibid., 31.
70 Field, *The Alchemy of Happiness*, 73.
71 Ibid., 74.
72 Ibid., 4–9.
73 Abrahamov, *Divine Love in Islamic Mysticism*, 9.
74 Known as Avicenna in the Latin translation. Friemuth, *God and Humans in Islamic Thought*, 136.
75 Abrahamov, *Divine Love in Islamic Mysticism*, 2.

76 Ibid., 8.
77 Quasem, 'Al-Ghāzālī's Conception of Happiness', 154.
78 Abrahamov, *Divine Love in Islamic Mysticism*, 3.
79 Quasem, 'Al-Ghāzālī's Conception of Happiness', 157.
80 Quran, 29/69.
81 Abu Hamid Al-Ghāzālī, *The Book of Knowledge*, trans. Nabih Amin Faris (New Delhi: Islamic Book Service, 1962), 43.
82 Field, *The Alchemy of Happiness*, 13.
83 Ibid., 31.
84 Friemuth, *God and Humans in Islamic Thought*, 136.
85 Ibid., 131.
86 Ibid., 130.
87 Ibid., 132.
88 Field, *The Alchemy of Happiness*, 78.
89 Friemuth, *God and Humans in Islamic Thought*, 136.
90 Field, *The Alchemy of Happiness*.
91 'Fitra' is the original state in which humans are created by God, http://www.oxfordislamicstudies.com/article/opr/t125/e666.
92 Abrahamov, *Divine Love in Islamic Mysticism*, 22.
93 Al-Ghāzālī, *Deliverance from Error*, trans. W. Montgomery Watt (Kuala Lumpur: Islamic Book Trust, 2005), 26–31.
94 Abrahamov, 'Al-Ghāzālī's Supreme Way to Know God', 142.
95 Al-Ghāzālī, *Deliverance from Error*, 30.
96 Gupta, *Maulana Rum's Masnawi*, 15.
97 Chittick, 'The Spiritual Path of Love of Ibn al-"Arabi and Rumi"', 11. For the meaning of 'fana', see Encyclopaedia Britannica Online, http://www.britannica.com/EBchecked/topic/201463/fana.
98 Gupta, *Maulana Rum's Masnawi*, i.
99 Ibid., 15.
100 Annemarie Schimmel, 'The Manifestation of Love', in *I am the Wind, You are the Fire: The Life and Work of Rumi* (London: Shambala Publications, 1992), 190.
101 Omaima Abou-Bakr, 'Abrogation of the Mind in the Poetry of Jalal al-Din Rumi', in *Journal of Comparative Poetics: Madness and Civilisation* (Egypt: American University in Cairo and American University in Cairo Press, 1994), 42. https://www.jstor.org/stable/521765?origin=crossref, accessed 28 August 2021.
102 Gupta, *Maulana Rum's Masnawi*, 5.
103 Reyold A. Nicholson, *The Mathnawi of Jalalu'ddin Rumi* (Cambridge: Luzac and Co., 1977), 5.
104 Safavi, *The Structure of Rumi's Mathnawi*, 65.
105 Schimmel, 'Mystical Poetry in Islam', 72.
106 Eric Schroeder, 'The Wild Deer Mathnawi', *The Journal of Aesthetics and Art Criticism* 11, no. 2 (1952): 125.
107 Kenan Rifai, *Listen: Commentary on the Spiritual Couplets of Mevlana Rumi*, trans. Victoria Holbrook (Louisville: Fons Vitae, 2011), 5.
108 Ibid., 3.
109 Schimmel, 'The Manifestation of Love', 174.
110 Schroeder, 'The Wild Deer Mathnawi', 125.
111 Rifai, *Listen*, 3.
112 Abou-Bakr, 'Abrogation of the Mind in the Poetry of Jalal al-Din Rumi', 38.
113 Schimmel, 'The Manifestation of Love', 181.
114 Schroeder, 'The Wild Deer Mathnawi', 125.
115 Schimmel, 'The Manifestation of Love', 177.
116 Rifai, *Listen*, 5.

6. A Comparison between the Ideas 149

117 Ibid., 7.
118 Abou-Bakr, 'Abrogation of the Mind in the Poetry of Jalal al-Din Rumi', 41.
119 Mannani, 'The Metaphysics of the Heart in the Sufi Poetry of Rumi', 166.
120 Abou-Bakr, 'Abrogation of the Mind in the Poetry of Jalal al-Din Rumi', 38.
121 King, 'Narrative Disjunction and Conjunction in Rumi's "Mathnawi"', 282.
122 Nicholson, *The Mathnawi of Jalalu'ddin Rumi*, 5.
123 Abou-Bakr, 'Abrogation of the Mind in the Poetry of Jalal al-Din Rumi', 40.
124 Mannani, 'The Metaphysics of the Heart in the Sufi Poetry of Rumi', 164.
125 Turkmen, *The Essence of Rumi's Masnevi Including His Life and Works*, 246.
126 Schimmel, 'The Manifestation of Love', 173.
127 Chittick, 'The Spiritual Path of Love of Ibn al-"Arabi and Rumi"', 223.
128 King, 'Narrative Disjunction and Conjunction in Rumi's "Mathnawi"', 281.
129 Field, *The Alchemy of Happiness*, 27.
130 Ibid., 26–9.
131 Ibid., 72.
132 Al-Ghāzālī, *Marvels of the Heart: Science of the Spirit*, trans. Walter J. Skellie (Louisville: Fons Vitae, 2010), 53–4.
133 See Field, *The Alchemy of Happiness*, 77 and Friemuth, *God and Humans in Islamic Thought*, 137.
134 Ibid., 138.
135 Ibid., 18.
136 Ibid., 52.
137 Friemuth, *God and Humans in Islamic Thought*, 131.
138 Ibid., 41 and 45.
139 Abrahamov, *Divine Love in Islamic Mysticism*, 35.
140 N. Hanif, *Biographical Encyclopaedia of Sufis: Central Asia and Middle East* (New Delhi: Sarup Book Publishers, 2002), 109.
141 Ibid., 67.
142 Ibid, 64 and 68–9.
143 Al-Ghāzālī, *On Disciplining the Soul and On Breaking the Two Desires*, trans. Timothy Winter (Cambridge: Islamic Texts Society, 1997), 156.
144 Ibid., 85.
145 Abrahamov, *Divine Love in Islamic Mysticism*, 29.
146 Friemuth, *God and Humans in Islamic Thought*, 137.
147 Muhammad Abul Quasem, *The Ethics of Al-Ghāzālī: A Composite Ethics in Islam* (New York: Caravan Books, 1978), 55.
148 Alessandro Bausani, 'Theism and Pantheism in Rumi', in *Iranian Studies*, vol.1 (Taylor and Francis Ltd, 1968), 8–24. Herbert L. Bodman Jr., '(untitled)'. Rev. of The Alchemy of Happiness, trans. by Claud Feild and rev. by Elton L. Daniel. *Journal of World History* (Fall 1993): 336–8.
149 Gupta, *Maulana Rum's Masnawi*, 14.
150 'Umar and the Ambassador', Nicholson (trans.), *The Mathnawi of Jalalu'ddin Rumi*, 77–8.
151 Chittick, 'The Spiritual Path of Love of Ibn al-"Arabi and Rumi"', 11.
152 Rifai, *Listen*, 3.
153 Ibid., 4.
154 Turkmen, *The Essence of Rumi's Masnevi Including His Life and Works*, 244.
155 Gupta, *Maulana Rum's Masnawi*, 12.
156 Ibid., 11.
157 Ibid., 14.
158 Schimmel, 'Mystical Poetry in Islam', 76.
159 Chittick, 'The Spiritual Path of Love of Ibn al-"Arabi and Rumi"', 10.
160 Schimmel, 'The Manifestation of Love', 175.
161 Schimmel, 'Mystical Poetry in Islam', 79.

162 King, 'Narrative Disjunction and Conjunction in Rumi's "Mathnawi"', 282.
163 Schimmel, 'The Manifestation of Love', 176.
164 Lewis, *Rumi. Past and Present, East and West*, 314.
165 Schimmel, 'Mystical Poetry in Islam', 78.
166 Lewis, *Rumi. Past and Present, East and West*, 172.
167 Ibid., 314.
168 Schimmel, 'Mystical Poetry in Islam', 79.
169 Schimmel, 'The Manifestation of Love', 174.
170 Abrahamov, *Divine Love in Islamic Mysticism*, 26, 40.
171 Scott Kugle, *Sufis & Saints Bodies: Mysticism, Corporeality and Sacred Power in Islam* (Chapel Hill, USA: The University of North Carolina Press, 2007), 1.
172 R. J. McCarthy, *Al-Ghāzālī's Path to Sufism: His Deliverance from Error* (Lousiville: Fons Vitae, 2000), 56.

Chapter 7

UNVEILING DESIRE

LOVE IN MODERN TURKISH POETRY[1]

Laurent Mignon

In a striking passage of his momentous *Storia della letteratura turca* (*History of Turkish Literature*, 1956), Alessio Bombaci wrote that, beside historiography, 'Ottoman classicism was mainly expressed through erotico-mystical lyrical poetry'.[2] The Italian orientalist had a point even though his statement underestimated other genres that flourished during the classical age. It is true, however, that the contrast between the classical age and the early years of the *Tanzimat* era could not be sharper than when focusing on love in the poetry of those two eras. Love, usually homoerotic and not necessarily mystical, largely reigned in the domain of poetry before the nineteenth century, but the reformist poets of the second half of the nineteenth century had little time for the theme of love in their verses. Indeed, the nightingale in Namık Kemal, the Young Ottoman firebrand's poetry, did not cry out for love and reunion with the beloved, but it yearned for emancipation: 'Even the nightingale annihilates itself for love of freedom', goes a verse in his most famous *murabba*'.[3] It was not only love that was being rejected by the advocates of political reform and literary regeneration. The whole classical Ottoman literary tradition was declared unfit for the new age and condemned to the recycling bin of history.

The theme of love was now being explored in new literary genres appropriated from the West, such as the novel and drama. From doomed forbidden passions, such as the loves of Hagop and Akabi in Hovsep Vartanyan's *Akabi Hikayesi* (*The Story of Akabi*, 1851) and of Talat and Fitnat in Şemseddin Sami's *Taaşşuk-ı Tal'at ve Fitnat* (*The Love of Talat and Fitnat*, 1872), to tragic femmes fatales, such as the murderous Mehpeyker in Namık Kemal's *İntibah* (*The Awakening*, 1876) and the jealous Ceylan in Ahmet Midhat Efendi's *Jöntürk* (*Young Turk*, 1910), novels explored gender relations and the societal status quo, occasionally challenging them, while also catering to the readers' thirst for intrigue and romance.[4]

The engaged poetry of the likes of İbrahim Şinasi, Namık Kemal and Ziya Paşa, though interesting from an intellectual and political point of view, was rarely poetically engaging. Things were to change in the era of Sultan Abdülhamid II, which was marked by increased censorship and political repression. While still exploring and combining the characteristics of often-conflicting French literary movements such as Romanticism and the *Parnasse*, the following generation of poets, inspired by the writings of Recaizade Mahmut Ekrem and, to a lesser extent, the passionate but unconventional poetry of Abdülhak Hamit (Tarhan), would chant, not unlike Paul Verlaine in his 'Art poétique', the supremacy of music and nuances over ideas and slogans. Ekrem's ideas on literature and the arts were to inspire the return of lyrical poetry and of love as a legitimate theme of modern poetry. A poet, playwright and novelist, as well as a much sought-after literary commentator, Ekrem defined literature as a quest for beauty and attributed an inspirational role in the creation of artistic beauty to love and women: 'From the point of view of human beauty and for the work of art, the woman is the principal entity. The creation of all great work of arts was the product of her inspiration, her beauty and her love.'[5] This was indicative of a truly revolutionary transformation: by declaring women a source of inspiration, contemplation and desire, the author of influential theoretical works, such as *Talim-i Edebiyat* (*The Teaching of Literature*, 1879) and *Takdir-i Elhan* (*The Appreciation of Songs*, 1884), not only reintroduced the theme of love, but also redefined its nature. As noted by the literary historian Kenan Akyüz, Ekrem brought an end to centuries of homoerotic love which had marked the classical tradition.[6]

At the turn of the century, Recaizade Mahmut Ekrem's followers, often associated with the *Servet-i Fünun* (*Treasury of the Arts*) journal, and also later nationalist advocates of the politicization of literature, inspired by folk poetry and decrying 'Byzantine emotions' – homosexuality – explored heterosexual love in highly stylized verses,[7] chanting either the illusive and elusive object of their desire, already encountered in Ekrem's verses, or the staunch village girl, incarnating national values. Love had been re-enthroned. Yet, were it not for the poetry of Ahmet Haşim, which was not devoid of an oedipal dimension, and its evocation of a melancholic beloved, her 'imaginary beauty' and 'inconceivable love',[8] little love poetry would have been written, which was of more than documentary interest. The author of two major collections with the titles *Göl Saatleri* (*Hours of the Lake*, 1921) and *Piyâle* (*The Chalice*, 1926), Ahmet Haşim was heralding the developments that were to come. The beloved in his poetry might still have been an illusion, a product of the imagination of the poetic I, but the desire aroused by this illusion was real and 'the fire of her lips, an invitation to madness'.[9]

In the years which followed, the representation of the beloved and the nature of the love expressed were to undergo several transformations, not the least because the Republic of Turkey, founded in 1923, was changing at a rapid pace: industrialization and the authoritarian implementation of Westernizing policies aimed at catapulting the new state into the Western world. By 1958 when Cemal Süreya, one of the leading figures of the modernist *İkinci Yeni* (Second Renewal) movement, published *Üvercinka*, his first collection of poems, poets such as the neo-classicist Yahya Kemal (Beyatlı), the socialist Nâzım Hikmet (Ran) and the avant-garde Orhan Veli (Kanık), whose works remained influential despite his untimely death in 1950 at the age of thirty-six, had developed clashing conceptions of poetry and novel interpretations of the theme of love, which left their imprint on the history of Turkish literature. All of them were at the centre of literary debates in the 1950s with followers and detractors.[10] This chapter will focus on the love poetry of Yahya Kemal,[11] Nâzım Hikmet,[12] Orhan Veli[13] and Cemal Süreya,[14] major figures of the era whose most significant works are also representative of the variety of poetics and the plurality of discourses in twentieth-century Turkish poetry.

'An ardent disciple of the tradition of those prophets who had no book',[15] according to Süleyman Nazif, an essayist and poet of uneven talents, Yahya Kemal never published any poetry collection during his lifetime. With the advocates of 'art for its own sake' of the previous generation, he considered poetry to be a continuous quest for musicality and beauty – 'a well-hidden gem' that needed to be cut again and again.[16] A perfectionist when it came to his own verses, he wrote little, slowly and always at a great price to himself, often revising minute details in poems that had already been published. The Yahya Kemal Institute, founded shortly after his death, undertook the posthumous publication of his complete works in accordance with his wishes. As a result, even though his poetry was well known among the literati, his two major poetry collections *Kendi Gök Kubbemiz* (*Our Own Firmament*, 1961) and *Eski Şiirin Rüzgâriyle* (*With the Breeze of Ancient Poetry*, 1962) were published for the first time when the landscape of Turkish poetry was being redefined by the modernist advocates of the *Second Renewal*, notably Cemal Süreya, who challenged the subjective realism of the *Garip* movement, spearheaded by Orhan Veli and the engaged poetry of the disciples of Nâzım Hikmet, who was agonizing in exile in Moscow. The belated publication of Kemal's works allowed his rediscovery by a generation of readers who had been entirely schooled in the Republican system. Yahya Kemal's neo-Ottoman aesthetics were thus granted a new life.

This was, perhaps, a form of compensation for a poet who belonged to a generation of intellectuals who had arguably lost their motherland twice. Born in Skopje in 1884 where he grew up, Yahya Kemal was never able to revisit those lands, which he had left as a rebellious teenager in 1902, because they became officially part of the Kingdom of Serbia after the treaty of London was signed in 1913. Some of the more radical cultural reforms implemented by Mustafa Kemal Atatürk after the establishment of the republic in 1923, such as the disparagement of Ottoman classical music which stopped being taught at conservatories and was even banned from the airwaves for a short period between 1934 and 1936, made him loose his cultural references, and turned him into a stranger in the new Republic. In particular the alphabet change of 1928 must have had a traumatizing effect, for the alphabet contained the very letters with which he, and others, exorcized their *mal de vivre* that were now condemned to oblivion. Quite a few writers and intellectuals of his generation sank into alcohol and drugs.[17] Yahya Kemal, however, was not one of them. His artificial paradise was an aesthetic quest incarnated in the figure of the beloved in his love poetry. He had travelled a long way, from his study of Ottoman history and literature while in Paris and a short period where he espoused the principles of Jean Moréas's *Ecole Romane*, to his later embrace of a form of Ottoman neo-classicism. Defending the *aruz*, the metrical system of *Divan* poetry, at a time when nationalist theoreticians and versifiers advocated the use of the *hece* syllabic metre of the folk tradition, he merged a Baudelairian spleen with identitarian interrogations, never hesitating to reinvent with a twist to the themes and *topoi* of the classical Ottoman tradition.

His love poetry is a case in point. Away from the stylized gardens of the classical tradition, Yahya Kemal set his poetry in Istanbul, the former capital of the Ottoman Empire. However, Istanbul, as the setting of love, was not a naturalist depiction of the city which in the 1910s was being altered by the beginning of industrialization and the influx of refugees from the Balkan wars. It was the capital of the Ottoman Empire that nationalist Republicans were to condemn for its cosmopolitanism and elitism. In his poetry, love was experienced in neighbourhoods and districts such as Bebek, Çamlıca, Erenköy, Moda, Kandilli, Göksu and Kanlıca and even the Princes' Islands, places of sojourn that were favoured by the Ottoman ruling elite in the final decades of the Ottoman Empires. These districts were associated with power but also with a certain Ottoman-ness and its aesthetics. It was the Istanbul of the privileged, neighbourhoods that also attracted the gaze of Western travellers, but which remained unknown to the great majority of the Istanbul population. In other words, it was the Istanbul which symbolized the very state that Atatürk's followers aimed to transform. Some of those districts, chanted by the poet, such as Bebek and Göksu, were also sceneries which suggested continuity with the Muslim neighbourhood of Skopje, with its mosques and minarets in the cosmopolitan setting of a Macedonian town.

Accordingly, Yahya Kemal's love poems are marked by a deep melancholy, an expression of his longing for a city and way of life that was now disappearing. Though the season of love is, like in the classical tradition, spring or summer, the point in time from which the poetic I makes his reminiscences is usually autumn:

> The grass that we trod last summer has faded, I saw
> My face has turned to ashes, like this failing season.[18]

The fact that the emphasis should be on remembrance is crucial in the poetry of Yahya Kemal, for love is an emotion experienced in the past. As a consequence the love theme is conjugated in the past tense:

> It was a dream-like summer. With passion, you created
> each moment, each colour, each poem from delight.[19]

Remarkably, while poets of the classical era longed for the *vuslat*, the union with the beloved, Yahya Kemal's lovers live in an era when the age of felicity, the era of togetherness with the loved one has come to an end. The *vuslat* is not longed for anymore; it is remembered with regret and nostalgia.

Yahya Kemal achieves a subtle renovation of the classical tradition when representing the beloved: the one who is often referred to as 'Canân', a common first name meaning 'beloved', is not only loved, but she is also an equal and active partner of the relationship – someone who loves, as in the verse that compares the pleasures of spring 'to the union between a loving woman and a loving man'.[20] Canân is far from being unreachable and untouchable. The *visâl*, the union of the lovers, 'starts and ends on the lips of the beloved'.[21] However, the kiss that the lovers of the classical tradition yearned for is not enough anymore:

> The longest kiss is not enough, you kiss and yearn for more
> The pleasure that induces thirst is the salt on the lips.[22]

The physical representation of the beloved too is different. While the *Divan* poet would have referred to the beloved with a variety of metaphors such as *servi* (cypress), *nihâl* (twig) or *şem* (candle) to refer to her stature and *nergis* (narcissus) or *bâdem* (almond) to evoke her eyes,[23] Yahya Kemal focuses on parts of the body of the beloved, like the lips, eyes and fingers and reinvents those images in such a way that they come to symbolize the independence of the beloved and her sensuality:

I saw her beautiful eyes, like a raptor's.
Her nails, pure gems, were the colour of blood.[24]

The subversion of mystical imagery is also obvious in the following verse:

A bloody rose in her mouth, a cup of wine in her hand
We drank, together, in one movement.[25]

The rose, usually longed for by the nightingale in Sufi poetry, is held between the teeth of the beloved, as in a tango. The cup of wine is not the symbol of spiritual knowledge leading to ecstasy anymore but an invitation to consummate sensual love. While this novel image of the beloved, combined with Western references, both undermines and reinvents the classical *Divan* tradition, its use remains nevertheless metaphoric. Indeed, one could argue that Canân is an incarnation of a disappearing Ottoman Istanbul, sensual and independent, yet conscious of her history. Past centuries can still be witnessed in her dark blue eyes and history is reflected on her face.[26] Merging metaphorical and autobiographical elements, Yahya Kemal's beloved is a figure that symbolizes the end of an age yet heralds the arrival of a new kind of beloved, well anchored in the realities of her time.

Literary critics and biographers of the poets have pointed to the possibility of an autobiographical dimension in some of the poet's love verses.[27] The fact that Canân might have been Celile Hanım, the mother of the enfant terrible of Turkish poetry, namely Nâzım Hikmet, is one timely reminder that, for much of the first half of the twentieth century, the 'writing class' in Ottoman, then Republican Turkey, was closely knit despite fundamental differences in matters of ideology and poetics. The teenage Nâzım is said to have threatened Yahya Kemal, his private tutor at the time, when he found out that the poet was ardently pursuing his mother. 'The house you entered as my tutor, you cannot enter as my father,' he scribbled on a piece of paper which he surreptitiously put into his teacher's coat pocket.[28] Less amusing was Yahya Kemal's refusal to sign a petition for the liberation of Nâzım Hikmet, jailed in 1938 on political grounds, which his mother, on hunger strike, had instigated – an indication of how profound a rift the Cold War had caused among the intelligentsia in Turkey.

In matters of love poetry, too, Yahya Kemal and Nâzım Hikmet followed different paths. The socialist poet, after his initial futurist phase, had explored ways of fusing modernist poetry with the folk tradition and the subversion of the ideological discourse of the classical tradition, for example, in his much underrated *Simavne Kadısı Oğlu Şeyh Bedrettin Destanı* (*The Epic of Sheikh Bedrettin, Son of the Qadi of Simavne*, 1936) and his *Rubailer* (*Quatrains*, published posthumously in 1966), thus pursuing an exploration into the nature of modern Turkish poetry, not unlike Yahya Kemal, but reaching a different conclusion and proposing a path which was poles apart. Hikmet's take on the theme of love was to be in clear contradistinction to the neo-classical poet's.[29] During an initial phase the young socialist poet questioned the legitimacy of love poetry in the revolutionary struggle. Unsurprisingly the figure of the beloved, if ever mentioned, appears as an obstacle to the realization of the political struggle of the poet. Her petty bourgeois aspirations in poems such as 'Mavi Gözlü Dev ile Minnacık Kadın ve Hanımelleri' (*The Blue-Eyed Giant, the Tiny Woman and* the Honeysuckles)[30] and 'Gövdemdeki Kurt' (The Worm in my Body), turn her into little more than a 'worm nibbling its way into the poet's brain'.[31] Yet it is also during those years that Nâzım Hikmet writes some of his most interesting works, namely the futurist epics *Jokond ile Si-Ya-U* (*The Gioconda and Si-Ya-U*, 1929) and *Benerci Kendini Niçin Öldürdü* (*Why Did Banardjee Kill Himself*, 1932), long poems where motives of colonial literature are parodied and European women are emotionally conquered by Asian males. In the 1929 epic it is not an ordinary woman who is seduced by an Asian communist student; it is the Gioconda, one of the most powerful symbols of Western art, who succumbs to Si-Ya-U, questions her own identity, appropriates the ideal of her lover and ultimately is condemned to death for treachery by a French war tribunal in China and is executed.

Nâzım Hikmet's 1932 Indian epic is partially constructed around a complex love story between an Indian revolutionary and a British woman who turns out to be a spy. In this text the poet again challenges colonialist discourse by rejecting the emotional involvement between subaltern people and the colonizers not on racial and racist grounds, as in colonialist propaganda, but by focusing on the political consequences of such associations in the context of national liberation struggles. Undeniably, in those epics, just like in his shorter lyrics of the same period, the beloved, and women in general, cut a poor figure as they are represented either as obstacles to the concretization of the narrator's ideals or, as in the case of the Gioconda, who is transfigured by her love for Si-Ya-U, they reach revolutionary consciousness only under the guidance of a male activist.

This negative discourse was to change in the 1930s after the poet's encounter with Piraye, his muse. Heartbreakingly he loved and reinvented her in poetry mostly written from behind prison bars as he was jailed between 1938 and 1950. The fact that she had become his wife in 1935 was an event that was not irrelevant in the context of the history of Turkish love poetry. For the first time, a wife became the centre of love verses with strong autobiographical elements: domestic life and the everyday concerns of the lovers were introduced as a legitimate topics into Turkish love poetry. The poetics of ordinary life were being invented in those verses. Nâzım Hikmet, himself, was very conscious of the change which he had undergone and of his new attitude towards love poetry. In a letter to Memet Fuat, Piraye's son from an earlier marriage, he wrote:

> I was somehow sectarian in matters of content before I met your mother. For instance, I never wrote about love relationships between human beings. I was saved from this attitude by the creative influence of your mother. I love and appreciate a love poem, but a true love poem, as much as I love and appreciate a politically engaged poem.[32]

He started to explore a theme that was also dear to other socialist poets, such as Pablo Neruda, Louis Aragon and Paul Eluard: the idea that the love felt towards a fellow human being could be sublimated into love for humankind. The gist of this idea had already been expressed in the predicaments of the Gioconda and in earlier poems such as 'Kerem Gibi' (Like Kerem):[33]

> Let me turn into ashes
>   Like
>   Kerem

>   burning
>   and burning.
> If I don't burn
>   if you don't burn
>   if we don't burn
>   how
>   will
>   darkness
>   turn
>   into
>   light . . .

Nâzım Hikmet was referring to the legendary lover Kerem in the folk tale *Kerem ile Aslı*. The anguish of the lover Kerem, consumed by fire because he was unable to unbutton the dress of his beloved on the wedding night, becomes the anguish of the politically engaged poet who must be consumed by the passion to serve the people. The text was a foretaste of the evolution that Nâzım Hikmet's love verse and literary project would undergo as it appropriated elements of folk and classical poetry and combined them with modernist elements and a politically engaged discourse. In this text, individual human love turns into love for the whole of mankind. Moreover the possible mystical reading of the ancient epic has also been subverted, and the ultimate aim of the lover is not the union with God, but the union with the people. In a letter that he wrote to Pirâye from jail, Hikmet stressed that he believed that 'love felt towards an individual was not in opposition to love felt for the whole of mankind, that it was one and the same thing'.[34]

Some of the most powerful verses that he wrote on this *topos* of socialist love poetry were dedicated to Pirâye. Just like the French surrealist Paul Eluard, the Turkish poet too presented the loving couple in his poetry as the founding principle of a loving, peaceful and humane society. Individual love was strengthened by becoming universal:

> They've taken us prisoner,
> They've put us into jail
>   me inside the walls
>   you outside.
> But that is nothing
> The worst is when you carry
> consciously or not
> the prison inside yourself. . . .
> Most people are forced to live like this;
> honest, hard-working, good people
> worthy of being loved as much as I love you.[35]

The collection from which this poem is excerpted has an interesting history in itself. While imprisoned in Bursa jail in 1945, the poet decided to dedicate one hour of each day to writing poetry about and for his wife. The title of the collection was accordingly *Pirâyem İçin Saat 21-22 Şiirleri* (*Poems for my Pirâye Written between 9 and 10 pm*), published posthumously in 1965. In those verses Hikmet created a new image of the beloved who was a wife, a mistress, a confidante and a comrade. More importantly, perhaps, Pirâye as a poetic character was an independent person with her own needs and a life beyond her marriage. This new creation was facilitated by the fact that the poems for Pirâye had the particularity that their primary audience was the beloved herself. The poems were love letters in verse. They were either included in letters sent to her or they were sent in place of letters and they often discussed everyday life, reflecting a sincere concern for the well-being of the addressee:

Damn! Winter is hard . . .
Who knows how you are, you and my virtuous Istanbul?

Have you got coal?
Did you manage to buy firewood?
Stick some newspaper around the window panes.

Go to bed early.
There must be nothing left to sell at home.
To feel the cold, half hungry and half fed:
that's the lot of most of us,
in the world, in this city and country of ours.[36]

The concern for the beloved evolves into a feeling of solidarity for all the downtrodden. Love is a necessary step, a necessary experience, to understand the predicament of the rest of humanity. Such verses, however, were perhaps the first time that the beloved was depicted as a real human being in the verses of a Turkish poet and not as an ideal, an illusion or the incarnation of lofty principles.

Verses that he would write after his release from jail in 1950 and his breakup with Piraye would be of a different nature altogether. After his flight to the Soviet Union, his love poetry would identify the figure of the beloved – Münevver Andaç – with the motherland. These verses remain today among his most popular love poems. Later works, mostly written about Vera Tulyakova, whom he had met in 1956 and married four years later, reflect an almost adolescent passion for his young partner. Yet in the poems about Piraye, too, sexual desire was openly expressed. This was a daring approach in a staunchly conservative society since the real-life identity of the beloved was no secret. But talking about desire was also part of a wider ideological agenda challenging the metaphorical nature of the Islamic poetic traditions. Indeed his quatrains dedicated to Piraye aimed at 'conveying the essence of dialectic materialism with *rubâis*'. 'I am sure that I will be successful', he wrote to his wife, 'because what Mevlana did, relying on the love of God and taking strength from it, I will do with my faith in your love. I will do exactly the contrary of what he aimed at: I will go in search for reality.'[37] While the quatrains also referred to the concrete reality of the poet's life – his imprisonment and the impossibility to touch the beloved – the focus on the physical existence of the beloved beyond the poet's verses and imagination was also a way of promoting his materialist world view. Though the poetic I 'cannot lie down and embrace [her] image', he knows that her 'flesh and bones', 'the red mouth whose honey he is deprived of', her 'whiteness he cannot touch' continue to exist in the city.[38] Her 'lips are as real as the universe'[39] and the human beloved is not a mere metaphor, a gate to the divine love the mystics were longing for.

Desire, however, could also be felt for figures other than the beloved. While this was rarely the case in Hikmet's verses, the exploration of ordinary desire was to become more common in the love poetry of Orhan Veli, a contemporary of Nâzım Hikmet and the leader of the *Garip* movement. Whether the exploration of sexual desire, independent of love, in the poetry of Orhan Veli could solely be ascribed to French surrealist influence, as suggested by some critics, is open to discussion.[40] Veli's interest in the relationship between the subconscious and sexuality is not unique in the history of post-*Tanzimat* Turkish literature, as can be seen in Abdülhak Hamit's (Tarhan) controversial 1918 play *Finten*. Freudian psychoanalysis and Bergson's work on time and consciousness had also fascinated authors such as James Joyce and Marcel Proust, who were known and appreciated by the members of the *Garip* movement.

The *Garip* (Bizarre) movement, the first Turkish literary group with a manifesto and a clear literary agenda, was constituted by Orhan Veli, Melih Cevdet (Anday), Oktay Rifat (Horozcu) and rejected all poetic conventions. Their stance was radical: until now poetry had been addressing the tastes of the ruling class. This had to change and *Garip* advocated the refutation of the literary tradition, of rhyme and metre and of the poetic language. Their aim was to strip the language to its bare essentials and to focus on ordinary subjective experiences.[41] Their call for a radical new definition of poetry was reminiscent of similar movements in France in the first quarter of the twentieth century, such as Dadaism and surrealism. Unlike most of the surrealists who saw links between literary innovation and social revolution, *Garip* had no clear political agenda. Despite their open appreciation of surrealist poets, Orhan Veli was uneasy with critical references to French surrealist influence, as this suggested, in between the lines, a lack of authenticity. He addressed the question directly in a defensive footnote of the *Garip* manifesto:

> Some people call us surrealists when they write about us. This is probably because we talked a few times with appreciation of surrealism or maybe because they did not read the surrealists or our poems. However apart from a few shared views [. . .] we have absolutely nothing in common with the surrealists and we are certainly not linked to any literary school.[42]

Be that as it may, Veli's questioning of the supremacy of love and of its transformative power would have been a stance that Paul Eluard and André Breton, the author of *L'Amour fou* (*Mad Love*, 1937), would not have wanted to associate with. In Turkey, since the rediscovery of love as a legitimate theme of poetry, poets from Recaizade Mahmut Ekrem to Nâzım Hikmet had celebrated its power. It was an overwhelming feeling that could lead the lover to comprehend the meaning of true beauty, or it could evolve into a feeling of universal solidarity and brotherhood. The mystics too saw human love as a bridge leading to celestial love and the union with the divine beloved.

Rejecting tradition and the works of his contemporaries, Veli studied new ways of writing about love. Set in urban surroundings, a kick in the side to nationalist advocates of Anatolianism such as the Five Syllabists, he develops a love poetry which does not focus on love as an emotion or on the beloved, but he explores the context that gives rise to the emotion. Hence love is not an overwhelming powerful emotion, but it is the product of particular circumstances: in 'Güzel Havalar' (Lovely Weather),[43] for instance, he mentions the impact of the weather. The ordinariness of love is brought to the fore by referring to other events provoked in similar circumstances – the speaker's resignation from the civil service, his taking up smoking, his forgetfulness of ordinary tasks and indeed his poetic endeavours:

> This lovely weather has brought on my ruin.
> One fine day like this I quit
> My job with the Pious Foundations Agency.
> In such weather I got used to smoking
> And on a day like this I fell in love:
> It was on such a day that I forgot
> To take home bread and salt;
> Time and again, in this weather
> My verse-making disease has recurred.
> This lovely weather has brought on my ruin.[44]

The establishment of such lists, which is not without reminding of Jacques Prévert's inventories, is a strategy used by the poet to trivialize the theme. The opening verses of 'Yaşamak' (Life),[45] a poem that he wrote on his deathbed, suggest that singing about the beloved is a task that is just as hard to achieve as is experiencing several other ordinary daily pleasures – walking under the stars, warming up under the sun and escaping to Çamlıca Hill, a popular park in Üsküdar on the Asian side of Istanbul. Similarly, in 'Ölüme Yakın' (Close to Death),[46] women are mentioned as a passion among others, beside fame and money. Recaizade Mahmut Ekrem's celebration of women as the great inspiration behind works of art could not have been more distant, even though only half a century had passed since he brought about this monumental change in Turkish poetry. Juxtaposing love with other feelings and experiences, focusing on the atmosphere that gave rise to the feeling and with a characteristic dose of humour, Orhan Veli subordinated love and thus defied the tradition. Rather than rejecting the theme, representing love not as a unique feeling but as an ordinary emotion experienced by common men made it a legitimate theme in a poetry that strove to be radically different.

By decoupling love and desire, which in the poetry of Nâzım Hikmet had been directed at the wife, a revolutionary innovation in itself, Orhan Veli made of sexual desire, on its own, a theme of poetry. The protagonists in his love poetry were unusual and brought together a wide range of characters from working-class people to the Istanbul *bohemian* – poets, artists, singers and prostitutes. 'I love beautiful women', he wrote, 'and I love working-class women. But what I love most are beautiful working-class women.'[47] However detractors of the *Garip* movement were quick to point out that their interest with the margins of society was in contradiction with the populist agenda – poetry for the people and about the people – expressed in their manifesto.

The poetic I in Orhan Veli's verses, a *flâneur* who is not without similarities to the narrator in Sait Faik's short-stories, bridges the gap between the working class and the bohemians. The helplessness of the poetic I in the face of desire is a truly novel theme in the context of Turkish poetry, as in the poem 'Şoförün Karısı' (The Cabbie's Wife):[48]

Cabbie's wife, don't ruin me;
Don't wave to me like that from your window
Dressed so flimsily.
You are out to get your brother-in-law,
I'm out to enjoy my youth,
I don't want to rot in prison;
Don't get me into trouble;
Have pity on me.[49]

The poem, a short monologue addressed to a flirtatious woman, is written in colloquial Turkish, a language particularly suited to the depiction of a relationship between ordinary people. The inability of the poetic I to look away from the playful cabbie's wife, probably undressing in front of the window, and his fear of the consequences of a possible affair (adultery was a criminal offence in Turkey in those years), is representative of the passive personality of Veli's *flâneur*. It is striking that it is not love felt for the woman in the window that makes him look at her, but her waving at him, dressed 'flimsily'. Hence, desire is not part of a loving relationship, but it is the product of circumstances – here a scantily dressed woman.

Similarly in his 1946 'Sere Serpe' (Nonchalantly) too,[50] social conventions are no obstacle to sexual desire. The poetic I observes a woman sleeping in a nonchalant manner and is unable to cope with his growing desire. Rather than looking away, he blames her, with the characteristic passivity of Orhan Veli's ordinary man.

She lied down, nonchalantly;
Her dress is pulled down, slightly
Her arm, raised; her armpit shows
She's holding her breast
She's no bad intentions, I know
No, neither have I, but . . .
Come on!
One shouldn't lie like that!

But, perhaps, more than the evocation of desire and the contextualization of love, it is Veli's humour that subverts the sanctity of love. Orhan Veli launched occasional ironic attacks on the very concept of love poetry. In the poem 'İş Olsun Diye' (Just for the Hell of It),[51] he claims to have written all his love poems 'just for the hell of it' even though

All the pretty women thought
The poems I wrote on love
Were meant for them.[52]

Veli's blend of sarcasm and melancholy was used here to undermine the commonly held assumption that love and poetry were closely linked. In 'Ben Orhan Veli' (I'm Orhan Veli),[53] he goes one step further by attacking literary scholars and challenging them to discover the real name of his beloved. The irony in those two poems reflects Orhan Veli's wish to confront traditional conceptions of love poetry and the critic's quest for biographical background. And yet, his poetry did not escape certain *topoi* of love poetry when he evoked his inability to write when in love as, for instance, in 'İstanbul İçin' (For Istanbul).⁵⁴ The idea that love is stronger than words is, of course, a well-worn cliché of world poetry. The theme is reiterated in the poem 'Şaheserim' (My Masterwork),⁵⁵ where the narrator again underlines that he is not used to writing poetry when in love. Nevertheless, in the more general context of his love poetry, it could be argued that this admission to his inability to write love poetry, when in love, could be interpreted as an ironic attack against both the literary tradition and much of contemporary, vaguely confessional or autobiographical poetry that celebrated love. The ground had been cleared for a new revolution: the emergence of the *Second Renewal* and the celebration of desire in the poetry of Cemal Süreya.

Though the name of the grouping *İkinci Yeni* (*Second Renewal*) might lead to the assumption that they were a literary movement with a well-defined agenda, this would be erroneous. In a programme on Turkish state television in 1988, Cemal Süreya reminisced on the emergence of this literary trend:

> In the years between 1953 and 1957, a group of young poets started to publish poems of a new type in magazines and they influenced each other. In those days poetry was too rationalist. The new poets brought an irrational element into poetry. Linear story-telling was excluded from poetry. Emphasis was put on sound and a search for internal harmony started. The horizons of poetry had to be broadened.⁵⁶

This was an adequate description. *İkinci Yeni* poetry was characterized by the rejection of linear narration and its focus on individual verses rather than the poem as a whole – in some ways a return to the structure of classical poetry based on the *beyit*. Language was not a tool for the poets; but it was the context in which they worked, the essence of literature. The term *İkinci Yeni* had been coined by the poet and critic İlhan Erdost in 1956 to describe these poets who rejected both what they saw as the lack of intellectual and aesthetic depth of much of post-*Garip* poetry, and the slogan-like verses of socialist realist poets. Süreya was only one among a group of poets who went in search of new poetic paths in the early 1950s. Many of them would mark the history of twentieth-century Turkish poetry such as Edip Cansever, Sezai Karakoç, Hilmi Yavuz and Gülten Akın. Their modernist outlook attracted much criticism, the socialist Atillâ İlhan calling their poetry a 'circus of meaninglessness',⁵⁷ the Islamist Rasım Özdenören denouncing their 'absolute estrangement to their own civilization and people'.⁵⁸ Other critics were quick to point out a possible surrealist influence and lack of authenticity, a charge rejected by Süreya, who argued that they were not aware of surrealism as a movement – a statement which beggars belief – but that surrealist elements could always be found in poetry throughout the ages.⁵⁹

While Süreya rejected the slogan-like poetry of some socialists, his own engagement on the socialist left forced him to discuss time and again the relation between poetics and politics. The fact that much of his poetry dealt with the theme of sexual desire and love played a central role in the legitimization of his literary endeavours: Süreya, who defined his poetry as erotic,⁶⁰ argued that erotica could be, in political terms, a progressive form of artistic expression. Indeed, he maintained that 'erotic art was an attempt to change the world'.⁶¹ Though vague on the changes that he implied, it seems that he was pointing to the societal taboos regarding sexuality in Turkey and gender segregation in traditional society. Hence the autonomization of desire in his poetry and indeed the eroticization of the beloved were ways of challenging the societal status-quo. Nonetheless, some of his verses espoused the socialist and surrealist principle that the love of two human beings was the founding stone of a more humane and solidary society, a challenge to dehumanizing oppression. But love, in Süreya's verses, is not limited to words, it is an act:

> Because whenever I kiss her mouth
> The more so, if it is your mouth,
> A huge rose grows behind us
> A challenge to oppression.[62]

Notably, the poetic I kisses also mouths other than the beloved's. While it is the embrace with the beloved which is more likely to engender the rose, transformed from a symbol of mystic love into a symbol of resistance, the libertine nature of the speaker subverts not only conservative mores but also the prudishness of the Turkish left. Süreya's revolution is not only erotic, but it is also humorous. While it can be argued that Nâzım Hikmet's defiance of social norms was that he caressed his wife in public verses, Süreya's subversion resides in his chanting love outside marital bonds. Within the socialist left in Turkey, many raised angry eyebrows at Süreya's poetic libertinage. To a point this was understandable. While communists were regularly accused of promoting a communal lifestyle, including the communal sharing of spouses, by the conservative and anti-communist populist media, with dire consequences for the wives and companions of political prisoners, the adoption of a moralistic discourse on love and sexuality was a natural response. Moreover, facts such as the ban in the Soviet Union of Alexandra Kollontaï's writings on love or the ignorance about Rosa Luxemburg's passionate letters to Leo Jogisches caused Marxists in Turkey to be largely unaware of a corpus of texts, anchored within the socialist tradition, that promoted love in a way that challenged soviet-type patriarchy. It should be noted that some of Nâzım Hikmet's love poems could have been added to those texts, and they too remained largely unknown in the Republic of Turkey before the 1960s because of censorship and repression.[63]

But it would be an oversimplification to claim that Süreya only wrote about sexual love outside marriage. Indeed, some of his most radical verses were focused on the marital bed, much more openly than Hikmet could have ever dared:

> Of my wife, her abdomen and her front
> Of my whore, her sides and her back
> All of these, all of these, all of these,
> How could I forget, I never did.[64]

The association of wife and whore is a step beyond what Hikmet could have imagined in his own attempt to depict the autonomy and complexity of the beloved as wife, lover, friend and comrade. Like Hikmet, Süreya incorporates desire into the depiction of a holistic relationship, like in the poem 'Sayım'[65], written at a time when he had abandoned many of the principles of İkinci Yeni's modernist stance. The poem describes the evolution of a relationship through the nature of kisses: a kiss on the wrist in the moonlight, a kiss on the lips, a kiss 'of the breath' in a doorway and a kiss on the groin in bed. These kisses that could also represent various stages of erotic foreplay are, however, accompanied by other kisses that indicate the deepening of the relationship between the poetic I and the beloved and partly reveal her identity: he kisses her child, indicating that she might be a single mother, he kisses her marrow 'in various houses', perhaps a reference to their publicly assuming their relationship and their emotional closeness, and finally he kisses her source, namely the street – a clear indication that the beloved is a woman from the real world:

> We were sitting in the moonlight
> I kissed your wrist
> Then I kissed you standing
> I kissed your lips
> I kissed you in the doorway
> I kissed your breath
> I took you home in my bed
> I kissed your groin
> We met in other houses
> I kissed your marrow
> In the end I took you to the streets
> I kissed your source

Following into the footsteps of Orhan Veli, but with more consistency, Cemal Süreya focused on women who were often denigrated by society: unfaithful wives, divorced women, single mothers and prostitutes. Even stripteasers could take the centre stage in his verses:

> Accompanied by a piano
> Quite close by
> With temper and passion
> She discards her clothes
> There is a 'si'
>   Here is a 'la'
>   sol
>   fa
>   mi
>   re
>   and dooo![66]

The closeness in sound between the musical note 'do' and 'don', the Turkish word for underpants leave little doubt as to the state of undress in which the stripteaser ends her performance. It would be wrong to believe that Cemal Süreya is trying to rehabilitate or to normalize the situation of marginalized women in Turkish society. His aim is different. By making them the focus of his love poetry he wishes to delegitimize the norms of society. Whether he does not perpetuate patriarchal clichés is open to debate, and he himself is conscious that his poetry is open to criticism from that point of view, hence his occasional reference to his wish to write poetry from a female perspective.[67] A reading of his journalistic writings and essays clearly indicates that he aims at questioning such stereotypes and transforming society by problematizing its attitude towards sexuality. Ultimately he argues that both 'poetry and love are illegal. Both end once legalized'.[68] Uttered in 1987, a few months after the publication of his *Complete Poems*, these words were a reflection on his work, on the two areas of struggle that he had focused on.

Thirty years earlier when he had published his first poetry collection, these words would have resounded with a very special meaning. Indeed, Nazım Hikmet's poetry, including his love verses, was still illegal. Yahya Kemal's neo-classical explorations in the Ottoman literary heritage, though now appropriated by the Turkish conservatives and religious nationalists, and indeed the Democratic Party government, the great victor of Turkish multipartyism in the 1950s, incarnated a cultural ideal in clear contradiction to Mustafa Kemal Atatürk's project. Orhan Veli, on the other hand, though arguably promoted in the 1930s and 1940s by Nurullah Ataç, the official literary critic of the İnönü regime, explored themes that would have estranged the largely rural and pious population of Turkey. Sezai Karakoç, an Islamist poet, with roots in the *İkinci Yeni* movement pointed out that Veli's depiction of impoverished milk- and *simit*-sellers lacked sensitivity and authenticity. They were, he argued, the fantasies and fancies of a bourgeois boy.[69]

Each of those poets was crossing lines, challenging the official legality or the wished-for legalities of others. The history of Turkish poetry is also a history of the clashes and conflicts that have shaped republican Turkish history. Aesthetic questions, such as the choice of metre, were eminently political. The *aruz* prosody promoted by Yahya Kemal had been condemned as 'foreign' by nationalist theoreticians, and most prominently by Ziya Gökalp, one of the founding fathers of Turkish nationalism. The free verse which Hikmet, Veli and Süreya championed had been denounced by a practitioner of neo-folk poetry supported by the nationalists as 'a meter cut into slices by the fingers of surgeons', the content of the poems as 'delirious nonsense tainted by the redness of a bloody world',[70] the redness being a not-too-subtle reference to the political sympathies of most, but certainly not all, free verse poets. Perhaps nowhere more than in love poetry this conflictual dynamic came to the fore: in the changing representation of the beloved and the changing emphasis on love and sexual desire. Yet it would be wrong to reduce the poetic landscape of the Republic of Turkey to the four figures studied in this chapter. From the mystical surrealism of Asaf Halet Çelebi to the syllabist poetry of Faruk Nafız Çamlıbel, from Bedri Rahmi Eyuboğlu's Anatolianism to Cahit Tarancı's subjective realism and indeed the neo-mystic poetry of the likes of Necip Fazıl Kısakürek and Sezai Karakoç, there were many other paths explored, a token of the diversity and pluralism existing within the Turkish literary world in the middle of the twentieth century. At a time when literary critics tend to depoliticize the history of literature and gloss over the nature of the conflicts that have shaped it – the reinvention of a depoliticized Nâzım Hikmet as the 'poet of Turkey' being a case in point, or to refer to the existence of an essential Turkishness that connects all of Turkish poetry beyond ideology and class – it is important to remember that Yahya Kemal's Canân dreamed of a world that was very different from the struggle of Nâzım Hikmet's Pirâye, that Orhan Veli's and Cemal Süreya's women would have been shunned by many of Yahya Kemal's readers. And indeed, things were to change even more. The apparition of Cemal Süreya on the literary scene was in itself indicative of a novelty. His family had been deported to Western Turkey in the aftermath of the Dersim massacres in 1937. Yet he was the carrier of an

Eastern sensitivity that questioned the oversimplified visions of Anatolia and Turkey in the works of the poets from Istanbul and other Western cities, a phenomenon that would gain more prominence in the years to come. The partly Kurdish East was writing back to the centre. Women too were to become much more present on the poetic scene, after the 1980s, openly challenging the patriarchal status-quo still very present even in the most avant-garde love poetry. Homoerotic love, after having been banned from poetry as a 'byzantine emotion', was to reappear, openly and self-consciously in the late 1980s. The beloved and the meaning of love were to take new forms again in new attempts to reinvent poetry and through poetry, the world.

Notes

1. The following chapter is partly based on findings of my 2002 PhD, *The Beloved Unveiled: Continuity and Change in Modern Turkish Love Poetry*, School of Oriental and African Studies, University of London, 2002 and published in my monograph *Çağdaş Türk Şiirinde Aşk, Aşıklar, Mekânlar* (Ankara: Hece, 2002).
2. Alessio Bombaci, *Storia della letteratura turca: Dall'antico impero di Mongolia all'odierna Turchia*, 2nd edn (Milano: Nuova Accademia Editrice, 1962), 291.
3. Namık Kemal, 'Murabba', in *Batı Tesirinde Türk Şiiri Antolojisi*, ed. Kenan Akyüz, 5th edn (Istanbul: İnkılâp Kitabevi, n.d.), 69.
4. For English-language sources on the emergence of the Turkish novel, see Robert Finn, *The Early Turkish Novel 1872–1900* (Istanbul: The Isis Press, 1984); Ahmet Evin, *Origins and Development of the Turkish Novel* (Minneapolis: Indiana University Press, 1983). See also Azade Seyhan, *Tales of Crossed Destinies: The Modern Turkish Novel in a Comparative Context* (New York: The Modern Language Association, 2008), 23–40.
5. Quoted by Akyüz, *Batı Tesirinde Türk Şiiri Antolojisi*, 84.
6. Akyüz, *Batı Tesirinde Türk Şiiri Antolojisi*, 84. On the homoerotic nature of classical Ottoman poetry, see, *i.a.*, Walter Andrews and Mehmet Kalpaklı, *The Age of Beloveds: Love and the Beloved in Early Modern Ottoman and European Culture and Society* (Durham and London: Duke University Press, 2005).
7. Ömer Seyfeddin, 'Yeni Lisan', in *Genç Kalemler Dergisi*, ed. İ. Parlatır and N. Çetin (Ankara: Türk Dil Kurumu, 1999), 76.
8. Ahmet Haşim, 'Şeb-i Muhayyel', in *Bütün Şiirleri* (Istanbul: Gözlem Yayınları, 1997), 66 and 'Şimdi', *Bütün Şiirleri*, 84.
9. 'Şeb-i Muhayyel', 68.
10. For sources in English on modern Turkish poetry see, Orhan Koçak, '"Our Master, the Novice": On the Catastrophic Births of Modern Turkish Poetry', *The South Atlantic Quarterly* 102, nos. 2–3 (2003): 567–98; Murat Nemet-Nejat, 'A Godless Sufism: Ideas on Twentieth Century Turkish Poetry', in *Eda: An Anthology of Modern Turkish Poetry* (Jersey City: Talisman House Publishers, 2004), 323–33; Güven Turan, 'The Adventure of Modernism in Turkish Poetry', *Agenda* 38 (2002): 3–4; Talat S. Halman, 'Poetry and Society: Propaganda Functions of Poetry in The Turkish Experience', in *Rapture and Revolution: Essays on Turkish Literature* (New York: Syracuse University Press, 2007), 154–90; Walter Andrews and Laurent Mignon, 'Ottoman, Azeri and Modern Turkish Poetry', in *The New Princeton Encyclopedia of Poetry and Poetics*, ed. Roland Green, et al. (Princeton, NJ: Princeton University Press, 2012), 1471–4.
11. For biographical studies of Yahya Kemal Beyatlı, see, *i.a*, Ahmet Hamdi Tanpınar, *Yahya Kemal*, 6th edn (Istanbul: Dergâh Yayınları, 2006); and Sermet Sâmi Uysal, *Şiire Adanmış bir Hayat: Yahya Kemal Beyatlı* (Istanbul: Yahya Kemal'i Sevenler Derneği, 1998).

12 For biographies in English on Nâzım Hikmet, see Mutlu Konuk Blasing, *Nâzim Hikmet: The Life and Times of Turkey's World Poet* (New York: Persea Books, 2013); and Saime Göksu and Edward Timms, *Romantic Communist: the Life and Work of Nazım Hikmet*, 6th edn (London: Hurst & Company, 2006).
13 For a study of the *Garip* movement, see Hakan Sazyek, *Cumhuriyet Dönemi Türk Şiirinde Garip Hareketi*, 2nd edn (Ankara: Türkiye İş Bankası Kültür Yayınları, 1999). On Orhan Veli, see Memet Fuat, *Orhan Veli* (Istanbul: Adam Yayınları, 2000); Semih Gümüş (ed.), *Orhan Veli Kanık* (Ankara: T.C. Turizm ve Kültür Bakanlığı Yayınları, 2011).
14 On Cemal Süreya, see Nursel Duruel and Feyza Perinçek, *Cemal Süreya: Şairin Hayatı Şiire Dahil* (Istanbul: Can Yayınları, 2008); Doğan Hızlan (ed.), *Cemal Süreya* (Ankara: T.C. Turizm ve Kültür Bakanlığı Yayınları, 2011).
15 Quoted in a letter to Ruşen Eşref Ünaydın, in Ruşen Eşref, *Diyorlar Ki* (Istanbul: Kanaat Maatbası, 1334, [1918]), 124.
16 Yahya Kemal, *Edebiyâta Dair*, 4th edn (Istanbul: Istanbul Fetih Cemiyeti, 1997), 48.
17 Beşir Ayvazoğlu, *Peyami: Hayatı, Sanatı, Felsefesi, Dramı* (Istanbul: Ötüken Neşriyat, 1998), 95–8.
18 Yahya Kemal, 'Şarkı', in *Eski Şiirin Rüzgâriyle*, 5th edn (Istanbul: Istanbul Fetih Cemiyeti, 1993), 120.
19 Yahya Kemal, 'Geçmiş Yaz', in *Kendi Gök Kubbemiz*, 12th edn (Istanbul: Istanbul Fetih Cemiyeti, 1999), 138.
20 Kemal, 'Moda'da Mayıs', in *Kendi Gök Kubbemiz*, 102.
21 Kemal, 'İstanbul'un o Yerleri', in *Kendi Gök Kubbemiz*, 73.
22 Kemal, 'Vuslat', in *Kendi Gök Kubbemiz*, 128.
23 For a comprehensive list of those attributes, see Kemal Sılay, *Nedim and the Poetics of the Ottoman Court* (Bloomington: Indiana University, 1994), 35–7.
24 Kemal, 'Ric'at', in *Kendi Gök Kubbemiz*, 152.
25 Kemal, 'Telâki', in *Kendi Gök Kubbemiz*, 130.
26 Kemal, 'Mihriyar', in *Kendi Gök Kubbemiz*, 71 and 'Bir Tepeden', in *Kendi Gök Kubbemiz*, 20.
27 Beşir Ayvazoğlu, *Yahya Kemal: Eve Dönen Adam* (Istanbul: Ötüken Neşriyat, 1996), 128.
28 Ibid., 126–7.
29 The following discussion of Nâzım Hikmet's love poetry is based on my article 'Venger Aziyadé', in *Regards sur la poésie du 20ème siècle*, ed. Laurent Fels (Namur: Presses Universitaires de Namur, 2009), 251–70.
30 Nâzım Hikmet, 'Mavi Gözlü Dev ile Minnacık Kadın ve Hanımelleri', in *Bütün Şiirleri*, 3rd edn (Istanbul: Yapı Kredi Yayınları, 2007), 356.
31 Hikmet, 'Gövdemdeki Kurt', in *Bütün Şiirleri*, 44.
32 Nâzım Hikmet, *Oğlum, Canım, Memedim: Mektuplar*, ed. Mehmet Fuat (Istanbul: De, 1968), 88.
33 Hikmet, 'Kerem Gibi', in *Bütün Şiirleri*, 204–5.
34 Nâzım Hikmet, *Nâzım ile Pirâye*, ed. Memet Fuat, 2nd edn (Istanbul: De Yayınları, 1976), 235.
35 Hikmet, '26 Eylül 1945', in *Bütün Şiirleri*, 623.
36 Hikmet, '14 Aralık 1945', in *Bütün Şiirleri*, 638.
37 Hikmet, *Nâzım ile Pirâye*, 235.
38 Hikmet, 'Rubailer', in *Bütün Şiirleri*, 733.
39 Ibid.
40 Şükran Kurdakul, 'Orhan Veli Kanık', in *Çağdaş Türk Edebiyatı 3: Cumhuriyet Dönemi 1 Şiir*, 2nd edn (Ankara: Bilgi Yayınevi, 1994), 189–90.
41 Orhan Veli, 'Garip', in *Bütün Şiirleri*, 38th edn (Istanbul: Adam Yayınları, 1999), 23–36.
42 Veli, 'Garip', in *Bütün Şiirleri*, 33.
43 Veli, 'Güzel Havalar', in *Bütün Şiirleri*, 53.

44 Translated by Talat Sait Halman in *Just for the Hell of It: 111 Poems by Orhan Veli Kanık* (Istanbul: Multilingual, 1997), 66.
45 Veli, 'Yaşamak', in *Bütün Şiirleri*, 133.
46 Veli, 'Ölüme Yakın', in *Bütün Şiirleri*, 89.
47 Veli, 'Quantitatif', in *Bütün Şiirleri*, 193.
48 Veli, 'Şoförün Karısı', in *Bütün Şiirleri*, 44.
49 Translated by Talat Sait Halman in Halman, *Just for the Hell of It*, 46.
50 Veli, 'Sere Serpe', in *Bütün Şiirleri*, 91.
51 Veli, 'İş Olsun Diye', in *Bütün Şiirleri*, 189.
52 Translated by Talat Sait Halman in Halman, *Just for the Hell of It*, 25.
53 Veli, 'Ben Orhan Veli', in *Bütün Şiirleri*, 194–5.
54 Veli, 'İstanbul İçin', in *Bütün Şiirleri*, 51.
55 Veli, 'Şaheserim', in *Bütün Şiirleri*, 207.
56 Cemal Süreya, *Güvercin Curnatası*, ed. Nursel Duruel (Istanbul: Yapı Kredi Yayınları, 1997), 174.
57 Feyza Perinçek and Nursel Duruel, *Cemal Süreya: Şairin Hayatı Şiire Dâhil* (Istanbul: Kaynak, 1995), 128.
58 Quoted by Turan Karataş, *Doğu'nun Yedinci Oğlu: Sezai Karakoç* (İstanbul: Kaknüs, 1998), 240.
59 Cemal Süreya, *Toplu Yazılar I* (Istanbul: Yapı Kredi Yayınları 2000), 419.
60 Süreya, *Güvercin Curnatası*, 27.
61 Ibid., 96.
62 Cemal Süreya, 'İngiliz', 20.
63 See, *i.a.*, Emin Karaca, *Nâzım Hikmet'in Aşkları*, 2nd edn (Istanbul: Gendaş, 1999), 169–81.
64 Cemal Süreya, 'Ülke', in *Sevda Sözleri*, 48.
65 Cemal Süreya, 'Sayım', in *Sevda Sözleri*, 119.
66 Cemal Süreya, 'Striptiz', in *Sevda Sözleri*, 157.
67 Süreya, *Güvercin Curnatası*, 65 and 201.
68 Ibid., 87.
69 Sezai Karakoç, *Edebiyat Yazıları II* (Istanbul: Diriliş Yayınları,1986), 51.
70 Quoted in Kurdakul, 'Orhan Veli Kanık', 3.

Chapter 8

LOVE, BELOVED AND ADORER

KURDISH *GHAZAL* POETRY IN THE NINETEENTH CENTURY AS A SPACE FOR MORAL PROTEST

Mariwan Kanie

Introduction

Love is the main theme of the Kurdish *ghazal* (love) poetry. Until the end of the nineteenth century, this form of poetry was the dominant form of literature that was written in Kurdish. Every Kurdish poet who wanted to write about love wrote *ghazal* poetry. Love in *ghazal* poetry is constructed as a strong and uncontrollable emotion connected to deep suffering, pain and patience. Difficult and unattainable, love is always in the process of developing, and the lover is in the process of falling in love, a stage of profound feelings in which the lover is careless for the social, cultural and religious taboos. Love is a heroic act; it is a strong protest against everything that works against it.

Although the description of the beloved's beauty is at the core of this poetry, the beloved's unfaithfulness, cruelty and indifference are also strongly present as the other side of the coin. The painful experience of the lover, his feeling of being deserted and the grief of being separated from the beloved form other important aspects in *ghazal* poetry. Love in *ghazal* poetry is also naked; both hetero and homosexual love, in which the body is celebrated as an erotic entity and as a space of sensuality, are celebrated.

This chapter will focus on the different conceptualization of love in Kurdish *ghazal* poetry in the nineteenth century. The article distinguishes between three main components of the Kurdish love poetry, namely *'ashiq* (lover or adorer), *ma'shuq* (beloved) and *'ishq* (love), and elaborates on these concepts in the works of three Kurdish poets of the nineteenth century, Nali (1797–1855), Salim (1800–66) and Kurdi (1809–49).

Short history of ghazal *poetry: From Bedouin poetry to a genre without borders*

Ghazal means 'talking to a woman about love';[1] it also means relating tenderly to a woman: the male in *ghazal* poetry is someone who is captivated and fascinated by women and speaks in a manner that pleases them.[2] The structure of the *ghazal* poem is usually seven double sentences with the same rhythm. The language is elegant, metaphoric and elitist. The poet often reveals his name in the last sentence, usually in *takhallus* (pen name or artistic name).

As a literary genre, *ghazal* has a long history and is regarded as one of the most successful literary genres in world literature.[3] Its emergence dates back to pre-Islamic Bedouin poetry in the Arab peninsula. *Ghazal* was known then as songs sung by minstrels and expressed the secular emotion of the longing for a heartless and cruel beloved, erotic feelings and the readiness of the lover to make sacrifices for the beloved. In the beginning stages, the literary and cultural status of this genre was so low that there was barely any mention of *ghazal* poetry as a specific genre.[4] But from the twelfth century onwards, *ghazal* was 'firmly established as the most important Persian lyrical form,[5] after it had gained prominence in Persia and was adopted by the Sufis. The appreciation for *ghazal* poetry went hand in hand with the growing interest of the Sufis in love poetry in the twelfth century and the adoptability of *ghazal* poetry to express the mystical love between God and the Sufis. In this spiritual love God became the beloved and the Sufis the adorers prepared to sacrifice everything to meet the beloved. Similar to *ghazal* poetry, love became the main theme in the life of the Sufis, and thus in Sufi poetry. Love is even seen as the fundamental experience of the Sufis, and they expect their souls to be purified through love.[6]

The influence of *ghazal* poetry on Sufi poetry remained significant while the Sufi poetry developed the genre further and distinguished three main forms of love.[7] The first form is natural, physical and secular love. This is the love as experienced by ordinary people. This form of love is corporeal and belongs to the experience of individuals who are physically attracted to each other. Instinctive and biological needs, and the urge towards bodily and sexual pleasure, are the flipside of this love. In Sufism this form of love has a lower status and is just above 'animal bohemianism'.[8] The second form of love is spiritual love. This type of love is related to the *khassa* (the elite). Spiritual love contains moments of physical, natural love but in its essence transcends this physical dimension by adding a strong mystical aspect to it. In spiritual love the soul, as well as the body, or the internal beauty and corporal attractiveness are connected, but in the end love rises beyond the instinctive and biological urges into a spiritual realm.[9] The third form of love is God-like or divine love. This form of love is to be compared with the love of God for the world and the love of the Sufi for God. It is higher than the two other forms of love. Divine love is total love; it contains the two other forms of love, while it transcends them and takes the divine form. The divine love is reserved only to the elite of the elite, for the Sufis who reach the apex of the spiritual development. Sufism contains 'a body of teachings and practices designed to help seekers of God experience the transformation of their own souls. The goal is conformity with the divine qualities that God instilled into human beings when he created them in his own image.'[10] Sufis seek unity with God through divine love, and it allows the Sufis to claim the presence of divinity themselves.[11]

When Sufis started writing poetry, they adopted various elements and forms of *ghazal* poetry in a manner that sometimes made it difficult to differentiate Sufi poetry from *ghazal* poetry.[12] In Sufi poetry secular and religious elements are intertwined, and the function of Sufi poetry is to catch the spiritual experience in a material form, to make the spiritual experience tangible in written words, poetic compositions and images. *Ghazal* poetry offered this opportunity.

After its interaction with Sufi poetry, *ghazal* poetry emigrated in the following centuries and now 'is spread over a vast geographical space of multiple literary languages: from Arabic it migrated via Persian into Turkish and the languages of India, in Spain into Hebrew via Arabic and, finally, transmitted via Persian models, it even emerged in the poetic canon of German literature.'[13] One can even speak of the existence of a literary sphere throughout the Ottoman Empire, Iran and India from the sixteenth century. Persian was the language of poetry not only in what is now known as Iran, Afghanistan and Tajikistan but also in other parts of the Indian subcontinent, Central Asia and Turkey.[14]

The influence of *ghazal* poetry through al-Andalus on the *troubadour* poetry of the Middle Ages in Spain is evident, and the Arabic *ghazal* poetry in al-Andalus helped 'troubadour poetry see light of day'.[15] In short, *ghazal* poetry crossed the borders of countries, languages, religions and cultures, and in the nineteenth century it spread to Germany, where Goethe began writing *ghazal* poetry and introduced it to European literature.[16] *Ghazal* poetry is used in the West to express 'highly personal experience', especially the sexual and erotic-related feelings 'which was otherwise prohibited by the repressive sexual morality of the Christian West'.[17] This continuous emigration of *ghazal* poetry is a marked example of literary interaction between various parts of the world in the nineteenth century and in the centuries prior to that. *Ghazal* poetry can thus be seen as an important global binding force in the first half of the nineteenth century.

The landscape of Kurdish ghazal *poetry in the ninetieth century*

Kurdish *ghazal* poetry is part of this universal literary phenomenon and interacts in the first place with the *ghazal* poetry written in Persian, Arabic and Turkish. Classic Kurdish poets commanded these languages and frequently wrote ghazal poetry in them. Due to similarities between Kurdish and Persian, Kurdish *ghazal* poetry was influenced more by the Persian *ghazal* poetry than Turkish or Arabic. The work of Persian poets such as Nizami (1141–1203), Rumi (1207–73), Hafiz (d.1390), Sa'di (d. 1292 or 1294) and Jami (1414–92) formed the main source of inspiration for Kurdish poets from the sixteenth century onwards. These Persian poets were cultural icons in classical Islamic literature and had a huge influence on the literary history of the whole region. When one reads nineteenth-century Kurdish *ghazal* poetry, references to those Persian poets will be found in the work of many Kurdish poets. The manuscripts of these poets were found in the Ottoman Empire and in India, and their poems were part of the curriculum of Kurdish religious schools in the Ottoman Empire and Iran.

As previously mentioned, the important names in the Kurdish literary landscape in the first half of the nineteenth century were Nali (1797–1855), Salim (1800–66) and Kurdi (1809–49). These poets belonged to the aristocratic and cultural elite of the Baban principality in the province of Suleimaniya in contemporary northern Iraq.[18] Despite the fact that these poets were not Sufis, their intellectual universe was formed by their religious education, in which studying and memorizing Sufi poetry played an important role.[19] The fact that these poets were not Sufis marks in itself a transformation in the development of Kurdish literature. Earlier Kurdish poets such as Jaziri (1570–1640), Besarani (1642–1701), Khani (1650–1707), Mewlawi (1806–82) and others were all Sufis.

It is important to underline that the language in which Nali, Salim and Kurdi wrote their *ghazal* poetry is complex, multilayered and elitist, with many Arabic and Persian words. Using such a complex language was not only a sign of the poet's breadth of knowledge but also that he was brought up in the elite culture of his time.[20] Poets regularly also referred to passages and events from the Quran and the Islamic tradition in their work. Thus, Kurdish *ghazal* poetry was mostly inaccessible to readers with limited knowledge of the Quran and Islamic tradition. This complexity of Kurdish *ghazal* poetry could be seen as the literary strategy to secure the elitist character of this poetry and its connection to the aristocratic sphere. Kurdish *ghazal* poetry belonged to high culture and was supposed to be protected from other forms of cultural non-elitist expressions, such as oral literature.

As I said earlier, the influence of Sufi poetry on *ghazal* poetry, including Kurdish *ghazal* poetry, of the nineteenth century is prominent. However, this does not mean that Kurdish *ghazal* poetry of that century is a repetition of Sufi poetry. The three Kurdish poets mentioned here were not Sufis, and what they wrote about love was not Sufi love. The experience of love in the work of Nali, Salim and Kurdi could be related to the first two forms of love that are already mentioned, namely the biological and spiritual love. Nali, Salim and Kurdi did not seek God in their poetry, and God is not the subject of their love; they rather sought the other two forms of love, the earthly and the spiritual. Love in their poetry is human love and the beloved is often, though not always, a woman. In the case of Kurdi, his beloved was a young boy called Qadir and his love poetry has a strong homosexual dimension. In the coming pages I will elaborate further on the homosexual dimension of love in the poetry of Kurdi. However, the poets did use the language, metaphors, imagery and symbolism of Sufi poetry and transformed it to catch the secular emotions of love. This means that the experience of love in the Kurdish *ghazal* poetry in the nineteenth century has a stronger secular dimension compared to Sufi poetry, while a spiritual interpretation of the experience of love in this poetry is still possible.

Let us look at the three important components of the Kurdish *ghazal* poetry in the nineteen century, namely *'ishq* (love), *'ashiq* (adorer) and *ma'shuq* (beloved), and see how these components are constructed and what meanings and characters are attributed to them.

'Ishq: Love

Lexicographers show us that the word *'ishq* goes together with the word *al-'ashaqa*, which is a kind of climbing plant that encircles objects near it.[21] In Kurdish *ghazal* poetry, the same Arabic word is used to express love. The metaphor of the climbing plant for love means that love encircles the whole existence of the adorer: 'Love encircles the *'ashiq* (the adorer) until all parts of his body are covered.'[22] In this sense *'ishq* is more than just normal love; as Ibn al-'Arabi mentions, *'ishq* is *ifrat al-mahabba*, the extravagant or extreme love.[23] To call love *'ishq* would mean that the love must develop itself to something higher than the normal feeling of being attached to someone; in *'ishq* the adorer is completely obsessed with love, sees the beloved everywhere and reduces the world to only the beloved. *'Ishq* contains then the two forms of love which are already mentioned, the corporal and spiritual love alike. In Kurdish *ghazal* poetry of the nineteenth century, this extravagant love has the following characteristics.

*'*Ishq *is a phenomenon which is not confined to age*

'Ishq in *ghazal* poetry forms the framework of human existence; it is 'the water of life', as formulated by the poet Salim.[24] Because it is the water of life, *'ishq* is not confined to a certain age; rather it is related to human life as life: young and old, men and women, rich and poor, even plants and animals fall in love.[25] Love as an eternal phenomenon, which the passing of time and changing of place cannot be weakened or diminished, can be in old age just as passionate as it is in youth. Salim illustrates this conception of love as follows:[26]

> *In my old age I still think of being with you*
> *Please do not let this affection go of my desires*

And

> *'*ishq *is a mission which must not cease.*
> *The cruelty of the beloved must not stop love.*

And

> *Whoever stops with* 'ishq *because the cruelty of the beloved*
> *Must mourn and cry in his grave until judgment day.*

*'*Ishq *overtakes the adorer's whole existence*

All the sensory energies of the adorer are focused on the beloved, and the beloved becomes the adorer's whole world. By being fully attached to the beloved, Nali loses his sense of reality and does not even know whether he is awake or asleep. Nali writes:[27]

> *Nali is so drunk by looking at your eyes*
> *That he does not know whether he is awake or dreaming or drunk*

In the same vein Salim writes:[28]

> *Salim's whole existence is devoted to* 'ishq
> *I should be filled with shame at the moment of the Last Judgment*
> *If I were to wish for paradise without you*

Love also comes only once: the adorer can only have one real beloved. As Salim says, the world is empty or impotent without this beloved:[29]

> *After your 'ishq mother earth has become impotent*
> *The mother of Christ also only gave birth once.*

As said earlier this love is an all-encompassing affection; the adorer loves everything about the beloved; all aspects of the beloved are meant for love, even the beloved's negative and cruel characteristics. The sweat of the beloved, for example, is precious and even works as a balm for the poet's wounds. Salim writes:[30]

> *Despite my terminal illness I know I shall recover soon*
> *If the physician would sprinkle your sweat on my wounds.*

'Ishq *as pain*

Pain is seen as the essence of love in *ghazal* poetry; without pain the true adorer could not be distinguished from those who claim to be and play the role of an adorer, the fake adorer. Pain is the parameter that differentiates between the true love from fake love. Pain is also essential in *ghazal* poetry since it is pain that can protect love from degenerating into mere cheap forms of sensuality. Nali describes his painful life as a life in hell, where he cannot live or die:[31]

> *Far from you don't ask how am I, my darling*
> *The condition of Nali is neither life nor death*

In this poem Nali refers to a sentence in the Quran, which describes the life of those in hell as something neither resembling death nor life.[32]

Ghazal poetry glorifies the pain of love, and the adorer is expected to be a sufferer who accepts the cruelty of the beloved and love itself as deeply painful experiences. Kurdi writes:[33]

> *If she wants to unjustly kill me,*
> *Nobody is allowed to stop her.*
> *If a leader is a kafir (an unbeliever)*
> *This injustice would be his manner of justice*

Kurdi completely surrenders himself to the unjust treatment of his beloved and accepts this as his fate. He calls his beloved *kafir*, and if a *kafir* is a leader, one cannot expect justice from her/him.

Pain in *ghazal* poetry also has another function: to attract the attention of the beloved. The adorer hopes that his beloved would show pity if she/he sees his pain. The adorer suffers in *ghazal* poetry from the ignorance and denial of the beloved; pain is a way for the adorer to make himself heard and visible.

Patience and loneliness as two aspects of 'ishq

Love in these poems goes hand in hand with a great deal of patience. The adorer must show a great fortitude in enduring the misconduct of the beloved, pain, criticism and reproach from society. The last aspect is called *lome* (reproach or reprimand). *Lome* can come from close friends and/or the community, but in particular from religious figures. The main figure who reproaches the adorer about his intense love is called *reqib* (the moral watchdog). The *reqib* represents the dominant morality within society, which is religiously coloured. The *reqib* can be male or female, and he/she watches over the two lovers to prevent them from meeting freely and talking freely to each other.[34] The adorer must be resistant against the reproaches of *reqib* and others and ignore them. The true adorer withstands critique and reproach from his friends, the community and religious orthodoxy, although this could mean social isolation and loneliness. Nali describes the dangerous fate of the lover where there will be no way to rescue himself:[35]

> *Every one has a safe path to move on further*
> *Only the unhappy lover has to take the road of fear and severity*

-The sensuality of 'ishq: Beauty, wine and eroticism

Ghazal poetry contains strong physical and erotic dimensions focused both on legitimate and illegitimate pleasures. *Ghazal* poetry gives love a corporal dimension and constructs it as erotic passion. The body of the beloved is detailed erotically in *ghazal* poetry: the eyes, eyebrows, lips, mouth, breasts, hips, hair, hands, belly, etc. The lips of Salim's beloved are as 'sweet as sugar', her eyes 'have taste of wine and her breasts are exceptionally tempestuous'.[36] Nali calls the nipples of the beloved a 'sweet button' and her breasts 'violet pomegranates'.[37] Salim desires nothing more than to put his hands on the breasts of his beloved.[38] In the same manner Nali writes:[39]

> *How the thirsty Sufi desires water, milk and honey from paradise*
> *In unison the lips of Nali long for the red lips of the beloved*

Also, the beloved's manner of walking, laughing and moving are objects of erotic passion. The longing to be alone with the beloved, to kiss and spend the night with the beloved are desires of the adorer. Salim writes:[40]

> *If I could have one kiss from your mouth*
> *Its sweetness would remain in my mouth until the Day of Judgment.*

This physical and erotic dimension of love is not only tied with the beloved's eroticized beauty but also with the circumstances in which the adorer and the beloved are in. The adorer often meets his beloved in a *meixane* (a wine bar), where music, alcohol and dancing bodies create an erotic atmosphere. The beloveds are the ones who pour the wine which are distributed by the *ghilman* (young teenage boys). The adorer combines his devotion for his beloved and his willingness to die for it with drinking wine and erotic desires. Young teenage boys, *ghilman*, could also be the object of erotic desire; there is a long tradition of love for young teenage boys in *ghazal* poetry and the Kurdish *ghazal* poetry in the nineteenth century continues it.

This erotic dimension in *ghazal* poetry goes hand in hand with an attack on four religious figures: the *wa'iz* (the counsellor), *zahid* (the ascetic), *wishkesofi* (the heartless ascetic) and *reqib* (the moral watchdog). The first three reflect the dogmatic religious authority, which play the role of protector of the 'true' faith, and the fourth represents the moralist who protects the dominant morality of the community. All these figures are presented as deceptive or deceitful characters in *ghazal* poetry; they are harshly criticized and ridiculed. They are constructed as figures who neither understand love nor religion. Nali compares *reqib* to 'a donkey',[41] or 'cold and lifeless.'[42]

From this perspective, *ghazal* poetry can be seen as a strong protest against the dominant moral order and all those social actors who speak in the name of this morality. One could even conclude that criticism of the orthodox practices in the first half of the nineteenth century was expressed mainly through *ghazal* poetry, and that this criticism took its form through defending love as the true faith, a faith which does not ridicule the secular materiality of body and its passions.

-'Ishq *versus rationality*

'*Ishq* in this poetry is represented as the opposite of rationality; *'ishq* cannot be united with a reasonable manner of thinking and doing. Comparing love to *junun* (madness) is one of the most common metaphors in Kurdish *ghazal* poetry.[43] In many poems Salim emphasizes the contrast between *'ishq* and rationality, for example:[44]

> *If the morning of* '*ishq shines*
> *The candle of rationality must be extinguished.*

The origin of love lies in the heart, and the heart follows other rules than the rules of rationality, namely *dewanei* or *junun* (madness).[45] Salim calls his heart the domain of *kufr* (disbelief) in which things happen that are not religiously permitted.[46] Salim writes:[47]

> *If my consciousness is absent for a moment*
> *My heart is already at work.*

And

> *The story of my* '*ishq is on everyone's lips, in every alley*
> *And yet my foolish senses continue to try to keep my* '*ishq a secret.*[48]

Majnūn, the hero of an Arabic love story, lost his sanity in his love for Layla, and ultimately died because of his love.[49] After his death Majnūn become the symbol of the martyr of love with whom Kurdish poets identify themselves. Nali compares himself to Majnūn and writes:[50]

I am as Majnun, if I lose you
Strayed I will be wandering in the desert

Kurdi also sees himself as Majnūn and compares his love for his beloved with that of Majnūn for Layla.[51]

Love in *ghazal* poetry is not controlled by reason nor could it be charged on religious ground. God does not hold mad people responsible for their actions and the punishments thereof.[52] This is also in accordance with sharia law: the implementation of religious obligations in sharia does not apply to people who are mad; mad people are unable to commit sins. By linking love to madness *ghazal* poetry creates an intellectual and emotional space outside the domain and supervision of religion, in particular outside the domain of religion's dogmatic and literal interpretation of holy texts. Madness offers the adorer the possibility to break free from the community's religious and cultural taboos. In this regard Salim belittles Islam's holiest spot, the *Kabah*, by saying that it only has value in relation to his beloved. He writes:[53]

What is the Ka'bah good for if not to be the soil under your feet,
What would I do with my soul if I could not sacrifice it for you

While the adorer ridicules religious symbols such as the *Kabah*, *ghazal* poetry presents him as someone who asks God for support in his unbearable and dangerous love. God in *ghazal* poetry takes the side of the adorer; God even bestows the title of martyr on him, should he die of or for love.

'Ishq as danger

'Ishq in *ghazal* poetry is a dangerous appeal as it determines a person's existence; it is irrational, in complete control of the adorer; it is a painful experience and is careless for reproaches and criticisms from society. To surrender to love means treading a difficult and dangerous path: a path, which could lead to the adorer's death, or martyrdom.[54] Love in *ghazal* poetry is often seen as an unsafe journey riddled with obstacles and difficulties and can only be completed by valiant people. According to Salim, *'ishq* is so dangerous that it could be a recipe to lose this world and the other world alike. Salim compares himself to Adam who was exiled from paradise and says:[55]

Because of my 'ishq for you
I was removed from paradise like Adam was.

Love needs, in the words of Henry Corbin, the 'courage of love'.[56] The true adorer distinguishes himself from the fake one by going through love's ultimate danger. A fake adorer, or one who plays the role of an adorer, seeks love without pain and danger and is not willing to overcome difficulties, and is certainly not ready to make the ultimate sacrifice. Nali calls the fake adorer *mudda'i*, someone who merely says he is one, a 'traitor of love'.[57]

The danger of love in these poems does not only have to do with love as an uncontrollably heavy emotion but also with its disregard of the social, cultural and religious barriers and taboos. The danger is part of this love as a specific kind of protest.

'Ashiq, the adorer

The adorer in *ghazal* poetry is a poet and he is often, if not always, a man: the one who speaks, falls in love, yearns, desires and has dangerous and painful experiences in the poems. He is also the person who is willing to sacrifice himself for his love and wants to become the martyr of love. Furthermore, he is the one who criticizes the religious orthodoxy and protests against the dominant morality. The adorer is the subject of *ghazal* poetry and basically everything revolves around him. The most important characteristics of the *'ashiq*, the adorer in the *ghazal* poetry could be reconstructed as follows.

The adorer is an active subject; the person who speaks, wishes and acts in *ghazal* poetry. But he constructs an image of himself which shows that everything he desires for himself, he actually wishes for his beloved. He loves his beloved more than himself, and the wishes of the beloved dictate his strivings if not his entire life. In total identification with the beloved, the adorer is ready to sacrifice his life and faith to his beloved. Kurdi writes:[58]

> I asked of you that the faith and heart of Kurdi
> Should not be seized, and yet you did just that.
> From now on you should just take whatever you could.

The adorer constructs himself as a person with a pure heart, someone who is honest in everything he does, says and wishes and he is faithful to his beloved under any circumstances. The adorer loves everything about his beloved: her good and bad traits, her faithfulness and unfaithfulness, her beauty and repulsiveness, her harshness and tenderness. The adorer has little or no specific ulterior motives; he only wishes to be together with his beloved. He is even prepared to exchange heaven for hell if that would fulfil his beloved's longing and wishes. Kurdi presents himself as a honest lover in these dramatic images:[59]

> Today I am left behind in the nook of loneliness.
> Humiliated, sick, and with no one to empathise with, today.
> My red tears and my yellowish face
> Are proof of my love, today.

The adorer literally adores his beloved and is even prepared to end his life if she so wishes. The adorer gives up his faith, wealth, name, reputation, peace, reason, will and even his life for his beloved. This readiness to sacrifice everything for love is actually the most important characteristic of the adorer in *ghazal* poetry. Kurdi:[60]

> Oh friends, come and kill me with a sword
> So I can be freed from my unfaithful beloved

The adorer looks forward to giving up his life for his beloved, and sometimes he does that for a kiss, a glance or a word from the beloved. Kurdi writes:[61]

> Besides a kiss on your eyes if I should wish for more
> God shall burn me without mercy with the fire of his rage

Kurdi further identified himself with the well-known Sufi al-Hallaj in three poems.[62] Al-Hallaj was a Persian mystic who lived in the ninth and tenth century. He was accused of heresy and burned; but even after his death, his ashes kept saying: 'I am the truth.' Kurdi also identified himself once with the famous Arabic Majnūn.[63] Through this identification, the adorer constructs his identity as an ethical and altruistic person.

Ma'shuq, *the beloved*

Ma'shuq is an important figure in *ghazal* poetry and in mystical Sufi poetry. While in the latter *ma'shuq* and God are identical, *ma'shuq* in *ghazal* poetry is certainly not God. It is even possible to ascertain the historical figure of the *ma'shuq* in many *ghazal* poems, to know who he/she really was as in the case of Kurdi. In many of his poems, the beloved was a young man called Qadir whom Kurdi was in love with and for whom he wrote a number of beautiful verses. The *ma'shuq* in *ghazal* poetry is often a woman but could also be a young man. As a rule, the *ma'shuq* is always absent; he/she is present in second or third person forms.[64] The most important characteristics of the beloved in *ghazal* poetry could be summarized as follows.

The beloved is constructed aesthetically as *houri* (the virginal feminine inhabitants of paradise), and also as *ghilman* (young men); both symbolize ultimate beauty. But the combination of *houri* and *ghilman* shows the ambiguous gender of the beloved in this poetry. Love for *ghilman* comes from the Sufi tradition, which positions love for a young man at the same level as love for beauty itself or as love of divine perfection.[65] But as the case of Kurdi shows, love for a young boy could be a secular love and part of a homoerotic relationship.

However, underneath the beloved's physical beauty is an ocean of cruelty, coldness, unfaithfulness, vengeance and sadism, always ready to raise hostility against the adorer. In this sense the beloved is someone without *insaf* (conscience). The image of the beloved as the murderer of the adorer is often found in *ghazal* poetry. The poet often describes the fingers of his beloved as red, painted by the blood of her adorer. Salim writes:[66]

> The colour of *henna* is too deep a red
> Do not use it to paint your fingers
> Use the blood of my heart,
> Which is a more beautiful kind of red

Comparing the poet's blood to *henna* with which the beloved paints her fingers is a dominant image and a recurring theme in *ghazal* poetry. The image of the beloved with a knife in her bloodied hand is also frequently found in these poems. Kurdi speaks of his beloved: 'You have a knife in your hands, your fingers are red from blood and your heart is dead.'[67] Or this even bloodier image of a beloved:[68]

> Today I am the martyr of the Karbala of your love
> Look how red your fingers are from my blood

The beloved is *maghrur* (arrogant) and proud and is not interested in the pain and suffering of the adorer. *Bewefai* (unfaithful) is the dominant characteristic of the beloved. Kurdi writes:[69]

> My beloved is not to be trusted and lies,
> She/he came and stole my heart
> Now she/he denies that she/he even knows me and says:
> Oh, you shameless person, I have never seen you

Salim begs his beloved hopelessly not to leave him, because he would otherwise die, and she will be held responsible in the afterlife for the death of an innocent poet. Salim writes:[70]

> Please do not abandon me, your departure would kill me
> I do not want my innocent and stewing blood, to testify against you in the afterlife

The beloved manipulates the adorer and uses his/her hypnotizing power to lead the beloved towards radical decisions such as denying his faith and sacrificing his life. Kurdi writes:[71]

> Because there were no witnesses present when I saw her for the first time
> I left my senses and my fate with her now she denies all of that

Ghazal *poetry and the masculine self-representation*

In *ghazal* poetry there are countless examples of self-representation of the adorer-poet as the martyrs of love, as someone who sacrifices his life for a deceitful beloved; a beloved not only untrustworthy but careless, cruel and sadist. Of course, the sacrifice of the adorer in this poetry is rhetorical; the poet doesn't literally suffer from pain and danger and does not seek death, but he rhetorically suffers pain and danger. The sacrifice does not go beyond the poet's written words, but it is actually embedded in the genre itself, *not* in the life of the genre's writer. All that happens in *ghazal* poetry is a language game, but still the poet glorifies his acts as courageous and heroic deeds, constructs his self-image as an honest and virtuous man who is ready to commit the ultimate sacrifice for his love. In this sense *ghazal* poetry is a literary instrument to create and distribute a glorified and altruistic form of masculinity, the masculinity of the poet-adorer.

At the beginning of this chapter I mentioned that *ghazal* has been defined as 'speaking about love with women', and thus the beloved is the most important subject in this poetry. But we can adopt a gendered perspective and emphasize that the essence of *ghazal* poetry is not so much about the love for a specific and imagined beloved but, rather, about the formation of a specific form of masculine identity: the identity of the poet or the adorer as a courageous, virtuous and altruistic man. The woman in *ghazal* poetry is often presented as an anonymous and abstract beloved: the idea behind this anonymization and abstraction is a dominant patriarchal strategy – a strategy which portrays the woman as an unfaithful and dangerous being who cannot become a true partner, even in love. Zizek underlines this point in his analysis of courtly love poetry in the West, which, in my opinion, can also be applied to *ghazal* poetry. Zizek says that the creation of a woman as an abstract ideal has nothing to do with spiritual purification but 'rather points towards the abstraction that pertains to a cold, distanced, inhuman partner – the Lady is in no way a warm, compassionate, understanding fellow creature'.[72] The anonymization of the female beloved strengthens the feeling of the reader of *ghazal* poetry that all poets in this genre are writing about the same beloved: an abstract woman who is constructed in the same manner and in the same content by all male poets. Following Sigmund Freud, we can say that the woman in *ghazal* poetry plays the role of 'the goddess of life and death' – woman as the cause of life and death. This, as Freud emphasizes, has to do with the wishes of the man to have power over death and to control it. 'For Freud', Clack writes, 'the explanation for making his connection between death and woman is simple: man is overcoming death by force of will, turning the uncontrollable reality of death into the controllable person of a beautiful woman.'[73]

Whether Freud is correct in this interpretation is less important than the fact that the man is the one who portrays the woman as the goddess of life and death. In relation to *ghazal* poetry, this means that the identity of the beloved in the poems is constructed according to the wishes of the male poet-adorer. As a subject with a voice, the poet-adorer sets down the identity of the beloved in such a manner as to establish his self-image as a courageous, virtuous and altruistic man. The beloved – the woman – in this poetry is presented as the traitor of love, one who is disloyal and unreliable and cruel, while the poet-adorer portrays himself as a courageous, loyal and altruistic person who does not hesitate to suffer pain, and even sacrifice his life, for his beloved. Sacrifice in *ghazal* poetry is a masculine act, or as Sered says, 'a male enterprise' and is part of the identity formation of the masculine man.[74]

The question that has an urgent relevance in this context is: Who were the public, the readers, of this poetry in the first half of the nineteenth century in Kurdistan? One thing is clear: the audience of *ghazal* poetry were not women, but men. De Bruijn confirmed this point as he speaks about the social and conceptual environment of *ghazal* poetry in the Islamic world: 'The environment alluded to is, both socially and conceptually, the atmosphere of male entertainment in gatherings to which the general term of majlis (literally "a place where one sits together") was applied.'[75] The three Kurdish poets discussed in this chapter belonged to the aristocrats of the Baban principality. Given the small number of literate people in Kurdistan during that period, and the difficulty and complexity of the language in the poems, the audience of *ghazal* poetry was small indeed and reduced to the minority that consisted of members of aristocratic families, religious scholars and the ruling elite. All these groups mainly if not exclusively consisted of men. Given this social environment, it could be said that *ghazal* poetry was poetry by men and for men. These poems were seldom authored and read by women. In this sense, *ghazal* poetry was not so much an expression of love for a woman but, rather, a representation of the poet as an ethical and courageous man in front of a male audience.

Ghazal poetry and love between men: The case of Kurdi

The theme of masculinity in *ghazal* poetry has another dimension: the homoerotic love between men.[76] The poet who falls in love with another man, and who presents this love as the theme of his *ghazal* poems, also sees himself as the martyr of love. He connects his love to another man with all forms of sacrifice, which is an important element of this genre. The love between the poet Kurdi and his beloved Qadir illustrates this. In eight *ghazal* poems, Kurdi describes in detail his love, and he does not hesitate to give the real name of his beloved.[77] In these poems Kurdi uses the notion of martyrdom or being a martyr of love four times, all of them in the context of his passionate love for Qadir.[78] In one of his famous poems this martyrdom appears as the following:[79]

> The martyr of love am I, my friends, I have no need of a shroud, a *kifin*.[80]
> My bloodied clothing is proof of my martyrdom for God.[81]
> The angels keep asking for my religion, in vain
> Qadir knows what faith is mine

In another poem Kurdi writes:[82]

> If one should ask of my faith and my guide
> Ali is my lord, Qadir is my guide and Mahmud is my sultan.

Kurdi also writes:[83]

> Even if I should be burned like Mansur
> My ashes will continue uttering: I am Qadir[84]

In the first poem Qadir refers to God and to his beloved.[85] In the second poem the name 'Qadir' is used to refer to Imam Ali, the fourth caliph in Islam, and next to the name of the Ottoman Sultan Mahmud II (1808–39), who was the symbol of the Ottoman Empire as a world power. In the third poem, the name 'Qadir' is brought in connection with the martyrdom of the famous Sufi al-Hallaj (*ca.* 858–922). It is noteworthy to see the manner in which Kurdi presents his beloved Qadir: appropriating religious language, images and figures. By adopting this religious strategy, Kurdi attempts to spiritualize his love for Qadir or, more precisely, to position his love in the tradition of Sufi male homosexual poetry. He tries to circumvent possible anticipated ethical criticism from the watchdogs of traditional religious morality. In Sufism, the Sufis meticulously use all emotions, desires and strengths in order to find God. Love between men was one of the proven ways in this search and part of an attempt to make the mystical spiritual experience possible.

Despite all these religious attempts, the love for Qadir, which Kurdi described, is not the same kind of love between men in Sufi poetry. In Kurdi's case, there is no such thing as a Sufi experience. Kurdi was not a Sufi, and Qadir was not an imaginary beloved, but a young man whom he was in love with. This love was so strong that Kurdi left his wife and children to pursue Qadir, who had moved from Iraqi Kurdistan to Iran.[86] The fact that Kurdi neither kept his love for Qadir secret nor saw it as something shameful proves the presence of a sexual morality which tolerated, at least on the level of discourse, homoerotic love. In this context, sexual conduct is not the practice that creates one's identity; there is still a moral space which allows ambiguity in sexual practices, and it seems that sexual relations were not markedly heterosexual or heterosexual. Qadir's beauty in Kurdi's poems is described in the same language and metaphors as those he uses to describe the beauty of a female beloved. There is no distinction in his poetry between the characteristics of beauty applied to men and women.[87] One can speak of the existence of homosexual conduct without homosexual discourse, the presence of homosexual deeds without homosexuality, by homosexuality I mean homosexual relationships as identity. It is at the end of the nineteenth century, when nationalism started gaining ground and the influence of Victorian morality became stronger in the Islamic world, that the existing ambiguity in sexual conduct and morality disappeared, as did the moral space which made that ambiguity possible.[88] Thus, *ghazal* poetry could be seen in the first half of the nineteenth century as a space of sexual protest against dominant moral values.

Conclusion

Ghazal poetry is a literary and intellectual space in which love takes a central place. This love is complex and multidimensional. On one side love belongs to the category of the spirit or soul, and it purifies a person's inner-self and transforms him/her into a better person. The pain, the undermining of the ego and persevering with patience, transcending the boundaries of rationality and enduring a lonesome existence are all important aspects of love as a spiritual power. However, this is not the only aspect of love in *ghazal* poetry, but love also has a strong physical and erotic dimension in which the body is a place of pleasure and sexual desire.

This multidimensionality makes love in *ghazal* poetry function as a literary, cultural and moral protest against the dominant sexual and religious taboos. The adorer in this poetry can criticize religious figures, social norms and present love as a truer faith than religion, transgressing various social formulas, religious rules and principles. Sexuality in *ghazal* poetry is not reduced to heterosexuality; the adorer could be in love with another man or a young boy. One can speak of the exultation of homosexual practices without the homosexual discourse: homosexuality in *ghazal* poetry is not presented as an identity, but it is a practice without a name, part of the love when the love is not totally heterosexualized.

Ghazal poetry also has a strong gender dimension; the beloved in this poetry is mainly a woman who is present through the discourse of the poet who is mainly a man. She is represented as a heartless, cruel and unfaithful female, who enjoys the suffering and the pain of the poet. The poet creates his image as a true lover, the one who is ready to undergo pain and difficulty, even to sacrifice his life for his love. In *ghazal* poetry the adorer-poet creates his identity as a courageous man.

Ghazal poetry had become a universal genre in the nineteenth century; not only poets from different parts of the Islamic world wrote this genre enthusiastically, but it had also entered European literature. However, at the end of the nineteenth century it came under attack of a new generation of poets who started to write more politicized patriotic and nationalistic poetry, with rigid perspectives on sexuality, manhood and morality.

Notes

1. Harbans Mukhia, 'The Celebration of Failure as Dissent in Urdi Ghazal', *Modern Asian Studies* 33, no. 4 Cambridge University Press (1999): 864.
2. Sirus Shmisa, *Sair ghazal dar shi'ri Farsi* (Teheran: Chapxana Ramin, 1997), 11.
3. Thomas Bauer and Angelika Neuwirth, *Ghazal as World Literature* (Würzburg: Ergon Verlag in Kommission, 2005).
4. J. T. P. De Bruijn, *Persian Sufi Poetry. An Introduction to the Mystical Use of Classical Persian Poems* (Richmond: Curzon Press, 1997), 55.
5. Ibid., 61.
6. Love is an important theme in Islamic intellectual tradition, virtually anyone who was involved in Islamic intellectual work has written extensively about love, including orthodox religious scholars, authors of collected stories and special encyclopedias, poets, oral storytellers and writers of folk tales and prose, Islamic philosophers, and of course the Sufis ('Abd al-Haq Munsif, *Ab'ad al-tajriba al-sūfiyya* (Afriqa: al-sharq Maghrib, 2007), 69–71).
7. Munsif, *Ab'ad al-tajriba al-sūfiyya*.
8. Ibid., 76.
9. Ibid., 83.
10. William C. Chittick, 'The Pluralistic Vision of Persian Sufi Poetry', *Islam and Christian-Muslim Relations* 14 (4 October 2003): 424.
11. Munsif, *Ab'ad al-tajriba al-sūfiyya*, 84–5.
12. De Bruijn, *Persian Sufi Poetry*, 3.
13. Bauer and Neuwirth, *Ghazal as World Literature*, 9.
14. De Bruijn, *Persian Sufi Poetry*, 1.
15. Bauer and Neuwirth, *Ghazal as World Literature*, 15.
16. Goethe got to know Oriental literature through the translated works of Hafiz in 1812–13 in German. Goethe was enthusiastic about Hafiz and called him a 'masterful poet'. He consequently published, under Hafiz' influence, his famous *West-Eastern Divan* in 1819 (Hendrik Birus, 'Goethe's Approximation of the Ghazal and Its Consequences', in *Ghazal as World Literature* 1, ed. Thomas Bauer and Angelika Neuwirth (Beirut: Orient-Institute, 2005), 419–20).
17. Bauer and Neuwirth, *Ghazal as World Literature*, 20.
18. See Aladin Sujadi, *Mejwî Edebî Kūrdî* (Bagdad, 1952). See also Martin Van Bruinessen, *Agha, Shaikh and State: The Social and Political Structures of Kurdistan* (London: Zed Books, 1992).
19. Up till the introduction of modern education towards the end of the nineteenth century, religious education in Kurdish regions of the Ottoman Empire was the only form of education. Studying and memorizing Sufi poetry of Iranian poets was among the mandatory subjects of that education (Sujadi, *Mejwî Edebî Kūrdî*; Kakai Felah, *Diwani Nari* (Iran: Intisharat, 2004)).
20. Felah, *Diwani Nari*, 6–7.
21. Adonis, *Al-Sufiya wa al-Suryaliya* (Lebanon: Dar al-Saqi, 1995), 105.

22 Ibid.
23 Ibid.
24 Giw Mukiryani, *Diwani Salim* (Hewler: Chapxanî Kurdistan, 1972), 34.
25 In the Islamic tradition, *'ishq* is not limited to human love, but animals and plants are also able to passionately fall in love with each other. In his books *Masri' al-'ushshaq*, Ibn Siraj presents love as a universal phenomenon. He speaks of love relationships between two date flowers, or the love between a ghost and a slave, or between a female goose who dies because her male goose was killed in front of her (Ibn al-Siraj, *Masari' al 'ushshaq* (Beirut: Dar al-Sadr, 1995), 31–3).
26 Mukiryani, *Diwani Salim*, 33.
27 Muhammad Mella Kerim, *Diwani Nali* (Bagdad: Kori Zanyari Kurd, 1973), 89.
28 Mukiryani, *Diwani Salim*, 28.
29 Ibid., 27.
30 Ibid., 33.
31 Mella Kerim, *Diwani Nali*, 128.
32 Ibid.
33 Giw Mukiryani, *Diwani Kurdi* (Hewler: Chapxani Kurdistan, 1973), 14.
34 For an extensive explanation of the *reqib*'s role in Sufi love poetry, see Abas al-Hadad, 'Al-'azl al-dini wa-l-ma'rifi fi al-shi'r al-sufi' (Suriya: Dar al-Hiwar, 2005). In this book various forms of *reqib* are distinguished from one another. *Ma'shuq*, the love object who could be male or female, is often afraid of the *reqib* and tries his/her best to keep the affair secret. Al-Hadad writes that in Arabic love poetry, *Ma'shuq*'s fear for *reqib* is so great that *Ma'shuq* would keep her love 'secret even from herself' (al-Hadad, 'Al-'azl al-dini wa-l-ma'rifi fi al-shi'r al-sufi', 75).
35 Mella Kerim, *Diwani Nali*, 120.
36 Mukiryani, *Diwani Kurdi*, 28, 29, 36.
37 Mella Kerim *Diwani Nali*, 538–46.
38 Mukiryani, *Diwani Kurdi*, 36.
39 Mella Kerim, *Diwani Nali*, 457.
40 Mukiryani, *Diwani Kurdi*, 22.
41 Mella Kerim, *Diwani Nali*, 585.
42 Ibid., 118.
43 Mukiryani, *Diwani Kurdi*, 108–9.
44 Ibid., 31.
45 In Islamic literature pertaining to *'ishq*, the link between *'ishq* and madness is frequently present. Ibn Siraj (417–500), in his famous book *Masari' al-'ushshaq* about *'ishq*, defines *'ishq* as madness (in Sheikh Zulfiqar Ahmad, *Defining Ishq*, 1998, https://www.thefcpm.com/images/seerah/articles/cr2.pdf, accessed on 28th August 2021).
46 Mukiryani, *Diwani Salim*, 6.
47 Ibid., 39.
48 Ibid., 32.
49 A. Schimmel, *Mystical Dimensions of Islam* (Chapel Hill: University of North Carolina Press, 1975), 292.
50 Mella Kerim, *Diwani Nali*, 127.
51 Mukiryani, *Diwani Kurdi*, 57. Schimmel writes about Majnūn: 'He has become one of the best-known symbols of true loving surrender, regardless of religious traditions, reputation, name, or fame' (Schimmel, *Mystical Dimensions of Islam*, 305).
52 Schimmel cites Iranian poets Jami to clarify this point. Jami says: 'God has freed them [the mad one. M.K.] from order and prohibition,' in Schimmel, *Mystical Dimensions of Islam*, 19.
53 Mukiryani, *Diwani Kurdi*, 52.
54 The link between *'ishq* and death is frequently found in the Islamic love tradition. Historical sources describe a tribe on the Arabic peninsula called Bani 'Udhra whose main cause of death within the tribe was love.

55 Mukiryani, *Diwani Salim*, 39.
56 Cheetham, Tom. *The Meaning of Imagination in Henry Corbin and James Hillman*. (Oxford: Spring Publications, 2015), 10.
57 Mella Kerim, *Diwani Nali*, 543.
58 Mukiryani, *Diwani Salim*, 71.
59 Ibid., 54.
60 Ibid., 16.
61 Ibid., 34.
62 Ibid., 28, 36 and 59.
63 Ibid. 57.
64 De Bruijn, *Persian Sufi Poetry*, 66.
65 Najmabadi explains the Sufi roots of this gender ambiguity: 'In Sufi practices, the figure of the young adolescent man as an object of desire was linked with the practice of gazing, "nazar". As Rowson has summarized, the practice of gazing (and consequently falling in love with) was directed at young adolescent males: "From a relatively early period- probably the mid-ninth century-some Muslim mystics claimed to see in the beauty of adolescent boys a 'testimony' to the beauty and goodness of God, and initiated the practice of gazing at such a boy as a form of spiritual exercise. The boy was thus known in Sufi parlance as a 'witness' (shahid)'" (Najabadi, Afsaneh. *Women with Moustaches and Men without Beards* (California: University of California Press, 2005), 17). Thus, the beauty of an adolescent boy is proof of God's beauty and symbolizes transcendent beauty.
66 Mukiryani, *Diwani Salim*, 52.
67 Ibid., 61.
68 Ibid., 62.
69 Ibid., 16.
70 Ibid., 23.
71 Ibid., 14.
72 Zizek Slavoj, *Trying With the Negative: Kant, Hegel and the Critique of Ideology* (Durham: Duke University Press, 1993).
73 Ibid., 77.
74 Susan Sered, Taxonomies of Ritual Mixing, in History of Religions, vol. 1. 47, No.2/3, November 2007. Chicago: University of Chicago Press, pp.221–238.
75 De Bruijn, *Persian Sufi Poetry*, 67.
76 The homoerotic love in *ghazal* poetry goes back a long way in the history of Islamic literature. The Arabic poet Abu Nawas (d. 814 or 815) is considered a representative of this subject. The poet had an enormous influence on the majority of poets who came after him. He is even seen as the one who 'formatively shape[d] Arabic love poetry for [the] entire millennium to follow'; Bauer and Neuwirth, *Ghazal as World Literature*, 24.
77 Mukiryani, *Diwani Salim*, 32, 39–40, 78, 80, 85, 87, 89.
78 Disney, Donald Bruce, Jr., 'The Kurdish nationalist movement and external influences', 1971, 39–43–62–47. https://calhoun.nps.edu/handle/10945/17624, accessed 28th August 2021.
79 Mukiryani, *Diwani Salim*, 39.
80 *Kifin* is the white cloth in which a corpse is wrapped in the Islamic world. The dead may not be buried in their own clothing.
81 According to Islamic burial laws, martyrs are allowed to be buried in their blood-stained clothes, and their bodies may not be washed. The bloodied clothing and body are witness of the person's martyrdom.
82 Mukiryani, *Diwani Salim*, 62.
83 Ibid., 36.
84 Kurdi refers here to the story of the famous Sufi al-Hallaj.
85 In Islam God or Allah has many names, one of which is Qadir.
86 Sucadi 1952, 297.

87 This phenomenon is not just present in Kurdi's case, but it was indeed widespread in the poetry of that period. Nali, for example, describes the male Baban soldiers in the same language used by Kurdi. For an excellent analysis of these matters in Iranian *ghazal* poetry and art in the same period, see Najmabadi 2005, 11-25.
88 For a thorough discussion of sexuality and sexual morality in the Ottoman Empire and Iran, please see Massad, Joseph. *Desiring Arabs*. (Chicago: University of Chicago Press, 2007) and Najmabadi 2005. One problematic point in the analysis of both authors is that they reduce the causes of this transformation in the Ottoman Empire and Iran to the influence of the oriental discourse and the contact that Iran and the Ottoman Empire had with Europe in the Victorian period. This not only overemphasizes the power of oriental discourse and Europe in the nineteenth century, but the authors also remove all forms of agency from the local actors. They also ignore the role played by the emergence of nationalism in the transformation of the representation of masculinity and femininity in sexual conduct.

Chapter 9

THE POLITICS OF MADNESS AND LOVE IN NEW IRANIAN POETRY IN THE 1950S–60S

THE LEGACY OF *MAJNŪN* IN *SHE'RE NOW*: AHMAD SHAMLU AND FOROUGH FARROKHZAD'S LOVE POETRY

Seyedeh Paniz Musawi Natanzi

Introduction

This comparative and interdisciplinary analysis examines the topological legacy of the mad man Majnūn, the poet in the epic love story of *Layla and Majnūn*, in the Iranian *She're Now* genre (New Poetry), with a focus on Ahmad Shamlu and Forough Farrokhzad's love poetry. The *topos* of Majnūn, the amorously mad poet who publicly declares his love for Layla, whom he is not allowed to marry, is present in Ahmad Shamlu and Farrokhzad's love poetry, in the form of a deeply loving *dramatis persona* whose social and political boundaries are distorted. The guiding question in this chapter evolves around understanding the potential of a gender-sensitive reading of *She're Now* to rethink the notions of love and madness as they have been normalized through classical Persian poetry.[1]

This chapter shows that as in the love poetry and life of her male colleague Ahmad Shamlu, Farrokhzad's love poetry blurs the boundaries between *dramatis persona* and poet and provides not just literary but also sociopolitical knowledge about what kind of 'madness' is at stake in mid-twentieth-century urban Iran. Using Majnūn's legacy in *She're Now* as part of the methodological framework, Shamlu's idea and articulation of love are classical in terms of the heteronormative and monogamous features of his love poetry, such as in the *topos* of Majnūn, but modern as it breaks the poetic conventions of classical Persian love poetry.

Adapting the *topos* of Majnūn to analyse Farrokhzad's poetic engagements with madness and love accentuates the need to consider a gender-sensitive approach to render visible the mulitple meanings that the relation between love and madness can take. Farrokhzad reflects in her love poetry on sociopolitical challenges, as politics shape individual living conditions. Disentangling Farrokhzad's early work by considering her sociopolitical positionality and poetic production renders intelligible the manifold meanings that politics of love and madness can have in *She're Now*'s love poetry: first, by providing insights into Farrokhzad's desire for intimacy in 1950s' Iran, as she has been widely praised for. Second, Farrokhzad introduces herself in her love poetry as a loving mother who cannot be a mother for her child and live up to social expectations. Third, Farrokhzad strives in her writings to be a poet: her love for the poetic vocation is another socially marginalizing factor, as her poetry and letters to her father show.[2]

Re-reading Farrokhzad's less scholarly celebrated early love poetry, I suggest that an interdisciplinary approach informed by insights from feminist geopolitics – emphasizing the epistemological relevance of the 'banal' and 'personal' of quotidian life – enables to assess the potential of a gender-sensitive reading of *New Iranian Poetry*, revisiting literary normalized and normative notions of madness and love in classical Persian poetry.

First, I develop the theoretical–conceptual framework: here, I apply my discussion of literary *topoi* to Majnūn's character and sketch out gender-sensitive readings in literary studies focusing on poetry. Additionally, I map out my use of feminist geopolitics in this chapter to critically examine the *New Iranian Poetry*. In order to underline the usability of the *topos* of *Majnūn*, I position Shamlu and Farrokhzad in Anglophone and Persian scholarly discussions. I focus on the instrumental use of *topos* to conceptualize the legacy of the *Layla and Majnūn* narrative within feminist geopolitics and feminist and gender-sensitive literary approaches to love and madness. Highlighting the sociopolitical conditions in which gendered bodies are labelled as mad for being in love or for not living up to the idea of 'proper' femininity or 'proper' masculinity, I show the reproduction of the 'metaphysics of substance', by naturalizing gender roles instead of considering the politics that gender relations are subject to.[3] The third part of the chapter engages with the analysis of the legacy of *Majnūn* in Shamlu and Farrokhzad's love poetry. I argue that what is significant about Farrokhzad's writing is not merely the engagement of a woman poet with love and carnal desire within the public sphere, but rather how in Farrokhzad's poetry on love and madness the reader can gain insights into the dynamic relation between multiple notions of love and its relation to madness and gendering processes through *She're Now* as an intrinsically political medium in modern Persian poetry of the twentieth century.

Literature review and methodology: Mapping gender-sensitive epistemologies on love and madness in Forough Farrokhzad's poetry

The genre of *She're Now*, established in the first half of the twentieth century by the Iranian poet Nima Yushij, embraces names such as Mehdi Akhavan-Sales, Sohrap Sepehri, Ahmad Shamlu and Forugh Farrokhzad. The New Poetry 'came to signify a type of poetry that featured lines of unequal length that rhymed only occasionally or sporadically'.[4] Yushij broke the canonical use of words and 'loosened the rules of poetic grammar observed by classical poets and considered inviolable by many among his contemporaries'.[5]

Majnūn provides a *topos* produced in the era of classical Persian poetry and is conceptually a very 'ambiguous term' in Islamic thought.[6] To assess Majnūn in terms of his topological legacy, I refer to *topos* in the sense of 'a framework', as Hunter suggests in her preface:[7] 'A topos provides a general setting for a discussion, a framework for arguments rather than a fixed set of rules, standards or axioms.' Hence, a *topos* is described here as a theme, but it does not force delineated categories onto an analysis.

Regarding this, the usage of *topoi* seems to enable to delve into a discourse without raising claims of completeness. It is a dynamic concept that enables one to re-evaluate the details of a certain discussion. Taking recourse to the linkages within Western European literature in the work of the Romanist Ernst Robert Curtius – who claims they are all connected through 'classical Latin' – Cherchi locates Curtius's notion of 'unity' in a 'tradition'. Curtius identifies 'a system, a code, a set of rules' that was ciphered in the late Latin period and in the Middle Ages. Those elements that appear 'repeatedly', Cherchi writes, are what Curtius calls 'topoi', describing them as 'the commonplaces – any theme, conceptual motif, image, or stylistic pattern – which recur repeatedly in varying forms at different periods'.[8] While the critics disapprove of Curtius's blurred definition of the term *topos*, fearing that its lack of clarity decreases the space for the 'individuality' of the 'artistic creation', Cherchi defends Curtius's approach arguing that 'in the hand of an artist, that topos acquires a meaning, a poetical meaning'.[9] Cherchi stresses the need to remember that the 'relationship between tradition and originality is not a mechanical one but rather a dialectic one'.[10] The synthesis is a 'paradox': 'whereas the topos seems to undermine creative originality, it is also true that it guarantees the communicability of this originality because it controls the literary creation from the side of the audience'.[11] In light of this, working out *topoi* can be seen as a productive process that creates theoretical space for interventions, challenging established notions and understandings of poetry. The use of a *topos* can take place absolutely independently from one writer to another,[12] for instance, through the use of the same imagery in independent works from the same era.

While Nizami's use of Majnūn is open to various interpretations, the character can be understood among others as mad for his 'obsessive love'.[13] Another way for understanding Majnūn's behaviour is, according to Dols's reading of Nizami, to see him as a victim of the 'evil eye' or 'fate'.[14] As Dols explains,[15] "love is a natural and desirable aspect of human existence, but obsessive love takes on the appearance of madness and its mysterious qualities. Majnūn is a 'romantic fool' who was included in society,[16] whereas in a European reading of his character, he would be described as a 'borderliner'" (Koenigsberg and Siever, 2000).[17] According to Dols, 'profane love' was defined as a form of madness when it reaches excessive features such as in Majnūn's case.[18] By the tenth century Majnūn's way of loving, an 'obsessive, melancholic love became a major theme of Islamic literature'.[19]

Nizami's concatenated his version of the drama about the two lovers who cannot be together to the story in the twelfth century.[20] In this era of classical Persian poetry the *dramatis persona*'s positionality is that of the normalized male articulating his love for God and his creations. In the narrative, before Majnūn goes mad, he is called Qays. Growing up together, Layla and Qays are deeply in love with each other.[21] Qays writes her poetry and reads it out loud in public. Despite being conscious of the rules within a paternally organized community, he is not scared of mentioning the name of his beloved, Layla, in the poems he dedicates to her. But when the young man asks for Layla's hand, the (law of the) father, feeling dishonoured and disempowered, rejects him. The young Qays loses the prospect of marrying Layla and is not able to keep on living as he used to. He runs into the wild and begins to live as an ascetic, telling poetry as he moves along to himself, stones, the people he encounters and the animals of the forest. This is when Qays becomes the Majnūn (mad man): 'A madman he became – but at the same time a poet, the harp of his love and of his pain.'[22] Dols writes in *Majnūn: The Madman in Medieval Islamic Society*: 'insanity can only exist against the background of an accepted standard of normal behaviour.'[23] Dols differentiates between three 'principal interpretations of mental illness': first, the 'traditional disease model' which claims that mental illness is a 'pathological' phenomenon. Second, Dols introduces the 'deviation model', which assumes that mental illness is a 'social issue or divergence from normative behaviour' which is observed and controlled for instance through psychiatry and its 'direct social control'. Finally, there is the 'intelligibility model'. This model suggests that mental illness can be judged on the basis of 'deprivation of rationality or the breaking of the constituency rules of reason'. The 'loss of "reason"' is nothing that needs to be treated: in contrast to European treatment of subjects who were assumed mentally ill and marginalized spatially and ideally from the public gaze, Islamic societies behaved in a diametrically opposite way towards 'mad' subjects.[24]

Problematizing gendering politics, madness and the idea of what comprises 'womanhood', feminist and queer scholars have rendered intelligible throughout the past decades the epistemologically crucial insight that context shapes how an individual experiences life and how his life is framed by societies, states and neoliberal economies based on ruling racisms and gendering regimes, mental and physical ableism and classism.[25] In the context of gender-sensitive literary studies,[26] Jan Montefiore pointed out how gendered relations in sociopolitical environments shape the interaction between the poet's aesthetic production and his audiences.[27] Gender-sensitive literature, taking the early works as serious as the later ones in terms of the sociopolitical knowledges they provide, has been examined with a focus on guiding themes such as love in relation to marriage,[28] as well as to 'freedom and rebellion'.[29] Instead of looking at the poets' love poetry as static with regards to concepts of love and madness, emphasizing the process of constantly 'becoming' something, it is helpful to consider the epistemological relevance of the 'banal' and 'personal' of everyday experiences.[30]

Making the banalized graspable by reducing the reproduction of identity politics, feminist geopolitics can accommodate Shamlu and Farrokhzad's work in the genre of *She're Now* as a source to understand 'embodied' knowledge.[31] Developed as a critique of critical geopolitics' methodology, which 'decentres the nation-state' and circumvents 'transformative or embodied ways of knowing and seeing',[32] feminist geopolitics sees 'the body as an active territorial agent in processes of border- and territory-making' as opposed to critical geopolitics prioritization of truth producing 'geopolitical cultures'.[33] The emphasis on the individual as a knowledge-producing entity renders visible epistemologies which cannot be easily accessed due to physical, material or ideal borders that exclude particular masses of bodies who circumvent the nation state and dominant ideas of 'proper' masculinity and femininity. Considering insights of feminist discussions into the linkages between embodiment, geographies and politics enables to read modern Persian love poetry, which is intrinsically political, through literary criticism and feminist lenses.

In the editorial to *Emotional Geographies*, Anderson and Smith discuss the silences caused by the feminization and devaluation of 'subjectivity, passion and desire' which are constructed as the opposite of the political realm which is masculine, strong and rational.[34] Christian, Dowler and Cuomo gender Michael Billig's concept of 'the banal',[35] showing how a heteronormative understanding of space, place and gender feminizes issues relating to 'subjectivity, private space, emotions, the body, the everyday and the banal' and positions them out of the realm of politics.

While these approaches highlight the omnipresence of subtle strategies of gendering derived from a heteronormative understanding based on which gender becomes a crucial factor determining the individual's place in a social formation (Oyěwùmí 1997),[36] the increase of women poets' publications from the late 1950s onwards provides today insights into the politics of privatized struggles depicted in the poetry of Audre Lorde, Adrienne Rich, Sylvia Plath and Anne Sexton, figures subjected to varying degrees of racialized, classist, sexual and ableist politics in the environments they lived in.[37] In light of the relatively young reflections on the particular and multitudinous challenges of women poets framing black feminist thought, Patricia Hill Collins refers to poetry as a source to research everyday thoughts, worries and challenges of black women in the US-context.[38] Farrokhzad's breaking of silences surrounding customary law of female modesty and introversion in 'public' reflects the absence of such voices in this temporal scenario.[39]

In modern Persian poetry of twentieth-century Iran, love and madness continue to be in a reciprocal relation;[40] however, social positionality renders visible particular sociopolitical scenarios in which the relation between love and madness vary from the *topos* of *Majnūn* and are not merely related to a romantic love that centres around a male *dramatis persona*. At the same time, the language and form of poetry go through a process of radical transformation: while the reading of *ghazal* demands education in classical Persian and the interpretation of metaphors, *She're Now* is, despite its sociopolitical depth, accessible for its narrative linguistic style, the language of the *kucheh* (alley, here in the sense of street) which has been examined in-depth by Shamlu and his partner Ayda Sarkisiyan.[41,42]

While in the classical era of Persian poetry universal ideas of philosophy provide poets with knowledge on *aleem wa adam* (world and human) through myths, faith and spirituality, modernity in Europe as well as in Iran is characterized by doubt, rationality, the individualization of poetry and the awareness of limits of knowledge acquisition.[43] Simidchieva argues that the 'dramatis persona is a literary character distinct from the person of the author who created it even in heavily autobiographical works'.[44] However, questioning the universality of the *topos* of Majnūn invites to render intelligible the relation between the social place of the poet and the *dramatis persona* to open epistemological potential to rethink gender, love and madness in modern Persianate poetry. Shamlu's poetry shows that the importance of social place and condition is not merely relevant when examining the making of women: as Papan-Matin explains,[45] Shamlu uses the first name of his partner Ayda Sarkisiyan, whom he marries in the beginning of the 1960s and transfers her into poetry.[46] Farrokhzad, on the other hand, describes her intimate encounters and lovemaking without naming her partners such as in the poem *Shab wa Havas* and *Buseh*.[47] When, in 1973, Ahmad Shamlu was honoured with the Forough Farrokhzad Price by the *Commite-ye Ahdayi jaizey-e Adabi-ye Forough Farrokhzad* (Committee of the Literary Honour Price of Forough Farrokhzad), his speech offered an insight into his idea of the role of poetry,[48] and he repeated that the distortion between *dramatis persona* and poet is not intrinsically 'feminine'. In his short political speech Shamlu links contemporary national politics to the necessity of the sociopolitical role of the poet and the literateur. Shamlu's speech proved that his comradeship went beyond gender stereotypes:[49] hence, the feminist slogan 'the personal is political' is interwoven with the Iranian *She're Now* of the 1950s and 1960s, as it was appropriated by artists informed by urban left-wing politics in their cultural production process.

By thematizing the distorted lines between *dramatis persona* and narrating poet, *She're Now* clearly distinguishes itself from classical Persian poetry. Farzaneh Milani has engaged in-depth with Farrokhzad's biography providing critical insights into her social and political environment, as well as individual struggles.[50] In her earlier works the emerging poet provides an 'alternative' to an androcentric and romanticized idea of love,[51] reaching like Shamlu did, masses of Iranians consuming and reciting their love poetry up until this day. Farrokhzad's iconic status might be due to the sensationalism around her love affairs, her tragic death and her provocatively sexual and intimate early poetry.[52] In comparison to later work, like *Tavalode Digar* (Rebirth),[53] her early production has been widely criticized in Persian and Anglophone literary discussions for its emotionality and lack of poetic complexity and depth.

However, the early poetry has provided social insights, if not necessarily lyrical perfection, which needs further discussion to challenge normative ideas of madness and love in Persianate love poetry: first, Farrokhzad broke with the shaming and silencing of female sexuality.[54] The geography of female sexuality was visible in popular realms such as *Film Farsi* cinema, cabarets and for male clientele in the brothels of *Shah-re Now*.[55,56] However, as Milani has highlighted, sexuality is one dimension of Farrokhzad's body of work. Re-reading *Asir*, *Diwar* and *'Esyan*,[57] it appears that Farrokhzad introduces herself as a loving mother who cannot be a mother for her child and live up to social expectations.[58] The poet does not centralize her life around the idea of creating a family organized in accordance with the law of the father, which characterizes the 'madness' she is caught in as a mother. Last but not least, Farrokhzad strives in her writings to be a poet: this love is entangled with 'madness' as the poetic vocation is not perceived as suitable for a woman as Farrokhzad's letters to her father underline.[59]

While there have been gender-sensitive readings in Anglophone scholarly discussions, as Milani's research shows, conceptual approaches offering a comparative feminist and/or gendering perspective on love poetry Persian-speaking discussions in general, and Farrokhzad's and Shamlu's love poetry in particular, have been rather absent until the past years. Two publications stand out using European philosophical concepts in conversation with local scholarly discourses to examine Farrokhzad.[60]

Nikbakht bases his analysis on the assumption that Farrokhzad's poetic journey can be understood through dialectics that run through the themes and poetic skills of the body of her work. Accentuating Farrokhzad's awareness in regard to her own place in society, Nikbakht argues that the poet locates the poetic Self in relation to the 'characteristics' (*khasayes*) of the time and space she is born into, thereby fulfilling 'the most important responsibility of art'.[61] As opposed to Simidchieva's clear distinction between *dramatis persona* and poet, Nikbakht observes a dialectical and ongoing reciprocal relation between the poetry and life of Farrokhzad. As in Anglophone discussions on Farrokhzad's poetic journey,[62] Nikbakht writes that Farrokhzad moves from creating cliché-like feminine poetry to poetic perfection dividing her poetry-life into three phases: *duran gomshodegi wa na-agahi-ye Forough* (the time of Forough's lostness and unawareness), *duran khud-yaftegi wa agahi-ye Forough* (the time of Forough's self-discovery and awareness) and *duran az khud guzashtegi wa rahaee-ye Forough* (the time of Forough's sacrifice and redemption). While Nikbakht's argument appears patronizing in it describes the banalized early poetry as immature and lost, it is exemplary for how the early intimate poetry of Farrokhzad has been depoliticized. In contrast to Farrokhzad, Shamlu's early work prior to his Ayda love poetry has been described as highly political by Alishan,[63] before the poet became frustrated with Iranian society and turned his attention to his partner Aida. Love poetry to Shamlu was hence also a way of accepting that the creation of political awareness is not necessarily triggering political action towards social and political justice. Love, on the other hand, seems, in Shamlu's later work, graspable in its amorphousness. What was perceived in Farrokhzad's early work as intimate and naive, in Shamlu's work it is seen as the peak of love poetry in *She're Now*.

Characteristic of Farrokhzad's first phase is the thematic discussion of the oppression of women and the individual alienation from society. For example, *Asir* was created in the era of the coup d'etat in Iran,[64] and the movement for the nationalization of Iranian oil, driven by Mossadeqh.[65] In *Asir*, *Divar* and *'Esyan* there is no presence yet – so argues Nikbakht –[66]of what Nima Yushij defines a poetic break with classical Persian poetry nor with the politically driven poetic movement in Iran. While Nikbakht mentions that Farrokhzad herself criticized, in later years, her early publications as 'banal words of the everyday', this era can offer an explanation of the politics of love and madness in *She're Now*; it also problematizes notions of what is considered 'banal', and for what reasons, all the way to modern-day Iran. Farrokhzad's *Tavalode Digar* establishes the start of the second phase of Farrokhzad's poetry, Nikbakht argues.[67] During this time, she has acquired knowledge of her Self (*khud*) and the Self's environment (*muhit*) while her use of metre, language, articulation and composition is also formed in this period. In the third phase of her life, the lines between *dramatis persona* and the poet become completely blurred, says Nikbakht;[68] this allows Farrokhzad to render visible, through her perspective (*negah*) and view of the world (*jahane vijeh*), the relations between human and world, crystallizing the dialectic nature of life: for example, she explores the relation between life and seasons, where the passing of death and decay gives space to life and rebirth in spring; since without winter, there can be no spring.[69]

Tavalode digar, which has been translated as 'Another Birth' and 'Rebirth',[70] carries the dichotomized relations between signifier and signified which have philosophically been intellectualized in German and French philosophy of the nineteenth century onwards, from Hegel to Marx to postmodern French philosophers. In an examination of the place of Shamlu and Farrokhzad's poetic work in the era of modernism, Iraj Amir-Ziaee also refers to European philosophical categories to analyse modern Persian poetry.[71] Amir-Ziaee argues that while classical Persian poetry was based on 'philosophical reflections' and related the universalized (male) poet with the realm of God's creations, 'the twilight of Persian poetry' begins after Jami and the political decline of *Iran zamin* (Earth of Iran), although he gives no explanation of what initiates the political regression; anything after the era of classical poetry is, according to Amir-Ziaee, imitation of Hafez's art of *ghazal*.[72] The era of philosophical and poetic decline, until the constitutional era at the beginning of the twentieth century, alienates poetry from thought and philosophy, writes Amir-Ziaee. The link is re-established when the Qajar and Pahlavi dynasties invest in the adaptation of cultural production inspired by the ruling elites' travels to the Ottoman Empire and modern Turkey, India and Europe.[73]

The use of non-native thought on the politics of madness and love in *She're Now* has been appropriated to an extent, by putting authors from geographies across the North-

Atlantic region and regional thinkers into a conversation. However, the marginalization of critical gender-sensitive thought is still dominant despite the increase in women and family studies in Iran over the past decade. Parvin Panahi's study argues that a comparative analysis of the place of 'anxiety' in Forough Farrokhzad work and that of Palestinian poet Ghada Al-Saman enables us to highlight something that is ignored about the *jahane sevum* (third world) dominated by *mard-salari* (patriarchy): a history of feminist organization within Asia such as the 'Congrees of the Women of the East' in Tehran in 1932.[74] While Panahi naturalizes the idea of feminity – which might be due to her being subject to censorship – the basis of her comparison is the upbringing of women poets in a misogynist environment hostile to women's call for equality.[75] A crucial statement in Panahi's introduction is what feminism is 'not', for example, the struggle for matriarchal rule (zan-salari), a powerful and dominant opinion not just across Asia and Africa but also in North-Atlantic ideas of feminist knowledges. While Panahi ignores so-called second-wave feminist scholars engaging with questions of alternatives to 'patriarchal rule' through the deconstruction of psychoanalytical discourses,[76] Panahi's analysis can be useful when considered as a form of 'strategic essentialism' in light of censorship-related limits of feminist thought production in Iran.[77] To highlight the need for feminist thought to render intelligible marginalized perspectives, Panahi refers to Al-Salaman's observation that women, making half of the population of the nation, cannot be disabled if the nation wants to thrive and turn away from 'American' ideas of equality.[78] As Panahi highlights throughout her literary review of Anglophone and Persian scholarship, with a critical assessment of Shokuh Navabinejad's work on *The Psychology of Women*,[79] the social and political conditions leading often to women's anxieties were not considered in the process of their medical treatment.

In contrast to the Iranian discourse, Anglophone discussions on the medicalization of 'loud', 'hysteric' and 'depressed' women have been subject to analysis since the late 1960s when social movements and white feminists' criticism of psychoanalyses and phallogocentrism emerged.[80] Examining the history of hysteria in England, Elaine Showalter explains, 'hysteria concerns feminists because the label has always been used to discredit women's political protest.'[81] While in recent years, hysteria has disappeared from consulting rooms, hospital wards and psychiatric textbooks, as many of its traditional symptoms were reclassified as anxiety, neuroses, obsessional disorders, manic depression or borderline personality disorders.[82] Hence, hysteria never disappeared but, rather, reconfigured its shape. One could also talk of the *topos* of hysteria that never really died. In the end of the nineteenth century 'hysteria, feminism, and political speech', writes Showalter, became one in the 'popular mind'.[83] particularly in England. The term 'madness' was equally used to describe sociopolitical women activists and mentally incapable subjects. Showalter's literary analysis of the power-knowledge relations, particularly perpetuated by the patient–doctor relation, enables to critically question the discourse on the 'hysteric woman' and can be read complementarily to Panahi's examination of Farrokhzad and Al-Saman.[84] Particularly, in light of the limited knowledge about women poets in the Qajar and Pahlavi era,[85] Farrokhzad's articulation of embodied experience becomes an important poetic, as well as sociological and political source of knowledge. Panahi's central focus on 'anxiety', while problematizing the genealogy of the term in the Iranian context and applying it among others to Farrokhzad's love poetry, does not consider the political economy behind the medicalization of women poets through psychologically oriented and banalizing explanations of Farrokhzad's idea of love and madness.

Hence, in order to problematize the idea of the young and mad woman poet, a comparative reading considering Shamlu's journey to love poetry and both poets' relation to the *topos* of Majnūn highlights the differing politics of love and madness *She're Now* they were subjected to depending on their social role and place in society.

Ahmad Shamlu's love poetry, Majnūn and the idea of destined love

In the early 1960s, Shamlu had reached a 'distinct period' in his poetry.[86] After having been imprisoned several times throughout the 1950s and 1960s Shamlu's 'anger at the cause of this sorrow' was directed at the people who did not show the activity he expected them to show. His will to change Iran's political landscape after the coup against Mohammad Mossadegh in 1953 was still the subject of his fourth poetry collection, *Hava-yi tazah*, published in 1957. Poems such as *Bimar* (*Sick*) express the hope of the narrator for change and a new sociopolitical direction in Iran.

While in Nizami's narration people give Quays the name 'mad', alluding to the fact that he is possessed by a jinn, Shamlu's love poetry has never led to questioning his mental health status in the first place. Shamlu's *dramatic persona* is comparable to the character of Majnūn in the oral and in the written story embodying a respected and productive poet, who creates as he walks and suffers, and a 'mad' man.[87] Khairallah writes about Majnūn's characteristics:

> love, madness, and poetry must be seen as archetypal channels for communion with the divine, channels that were fused in one legendary character who symbolized different quests in different contexts. In all those contexts, however, Magnun represents the rejection of established intellectual, social, and psychological limitations and symbolizes the basic yearning of the 'I' to be at one with the Other.[88]

The 'Majnūn legend', unifying 'love, madness, and poetry', is hence not referring to an understanding of madness, as in the modern central European making of the mad body and mind.[89] Rather, madness for love and the poetic product of this combination are understood as a divine intervention. Khairallah reminds that also the prophet Mohammed was accused in his days of being a 'poet and mad man'.[90] The explanation that Majnūn, meaning '"possessed by a jinn or demon"' or simply '"possessed"', makes sense within the rationality of the time and space of the story.[91] Later Sufist interpretations suggested, Majnūn's love goes beyond the love for a human subject but is directed towards God.[92] Clinton argues that Majnūn's madness frees him in the same way it 'liberates' Sufis from 'the ordinary conventions and constraints of society'.[93] From this perspective, madness becomes the opposite of what modern European psychoanalysis and psychology have established as madness. However, Nizami's idea of the origins of Majnūn's 'madness' is based on his boundless love for Layla. The immeasurable character of his affection subsequently elevates her to a silent 'goddess' that can also be found in Shamlu's poetry for his wife,[94] particularly in *Ayda in the Mirror*. Majnūn is not being marginalized or imprisoned by the community for his 'abnormal' behaviour but, rather, admired for the creative and moving production of his mind. People express pity for the possessed and brilliant mad poet.

Attempting to reflect peoples' pain and fears of trespassing political boundaries, Shamlu, who believed that poetry is the 'weapon' of the people,[95] regarded himself as a tool or channel to articulate the frustrations and hopes of the people in Iran. Alishan suggests that from the 'mid-1960s onward, Shamlu ceases to search for or to believe in an ideal audience' and intensively engages with love poetry.[96] From that perspective love 'replaced' the political to a certain extent in Shamlu's work. Finally, in *Ayda, the Tree, the Dagger, and a Memory* that was published in 1965, Alishan writes, 'the people's poet was turning away from the people'.[97] Karimi-Hakkak explains in his analysis of Shamlu that the poet wants to be 'remembered and judged as the poet of collections such as Aïda in the Mirror'. While the 'early Shamlu' was 'a man of power, persuasion and determination' the older Shamlu is introverted in his work.[98]

Although the poet's focused escapism into love poetry culminated in the 'Ayda' poetry, he already developed a distinct poetic engagement with the beloved subject in *Hava-yi tazah*, in the poem *Roxana*.[99] Here, Shamlu introduces an 'idealized' woman, an 'image of obscure and evasive desire', a mysterious symbol of what the narrator has not yet found in his life; someone who in contrast to Ayda is

> the account of the unrequited love between the narrator/lover and his beloved. On the surface, it is a familiar tale. But, as a result of his rejection and abandonment, the lover falls into self-contemplation.[100]

If Roxana was the young man's longing for a female body he cannot reach, Ayda is the materialization of a desired lover who brings stability and order to the unpredictability of the narrator's melodramatic relation to the unattainable Roxana. Shamlu's poetry collection *Hava-yi tazah* embraces sociopolitical poems alongside love poetry, although the latter are not a central theme in this work. The poet's idea of love is reliable; without surprises, it is the longing for stability. The title 'fresh air' alludes, on the one hand, to the longing for political change initiated from the grassroots, but simultaneously it can be understood as the feeling of being reborn through the loved 'other'. Shamlu's amorously longing for women in *Hava-yi tazah* – who, in contrast to *Roxana*, are nameless – reflects his ideal of a partner who complements him. He approaches a beloved 'other' in *Esgh- e Umumi* (*Public Love*). Here already one can trace the organized examination of the lover as it appears in the Ayda poetry. The *dramatis persona* philosophizes:[101]

> A tear is mysterious
> A smile is mysterious
> Love is mysterious

The composition embraces physically perceivable phenomenon, while the last one, 'love' is an abstract idea. A tear and smile can be felt, tasted and seen. Nevertheless, what initiates it is scientifically as 'mysterious' as the idea of love. The narrator links the three phenomena and creates a sense of mysteriousness:

> That night, tears were the smile of my love

The narrator makes love verbally palpable for himself. The following stanza is a number of things that the narrator claims not to be:

> I am not a story that you can tell
> I am not a melody that you can sing
> I am not a sound that you can hear
> Or something obvious that you see
> Or something obvious that you know

The repetitions of what the narrator claims he is not are strong statements that attempt to clarify that the narrator is neither of these abstract things that can be again perceived through the body's senses. The narrator is beyond the aesthetics of the story, melody and sound. All three terms are rather positively connoted in contrast to what the narrator claims to be:

> I am the shared pain
> Cry me out.

The *dramatis persona* is a part of the loved one's inner life and thereby intrinsic to the subject. He is not what can be perceived through the senses but felt from within. The poem continues by portraying the inner life of the 'self':
Within oneself, one holds speeches with the forest

> The grass with the plain
> The star with the galaxy
> And me with you, we hold speeches.

The elements are part of the same system; the narrator suggests that he and the subject are part of the same system. The narrator is part of the loved one's inner life, as the loved subject is part of his. The theme of this reciprocal relationship is transferred by the narrator back to the outer-body experience where he wants to know the subject's name, he wants to hold her hand, he wants to listen to her and literally asks her 'give me your heart'.[102] The *dramatis persona* conceptualizes the love for the subject's body, and particularly her lips, as the source of his poetic inspiration. This classic, heterosexual, all-embracing form of love is nourished by the idea that *being* means to *be* with the loved one. Even among those who are not anymore:

> (...)
> And in the dark cemetery
> I sang with you
> The most beautiful anthems
> Because this year the dead
> Were the liveliest lovers.

Shamlu's unique love takes place in a time when no one else seems to understand this type of dedication that spans physical and platonic love. The repetition of what they are 'like' throughout the subsequent stanza is a series of comparisons such as cloud and hurricane, rain and ocean, bird and spring and tree and jungle. The latter couple refers to the above-mentioned inner speech where the narrator describes the self's dialogue with the inner forest. Now he replaces the abstract self with a tree, the tree that is not just a part of the forest but gives the forest its meaning. The *dramatis persona* concludes the tree–forest relation by establishing himself as the soil of the forest that welcomes the tree's roots. Just as the narrator associates tree and soil as undividable unities, he perceives himself and the loved subject as a holistic and 'natural' entity within a bigger system.

The love poems in *Ayda dar Ayneh* give the loved subject in *Hava-yi tazah*, not just a name but the shape of Shamlu's wife and best friend Ayda.[103] As mentioned earlier, this poetry collection introduced a shift in Shamlu's choice of subjects. He moved from reading the subject's body within a sociopolitical context to the inner life of the subject and his bodily desires. While the nation, the political, the people and the politicization of the people were in the focus of the preceding works, *Ayda dar Ayneh* is the manifestation of the shift from the politics loving poet caught in the political act of poetic negotiation to the loving poet articulating destined affect.[104] Shamlu's idea of love is a reflection of a classic idea of love characterized by an intense emotional relation between two subjects, a heterosexual and monogamous idea of love. He is analytical and rational in his engagement with the beloved one. This becomes particularly obvious in the most famous poem and name giver of the collection, *Ayda dar Ayneh*, where the dramatis persona sings a hymn to the beloved Ayda. As Papan-Matin suggests, the narrator might speak to the beloved subject through the poem or an audience.[105] Although Ayda is not mentioned throughout the poem, the narrator uses the second person singular to express himself when gazing at Ayda's reflection in a mirror. In contrast to Farrokhzad who uses the symbolism of the mirror to 'express herself as a feminine, modern and anti-transcendentalist poet' allowing herself to articulate via the mirror 'desires, fears, anxieties, doubts and many other feelings' but also to capture the development and change within the self,[106] Shamlu uses the mirror to describe the silent beauty of Ayda's body and personality. Previous notions of the beloved woman and particularly that of the Ayda poetry elevate her to 'goddess' whose characteristics are not static but, rather, change in their beauty and uniqueness from poem to poem.[107] In Shamlu's work the female subject is flawless and exerts, through her aesthetic being and sexual charisma, her power over the male narrator:[108]

> Your lips, delicate as poetry
> Turn the most voluptuous kiss into such coyness
> That the cave-animal uses it
> To become human.

At first sight, the first stanza seems to express carnal desire for the admired subject starting with the description of her 'lips' that perform 'the most erotic kisses'.[109] The subsequent portrayal of the power of her lips transforming even a 'cavemen' into a mature and sophisticated human being underlines her goddess-like nature that is beyond sexual desire. The narrator admires her intellect as much as her lips, a very sensual and sexual part of the body and simultaneously the channel to articulate thoughts verbally. From her lips the narrator moves to describing her cheeks and the 'oblique lines' surrounding her mouth, again accentuating the aesthetics of the seen.[110]

The narrator then links physical beauty to intellect when he writes that these checks and lines lead her 'pride' and determine his 'destiny' by enchanting him even stronger through her spoken words. The *dramatis persona* tries to portray the breathtaking being he sees in the mirror. He complements what he sees by drawing epic comparisons when he writes, 'and your love/is the victory of a man/as long as he rushes to the destined war'. The war symbolizes the relationship that is worth fighting for, underpinning his success at winning her love eventually. This strong visual scenery is followed by the portrayal of her 'bosom' that protects the man like a new born child while the lovers are exposed to the gossiping of the people:[111]

> And your bosom
> a tiny place to live
> a tiny place to die
> and an escape
> from the city
> that accuses the purity of the sky
> shamelessly with a thousand fingers.

The narrator is not just safe with her but was also saved by her:

> A mountain begins with its first rocks
> And man with the first pain in me there was a cruel prisoner
> not used to the clanking of his chains
> I began with your first glance.

Her hands are 'reconciliation'. Her lips, cheecks and bosom make him feel peaceful and forget his 'enemies', symbolizing worries and fears of the self.[112] Towards the end of the poem the *dramatis persona* moves his eyes from her hands back to her face where he describes her forehead as 'a long mirror'.[113] The 'seven sisters', the mythological daughters of the titan Atlas and the nymph Pleione, strive to have a forehead like this, the narrator praises:

> Your presence is a paradise
> justifying escape from hell
> it is an ocean overwhelming me
> to wash me clean
> of every lie and of every sin.
> And the dawn awakens with your hands.

The glorified love purifies him from his 'sins and lies'.[114] The almost fetishisation of the loved one culminates in the beginning of a new day and her first touch. Similar to Majnūn's love for Layla, Shamlu's love for Ayda articulates 'obsession' for the loved partner, as if possessed by her body and mind which inspires the poet/*dramatis persona* to make himself vulnerable by articulating his love.

Shamlu discovers the loved subject's body without reducing her to carnality. In order to avoid her pure sexualization, the narrator draws parallel between her enchanting eroticism and her intellect. Therefore, Shamlu presents an analysis of his love relation that is based on balance and order. The amalgam of sophistication and almost motherly safety that she gives him characterize the narrator's popular idea of love. In contrast to the love he describes in *Roxana*, the poet shapes for his nameless lovers, and for Ayda, a love poetry that equates their relation to the law of nature: a destined relation that grew organically and in accordance with the procedures of the universe. Although the poet is not alluding to a religious notion of 'destiny', love makes his poetry indeed spiritual. The materialization of love, of which Ayda is the epitome, introduces emphasis smooth and destined movements and shifts that marginalizes any notion of madness in view of the poet satisfying his longing.

Forough Farrokhzad's love poetry, Majnūn and the predicament of love

In contrast to Shamlu, Farrokhzad's loved subjects have no names. Nevertheless, her early poetry collections consist of works that seem to be dedicated to Parviz Shahpour to whom she was married from 1952 to 1958.[115] In her later poetry Farrokhzad portrays lovers, but the lovers are still nameless. The bodily interaction creates an intimate space in-between the interchangeable lovers that Farrokhzad captures in her poetry.

As a result of Farrokhzad's openness about bodily intimacy, her 'contemporaries' perceived it as inappropriate, which contributed to her work being understood as scandalous:[116] 'Farrokhzad's early verses caused a stir in a culture traditionally censorious of exposing the realm of the intimate to the public gaze.'[117] Although other female poets such as Tahereh Quorratol'Ayn and Parvin E'tessami established themselves prior to Farrokhzad, she was indeed the first to articulate her love and desire for the male 'other'. In Milani's words, 'she literally creates an- other voice' particularly by becoming the 'storyteller' herself and instead of 'effacing men', in the way Parvin E'tessami did, she 'uncovers them'. Farrokhzad breaks the tradition that wants the madly loving poet to be male: Farrokhzad identifies herself primarily as a poet and second, as a gendered subject.[118] While staying with her older brother Amir in Munich, Germany, in 1957 Farrokhzad wrote in a letter to her father: 'I want to become a great poet: I love poems. I never had any other job apart from that; so since I know myself I love poetry.'[119] Farrokhzad is living for the 'conventionally forbidden: textual and sexual'.[120] She writes to her father that nothing material can satisfy her needs the way poetry can. She writes that if she looses 'the power to write poetry I will kill myself'.[121] If Shamlu's 'goddess' is Ayda, Farrokhzad's is manifold. Apart from lovers and her son, there is poetry. But she has a vicious relation to poetry: while she praises it, she simultaneously despises it, since it has torn her apart from her father, former husband and son.[122] Her love relation can go beyond a physically present subject: she is also in a passionate loving relationship with her vocation as a poet. In the piece *Esyan* (Rebellion) included in the collection titled *Asir* the narrator chooses even poetry over her lover/husband.[123] So, the love relation between Farrokhzad and poetry shows that performing the beloved practice does not necessarily resolve the problem but, rather, nourishes the vicious cycle, just like Majnūn's continued poetic love declaration for Layla shows. In her early poetry Farrokhzad does not just unveil herself but 'unveil men'. Milani highlights that the poet does so by portraying men beyond conventional guidelines, by freeing them from the stereotype of masculine power and virility.[124]

Farrokhzad's first, second and third collection – *Asir* (*Captive*, 1955), *Divar* (*The Wall*, 1956) and *Esyan* (*Rebellion*, 1958) – have been marginally analysed by scholars who argue that they lack in quality and have not yet captured the virtuosity of the poet of *Iman biavarim be aghaz-e fasl-e sard* (*Let Us Believe in the Beginning of the Cold Season*) and *Tavalod-e Digar* (*Another Birth*).[125] Milani compares Farrokhzad's development to that of a protagonist in the German '*Bildungsroman*': 'a personal history of growth and change'.[126] In light of this comparison, Farrokhzad's early poetry seems as important as her later, more perfected work. The young and 'sinful' Farrokhzad opens up new perspectives on the legacy of Majnūn in contemporary Iranian poetry. Nevertheless, Farrokhzad's work and the narrator's voice cannot be fully examined within the *topos* of Majnūn. Her voice is far more complex than that of the mad man of the Middle Ages and raises, in contrast to Shamlu's love poetry for Aida, questions in regard to the multiple meanings of love and madness.[127] Describing her as a *majnūna* allows us to grasp the boundaries she trespasses and her de-mystification of a type of love and madness that is limited to romantic love.[128]

The first poetry collection is very sensual. Farrokhzad's *dramatis persona* articulates through poetry her longing for the 'other' such as in *Shab va Havas* (*Night and Desire*) portraying her 'fiery moments of desire' and explicitly articulating 'I want him'.[129] The poem *Buseh* (*The kiss*) begins with the description 'From his two eyes smiled sin'.[130] The narrator continues portraying the intimate interaction between her and the desired subject. What is significant is that in contrast to Majnūn, whose love is purely platonic and who is eventually in love with an idea of the desired subject, Layla, Farrokhzad mixes love and carnal desire; in poems such as *Buseh* she describes her love and desire for bodily intimacy.

Contrary to the two above-mentioned pieces, Farrokhzad presents also another side of the loving self-identified woman in the same collection. In *Hasrat* (*Regret*) the poet depicts the loss of a lover with whose absence diminishes her will and desire to seek for the same satisfaction. She writes, 'You are gone and with you my happiness and hope / How can I ever wish for love like yours.'[131] The *majnūna* embraces the pain knowing she cannot erase it. Her suffering is as intense as her moments of intense longing and desire. A climax of suffering and unfulfilled love is reached in the poem *Bimar* (*Sick*) in which the *dramatis persona* feels sick and tired from loving and longing and prays to god to take her life:[132]

> Sometimes when I fear loneliness
> I ask myself what is there in the end
> my tear floats down my cheeck
> as I hear its name through my own whine

The *majnūna* is full of self-pity for not being able to reach the desired subject and stumbles into melancholic and nostalgic thoughts:

> I remember that he asked for kisses with charming and drunken laughs
> Or he sat with impatient glance
> Longing to consume breakfast

The love expressed in this poem is directed at Farrokhzad's son Kamyar and is a purely motherly love. *Bimar* extends the idea that love, desire and madness are – within a heteronormative mind-set – merely a phenomenon of a love relationship between two subjects of opposing sexes. The tragedy lies in the fact that the loving mother cannot show and articulate her love towards her absent son. Failing in performing idealized motherhood, the poetry becomes an instrument to articulate sickening love.

In her second poetry collection, *Divar*, which was 'dedicated to her former husband Parviz',[133] Farrokhzad published the poem *Bar Gur-e Leili* (*Upon Layla's Grave*).[134] In this Farrokhzad shares a soliloquy between herself and the absent Layla. In this way, Layla can be kept as silent as in Nizami's version of the love story. While Majnūn is developed as a round character with agency, Layla becomes a silent symbol, an 'idol' rather an active part of the storyline.[135] Clinton explains:[136] 'Leili the person has been replaced by Majnūn's idealization of her, an entity that he can sustain quite independently.'[137] Despite Layla's silence, Talattof argues that she is rather an exception. Nizami's 'unlikely heroines' are generally round characters who are portrayed in 'their role as lovers, heroines, rulers, and even educators and challengers of men' in the diverse contexts.[138] Talattof describes this phenomenon as 'anachronistic, unlikely, and puzzling'. There were rather chauvinist attitudes towards female-identified bodies that were pronounced in prose and epic poetry of Nizami's era.[139] According to Farrokhzad, her beauty did not help her in any way. She was not able to make her own decisions and have something of her own apart from those 'black eyes'. The narrator braces Majnūn's Layla:[140]

> In the end it was opened, that mysterious curtain
> In the end you recognized me, oh familiar eye
> Because another shadow of your ominous delusion
> I am that lengthy bride of imaginations
>
> It is my eye that you are staring at
> Who was Layla? What is the story of the black eyed ones?
> Do not think why my eyes are not
> Like Layla's wild eyes black

The mysterious *dramatis persona* begins with the end. The end seems to have brought enlightenment and clarification. Talking to Layla – or maybe an audience – the narrator shows in stanza one and two the aesthetic power of the narrator's eye and the 'familiar eye'. In the second stanza Layla clarifies that she herself wants to be the protagonist of the poem. But asking 'Who was Layla?' supplements the mysteriousness of women with black eyes. Again the author relativizes the exotic aura surrounding Layla and invites the reader to think of her as just as interesting and secretive as Layla. The third stanza continues and intensifies the description of the eyes.

> If night was blossoming in Layla's eyes
> Then in my eyes the fiery flower of love blossoms
> On the blossom of my silent lips
> Many of those stories of the pleasant twists and bends of love

The narrator compares her eyes in the tone of a jealous teenager to Layla's that are as dark as 'night', in contrast to hers which are full of passionate 'fiery flowers' when in love. They glow and shine and express their love brightly, while Layla remains mysterious and silent. Although the narrator's eyes seem to speak, her lips are 'silent'. While she most certainly has a story to tell, she raises the interest in her person by alluding to her many encounters with love that she keeps though to herself. Towards the end of the poem the narrator directs her speech towards Layla claiming:

> Yes . . .why shouldn't I mention to you, oh familiar eye
> I am that bride of lengthy imagination
> I am that woman who has set foot lightly
> Upon the cold and silent grave of the unfaithful Layla.

Reiterating the statement from the first stanza, the *dramatis persona*'s claims again to be 'the bride of lengthy imagination'. She is the one who people dream and think of, not Layla. She is also the strong and living one who is walking on Layla's grave who moved long ago from the living silent, to the silent dead. The narrator does not feel bad about demonstrating her power 'upon Layla's grave' when she unveils finally that the mysterious Layla was not loyal to someone. She seems to suggest that Layla does not deserve all the attention she receives, while the narrator does. Despite not having black eyes and the mysterious aura of Layla, in the end of the poem, the narrator has the power to declare that the introductory allusion to the opening of 'the mysterious curtain' of her eyes reveals the hidden secret that these wild dark eyes were 'unfaithful'. If Farrokhzad actually alludes to the love story in which Layla marries Ibn Salam after her parents reject Majnūn's request for their daughter's hand, she judges her submissive behaviour.[141] Farrokhzad's narrator seems confident in her judging. Building upon the assumption that Farrokhzad's relationship to her *dramatis persona* is intensively intertwined in her early works she alludes to her own rebellion. Despite her parents' rejection of Parviz Shahpour's proposal, Farrokhzad decides to run away with him at the age of sixteen and get married.[142] At this point, several years before her divorce from Shahpour and the birth of her son Kamyar, Farrokhzad is proud of her decision to challenge paternal law and to embody the 'new woman'.[143] Layla dies 'alone', away from her Majnūn. Farrokhzad does not allow this to happen. Layla did not leave anything behind apart from herself. But Farrokhzad is 'lengthy' as she is producing and writing to declare her love, just as Majnūn did, who is unmentioned in this poem.

In the poem *Junūn* (*Madness*) in Farrokhzad's third publication, *Esyan*, the narrator, bemoans the loss of a beloved person. The sorrow of loneliness – in contrast to solitude – drives her mad:[144]

> What will my deluded heart do
> with spring arriving
> with the need to color
> the body of the dry and black branches?

The feeling of desperation and need to have someone to feel complete is created by 'spring', representing, on the one hand, the renaissance of nature; on the other hand, spring comes with the expectation to not just find rebirth in nature but also through an 'other' subject for the narrator herself. But the sorrowful tone suggests that she suffered so much that she does not know how to start anew:[145]

> My lips burn from the song
> My breasts burn amorously
> My skin bursts from excitement
> My body burns from its core

The focus on the narrator's self reveals the anxiety of losing control of the self. The imagery of bursting and burning powers seems to affect the narrator's mind and give her the feeling of restlessness. There is something narcissistic about the mad poet: the self is in the centre of the event and describes the productive destruction of the poet:[146]

> Oh spring, oh charming spring
> I am waiting for him
> In your madness I forgot myself
> I have turned into a song, a cry, a wish

The narrator's desperate search for someone to share spring with finds its climax in the expression that there is nothing left of her apart from the words of the poem, moaning for a love that fulfils physical and intellectual desires. The poem ends as it started, with the wailing expression of what shall be done with her deluded and saddened heart.

Dols writes about the 'destructive aspects of love's power' since 'all who are touched by Majnun's passion are either altered or destroyed by it',[147] such as his parents, who passed away after trying without success to bring Majnūn back home. Likewise, Farrokhzad's love had a great impact on those she was involved with; but also their behaviour towards Farrokhzad had a significant influence on her being: especially with relation to her former husband Shahpour who denied her the right to see their son, which resulted in a 'nervous breakdown' in 1955;[148] or to the impact Farrokhzad's affair with Ebrahim Golestan had on the filmmaker's marriage.[149]

Farrokhzad's later work, such as *Delam bara-e Bakhshe Misuzad* (*I feel Sorry for the Garden*) in the posthumously published *Iman biavarim be aghaz-e fasl-e sard*,[150] and *Ey Marz-e Porgohar* (*O Realm Bejewelled*) in *Tavalod-e Digar* are socio-politically critical poems full of empathy for the Iranian people. The title *Ey Marz-e Porgohar* refers to the Iranian national anthem during the rule of the Pahlavi dynasty starting with 'Oh Iran, o realm bejewelled'. The mature poet describes the creation and maintenance of 'stability and silence' in 1960s Iran. Upon receiving an ID card, she describes sarcastically how now she has become an acknowledged subject.[151] The poem deals with a number of critiques, directed towards political control and the creation of 'constructive citizen', the pretentiousness of men, capitalization of the urban space through billboards and flashing lights, and the commodification of female bodies that are being sold as 'art'.[152]

Conclusion

This chapter examined the politics of love and madness in 1950s–60s New Iranian Poetry to understand the legacy of the *topos* of Majnūn in Ahmad Shamlu and Forough

Farrokhzad's love poetry. The guiding question in this chapter was to examine the potential of a gender-sensitive reading of *She're Now* to rethink the notion of love and madness as it has been normalized through classical Persian poetry.

The comparative and interdisciplinary analysis allowed to link crucial insights on the instrumental use of *topoi*, feminist and gender-sensitive literary studies and feminist geopolitics – the latter used here as a methodological tool to critically trace the making of knowledge in particular temporalities and spaces – to frame the topological legacy of the mad man poet Majnūn in the epic love story of *Layla and Majnūn* in Forough Farrokhzad's love poetry.

A feminist methodology allows us to highlight the gendered politics that the love poetry of Shamlu and Farrokhzad was subjected to in light of grassroots ideas of normative gender roles and relations. The distorted boundaries between *dramatis persona* and poet in the love poetry of Farrokhzad and Shamlu provide not just literary but also sociopolitical knowledge in terms of the type of 'madness' that is at stake depending on the poets' social and political place in urban Iran. Gender is crucial in light of the era of interest, the 1950s to 1960s, and scholarly discussions on Farrokhzad and Shamlu in contemporary Iran have been provided by Nikbakht, Amir-Ziaee and Panahi. In order to critically assess the politics of madness and love, an epistemological bridging has to take place, linking contemporary and past Anglophone and Persianate epistemologies – comprising today's Iran, Afghanistan and Tajikistan – to question normalized androcentric and romanticized notions of love and madness. By emphasizing positionality in poetic production, epistemological processes can accommodate for an increased awareness of the limits and accessibility of knowledge across geographies and develop concepts to rethink normalized ideas of the limitations and advantages posed by the use of tropes such as the 'mad man' Majnūn. There is nothing intrinsically feminine about Farrokhzad's narratives of love and madness. Rather her embodied experiences challenged her into articulating maddening love beyond romantic affect. In relation to her male colleague Shamlu, both seem to have numerous similarities that need to be examined in terms of the impact of their positionality on their love poetry.

Notes

1. Firoozeh Papan-Matin, *The Love Poems of Ahmad Shamlu* (Washington: Ibex Publishers, 2005); Ghulam Husayn Yusufi, Bihruz Shahib Ikhtiyari and Hamed Baqirzadeh (eds), *Aḥmad Shamlu, Shaʻir-I Shabanah'ha va ʻashiqanah'ha*, Chāp-I 1 (Washington Tihran: Hirmand, 2003).
2. Farrokhzad, 'A Letter from Forugh to Her Father', in *Another Birth: And Other Poems*, Updated and revised edn (Washington, DC: Mage Publishers, 2010a), 181–2.
3. Judith Butler, *Gender Trouble : Feminism and the Subversion of Identity*, 2nd edn (New York and London: Routledge, 1999), 14–15, 22–33.
4. Ahmad Karimi-Hakkak and Kamran Talattof (eds), *Essays on Nima Yushij: Animating Modernism in Persian Poetry*, Brill Studies in Middle Eastern Literatures, v. 31 (Leiden; Boston: Brill, 2004).
5. Ibid., 4–6.
6. Michael W. Dols, *Majnūn: The Madman in Medieval Islamic Society* (Oxford: Clarendon Press, 1992), 10.

7   Lynette Hunter, *Critiques of Knowing: Situated Textualities in Science, Computing and the Arts* (London and New York: Routledge, 1991), viii.
8   Paolo A. Cherchi, 'Tradition and Topoi in Medieval Literature', *Critical Inquiry* 3, no. 2 (1976): 285.
9   Ibid., 286.
10 Ibid.
11 Ibid., 286–7.
12 Ibid., 287–8.
13 Dols, *Majnūn*, 339.
14 Ibid., 339.
15 Ibid., 12.
16 Ibid., 4. There used to be more than one story of Layla and Majnūn. The story is based on a 'semi- historical character' from which many versions were derived (A. A. Seyed-Gohrab, *Laylī and Majnūn: Love, Madness, and Mystic Longing in Niẓāmī's Epic Romance*, Brill Studies in Middle Eastern Literatures, v. 27 (Leiden and Boston, MA: Brill, 2003).
17 Koenigsberg and Siever, *The Frustrating No-Man's Land of Borderline Personality Disorder* (Cerebrum Dana Foundation, 2000), see website: https://www.dana.org/article/the-fr ustrating-no-mans-land-of-borderline-personality-disorder/ last accessed 21 July 2021.
18 Dols, *Majnūn*, 313.
19 Ibid., 314.
20 Kamran Talattof, 'Nizami's Unlikely Heroines: A Study of the Characterizations of Women in Classical Persian Literature', in *The Poetry of Nizami Ganjavi: Knowledge, Love, and Rhetoric*, ed. Kamran Talattof, Jerome W. Clinton, and Kenneth A. Luther (Houndmills, Basingstoke, Hampshire and New York: Palgrave, 2000), 4.
21 Nizami Ganjavi, *The Story of Layla and Majnun*, ed and trans. Rudolph Gelpke (New Lebanon, NY : Omega, 2011), 4–5.
22 Ibid., 10–11.
23 Dols, *Majnūn*, 5; see also Michel Foucault, *Madness and Civilization: A History of Insanity in the Age of Reason*, Vintage Books Ed. (New York: Random House, 1988); *The Birth of the Clinic: An Archaeology of Medical Perception*, World of Man (London: Routledge, 1989).
24 Rivanne Sandler compares Farrokhzad and Majnūn in her anthology *Forugh Farrokhazad, Poet of Modern Iran Iconic Woman and Feminine Pioneer of New Persian Poetry*, ed. Dominic Parviz Brookshaw and Nasrin Rahimieh, Iran and the Persianate World (London: I.B. Tauris in association with Iran Heritage Foundation, 2010), 59. However, the analogy stops at the observation that in the later poem *Ma'shuq-e man* (The One I Love) 'the beloved is like the wild lover Majnun, who (like Farrokhzad) loves recklessly, and insanely'.
25 Butler, *Gender Trouble*; Donna Haraway, 'Situated Knowledges: The Science Question in Feminism and the Privilege of Partial Perspective', *Feminist Studies* 14, no. 3 (1988): 575–99; Sandra G. Harding, *Whose Science? Whose Knowledge? Thinking from Women's Lives*, (Ithaca, NY: Cornell University Press, 1991); Bell Hooks, *Yearning: Race, Gender, and Cultural Politics* (Boston, MA: South End Press, 1990); Deniz Kandiyoti, 'Bargaining with Patriarchy', *Gender and Society* 2, no. 3 (1988): 274–90; Jasbir K. Puar, *Terrorist Assemblages: Homonationalism in Queer Times* (Durham: Duke University Press, 2007); Gayatri C. Spivak, 'Can the Subaltern Speak?', in *Marxism and the Interpretation of Culture*, ed. Cary Nelson and Lawrence Grossberg (Urbana: University of Illinois Press, 1988), 271–316.
26 I consciously use here the terminology 'gender-sensitive' instead of 'feminist' because first, not all gender-sensitive approaches are necessarily driven by feminist politics. Second, due to the infamous politics of feminism in Iran to the disadvantage of diverse feminist argumentations from manifold positionalities across the secular and religious specter, I try to emphasize here that a methodology informed by feminist geopolitics is

not merely about gendering the subject of interest but, rather, to render visible ideas that have been neglected for their 'banality' and subsumption to the allegedly realm of the depoliticized 'private'.

27 Jan Montefiore, *Feminism and Poetry: Language, Experience, Identity in Women's Writing* (London and Chicago: Pandora, 2004). See for literature with focus on North Africa and West Asia: Zakia Belhachmi, 'Al-Salafiyya, Feminism, and Reforms in the Nineteenth-Century Arab-Islamic Society', *The Journal of North African Studies* 9, no. 4 (January 2004): 63–90. https://doi.org/10.1080/1362938042000326290; Nawar Al-Hassan Golley, *Reading Arab Women's Autobiographies: Shahrazad Tells Her Story*, 1st edn (Austin: University of Texas Press, 2003); *Arab Women's Lives Retold: Exploring Identity through Writing*, 1st edn (Syracuse, NY: Syracuse University Press, 2007).

28 Marta Simidchieva, 'Men and Women Together: Love, Marriage and Gender in Forugh Farrokhzad's Asir', in *Forugh Farrokhzad. Poet of Modern Iran, Iconic Woman and Feminine Pioneer of New Persian Poetry*, ed. Dominic Parviz Brookshaw and Nasrin Rahimieh (London and New York: I.B. Tauris, 2010), 19–34.

29 John Zubizarreta, 'The Woman Who Sings No, No, No: Love, Freedom, and Rebellion in the Poetry of Forugh Farrokhzad', *World Literature Today* 66, no. 3 (1992): 421. https://doi.org/10.2307/40148358.

30 Jenna Christian, Lorraine Dowler, and Dana Cuomo, 'Fear, Feminist Geopolitics and the Hot and Banal', *Political Geography* 54 (September 2016): 64–72. https://doi.org/10.1016/j.polgeo.2015.06.003.

31 Jennifer Hyndman, 'Mind the Gap: Bridging Feminist and Political Geography through Geopolitics', *Political Geography* 23, no. 3 (2004): 307–22. https://doi.org/10.1016/j.polgeo.2003.12.014.

32 Laura Jones and Daniel Sage, 'New Directions in Critical Geopolitics: an Introduction: With Contributions of Gearóid Ó Tuathail, Jennifer Hyndman, Fraser MacDonald, Emily Gilbert and Virginie Mamadouh', *GeoJournal* 75, no. 4 (2010): 317. https://doi.org/10.1007/s10708-008-9255-4.

33 Sara Smith, Nathan W. Swanson, and Banu Gökarıksel, 'Territory, Bodies and Borders', *Area* 48, no. 3 (2016): 259. https://doi.org/10.1111/area.12247.

34 K. Anderson and S. Smith, 'Editorial: Emotional Geographies', *Transactions of the Institute of British Geographers* 26, no. 1 (2001): 7–10.

35 Michael Billig, *Banal Nationalism* (London and Thousand Oaks, CA: Sage, 1995).

36 Oyèrónkẹ́ Oyěwùmí, *The Invention of Women: Making an African Sense of Western Gender Discourses* (Minneapolis: University of Minnesota Press, 1997).

37 Audre Lorde, *Sister Outsider: Essays and Speeches*, The Crossing Press Feminist Series (Trumansburg, NY: Crossing Press, 1984); Nathalie Handal, *The Poetry of Arab Women: A Contemporary Anthology* (New York: Interlink Books, 2001).

38 Patricia Hill Collins, *Black Feminist Thought: Knowledge, Consciousness, and the Politics of Empowerment*, 1st edn (New York: Routledge, 2008), 9.

39 Michael Craig Hillmann, *A Lonely Woman: Forugh Farrokhzad and Her Poetry*, 1st edn (Washington, DC: Mage Publishers, Three Continents Press, 1987); Farzaneh Milani, 'Love and Sexuality in the Poetry of Forugh Farrokhzad: A Reconsideration', *Iranian Studies* 15, no. (1/4) (1982): 117–28; Eve Kosofsky Sedgwick, *Between Men: English Literature and Male Homosocial Desire* (New York: Columbia University Press, 1985).

40 Ahmad Karimi-Hakkak, *Recasting Persian Poetry Scenarios of Poetic Modernity in Iran* (Milton Keynes: Oneworld Publications Ltd, 2012), 2–7.

41 Aḥmad Shamlu, and Ayida Sarkisiyan, *Kitāb-I Kūchah: Jāmi' Lughāt, Iṣṭilāḥāt, Ta'bīrāt, Ẓarb Al-Maṣal'hā-Yi Fārsī (Book of the Street: A Collection of Words, Idioms, Expressions and Sayings in the Persian Language)*, Chāp. 2 (Tihrān: Intishārāt-i Māzyār, 1998).

42 Apart from German and French philosophy, the literary and poetic production of Berthold Brecht in Germany during the first half of the twentieth century informed the use of 'provocative' and 'communicative' themes and language through problematizing

narration rather than the presentation of a moral and truth (Klaus-Detlef Müller, *Bertolt Brecht: Epoche-Werk-Wirkung*, Arbeitsbücher Zur Literaturgeschichte (München: Beck, 2009), 24) in *she're now* (Iraj Amir-Ziaee, *Modernism Dar She'r-E Forough Wa Shamlu* (Tehran: Haft Wadi, 2011), 39–40).

43   Amir-Ziaee, *Modernism Dar She'r-E Forough Wa Shamlu*, 32–3.
44   Simidchieva, 'Men and Women Together', 19.
45   Papan-Matin, *The Love Poems of Ahmad Shamlu*, 18.
46   Aḥmad Shamlu, 'Ayda in the Mirror', in *An Anthology of Modern Persian Poetry*, ed. and trans. Ahmad Karimi-Hakkak, Modern Persian Literature Series, no. 1. (Boulder, CO: Westview Press, 1978), 62–4.
47   Forugh Farrokhzad, 'Dar Khiyaban-ha-ya Sard-e Shab', in *Tavallodi Digar* (Tehran: Morvarid, 4th printing, 1969), 83.
48   The committee honoured annually in Iran on Forough Farrokhzad date of death, 13 February 1967, the country's best poet, writer and other artists of the year. The first prize in 1972 was given to Jalal Al-Ahmad. The price was awarded from 1972 until 1978 (Shams 1991, 254–5; Yusufi et al., *Aḥmad Shamlu, Sha'ir-I Shabanah'ha va 'ashiqanah'ha*, 141–3).
49   Shams Langaroodi, *Tarikh Tahili Sher Now* (Iran: Nashr Markaz, 1959), 256–7.
50   See Milani, *Forough Farrokhzad: A Literary Biography with Unpublished Letters (Forough Farrokhzad: zendegi name-ye adabi hamra banameh-hae chap nashode)* (Persian Circle, 2016); Leila Rahimi Bahmany, 'Bewildered Mirror: Mirror, Self and World in the Poems of Forugh Farrokhzad', in *Forugh Farrokhzad. Poet of Moder Iran, Iconic Woman and Feminine Pioneer of New Persian Poetry*, ed. Brookshaw Brookshaw Dominic Parviz and Nasrin Rahimieh (London and New York: I.B. Tauris, 2010), 69–82; John Zubizarreta, 'The Woman Who Sings No, No, No: Love, Freedom, and Rebellion in the Poetry of Forugh Farrokhzad', *World Literature Today* 66, no. 3 (1992): 421. https://doi.org/10.2307/40148358
51   Forugh Farrokhzad, *Asīr*, Chāp-I 4 (Tihrān: Amīr Kabīr, 1967); *Dīvār* (Tehran: Jāvīdān, 1967); *'Isyān* (Tehran: Amir Kabir, 1968).
52   Homa Katouzian, 'Of the Sins of Forugh Farrokhzād', in *Forugh Farrokhzad, Poet of Modern Iran: Iconic Woman and Feminine Pioneer of New Persian Poetry*, ed. Dominic Parviz Brookshaw and Nasrin Rahimieh, International Library of Iranian Studies (I.B. Tauris, 2010), 7–18.
53   Milani, 'Love and Sexuality in the Poetry of Forugh Farrokhzad'; *Veils and Words: The Emerging Voices of Iranian Women Writers*, 1st edn, Contemporary Issues in the Middle East (Syracuse, NY: Syracuse University Press, 1992); *Words, Not Swords: Iranian Women Writers and the Freedom of Movement*, 1st edn Gender, Culture, and Politics in the Middle East (Syracuse, NY: Syracuse University Press, 2011); Mahmud Nikbakht, *Az Gomshodegi-Ye Tarha-Ee. Dialektik-E She'r Wa Zendegi-Ye 'Forough Farrokhzad' Dar Teknik She'ri-Yee Ou* (Tehran: Nashr-i Gamān, 2016); see also the anthology Dominic Parviz Brookshaw and Nasrin Rahimieh (eds), *Forugh Farrokhzad, Poet of Modern Iran: Iconic Woman and Feminine Pioneer of New Persian Poetry*, International Library of Iranian Studies 21 (London: I.B. Tauris in association with Iran Heritage Foundation, 2010).
54   Milani, 'Love and Sexuality in the Poetry of Forugh Farrokhzad'.
55   The red light district of *Shah-re Now* has been destroyed and renamed after the Islamic Revolution *Gomrok*.
56   For a series of images on the 'New City', see Kaveh Golestan, Malu Halasa, Maziar Bahari, and Hengameh Golestan, *Kaveh Golestan: 1950–2003; Recording the Truth in Iran* (Ostfildern: Hatje Cantz, 2007).
57   Farrokhzad, *Dīvār*; *'Isyān*.
58   Nira Yuval-Davis, *Gender and Nation* (SAGE, 1997); Lisa Wedeen, *Ambiguities of Domination: Politics, Rhetoric, and Symbols in Contemporary Syria* (Chicago: University of Chicago Press, 1999).

59 Forugh Farrokhzad, 'Az Miyan-E Nameha-E Forugh Farrokhzad', in *Yad Nameh Forugh Farrokhzad. Zan-E Tanha*, ed. Hamid Siyahpush (Tehran: Muasse Intesharat Nigah, 1997a), 197–201; 'Du Nameh Tshab Nashodeh Az Forugh Farrokhzad: Faghat She'er Mara Razi Mikonad', in *Yad Nameh Forugh Farrokhzad. Zan-E Tanha*, ed. Aydin Aghdashloo (Tehran: Muasse Intesharat Nigah, 1997b), 207–14.
60 Nikbakht, *Az Gomshodegi-Ye Tarha-Ee*; Parvin Panahi, *Ezterāb Dar Ash'a-Er Forough Farrokhzad Wa Ghada Al-Saman - Naqd-E Tatbiqee (Anxiety in the Poetry of Forough Farrokhzad and Ghada Al-Saman), Comparative Criticism* (Tehran: Roshangaran & Women Studies Publishing, 2015).
61 Nikbakht, *Az Gomshodegi-Ye Tarha-Ee*, 11–12.
62 Brookshaw and Rahimie, *Forugh Farrokhzad, Poet of Modern Iran*; Hillman, *A Lonely Woman*, and Milani, 'Love and Sexuality in the Poetry of Forugh Farrokhzad'.
63 Leonardo Alishan, 'Ahmad Shamlu: The Rebel Poet in Search of an Audience', *Iranian Studies* 18, no. 2 (1985): 384–5 and 390–1.
64 Nikbakht, *Az Gomshodegi-Ye Tarha-Ee*, 12.
65 Ervand Abrahamian, *The Coup: 1953, the CIA, and the Roots of Modern U.S.-Iranian Relations* (New York: The New Press, 2013).
66 Nikbakht, *Az Gomshodegi-Ye Tarha-Ee*, 17–18.
67 Ibid., 12.
68 Ibid., 13.
69 Ibid., 130.
70 David Martin (trans.), *A Rebirth: Poems by Forugh Farrokhzaad* (Lexington (Kentucky): Mazda Publishers, 1985); other collections of poetry by the same author, in English translation, are *Bride of Acacias: Selected Poems of Forugh Farrokhzad*, Modern Persian Literature Series, no. 5. (Delmar, NY: Caravan Books, 1982); Hasan Javadi and Susan Sallée (trans.), *Another Birth: And Other Poems*, updated and revised edn (Washington, DC: Mage Publishers, 2010b).
71 The author also uses instead of the Anglicism 'modernism' the Persian term 'now-gerayee' (Amir-Ziaee, *Modernism Dar She'r-E Forough Wa Shamlu*, 39).
72 Amir-Ziaee, *Modernism Dar She'r-E Forough Wa Shamlu*, 7–9.
73 Ibid., 7–8.
74 Ellen Carol DuBois and Haleh Emrani, 'A Speech by Nour Hamada: Tehran, 1932', *Journal of Middle East Women's Studies* 4, no. 1 (Winter 2008): 107–24.
75 Panahi, *Ezterāb Dar Ash'a-Er Forough Farrokhzad Wa Ghada Al-Saman - Naqd-E Tatbiqee*, 16 and 65.
76 See Butler, *Gender Trouble*.
77 G. C. Spivak, *In Other Worlds: Essays in Cultural Politics*, Routledge Classics (London; New York: Routledge, 2006).
78 Panahi, *Ezterāb Dar Ash'a-Er Forough Farrokhzad Wa Ghada Al-Saman - Naqd-E Tatbiqee*, 16.
79 Shokuh Navabinejad, *Ravanshenasi-Ye Zan (The Psychology of Women)* (Tehran: Elm, 2012).
80 Butler, *Gender Trouble*; Teresa De Lauretis, *Freud's Drive: Psychoanalysis, Literature and Film* (Houndmills, Basingstoke, Hampshire and New York: Palgrave Macmillan, 2008). http://public.eblib.com/choice/publicfullrecord.aspx?p=416839;Luce Irigaray, *This Sex Which Is Not One* (Ithaca, NY: Cornell University Press, 1985); Julia Kristeva, *In the Beginning Was Love: Psychoanalysis and Faith*, European Perspectives (New York: Columbia University Press, 1987); *Black Sun: Depression and Melancholia*. European Perspectives (New York: Columbia University Press, 1989).
81 Elaine Showalter, *Hystories: Hysteria, Gender and Culture* (London: Picador, 1997), 10.
82 Ibid., 17.
83 Ibid., 49.
84 Ibid., 88.

85 Panahi, *Ezterāb Dar Ash'a-Er Forough Farrokhzad Wa Ghada Al-Saman - Naqd-E Tatbiqee*, 65; Milani, 'Love and Sexuality in the Poetry of Forugh Farrokhzad' and 1992.
86 Alishan, 'Ahmad Shamlu', 384.
87 Nizami, *The Story of Layla and Majnun*, 10–11.
88 As'ad E. Khairallah, *Love, Madness and Poetry: An Interpretation on the Magnun Poetry*, In Kommission bei F. (Steiner Verlag, 1980).
89 Foucault Michel, *History of Madness* (London: Routledge, 2009).
90 Khairallah, *Love, Madness and Poetry*, 37.
91 Clinton, *The Poetry of Nizami Ganjavi*, 21; Dols, *Majnūn*, 3, 10, 339.
92 Khairallah, *Love, Madness and Poetry*, 11.
93 Clinton, *The Poetry of Nizami Ganjavi*, 25.
94 Papan-Matin, *The Love Poems of Ahmad Shamlu*, 14.
95 See Shamlu's poem *She'ri keh zendegi-st* (A Poetry that is Life) from 1956 in which he writes: 'Today/ poetry/ is the people's weapon;/For the poets/are but a branch from the forest of the people,/not Jasmines or Hyacinths of someone's greenhouse' (A. Shamlu, *Havā-Yi Tāzah : Majmū'ah-I Muntakhab-I Shi'r* (Tehran: Nil, 1976), 87–99).
96 Alishan, 'Ahmad Shamlu', 384–5 and 390–1.
97 Ibid.
98 Ahmad Karimi-Hakkak, 'A Well Amid the Waste: An Introduction to the Poetry of Ahmad Shamlu', *World Literature Today* 51, no. 2 (1977): 201, 206. https://doi.org/10.2307/40133284
99 Shamlu, *Havā-Yi Tāzah*, 265–84.
100 Papan-Matin, *The Love Poems of Ahmad Shamlu*, 47, 57.
101 Shamlu, *Havā-Yi Tāzah*, 198.
102 Ibid., 200.
103 Yusufi et al., *Aḥmad Shamlu, Sha'ir-I Shabanah'ha va 'ashiqanah'ha*, 128–9; Farāmarz Khabiri, *Shinākhtnāmah-'i Aḥmad Shāmlū*, ed. Javād Mujābī, Chāp-I 1, Silsilah-I Intishārāt-I Nashr-I Qaṭrah 161. (Tihrān: Nashr-i Qaṭrah, 1998), 222–7.
104 Researcher and tim of Shamlu, Karimi-Hakkak explains: Shamlu's followers adored him for his political poetry. He was the 'poet of *azadi*' (freedom) and his poetry a 'euology, even a apotheosis to freedom' (conversation with Dr Karimi-Hakkak, 30 October 2014). With the poetry collection *Shikuftan dar mih* (Blossoming in the Mist) Shamlu returned properly to a poetry that was supposed to shake the grounds of Iranian politics bottom-up (A. Shamlu, *Shikuftan Dar Mih*. Chāp-I 2. Shi'r-I Zamān 4 (Tihrān: Zamān, 1973).
105 Papan-Matin, *The Love Poems of Ahmad Shamlu*, 14.
106 Rahimi Bahmany, 'Bewildered Mirror', 69.
107 Papan-Matin, *The Love Poems of Ahmad Shamlu*, 14.
108 Shamlu, *Ayada Dar Ayinah*, 62–4.
109 Ibid., 69.
110 Ibid., 70.
111 Ibid., 71.
112 Ibid., 72.
113 Ibid., 73.
114 Ibid., 74.
115 Milani, *Veils and Words*, 134.
116 Simidchieva, 'Men and Women Together', 21.
117 Ibid., 19; see also Milani, *Veils and Words*, 127–52.
118 Farrokhzad, 'Az Miyan-E Nameha-E Forugh Farrokhzad'.
119 Ibid., 207.
120 Milani, *Veils and Words*, 137–8.
121 Farrokhzad, 'Az Miyan-E Nameha-E Forugh Farrokhzad', 210.
122 Ibid., 210.

123 Simidchieva, 'Men and Women Together', 28–9.
124 Milani, 'Love and Sexuality in the Poetry of Forugh Farrokhzad' and 1992.
125 See Homa Katouzian, 'Of the Sins of Forugh Farrokhzād', in *Forugh Farrokhzad, Poet of Modern Iran: Iconic Woman and Feminine Pioneer of New Persian Poetry*, ed. Dominic Parviz Brookshaw and Nasrin Rahimieh, International Library of Iranian Studies (I.B. Tauris, 2010), 7–18; Farzaneh Milani, 'Love and Sexuality in the Poetry of Forugh Farrokhzad', *Iranian Studies* 15, no. (1/4) (1982): 117–28. London: Taylor & Fracis Online: https://www.tandfonline.com/doi/abs/10.1080/00210868208701596, accessed on 29th August 2021.
126 Milani, *Veils and Words*, 136.
127 See for instance, *Mechanical Doll* (Farrokhzad, 1982), 44–5. https://www.encyclopedia.com/arts/culture-magazines/mechanical-doll-and-other-poems, accessed on 29th August 2021.
128 One of the characters that Showalter introduces in *The Female Malady* is the 'wronged Romantic madwoman', Crazy Jane, whose story goes back to the end of the eighteenth century. Crazy Jane, a poor servant girl, who is abandoned by her lover, or he is dead, goes mad. She wanders out into the wild, talks to herself in her solitude, but tells also people the reason of her wandering. Her being is defined by the maintenance of the memory of her absent lover (Showalter, *The Female Malady: Women, Madness and English Culture 1830-1980* (London: Virago, 1987), 13).
129 Farrokhzad, *Aṣīr*, 11–14.
130 Ibid., 37.
131 Ibid., 33–4.
132 Ibid., 119–20.
133 Milani, *Veils and Words*, 134.
134 The poems *Bar Gur-e Leili* and *Junun* are my translations (based on Farrokhzad, *Aṣīr*).
135 Talattof, 'Nizami's Unlikely Heroines'; Clinton, *The Poetry of Nizami Ganjavi*, 4, 23.
136 Clinton, *The Poetry of Nizami Ganjavi*, 24.
137 Layla is also referred to as Leili.
138 Talattof, 'Nizami's Unlikely Heroines', 53. Another example that Talattof refers to is *Chosrou and Shirin*. Shirin is an active character in this love story who has agency: she decides to look for Chosrou while he is looking for her too. Since they cannot be together in life, Shirin decides to commit suicide to be with Chosrou (Ganjavi Nizami, *Chosrou Und Schirin*, Manesse Bibliothek Der Weltliteratur (Zürich: Manesse, 1980).
139 For instance, in Jami's work women are characterized by 'negative' features and stereotyped through 'generalizations', according to Talattof ('Nizami's Unlikely Heroines', 53–7, 69), such as 'betrayal, deceit, and his disgrace'.
140 Farrokhzad, *Dīvār*, Chāp-I 7 (Tihrān : Amīr Kabīr, 1976), 65–6.
141 Nizami, *The Story of Layla and Majnun*, 80–7.
142 Milani, *Veils and Words*, 134.
143 Semidchieva, 19.
144 Farrokhzad, *Aṣīr*, 121.
145 Ibid., 122.
146 Ibid., 123.
147 Dols, *Majnūn*, 324, quote by Julie S. Meisami.
148 Milani, *Veils and Words*, 134.
149 Nasser Saffarian, *Sard-E Sabz (The Green Cold)*, 2003. https://www.youtube.com/watch?v=ILTOIt-0ezc.
150 Farrokhzad 1975, 49–60. In Heliotricity Reviews. see website for the poems: http://www.heliotricity.com/forughfarrokhzad.html, accessed on 29th August 2021.
151 Farrokhzad 1982, 82, 86.
152 Ibid., 83, 85.

Chapter 10

LOVE AND CONFLICT IN MODERN ARABIC POETRY
THE CASE OF NIZAR QABBANI AND MAHMOUD DARWISH

Atef Alshaer[1]

Introduction

This chapter which builds on the ideas introduced in Chapter 5 turns to the modern period. It will show how the experience of the newly emerging nation states in the Arab world, and the wider Middle East, as well as the establishment of Israel as a state in Palestine, marked the poetry of love. There is continuity with the early Arabic tradition where there is an oscillation in the writing of the poets between the psychical and natural dimensions that love engenders and the sociopolitical structures that set limits on personal freedoms and other existential possibilities. The chapter is devoted to the poetry of Syrian poet Nizar Qabbani (1923–98) and Palestinian poet Mahmoud Darwish (1941–2008), innovative poets whose poetic journeys mark significant evolutions and manifestations within the Arabic tradition of love poetry.

Their poetry echoes psychical and political realities and meanings that represent continuities and discontinuities with the tradition of love in Arabic poetry. The two poets are particularly important because their love poetry springs from vivid political and social contexts within which they were embedded, and which are in turn illustrative of the state of the Arab world in the twentieth century, as a world ridden with conflicts, archaic taboos and traditions, loyalties and modernist aspirations. Needless to say, there are countless Arab poets who treated the subject of love in their poetry throughout the centuries. In fact, some produced versatile and expressive accounts of love that carry significant meanings at several levels. In terms of literary themes, love is at the heart of Arabic poetry.[2]

Against this backdrop, this chapter intends to put forward and explore a number of ideas and arguments. To being with, Nizar Qabbani attempts at advancing modernist agenda, albeit often with traditional means. His love poetry reveals and chides a wounded masculinity. It masquerades a discourse of enlightenment that in itself is not embodied with its nuances and consequences beyond the rhetoric of its liberating potential. The psychology of love in Qabbani's poetry is not borne of free contexts. In that, love is often a metaphor for structures that curtail the realization of its subjective outcomes in relation to love's own dynamics. Love is a victim crying out to be rid of societal shackles. Therefore, Nizar adopts a grand narrative in his poetry, which is characteristic of modernist discourses,[3] in order to make love premised on free choice, possible. Hence, the details of love, its dynamics in their material sense, do not feature or preoccupy Qabbani's poetic creations in serious and genuine ways. Instead, it is the change from traditional societal structures, which the poet is ironically steeped in, to modern ones, which animate the spirits of his poetry. Then love can flourish or flounder, but it does so within a context of freedom, not under the pressure of familial, communal or religious or state or party-related supervisions and coercions.

On the other hand, Mahmoud Darwish, in so far as his love poetry is concerned, treats love in postmodernist tones. Love in Darwish's poetry is narrated through details. Romantic gestures and absorbing thoughts that constitute the initial stages of love give way to a fully engaged relationship that negotiates the running of love, including its ordinariness. Then there is the sustenance of love or its potential breakup – love is maturity in handling its details, living all its blessings, shades and disappointments. In particular, the breakup of love in Darwish's case requires careful negotiation to maintain one's sanity and long-term well-being so as to withstand the withering of spirits and potential decay of one's humanity. This treatment of love, I suggest, is postmodernist. In that, it is not concerned with grand narratives,[4] and it deals with the manifestations, consequences and etiquettes of love at all stages. It is the subjectivity of love as lived by two subjects, even though it is clouded with communal constraints impeding or colouring it. Nonetheless, Darwish, as in much of his poetry, undergoes a journey which moves from the collective to the subjective in his love poetry.

The poetics of Nizar Qabbani

One of the periodic descriptions applied to Arabic poetry in the twentieth century includes that of the Romantic Movement, which appeared at the turn of the twentieth century and flourished in the thirtieth and fortieth of the same century.[5] But the romanticism of this period is not solely devoted to relations between men and women or the nature of each sex's world but more so to individual freedoms and liberties in general. One of the most remarkable poets of that movement is the Tunisian poet Abu al-Qassim al-Shabbi. Al-Shabbi is not necessarily concerned with love in its romantic and erotic sense, but with the state of a patriarchal society lacking in liberty, openness and generally suffering the dark forces of dictatorship and narrow traditional forms of living, and so was the case of the great Lebanese poet Gibran Khalil Gibran (1883–1931).[6]

It would take until the appearance of the Syrian poet Nizar Qabbani on the Arab scene for love in a revolutionary sense to be thrust into the public arena and for Qabbani to be its poetic spokesperson. Nizar, as the Lebanese critic Bassam Frangieh wrote, 'gave the theme of love distinct dimensions that guaranteed its independent existence, and as a result, he was named the poet of love'.[7] He, as Salma Jayyusi, wrote

> aimed his well-honed pen at the most sacrosanct taboos in Arab traditional culture: the sexual. He called for the liberation of both body and soul from the repressive injunctions imposed upon them throughout the centuries, awakening women to a new awareness of their bodies and their sexuality, wrenching them away from the

taboos of society, and making them aware of its discriminatory treatment of the sexes, of its inherent cruelty.⁸

Love and sex, which were not such prominent considerations in the formation and dynamics of the nation states in the Arab world and the wider Middle East, suddenly became important and a factor accounting for the conservative and patriarchal makeup of these nations.⁹ The lack of basic freedoms severely curtails the progress of societies and elevates particular figures and groups over others in ways that sow mistrust and resentment and darken the spirit of societies. And this is what Nizar Qabbani aimed to awaken, a consciousness of the spirit in a region mired in unproductive ideological shackles and implications. The fact that his poetry was well received and widely used all over the Arab world, and that he became an icon of freedom and liberation from sexual repression and traditional conservatism is an indication as to how important the issue in question is and how resonant his poetic discourse was.

To this end, it is not farfetched to think of Qabbani with the simplicity and directness of his love verse, expansively opening his heart in a world where the hearts are veiled with excessive values of modesty and piety, as an *'Udhrī* poet,¹⁰ but with a new twist. He enjoyed a fulfilled love, albeit the passing of his beloved wife Balqees was tragic, resoundingly invoked and commemorated in his poem 'Balqees'. Yet, it is the rebellious and conversant nature of his love poetry that links him to the tradition of *'Udhrī*, in addition to his idolizing and almost metaphysical love to women that invites the comparison.¹¹ But there are differences from the past, and it is worthwhile reflecting on this with the broader sociopolitical context of the modern Arab world in mind.

If the *'Udhrī* poets pierced through the Islamic scene and challenged the narrow ways of living Islam, Qabbani challenged the nation state and the sociopolitical traditions that consign women to obscurity by restricting the understanding of the nation state to political maneuverers and routines, lacking in existential and psychological implications and manifestations. In Qabbani's view, the nation state, *ad-dawla*, or the homeland, *al-watan*, should be categories of emancipation and inclusivity, not restriction and exclusivity where women are treated as second, or even less than that, class citizens. In his revealing autobiography, *My Story with Poetry*, he wrote in a way that applies and illuminates the nation state, as much as it applies and illustrates the *'Udhrī* poets who expanded the theological and existential basis of Islam:

> My understanding of the nation-state and nationalism is multi-layered and panoramic. My portrait of the nation-state is that of a symphonic structure. It is composed of a million things, starting with a raindrop to a tree leaf, to a loaf of bread, water pipes, the letters of love, the smell of books, the kites, the nightly dialogues of cockroaches, the comb holding the hair of my beloved in her travel, the prayer mat of my mother, to the time engraved on the forehead of my father . . . from this perspective, which is open to the inner and outer-self of man, allow me to say with a loud voice, that my entire poetry, from the first comma to the last full stop and regardless of the primary materials of which it is constituted, and the people who populate it, whether they be men or women, and the experience that inflicts it whether it be an emotional or political experience . . . it is a nationalist poetry.¹²

Like the 'Udhrīs who did not attack or undermine Islam per se, Nizar does not extricate himself from the nation state as a solid reality of the modern age. Instead, he enlarges the scope of its meaning, its tolerance and its humanity, foregrounding human beings in the historicity of their agency and their contexts. While the voice of women in the 'Udhrī movement cannot be seriously heard, in the new poetry that Qabbani led, the women speak through him about their desires and the world they inhabit. Qabbani wrote:

> I thought that the problem lies with us, not with love, and that love is a natural motion where life expresses itself, but we have complicated and crucified love on the cross of superstition. . . . In our (Arab) countries, the poet of love fights on muddy grounds; he fights amidst an extremely aggressive atmosphere; he sings in a forest inhabited with harmful creatures and ghosts.[13]

Consciously and directly, Nizar critiques the prevailing structures of archaic protectionism as opposed to open intimacy. Unlike the 'Udhrī poets, Nizar is often erotic in his poetry, whereas the 'Udhrī poets were more spiritual and psychical on their reflections as unfulfilled lovers. Sex being one of the taboo topics in the Arab world spurred Nizar to evoke it as a natural instinct that should not be hypocritically concealed and darkly conceived. What his poetry persistently shows is the interaction with political and societal structures that restrict women's voice and undermine their humanity and independence. Alongside his celebration of women, their physical beauty and the blessings of love, Nizar had an agenda of humanistic enlightenment, an enlightenment that starts with the basic needs of society, the individuals, whether they be men or women. In this respect, his poetic conversation is not with religion and its immediate sanctions and prohibitions, as was the case with the 'Udhrī poets, who had just emerged from the throes of a religious revolution in Arabia, but more so with the Arab societies as a by-product of historical and sociopolitical norms and developments. He is not a shy lover, as the 'Udhrī poets largely were, but a forthcoming poet, whose desires are intermingled with political aspirations that enlarge the scope of the Arab world in its largely limited relational and sexual dynamics. He further explained the rationale behind his poetry as follows:

> I want to humanise the relation between the Arab man and the Arab woman. I want to make it more transparent . . . the Arab body cannot be free if the Arab mind is not free, and the Arab opinion free. Sexual repression is like economic repression and it is one of the repressive circles. As for reproduction and procreation (tanāsul), they do not mean anything in my opinion, because cows in Australia reproduce and recreate without feeling the need for any coup or revolution.[14]

The humanization of relations between the Arab man and woman stands for the universalization of love. In this universalization, the man and the woman chose their beloved and their partners and are not forced into locking themselves in relations imposed on them by the various oppressive apparatuses of their society, including the parents, the relatives, the extended family and ultimately the nation state. Such customs are perceived as old in the negative sense in Qabbani's view, but they have also been voiced before by Majnun and Buthaina and others, where they cry out for freedom of love and fluidity in human relations, away from the tribal shackles. Majnun and Buthaina might not have been modernists in the modern sense of the term: they voiced their predicament which conjured in them aspirations of freedom and justice with love being at the heart of these universal rights; but they remained 'Udhrīs, pure fixated lovers, effectively repressed. But Nizar, not being fixated on one woman, in particular, is keen to reform the customs of the era in which he lives in a radical and revolutionary manner. His love poetry is more rebellious, not markedly dialogic, as the poetry of the 'Udhrī poets was. He does not want to convince and plead with the society per se but to release revolutionary messages as to what 'freedom in love' means. He thus places freedom at the heart of love the way the 'Udhrīs invoked love beyond religious and tribal restrictions. His poem 'Language' clearly expresses the need for renewal and openness in the Arab world:

Language
When a man is in love
How can he use old words?
Should a woman
Desiring her lover
Lie down with grammarians and linguists?

I said nothing
To the woman I loved
But gathered
Love's adjectives into a suitcase
And fled from all languages.[15]

Love is universal; that is what the message of the poem reveals at the end. The modernity embodied in this poem is consciously crafted; it is immersed in the present of love and its imperatives; it is borderless in its use of language. Here, love is psychically invoked, and hence, it cannot be tied to any rules including that of language itself. In short what is suggested is a freedom where there is modernity in the very language that expresses love, but also love that is not confined and restricted through societal and political borders: if there is a conversation in Qabbani's poetry, it is with the Arab family and the nation state. Islam and the Quranic language and discourse are not so immediate to Qabbani discourse, even though they are used and subverted as the 'Udhrīs did, as was shown in Chapter 5. The following poem brings radical meanings and subversions that put love at the heart of any prophetic message:

I am the prophet of love,
Carrying surprises to women.
Had I not washed your breasts with wine,
They would have never blossomed.
My modest miracle
Made your nipples bloom.[16]

Qabbani starts with a grand title and ends with purportedly a modest miracle. The entire structure of the poem is a play on Islamic and Christian ideals, subversions spilling rebellions, from his declaration of prophecy (of love, not monotheism) to his performing of a miracle, each in their own is the forte of Prophet Mohammad, and the message of Islam he brought, and Jesus and the miracles he performed to authenticate his status of divinity. Like the earlier prophets, Qabbani is suggesting that he made women aware of the charms and treasures contained within their bodies, thus releasing energy of open love that traditions conceal. The poem is ingenious in fusing religions, Islam and Christianity together, using their miracles and highlighting the fluidity of the human subject who bears love – among other emotions. Love is the source of miracles and of human progress. It precedes religion, and therefore, religion or any customs for that matter cannot contain and dictate it. Poetry here is a source of prophecy that engenders change in sensibility and understanding of one's inner world towards a new reality that embraces and endorses love not only as a private affair but as a sentiment to be expressed and celebrated.

Thus, it is the modernization of discourse that Qabbani seeks. This is very clearly expressed in his poem, 'What Is Love':

What is love?
We have read a thousand treatises on it
And still do not know what we have read
Read works of interpretation, astrology and medicine
And do not know where we began
And we have memorized the whole of folk literature
Poetry and song
And remember not a single line
We have asked the sages of love about their state
And discovered that they knew no more than we do.

Nizar continues along the same line, emphasizing that nobody knows what love is. He ends his poem with the following noteworthy stanza:

We turned to the princes of love in our history
We consulted with Layla's demented lover
We consulted with Lubna's demented lover
And discovered that they were called princes of love
Were never happier than we were in their love.[17]

In both stanzas, the mystery that love will always stand for is clearly present; but the last stanza is clear in its emphasis on the fact the Arab past is neither solely glorious, as it is said to be in popular Arab imaginaries about the past, nor the present for that matter. Here, love is linked to experience. Therefore, the stories of Majnun Layla and other ʿUdhrī lovers in general represent repressive characters, a repression with which the present is marked. Yet these stories are glorified and celebrated; they make their readers happy, representing a state of submission to a complex tradition rather than having critical attitudes towards it. The cycles of repression have not stopped, mainly because the various authorities that administer such repression are still the same, and therefore, a change that respects the fluidity of relations between men and women and the freedom that such fluidity entails has to be comprehensive. As Bassam K. Frangieh wrote of Qabbani's poetry:

Kabbani's message is clear and consistent: the political and social structures in the Arab world must change to better represent the people. He vowed publicly to maintain his vigil on Arab governments and societies until real change took place, and he held to his course.[18]

However, Nizar appears guilty of what he preaches. His idyllic view of women, while different from that of the 'Udhrīs, is also maintained in a number of poems. But it is an idealism that rings with a particular sincerity where there is appreciation of beauty and female charm. Nizar was a consummate romantic, with his poetry being mediated through modernist consciousness. In the grandly titled poem *Thus I Write the History of Women*, he writes:

> *I want you female as you are.*
> *I claim no knowledge of woman's chemistry*
> *The sources of woman's nectar*
> *How the she-gazelle becomes a she-gazelle*
> *Nor how birds perfect the art of song*
>
> *I want you like the woman*
> *In immortal paintings*
> *The virgins gracing*
> *Cathedral ceilings*
> *Bathing their breasts in moonlight*
> *I want you female . . . so the trees will sprout green*
> *And the misty clouds will gather . . . so that the rains will come.*[19]

There is a lofty understanding and appreciation of beauty; and it is one that draws on the past to consecrate, elevate and celebrate beauty. Women are portrayed as the bearers of beauty, fertility and renewal. Meanwhile, love is the brainchild of chemistry and experience. The underpinnings of relations being grounded in such psychical considerations cannot be beset by sociopolitical rules and inhibitions. To this end, Qabbani opens a clear modernist path where men and women should be free and immune from the cultural and political curtailments that impose restrictions on love, particularly on women.

The modernist sensibility of Qabbani, albeit poignant and tragic, is acutely felt in the startling and moving poem which he wrote to commemorate the tragic killing of his beloved Iraqi wife, Balqees. Her assassination in front of the Iraqi Embassy in Beirut in 1981 within the context of the Lebanese civil war (1975–89) harnessed the poetic energy towards a form of rebellion that condemns the entire structure of Arab society. There is an epic condemnation of the state of the Arab world. It is possible to read through it the inter-Arab infighting and discord, which Qabbani detested and fought against in favour of Arab unity.

The consequences of love

The searing lamentation, remembrance, nostalgia, accusation and sorrow overwhelming the poet's world subsequent to his wife's killing show the traumas of a unique voice, tormented beyond repair. Here, he does not converse but more so describes, condemns and declares within a poem packed with successive emotional and metaphorical intensity. In doing this, Qabbani shows that the Arab nation state did not have a mature discourse to engage with but more an imposed template of governance with domestic producers and consumers, trading in violence and suppressing dissent or counternarratives – this evidently applies to his native Syria. And it is this tragic state of affairs which is responsible for the killing of his wife. Therefore, Qabbani dictates in fits and bursts of fury, mourning, remembrance and love, rather than converse. He is pained, emboldened and comforted all at the same time by the power and therapy of the poetic word: this gives him a semblance of anchored existence through the historical and eternal voice of poetry, as an Arab battered and betrayed by his own people. The voice inhabiting the poem is broken, just as the nation state with its violent routine, its oppression and its distance from humanity, lacking in the elements of progress and civility that the historical experience of other nations and communities, including that of the Arabs themselves, suggest are possible.

> Thank you . . .
> Thank you . . .
> My beloved has been killed . . .
> It behoves you to drink a glass over the grave of the martyr
> And my poem has been assassinated . . .
> Is there a nation on earth except us which assassinates the poem . . .?
> Balqees was the most beautiful queen in the history of Babylon
> Balqees was the tallest palm tree in the land of Iraq . . .

> Which nation is this that assassinates the sounds of nightingales?

>> *Beirut kills one of us every day*
>> *And looks for a victim every day*
>> *Death is in our cup of coffee . . .*
>> *In the key to our apartment . . .*
>> *In the flowers of our balcony . . .*
>> *In the papers of our newspapers . . .*
>> *And in the alphabets . . .*
>> *Here we are Balqees, again, we enter the age of ignorance*
>> *We dwell deep in savagery*
>> *Deep in backwardness, gruesomeness and degradation*
>> *We enter the barbaric ages*
>> *Where writing is a journey*
>> *Between one bomb and another*
>> *Where the killing of a butterfly in her throat*
>> *Has become a cause*
>> *Balqees, this is not a eulogy*
>> *But a farewell to the Arabs*
> *Balqees, we are yearning, yearning, yearning . . .*
> *Balqees, sadness digs holes inside me*
> *Beirut which killed you does not know its crime*

And Beirut which loved you
Is oblivious that it had killed you who loved it
and switched off the moon . . .
The memory of the small details in our relations kills me
and the minutes and seconds lash at me . . .
Balqees: it is so difficult for me to migrate away from my blood . . .
and I am the besieged, consumed by fire . . .
Balqees, the princesses, here you are,
Burning in the war between one tribe and another
What can I write about you after your passing? . . .
We wonder if this grave is yours
Or the grave of the Arab nation . . .
Our Arab fate is that we be assassinated by Arabs . . .
Our flesh will be eaten by Arabs . . .
And our bellies would be stabbed by Arabs . . .
And our graves would be opened by Arabs . . .
How can we flee this Arab space? . . .
Now I know the dilemma of words . . .
I know the morass of impossible language
And I am the one who invents letters . . .
Balqees, all the civilisation is you and civilisation is a woman . . .
Balqees, my moon that was buried under the stones
Now the curtains have been lifted
The curtains have been lifted
At the interrogation, I would say
I know the names, the things and the prisoners
The martyrs, the poor and the weak
And I know the sword bearer: the killer of my wife,
and the faces of all the spies . . .
I will say: all our purity is prostitution
And our piety is dirtiness
I will say: our struggle is a lie
And that there is no difference
between politics and prostitution!!
I will say at the interrogation that
I knew the killers
And that our Arab age is devoted to the killing of jasmine
And the killing of prophets
And the killing of messengers . . .
I wondered: Is the killing of women an Arab hobby?
Or are we in origin professional criminals?
Balqees, I am ashamed of all my history
Balqees, the most beautiful homeland,
One does not know how to live in this homeland
One does not know how to die in this homeland . . .
The sky has willed it that I should be alone . . .
Like the leaves of winter
Are poets born from the womb of misery? . . .
What can poetry say in this populist age? . . .

And the Arab world is oppressed, brutalised
its tongue is cut . . .
I know so well that those who have killed you meant to kill my words!!!
After you, poetry is impossible . . .
And womanhood is impossible . . .
Generations upon generations of children
Will be asking about your long braids
And generations of lovers will be reading about you
The true teacher . . .
Arabs will one day know that
They have killed the prophetess
They have killed the prophetess . . .[20]

This is clearly a husband, lover and poet in profound mourning over the tragic and premature passing of his wife. Like the 'Udhrī poets, his predicament is uncompromisingly mediated through the powerful medium of poetry in a way that depicts the dramatic truth of his own experience. The poem insistently condemns the Arab world with its wars, violence and cruelty, as well as its traditions; it sees and foregrounds the killing of his wife as an immediate, rather than urgent, example of a world steeped and stuck in chaos and savagery. If such symbols of innocence and sanity, Balqees and his poetry, the psychical essence of his own identity, could be targeted and obliterated in this way within the context of the civil war that consumed so much of Lebanon – and has been doing the same and worse for his native Syria – what drives the Arab nation towards such practices, leading it to wilfully sleepwalk and mire itself in disasters? Qabbani addresses the question through his expression of love and cries of passion for women and poetry. In this context, love, poetry and women are not disconnected as a category. While these might seem honoured and respected on the open in some places, they are disfigured and manipulated by the political elites and their mercenaries driving the wars in the Middle East and sustaining traditions and practices that ensure unproductive and unidirectional continuity where critical voices are denied their voice and the majority of society is left disdainfully obedient, wasted and neglected. This latent and indeed manifest stratification in the understanding of people's humanity that authoritarian regimes, permeated by varying degrees of violence and cruelty, sustain is what the poet has consistently resisted and spoken against. His wife and him understood the underlying forces that the subject formation, an inhumane one, engendered by politics of exclusion and grand masculinities that reduce the other, most visibly women, to an irrelevant and powerless category. The poet bears witness to his dramatic humanity as a force of introspection and perception, targeted in his most beloved symbol of normality and stability. The nation state is averse to any truth that contradicts or challenges its severe and narrow conception of itself. Its cruelty is multifaceted, far-reaching, and it is shameless in its pursuit of authoritarianism. Beirut, the capital of Lebanon, in the context of the civil war with its violence and loss of life, is a metaphor for an Arab world seriously wounded.

Qabbani was not alone to shed light on Arab inter-fighting and its consequences on conscientiousness and outspoken individuals like him, but the war had touched him so personally that it sharpened and darkened his poetic vision. He declares towards the end of the poem that 'they have killed the prophetess'. It was seen earlier how

Qabbani declares himself a prophet of love. Balqees is depicted as one who predicted her own killing but also as one who animated and sustained his poetic energy. The love for women that he has and the understanding of them as enablers of renewal and enlightenment is the source of new prophecy that Balqees guarded and understood. If all the Arab and religious prophets were males before, this age calls for a prophetess, a woman like Balqees whose thoughtful and graceful existence and sacrifice for him, as a poet carrying messages of openness and enlightenment, is a source of pride and continuity. Instead of sulking in fear and accepting defeat, Qabbani seals his poem with another sign of rebellion and defiance. He declares and anoints his wife as a prophetess who has been killed by a patriarchal society within a futile war that kills and destroys any sign of beauty or ambitious normality, a war that desecrates the Arab nation and any dream of independence and self-respect, as if he is forewarning and lamenting what will happen in his native Syria. The declaration is a sign of continuity on the part of the poet to be the voice of the oppressed, marginalized and voiceless; and it revolutionizes the Middle Eastern region, which had not experienced any woman as a prophet. Balqees is not only a prophetess who had predicted her own assassination, who the poet Qabbani claims to know, but also a prophetess in the general and in the grand sense, a prophetess of enlightenment and change, led by a woman of insight and dignified fortitude and beauty.

Even though Qabbani's production is embedded in the Arab tradition, the poet's relation with tradition is one of conventional tension, thanks to the overwhelming resonance of the Arabic language and its illustrious history of powerful poetics. His sharper sentiment is one of rebellion and change, embracing modernity as an enabler of liberation and equality that recognizes all Arab citizens as equal, aware of their rights and obligations. The definition of modernity by David Harvey applies to the case at hand: 'Modernity, therefore, not only entails a ruthless break with any or all preceding historical conditions, but is characterized by a never ending process of internal ruptures and fragmentations within itself.'[21] Thus, in Nizar's poetry, as was shown before, 'all that is solid melt into air', as Marx said in reference to the modern age of the nation state in Europe.[22]

Qabbani is painfully fragmented in his loyalties and feelings in the poem. While the archetypal node of loyalty, which functions as the prime mover of the poem, is for his wife, he is also critically attached and loyal to the Arab world: in it, he sears his love while advocating for better sociopolitical conditions. As such, he is an important voice of modernity. Yet, it is a modernity that emerges from the woes of ongoing wars and tragedies, not from systematic and well thought-out considerations of the modern age and its complexities. Qabbani's modernity is impelled by personal sensibility, circumstances and his reading into the present Arab age as one of chaos, injustice and hypocrisy. He has several poems that critique the Arab world, its traditions, politics, the misuse of its wealth, particularly the oil, the loss of Palestine and the treatment of women, as well as women's limited understanding of themselves and their roles, given the dominant patriarchal and hierarchal nature of their societies.[23] Though Qabbani is a poet of enormous talent and appeal, as much as his poetry is about women in the contemporary Arab world, it is also about him and the Arab men of his generation and beyond and their frustrated sexual and romantic impulses that underscore the general sensibilities. The direct nature of his poem makes him modernist enough, but still within the tradition of poetry that describes, preaches and declares and does not necessarily explore the depths of the meanings of love, its many contradictions and manifestations. In this sense, his is a romance reiterated and consummated within the realm of the Arabic tradition of *ghazal* writing. Love is populated with images of longing, sensuality, sexual thirst and populist directness. While it characterizes the nature of relations underpinning the formation of Arab societies and celebrates love in erotic and open ways, it is situated within a traditional context. It lacks the philosophical depth characteristic of other poets of love, where the complexity of the emotions involved as well as their malleability calls for a multiplicity of meditations beyond the binary nature of love, its loveliness and its lack thereof.

Against this backdrop, love, like life itself, posits diverse faces and significations that are accentuated in one way or another in congruence with the experience and vision of the lover. Whereas for one poet, love means fulfilment and contentment, for another, it signifies pleasure tinged with tension and contradictions. To this end, the Palestinian poet Mahmoud Darwish is another Arab poet whose poetry of love occupied a significant place in his poetic vision and journey. Being another figure of poetic modernity alongside Qabbani and others, Darwish offers a challenging and not so conventional panorama of love.

Postmodern considerations: Love in the poetry of Mahmoud Darwish

Unlike Qabbani, whose poetry followed a relatively linear line driven by a resounding discourse of liberty, Mahmoud Darwish's poetry of love is discursive; it evolves within various stages, marking an illustrious poetic journey for the poet himself as a poet-philosopher.[24] Darwish grew deeply concerned with the meaning of love and the varied contours of its manifestations and complexities. In what follows, I draw on the love poetry of the Palestinian poet Mahmoud Darwish, the second most important popular and famous Arab poet after the passing of Nizar Qabbani in 1998. His poetry is important for the nuances that show the seeds of the Arabic tradition while exploring it further and infusing it with other poetic traditions. Thus, if Nizar's poetry carries elements of modernity in its direct and popular calls for openness and freedom, Darwish's love poetry can be read as an instance of postmodernity as being rooted in aesthetics of emancipation, giving rise to a subjective responsibility of vision and understanding. It is also interesting because it emanates from particular love experiences the poet had. But unlike Qabbani, the reflective and meta-poetical nature of meditation employed in Darwish's love poetry is more manifest and systematic. It shows his poetry as a unique example of a poet-philosopher not only invested in the natural sentiments of love and their consequences but also the intrinsic politics and metaphysics of love as an engaging and genuine realm of contradictions and tension. In addition, Darwish's poetry of love is multifaceted in the sense that it develops from being rich with political metaphors and insights, where love in its natural sense clashes with imposing political contexts, to love as a metaphysical and mysterious experience. In particular, there is emphasis on the perplexing independence of lovers even as they engage in the sentiments of love and experience its intricate paths.

The title of Darwish's first volume of poetry, *A Lover from Palestine*, demonstrates an archetypal sensibility that runs throughout his poetic oeuvre. While this sensibility developed and morphed into varied streams of introspections and revelations where the understanding of love is enriched with an ever-startling language of composition and thought, love as a basic human sentiment and an intellectual attitude foregrounds the journey of the poet. A simple explanation of the title in question shows attachment to two terrains that belong to different yet related templates of belonging, namely love and Palestine. If love reflects emotions of profound nature, connected to human needs, bonding and aspirations, Palestine, in this visceral case, stands for politics and history in their most immediate and urgent sense. Seven years after the poet was borne in 1941, he was forced into exile from his homeland, Palestine. In 1948, Palestine experienced a traumatic process of disfigurement that involved the renaming and reshaping of its historicity to befit the newly established state of Israel with its Zionist project of depopulating the land of its native Palestinian inhabitants and filling it with new Jewish arrivals. This experience of dispossession that touched entire generations of Palestinians and indeed continues to reverberate in various ways today introduced the poet to politics as a core element of life that has to be painfully understood and engaged with. The attachment to land and sociopolitical identity, which would have been tacitly assumed had not such a colonial state of affairs arisen, would not have triggered the consciously crafted emotions of attachment with which the poems of Darwish continuously ring.[25] In this respect, Salma Jayyusi's general observation regarding the motivating grounds behind the poet's poetics resonates with particular truth:

> The fact is that his commitment is not solely to a major political issue, but also – in fact primarily – to revelation of the daily human tragedy springing from it. This applies equally to the poetry dealing with his private experiences, which has as its source the deep well of Palestinian tragic experience. His primary incentive, then, is to consider the human condition; and it is this, not politics, that makes him a world poet.[26]

In this case, the first anchor of love is that of the land with its unassuming simplicity of being the seat of the poet's birthplace and early childhood, with its sights of normality, stability and continuity that the poet's family had relied upon and embodied for centuries. With the loss of the land, Darwish asserts his love in visceral terms, constantly employing the language of love usually reserved for romantic and even Sufi attachment to speak of the land and reclaim its significance to his spiritual and emotional formation – and by extension to that of the Palestinian people. The poet's childhood and his elemental feeling of love are related to the predicament of the land whence love first sprung. The poet is inseparable from his disposition for love (most materially to women) and his condition as a sociopolitical subject born and raised amidst a ravaging political context of dispossession and struggle. This triplet of attachment is resounding and absolute, particularly for a poet at the prime of his youth, confronting an ever shocking reality turned topsy-turvy by dramatic changes that touch him, his family and nation so directly:

> *Your eyes are a thorn in my heart*
> *Inflicting pain, yet I cherish that thorn*
> *And shield it from the wind.*
> *I sheathe it in my flesh, I sheathe it, protecting it from night and agony,*

And its wound lights the lanterns,
Its tomorrow makes my present
Dearer to me than my soul.
And soon I forget, as eye meets eye,
That once, behind the doors, there were two of us . . .

Her eyes and the tattoo on her hands is Palestinian,
Her name, Palestinian,
Her dreams, and sorrow, Palestinian,
Her kerchief, her feet and body, Palestinian,
Her words and her silence, Palestinian,
Her voice, Palestinian,
Her birth and her death, Palestinian . . .[27]

That the land is endowed and decorated with feminine attributes does not necessarily entail fixing women's roles as deposits of fertility and charms nor that they are stereotyped beyond agency. The land connotes normality and stability, like the mother and the lover; both are anchors of secure existence. Here, passion is the fuel of metaphors invoking an unforgettable rich experience of belonging, which in this instance has been severely disrupted and denied through the Israeli conquest and remapping of the land.[28] It is a case of separation and estrangement here that invites lamentation, remembrance and reclamation over the land (*That once, behind the doors, there were two of us*), as a lover would have lamented the disappearance of his beloved from his life with a constant revisitation of memories. Loss breeds a new form of consciousness that didn't exist before. As an individual voice speaking in the collective poetics of responsibility that the poet embodies, Darwish's love life had been fated to be linked with his own initial predicament as a child refugee and a Palestinian in conflict with Israeli Zionism as an aggressive ideology of expansionism and domination.[29] In this respect, Israel represents an occupation whose conduct has been contradictory to every aspiration of dignity and security that the poet has, establishing a dilemma that touches the very sentiment of love and bonding with the other. The story of Darwish's love for the Jewish Israeli girl named in the poem as Rita and its invocation in his early poetry testifies to a powerful instance where nationalism competes and clashes with love and ultimately destroys it, showing how love is not immune from the political structures that permeate our lives, and how it can be a victim of it:

Between Rita and my eyes
There is a rifle
And whoever knows Rita
Kneels and prays
To the divinity in those honey-colored eyes
And I kissed Rita
When she was young
And I remember how she approached
And how my arm covered the loveliest of braids
And I remember Rita
The way a sparrow remembers its stream

> *Ah, Rita*
> *Between us there are a million sparrows and images*
> *And many a rendezvous*
> *Fired at by a rifle*
>
> *Rita's name was a feast in my mouth*
> *Rita's body was a wedding in my blood*
> *And I was lost in Rita for two years*
> *And for two years she slept on my arm*
> *And we made promises*
> *Over the most beautiful of cups*
> *And we burned in the wine of our lips*
> *And we were born again . . .*[30]

It is noteworthy that residues from the physical elements in the pre-Islamic and the psychical intimations of the ʿUdhrī s and the romantic and erotic celebrations of love in Nizar Qabbani can be encountered here. Therefore, underlying the poem is a pluralistic voice grounded in what T. S Eliot calls 'the historical sense', where the talented poet creatively situates and infuses his own experience, passion and vision with a rich historical narrative to enliven and synthesize his poetry with exalted voices, crafting his own historicity and timelessness and thus his cultivated sense, while at the same time being in harmony with his own conditions and emotions. All the invocations in question are inflicted with the dark spectre of the rifle that shoots love down, demonstrating the ominous threat of different narratives and nationalities locked into bitter conflict. As Verena Klemm wrote, 'poetic imagery and political reality are interposed . . . love is portrayed as an erotic and spiritual unity. It is destroyed by the rifle and the city, which both stand for an aggressor attacking from an outside. The destruction of love by purely external factors is a traditional motif familiar to us from classical Arabic love poetry.'[31]

As in the ʿUdhrīs poetry, Rita is depicted as God with the associated obligations towards the divine involved, as subscribed in the religion, including the Islamic ritual of kneeling and praying. Her divinity is remembered and heightened through the sexual experience the poet had with her. Remembrance is all that is left to the poet, with such Sufi symbols like the wine that burns the lips from such intense devotion and passion to God, intensifying the union of the two lovers into one, making God a resident of the bustling earth.[32] Moreover, Darwish paints a double picture which features the land and the beloved, constituting belonging and intimacy with a natural continuity that no longer exists. The real love story between Rita (Tamar is the real name) and Darwish, which lasted for two years, is cut short and tainted by the 1967 war when Israel occupied further Arab territory and colonized all of Palestine, including Gaza, the West Bank and East Jerusalem. Rita was summoned to serve in the ever-expanding and destructive Israeli army, an army devoted to maintaining the Israeli occupation with all the violence and oppression involved.[33] In this poem, Darwish portrays the harsh reality of a love borne and besieged by such an intense nationalist conflict in which his people are the primary victims. As Abdullah Al-Shahham explained in his study of the poems devoted to Rita:

> Regardless of what may be said about this poem, such as that it establishes
>   an unequal relationship between two lovers associated with differing nationalistic

identities (between a Palestinian Arab man and an Israeli Jewish woman),
it is, in fact, the outcry of a mighty love in the face of barbarity and
destruction. Undoubtedly this cry produces a deep echo which resounds in the
heart of all high-minded people, because it is replete with honesty, strength of
character, and clarity.[34]

Love did not survive the nationalist conflict amidst which it blossomed. Yet, Rita appears in other poems, eternally symbolizing love that could not transcend the nationalist mundane intricacies of the conflict, and love in which passion, intimate humane interactions and the hope for a bright future are abundantly present, but severely undermined and ultimately ended with the menacing violence of the Israeli occupation. As a Palestinian Arab poet with critical sensitivity of his background and the aspirations of his people for liberation, his lover Rita, who at one point carries a gun and fights in the Israeli army, becomes another emblem of oppression and violence, aspects which are irreconcilably contradictory to love in its innocent and passionate drive towards fulfilment and contentment. In this case, love is forced to seek the metaphysical refuge of poetry in order to be remembered and lamented as a fact of human conditions and a victim of them, too.

Darwish and his pursuit of love are not restricted to the story highlighted above and the lessons from it. In fact, Darwish's poetry in all its stages brims with love. This applies to his poetry in Palestine before he left in 1970; to Cairo where he stayed for two years; to Beirut, where he further evolved into an epic poet merging nationalist, humanist and metaphysical evocations; to Paris, Tunisia, Ramallah and so on where he continued to perfect the merger of ideals and the song. In all these places which embodied varied significations for the Palestinian identity and its development, there have had always been love references in Darwish's poetry, which witnessed an organic and evolutionary process of introspection and understanding as reflected in the compositions and the attitudes in the poems. These references corresponded to actual contexts of romantic encounters including his two (short-lived) marriages and his general philosophical intimations about love as such an abiding psychical and existential call, felt with persistent profundity by such a poet of wondrous and responsible character,[35] expanding the narrow horizons of his disruptive existence, as most symbolized through exile.

One particular poem which was inspired and devoted to his second artist wife Hayat al-Hayni from Egypt shows a nuanced, dual, albeit lyrical, sense and perception of love. The poem *The Doves Fly, the Doves Come Down* was put into music by the Lebanese singer Marcel Khalifa.[36] It includes depths and twists that show the dynamics of living love through the character of a poet increasingly mindful, enriched and perhaps struck by its contradictions. The poem is studied with love to his wife and the charms of life that their union brought, but it is not free of the angst and anxieties love might bring.

The doves fly,
the doves come down . . .
Prepare a place for me to rest.
I love you unto weariness,

your morning is fruit for songs
and this evening is precious gold
the shadows are strong as marble.
When I see myself,
it is hanging upon a neck that embraces only the clouds,
you are the air that undresses in front of me like tears of the grape,
you are the beginning of the family of waves held by the shore.
I love you, you are the beginning of my soul, and you are the end . . .
the doves fly
the doves come down . . .

I am for my lover I am. And my lover is for his wandering star
Sleep my love
on you my hair braids, peace be with you . . .
the doves fly
the doves come down . . .

Oh, my love, where are you taking me away from my parents,
from my trees, small bed and from my weariness,
from my visions, from my light, from my memories and pleasant evenings,
from my dress and my shyness,
where are you taking me my love, where?
You take me, set me on fire, and then leave me
in the vain path of the air
that is a sin . . . that is a sin . . .
the doves fly
the doves come down . . .[37]

The choice of the bird 'dove' is not random. There is a reference to the great treatise of Ibn Hazm, namely 'The Dove's Necklace', which was mentioned in Chapter 4. The necklace adorns the bird and enhances its beauty, but it also shackles the humble dove and takes away from its sovereignty. In the poem here, love soars in metaphysical spheres of mystery and enchantment, but it also inevitably lands on earth, like the bird itself, where it acquires materiality of concrete and immediate sense. This soaring and landing associated with love are meaningfully and aurally rendered in the first stanza. The poet calls his wife to prepare for his return from his flights of love, where nature is seen at its most sublime and metaphors easily yield to the charms that love endows his sight with. Love does not manifest itself as a state of an unbridled ecstasy in this poem, but more as a human aspiration and instinct that swings between flight and restfulness and resignation inflicted with anxiety. As Roland Barthes aptly put it, 'amorous anxiety involves an expenditure which tires the body as harshly as any physical labour.'[38]

While in action, love takes the lover away; it affects and blurs the essential and the constructed in the very being of man. Love holds within its dynamics that sense of unstoppable union and unity that takes place between two people and, in the process, excludes others, including the immediate family and the earlier routines and memories that so far shaped the lover-poet's understanding of himself and his own identity. Love nourishes and instils devotion in the lover. It does so by showing him everything in a new light, growing and implanting in his consciousness another order of things. But whatever union love creates, this unity which it thrives on includes an important and indeed productive and necessary illusion that one is entirely safe, one is two; and in that duality, the one is dissolved. But the reality before, within and after and beyond love is that one is one; and this one discovers himself or herself on earth, when the lover lands, away from that soaring state of love where the two souls are inseparable. And gravity facilitates the soaring of the bird; without it, flight would not be possible. Therefore, in love, there are the concrete manifestations of spiritual effects becoming psychical imperatives. Poetry seems to be that space in between, the bridge that connects and holds the balance of that space. The poet in this poem is attempting to preserve this balance, a balance that is ever perplexing and provoking and often tilts towards an absolute union that knows no sense of independence or sovereignty for any of the lovers. Then the calls of nature, of which love is a great manifestation, are irreversible. Yet, the sensibility of the poet is endowed with such spaces that cannot afford to be extricated of their own material of language with its natural fluidity and its imperative of presence – and one might even say, its mercy or critical attachment to love.

Love as a stranger's journey

The themes of inseparability and independence, presence and absence, union and estrangement, rapture and antipathy, exile and history are at the heart of Darwish's *diwan* on love, namely *Sareer al-Ghareebah*. *Sareer al-Ghareebah* (*The Stranger's Bed*) is the most important collection devoted to the theme of love. And it is one where modern images and sensibilities jostle with traditional tendencies and evocations. The collection, published in 1996, is accumulative and latent in its overall tone. It echoes and consecrates all the earlier experiences and perceptions of the poet; and yet it rises above them, using them as lessons and thoughts about love, but not dwelling in their specificity. The voice of experience, wisdom and considered understanding of human nature in love is profoundly meditative, lightly rendered with lyrical dexterity and nuance. The words and constructions are chosen and chiselled with deft care – the portrayal of love is meant to appear and feel the way love is in nature, in reality and from afar. A recurring theme and feel in the collection relates to history and exile and how both inflict love, rooting it on nostalgic terrains imbued with robust, gothic even, dreams of belonging that love substantiates and enlivens. Throughout the collection, the theme of exile is powerfully present. The outcome is that exile becomes the brainchild of mature visions, seated on an earth lit with tension and longings.

In this respect, it is noteworthy to consider Subhi Haddidi, the Syrian literary critic's observations, in order to foreground the discussion to follow:

> At first glance, it does not necessarily occur to us to think of the poems gathered in the collection Sarīr al-Gharība (The stranger's bed) as love poems. They are not poems of pleasure, or ghazal in the classical sense, nor do they speak of sensual and fascinated courtship, or lament past courtship . . . it is, however, relevant to note that Darwish's love poems differ from others' in terms of their aesthetics, which is of crucial importance at the artistic level . . .

Instead of being introspective, as is the case in the Arabic poetic tradition, Darwish's love poems contemplate history. Instead of describing the calm of a lovers' meeting, his poems evoke the pains of exile.[39]

If exile is central to the poems of *The Stranger's Bed*, this exile is a 'private exile',[40] as Fady Joudah put it. This private exile would have been felt by the 'Udhrī lovers discussed in Chapter 4. It is an exile where the poet is confronted with the depths of his own vision in an overwhelming yet alienating context of love amidst a society preoccupied with routines and norms that do not acknowledge or pay enough attention to the privacy of such an exile, hence, 'no cultural solutions for existential concerns' and 'no collective solutions for personal scruples', as Darwish puts it in the first poem of the collection.[41] Furthermore, Fady Joudah's is of the view that the collection is firmly rooted in the Arabic love poetry. Here, he clarifies and perhaps contradicts Subhi Haddadi's assessment of the poems that they stand apart from the Arabic tradition. By relating the collection to the Arabic tradition of love poetry, Joudah assists in deepening and stretching the analysis of the poems as situated within a long-standing historical experience of Arabic and indeed universal love poetry to which Darwish is an important contributor. In this respect, Joudah writes:

> Arabic love poetry is a primary wellspring here. Whether in the Jahili night, in Majnoon Laila and Jameel Bouthaina fourteen centuries ago, in a Sufi east or an Andalusian west, it has always had its roots in an exile that slackens the bind to 'the gravity of identity's land'.[42]

Indeed, this description of the entirety of the love poems is in concurrence with T. S Eliot's vision of the talented poet, as alluded earlier. In this case, the talented poet commands a historical sense, which T. S Eliot defines as follows:

> This historical sense, which is a sense of the timeless as well as of the temporal and of the timeless and of the temporal together, is what makes a writer traditional. And it is at the same time what makes a writer most acutely conscious of his place in time, of his contemporaneity.[43]

To analyse the historical sense in the collection at hand, the first poem can serve as a litmus test, in that the poem starts with the theme of separation, and it connects the past with the present of love through the vivid construction, كان ينقصنا حاضر 'we were missing a present'.[44] The lovers' time together was not ripe enough to carry them through to the present. Pointedly, the entire edifice of pre-Islamic poetry evokes the theme of separation as an opening for the poems. Separation and loss are what cause the search, the journey and the discovery that one is alone after all,[45] and that the psyche that has been veiled through social and intimate preoccupations is suddenly opened onto the reality of its emptiness. Darwish is firmly rooted in the Arabic tradition in opening his illustrious – at times austere and ascetic perhaps – *diwan*: he draws inspiration from the Arab literary past, showing an awareness that some elemental psychological facts recur throughout the ages and indeed in all traditions. Yet, the poem and the entire collection are modern in their vivid linguistic energy and philosophical attitudes.

Unlike the pre-Islamic or the ʿUdhrī Arab lovers, Darwish does not lament in this poem or seek solutions, immediate or long-term ones. Instead, he describes with rare reflective coolness the state of separation while sagely intoning that the cessation of love, not so unlike its initiation, is also normal and natural.[46] It happens. In such a context, love as a feeling is being exhorted to turn into love as a human value. Thus, the lovers, while beset by remembrance, can also prepare themselves to be themselves in their uncorrupted sense and to be kind (and another translation might render the word *Tayybīn* as 'good', as a wider – critical perhaps – category of being than 'kind'):

> *Let's go as we are*
> *A free woman*
> *And a loyal friend,*
> *Let's go together on two different paths*
> *Let's go as we are united*
> *And separate,*
> *With nothing hurting us*
> *Not the divorce of the doves or the coldness between the hands*
> *Nor the wind around the church . . .*
> *What bloomed of almond trees wasn't enough.*
> *So smile for the almonds to blossom more*
> *Between the butterflies of two dimples*
>
> *And soon there will be a new present for us*
> *If you look back you will see only*
> *The exile of your looking back:*
> *Your bedroom,*
> *The courtyard willow,*
> *The river behind the glass buildings,*
> *And the café of our trysts . . . all of it, all*
> *Preparing to become exile, so*
> *Let's be kind!*[47]

Throughout the poem *Let's Be Kind* is a gentle refrain that reflexively attempts to transcend the heat of potentially disturbed psyches once in union unable to foreground their past in any sentiment other than fixation and enslavement to that past and its burdensome consequences. The modern age is one that rightly gives voice to all, women and men – or at least this is the philosophical, aspirational and political assumption. The distant past, as literature reveals, is full of dominant masculine voices, crippled and indulgent beyond repair by their loss and the societies that ignore their loss. Then, the claim here is that the poetic word often carried a significant therapeutic value before it assumed a philosophical one. Therefore, the unconscious significance of what was revealed is vast and profound. However, in the modern age, and despite the inescapable force of the unconscious in the release of poetry, the conscious is at work in notable ways. This cannot be said for all modern Arab poets. But it gains some currency in the case of Darwish, particularly in his later stages of poetry writing, where certain metaphors and constructions from the Arab and other literary traditions are consciously incorporated, resonating with intent and purpose and still exuding poetic energy. In this poem, as indeed the other poems, philosophical attitudes are sought and invoked, including other important facets of life, as exile and history in Darwish's case. The poet reflects collectedly, refining the psyche beyond its infantile stage of inexperience and uninformed innocence. Thus in the same poem, when the duality of the lovers presents itself in the absolute, the two-into-one sense, the lover asks before deconstructing and abandoning his own question:[48]

> *Am I another you*
> *And you another I?*
> *'This isn't my path to my freedom's land'*
> *This isn't my path to my body*
> *And I won't be 'I' twice*
> *Now that my yesterday has become my tomorrow*
> *And I have split into two women*
> *So I am not of the east*
> *And I am not of the west,*
> *Nor am I an olive tree shading two verses in the Quran,*
> *Then let's go.*[49]

The 'I' desires to regain its sovereignty to be what it chooses to be. It wants freedom – the authentic house of being. This urge for freedom (let's . . .) is not through a poetic journey as such – an unconscious one – as was discussed in pre-Islamic poetry, but through philosophical attitudes and aspirations. The 'I' realizes a variety of states it can potentially occupy and seizes on the one where it feels most free and unshackled, where it resumes its agency, the seed of its power, recovery and continuity, whatever the limitations of these are. The postmodern 'I' is unfixed, fragmented and limitless in its pursuit of self-deconstruction, instinctively rooted in freedom. The poet realizes that freedom is essential in the absence of a full-fledged duality that facilitates the founding of another union and growth and freedom within that union. In the poem, the context is given prominence 'we were missing a present to see where we were'. Principally, the poet is in an intimate conversation with the previous beloved, explaining his context not only in relation to his own psyche but also to the sociopolitical and psychological structures that surround them: the mature voice of experience is bearing on the outcome. This is not a poem that wholly overcomes love, as this is impossible, but it's one that gives it value in relation to its very constitutive elements concerning human possibilities that evolve, strive and plant love in a multitude of ways – it is not a poem of fixation, once and for all.

The thematic spectres of the first poem are scattered throughout the collection, consecrating times and trends, including traditions, modernist and postmodernist sensibilities and tendencies. Darwish situates love at the intersection of several realities, as wedged between duality and singularity; and this is the broader intent of the collection. There is an instinctive search and attraction to the female other and the union thereof, and there is the nostalgic and powerful entrenchment of the self in its constitution and the betwixt position of the human subject who experienced the dynamics and effects of both. Each ebbs and flows and compromises one or the other; and each echoes the other. The female voice gives rise to its own presence. It exercises its own agency, widening the imagination as to what love is in its varied embodied manifestations beyond the definitional frames set by masculine forces. Love appears as a journey of singular strangeness that ironically nurses duality.

In the poem, *The Stranger Stumbles upon Himself in the Stranger*, the refrain is, 'we are one in two'. The duality of the lovers unfurls along their evolved togetherness. The present tense exhorts the past tense to bear witness to its pastness and wear its tomorrow:

> *We are one in two [. . .]*
> *We need to see how we were here,*
> *stranger, as two shadows opening and closing on what*
> *has been shaped of our shape: a body disappearing then reappearing*
> *in a body disappearing in the mystery of the eternal*
> *duality. We need to return to being two*
> *to embrace each other more. There's no name for us,*
> *when the stranger stumbles upon himself in the stranger.*[50]

The love poem as marked is riddled with contradictory tendencies. Ibn Hazm is aptly relevant when he describes the entanglements of love, which the poem in question reflects as 'discord in opposites and agreement in separation, and struggle in resemblance'.[51] The name of the person is the primary address of his identity; but this address with all its particularity and historicity becomes more real and authentic when it stumbles upon an 'other' with whom it constructs a union. The strange irony is that despite the singularity of the human self and its visible urges, this singularity does not realize itself in its fullness and meaningfulness except through that cardinal experience with an 'other'. Love is the maximum epitome of that otherness and sameness at the same time, as it exercises the entire faculties and functions of the human, as a holistic apparatus bent on holistic fulfilment that includes the body, the mind and the soul.

In particular, Darwish seems adept at invoking the in-between spaces of love. Having not settled into a normative union of love, and yet experienced it amidst the pressing condition of his Palestinian identity and the meanderings of exile, his position remains that of the stranger, whose full sense of duality did not endure and remained interrupted. His singularity seems always to assert itself, while it yearns from a place of distance, reflexivity and loving ingenuity for fulfilling and enriching duality in love. In the absence of duality, the nostalgic lover pursues self-deconstruction and understanding in relation to defining experiences and abiding thoughts. Places brimming with exilic and spiritual enrichment guide the poet-lover and return him to an earlier self. In the poem *Take My Horse and Slaughter It . . .*, Darwish asserts the essence of his searching self, defying love stuck in discord and lacking in 'struggle in resemblance', consuming the psyche of the lovers and rendering them opposites in despair, irreconcilable singularities. The voice of experience is palpable in the poem, and the philosophical attitude of a self-sheltered in and moved by wisdom endures:

> *Take my breath the way a guitar responds*
> *to what you demand of the wind. All of my Andalus [Andalusia]*
> *is within your hands, so don't leave a single string*
> *for self-defence in the land of my Andalus.*
> *I will realise, in another time,*
> *I will realise that I have won with my despair*

*and that I have found my life, over there
outside itself, near my past
take my horse
and slaughter it, and I will carry myself dead and alive
by myself . . .*[52]

Here is a statement of agency emanating from the self-finding itself in its rediscovered self. While he is rendered defenceless even over the precious Andalusia of his memory, that memory and stable identity being targeted, he will 'rise'. Resurrection is not restricted to one incident in human history. Lovers are renowned for it. So while the 'horse', the symbol of fertile and unstoppable manliness, is tickled with obliterating indignity, the poet-lover still finds himself suspended between death and life. Spurred by alarms at his psychotic state, the lover can breed and give way to visions of recovery. Here, there is an apt instance of postmodernist sensibility, which resonates with Frederic Jameson's definition that 'Postmodernism is what you have when the modernisation process is complete and nature is gone for good. It is a more fully human world than the older one, but one in which "culture" has become a veritable "second nature".'[53]

To this end, Darwish situates his understanding of love in memory of places where things are not irreversible; and whatever stages the human being reaches, her humanity in its very ordinariness is the key to its enlivened presence and power. In this stance, it is the culture of the human, more than his nature, if such a distinction can be maintained, that is at work. The collection reinforces the voice of the willed and hopeful lover even amidst confusion and tension. The invoked 'I' is not necessarily masculine or feminine. Even though, linguistically, the masculine references are sometimes clearly demarcated from or mixed with feminine ones, the two are still interrelated, revealed by the ordinary evocation of their genderless agency. When the woman is clearly given the poetic platform, her discourse is straightforward:

I am a woman, no more and no less

*I am who I am, as
you are who you are: you live in me
and I live in you, to and for you
I love the necessary clarity of our mutual puzzle
I am yours when I overflow the night
but I am not a land
or a journey
I am a woman, no more no less*

*And I tire
from the moon's feminine cycle
and my guitar falls ill
string
by string
I am a woman, no more
And no less!*[54]

So many Arab poets, including Darwish at his early stages, dwelt in attributing to women transcendental feminine powers. The woman became celebrated, not for her actions or practices but for her sheer femininity: delightful scenes and mutations of nature and her were made into exchangeable synonyms, objectified to be an ambassador of nature rather than herself and her culture. She became an object of tokenism invoked in contexts of land colonized, love repressed or societies mired in traditional immobility. The woman as a questioning and searching human being and agent, in addition to the physical charms, had been overlooked. Darwish involves the woman in the construction of the duality of love and lovers. This duality with all its ambiguity and necessity for the endurance of love is the essential identity that lovers, whether they be men or women, seek. Femininity is embedded in the constructs that masculinity sets up for it, whereas womanhood has its frames of reference within its own ordinariness and aspirations.

To this end, Darwish's *diwan*, Sareer al-Ghareebah is constructed with the care of somebody who felt, lived and observed varied experiences and manifestations of love. It veers towards philosophical tendencies that diversify and elevate the voices within the experience of love. And it mixes the tenses: what was love and how it felt, and what it really is from a distance trailing with abiding echoes. This is while certain thematic currents run throughout the *diwan* which are unmistakably Darwishian. In that, they colour the broad silhouettes of Darwish's life. These include exile and history, the former as the embodiment of all the stages of his life, childhood, youth and old age, and the latter as the reference to the Palestinian experience with its profound sense of historicity and the struggle for a historical restoration. Darwish is a multiple subject with multiple visions.

In the signature poem, *Who Am I, Without Exile?*, what connects the poet to the memory of his love is the river, more specifically water: 'A stranger on the riverbank, like the river . . . water binds me to your name . . . what will I do without exile, and a long night that stares at the water?'[55] Water is eternally in motion, and so is the stare of the lover, 'and the scene consecrates the object I am going to love', as Roland Barthes intones.[56] It is the mobility within the most mobile and moving of nature's gifts, water, which the lover hangs on to, after everything has disappeared, the road, the house and the nation. Already the Islamic tradition teaches that water is the primordial source of life, 'We made from water everything living', the Quranic verse confirms.[57] Exile targets the human memory in order to subject it to repression to assume a different present from the one it used to have. However, memory is resilient, particularly that of love: it recreates the past while expanding physical localities and wearing symbols of continuity and mobility. Water, like love and the eye that first wears it, is a substance that requires no substantiation; it combines permanence and mobility. 'Water is another matter', the great Chilean poet Pablo Neruda wrote, 'has no direction but its own bright grace'.[58] Water in this poem serves as a connecting element to history and love, as a source of nourishment to both, as a source that no matter what locality it inhabits, it remains rooted in its source, assuming an identity of timeless and searching love. The soothing sight of water in the face of absence reminds one of his best alliances in nature. In his poem 'Tree of the East', the Syrian poet Adonis renders the relationship between lovers and their thirst for what they have lost and water in elegant and luminous verses: 'I have begun to see you as two/ you and this pearl swimming in my eye. / Water and I have become lovers. / I am born in the name of water, / and water is born within me. / We have become twins'.[59] The lover in exile holds on to his beloved through the very object with which he first saw her, the watery light of his eyes. With water, he washes the pain and sees within the intricate twists of his identity an origin like that of water, love reproduced and eternally reflective of its own, ever, renewable self. Exile, therefore, is not without its water. It substantiates love and enriches the loves, invoking in him permanence and fluidity, ancientness and newness that characterize his conditions of exile and love. Exile grows, and so does the lover to the point that exile becomes an active and mobile identity integral to the poet-lover's formation, hence 'what will we do without exile?'[60]

If modern exile and its symbols nuance love and enrich the lover, tradition with relevant echoes of love and struggle deepens the historical sense and the pressing transience and fluidity of the human subject. In the last three poems in the *diwan*, namely *Jameel Bouthaina and I, A Mask for Majnūn Layla* and *A Lesson from Kama Sutra*, love is conjured up as an exilic experience rooted in timelessness that derives its sustenance from the disruptions and continuities of history. Love is an internal exile: it exiles the lover from his surroundings while connecting him to a deathly instinct within him, bursting with living emotions of ancientness, desire, hope and fragility. The earth, not only the land, becomes the theatre of the wandering and beguiled lover. Darwish explores the very historic terrains of imagination that once preoccupied lovers and poets, as Jameel Bouthaina and Majnūn Layla. The poet constructs mirrors for his own humanity while feeling through it the timeless aspiration for love, whatever puzzlement it generates:

> It's love, my friend, our chosen death
> one passer-by marrying the absolute in another . . .
> No end for me, no beginning for me. No
> Bouthaina for me or me for Bouthaina. This
> is love, my friend. I wish I were
> twenty doors younger than myself
> for the air to be light on me, and for her side-profile
> at night to be clearer than a mole
> above her navel[61]

The invocation of history and the questioning affiliation with its resonant vicissitudes make the present moment and experience critically historical. History is consulted as a space of exploratory visions, not as an immutable reference of ideology. In this respect, Jameson's writing regarding the postmodernist's relation to history is noteworthy: 'It is safest to grasp the concept of the postmodern as an attempt to think the present historically in an age that has forgotten how to think historically in the first place.'[62] History ceases to be only about events and becomes more of an eternal child of psychological permutations, in its past contexts and present appearance, distilled to inject confidence in the present. By walking and conversing with the ancients, 'my friend', which in another translation can be rendered as 'my companion', as recurrently appears in several classical *qasīda* poems, Darwish recreates the relevant dilemma of the lover Bouthaina as a wise man seeing love from a place of revelation and nostalgia. In *Majnūn Layla*, Darwish conjures up the old 'Uhdri saying, 'I am one of those who die when they love.'[63] He dissolves and deconstructs himself, moving from a historical affiliation towards fragmentation and dissolution till the subject becomes infinitely no one: 'I am Qays Leila, I am and I am . . . no one.'[64] The human psyche in love is one. It dissolves itself with and in the beloved within a postmodernist context where the fragments of the self are only united in death. Self-deconstruction is destruction and reconstruction. Its death is the living certificate of its love. Darwish identifies with the eighth-century Bouthaina and the Majnoon and incorporates their wandering and questioning sentiments into his modernist poetics, relevant poetics of nostalgia, alienation and love bleeding with wisdom.

In the last exhortation Darwish gives to the lovers in *A Lesson from Kama Sutra*, love is an instinctive hunt endowed with echoes of productive death, which needs to be graced with patience and spiritual elegance. Last but not least, love is about self-cultivation that sees deeply into its very conditions, down to their last vestige of life:

You are the only two left in the universe
so take her, gently, to your desired death
and wait for her!...[65]

Conclusion

It is striking how much the theme of love has affected modern Arabic poetry. The Arab world is particularly sensitive and attuned to verses of love considering that the sociopolitical structures underscoring this sentiment are permeated with strictures on flexible and fluid emotional bonds. Love is sung about, invoked endlessly in poetry and discussed as a cultural value to strengthen the social and even political affiliations, but it is not considered sufficiently in a psychological or existential light. Poetry and art in general unearth the habits of society by pronouncing and reiterating their silences, what they most render invisible through discourses of virtue and decorum. The early Arab romantics were adept at invoking and criticizing the strict structures of the Arab world and some of its dominant patriarchal and limited references and archaic discourses. This background promoted Arab poets in the 1950s and 1960s to use love poetry and popularize its sentiments, to normalize love as a practice of social freedom in the public sphere. The first poet to cut through towards public endorsement and admiration and to occupy the throne of Arabic love poetry in the modern age is Nizar Qabbani. Qabbani's poetry celebrates and revers love between the sexes. It celebrates it in its most sensitive aspect, namely in its sexual dimension. Women are celebrated, not only as mothers and housewives but as lovers and beings of desires with agency and voice. Qabbani exults as a lover. He dissects his personal experiences of love, expresses his pain for its absence, the joys of its attainments and invokes its mysterious regions when lovers are locked into physical and psychical union.

Methodologically, Qabbani uses the Arabic tradition in which he is steeped in and particularly its sentimental aspects but flaunts its rules through modernist poetry attendant to free poetic energy equipped with modernist sociopolitical attitudes. The tradition is made to inspire the modern present not to imprison it in its own contexts and particularities. Therefore, one of the particular reiterations of Qabbani in his poetry relates to renewing the language and injecting the public sphere with a sense of freedom and openness so that love can be practised without traditional restrictions and not be subject to the violence of the modern nation states and the grip of its patriarchal underpinnings, a sentiment that was echoed by earlier Arab romantics, such as the Lebanese poet Gibran Khalil Gibran (1883–1931) and the Tunisian poet Abu al-Qasim al-Shabbi (1909–34). Qabbani concentrates on freedom in love and extends it to men and women as a universal right concurrent with universal psychical grounds, presently haunted by restrictive and limited understanding of freedom and love. Most poignantly, in the poem devoted to his assassinated wife, Balqees, Nizar Qabbani laments the fact that this hope of free and humane love that should be protected and guaranteed by the sociopolitical structures has been shattered by an Arab world mired in limited references and tendencies that breed oppression and violence.

If Qabbani is a poet of love and freedom away from societal restrictions, Darwish is a poet of love rooted in reconciliation and evolution that leads to productive duality that houses the singularity of lovers. The grandness of Qabbani's tone contrasts with the intimate and private voice of Darwish where the ordinariness of love is philosophically and lyrically rendered through its tensions, contradictions and traces inside the searching self. The initial experiences of love for Darwish with an Israeli Jewish girl introduce him to the ecstasy and divinity of love that the glaring reality of the Israeli-Palestinian conflict disrupts. Memory is seared with the pain of separation that the political conflict ultimately caused. In this instance, the celebrated poet of resistance could not reconcile with love being haunted by the beloved who carries a gun and directs it towards his people, whom he is the most versatile poetic chronicler of their pain and dispossession from their homeland.[66] This particular experience of love and its lessons shapes Darwish's earlier sensibility and understanding of love as an abiding human sentiment that cannot flourish without reconciliation and an expansive sense of humanity. Thus, in the latter stage of his love poetry writing, Darwish invokes the agency of lovers, be they women or men, and deconstructs their relation to its constitutive elements. In his case, love, exile and history are inseparable in their effect and resonance. In *The Stranger's Bed*, Darwish shows several instances of love, interweaving traditional with postmodernist narratives about the human subject and the fluidity love induces. The self is seen in fragments and memory is host for reconstructive and deconstructive understanding and portrayal of love: love in context of separation, love mired in psychical blockages, love invoking and associating with historical figures and symbolic icons of its upholders, love as a hope bred with patience and spiritual fortitude, and love as reconciliation with the death of the self itself for the sake of duality that produces and reproduces itself and humanity.

Against this background, we stand before experiences and renderings of love springing from different positions and contexts but all emergent from and within a renewed and radically deconstructed Arab tradition and life. Future Arab poets and researchers of love can benefit from such a rich legacy of poets-lovers keenly committed to and conversant with love as a liberating experience that requires liberating societal and political structures and spaces to engender and grow.

Notes

1   All the translations in the text are the author's, unless indicated otherwise.
2   For an exploration of the theme of love in Arabic literature, see, for example, A. Roger, K. Hilary and M. Ed de, *Love and Sexuality in Modern Arabic Literature* (London: Saqi Books, 1997).

3   Jean Lyotard, *The Postmodern Condition: A Report on Knowledge* (Manchester: Manchester University Press, 1984).
4   Lyotard defines postmodernism as 'incredulity toward metanarratives. . . . The narrative function is losing its functors, its great hero, its great dangers, its great voyages, its great goal. It is being dispersed in clouds of narrative language elements – narrative, but also denotative, prescriptive, descriptive, and so on. Conveyed within each cloud are pragmatic valencies specific to its kind. Each of us lives at the inter section of many of these.' Lyotard, *The Postmodern Condition*, 1.
5   See Salma Jayussi, *Trends and Movements in Modern Arabic Poetry* (Leiden: Brill, 1977). See also R. C. Ostle, 'The Romantic Poets', in *Modern Arabic Literature*, ed. M. M. Badawi (Cambridge: Cambridge University Press), 82–132.
6   See Atef Alshaer, *Poetry and Politics in the Modern Arab World* (London and New York: Hurst and Co. 2016).
7   Bassam K. Frangieh, *Introduction to Nizar Qabbani: Arabian Love Poems* (London: Lynne Rienner Publishers, 1999), 9.
8   Salma Khadra Jayyusi, 'Introduction: A Lover for All Times', in *On Entering the Sea: The Erotic and Other Poetry of Nizar Qabbani*, ed. Lena Jayyusi and Sharif Elmusa (New York: Interlink Books, 1996), vii.
9   On the topic of patriarchy and its consequences in the Arab world, see Hisham Sharabi, *Neopatriarchy: A Theory of Distorted Change in Arab Society* (Oxford: Oxford University Press, 1993).
10 See Chapter 5 in this book.
11 It is noteworthy to pay attention to the German critic Stefan Wild's observation: 'Nizār Qabbānī the rebel is at the same time Nizār Qabbāni the eternal child. The woman who wants to be loved by him must liberate herself from all the fetters of traditional Arab society but must at the same time play the role of his mother; she must be completely Arab but in many ways resemble a caricature of an emancipated Western woman.' Stefan Wild, 'Nizār Qabbānī's Autobiography: Images of Sexuality, Death and Poetry', in *Love and Sexuality in Modern Arabic Literature* (London: Saqi Books, 1997), 209, 200–9.
12 N. Qabbani, *Qisatī ma'al-Sh'ir* (Beirut: Manshūrāt Nizār Qbbanī, 1973), 174.
13 Ibid., 134–5.
14 N. Qabbānī, *Rihlat al-Sh'ir wal-hayāh*, ed. Deeb Ali Hassan (Beirut, Damascus: Dār al-Hikmah, 2000), 112, 113.
15 Lena Jayyusi and Sharif Elmusa (eds), *On Entering the Sea: The Erotic and Other Poetry of Nizar Qabbani* (New York: Interlink Books, 1996), 21.
16 Nizar Kabbani, *Arabian Love Poems*, eds and trans. B. K. Frangieh and C. R. Brown (Colorado Springs: Three Continents Press, 1998), 45.
17 Ibid., 68–70. It is worthwhile that Qabbani's reference (e.g. 'Lubna's lover') here is influenced by Saddiq Jalal al-Azm's book which condemned past Arab poet lovers and chided those who aspired to be like them in the modern period.
18 Frangieh, *Introduction to Nizar Qabbani*, 14.
19 Jayyusi and Elmusa, *On Entering the Sea*, 15.
20 See N. Qabbani, *Ahlā Qasā'id* (Lebanon: Kitabouna, 2006), 217–36, my translation.
21 David Harvey, *The Condition of Postmodernity: An Enquiry into the Origins of Cultural Change* (Cambridge and Oxford: Blackwell, 1990), 12.
22 See Marshal Berman's book, which bear the title at hand: *All That Is Solid Melts Down into Air: The Experience of Modernity* (London: Verso, 2010).
23 For some of these poems, see the section under the title, the forbidden poems, in *Ahlā Qasā'id* (Lebanon: Kitabouna, 2006), 237–74.
24 For the study of these stages from various thematic standpoints, see Atef Alshaer, 'Violence, Nationalism and Humanism in Mahmoud Darwish's Poetry', in *Poetry and Warfare in Middle Eastern Literature*, ed. Hugh Kennedy (London: I.B. Tauris, 2014), and As'ad E. Khairallah, 'Mahmoud Darwish: Writing Self and History as Poem', in *Poetry and*

History: The Value of Poetry in Reconstructing Arab History, ed. B. Ramzi, et al. (Beirut: AUB, 2011), 335–61.
25. See Faisal Darāj, 'Dalālat al-Ard fī Qasīdah Mutahwwilah', in *Hakadhā Takalma Mahmoud Darwish: Dirasāt fī Dhikrah Rahīleh* (Beirut: Markaz Dirasat al-Wihda al-arabiyya, 2009), 27–51.
26. Salma Khadra Jayyusi, *Foreword: Mahmoud Darwish: Exile's Poet: Critical Essays* (Northampton, MA: Olive Branch Press, 2008), vii–xiv, ix.
27. Mahmoud Darwish, *A Lover from Palestine*, in Khalid Sulaiman, *Palestine and Modern Arab Poetry* (London: Zed Books, 1948).
28. On theme of mapping and renaming, see Meron Benvenisti, *Sacred Landscape: The Buried History of the Holy Land Since 1948* (Berkeley, Los Angeles and London: University of California Press, 2002).
29. See Atef Alshaer, 'In the Company of Frantz Fanon: The Israeli Wars and the National Culture of Gaza', in *Gaza as A Metaphor*, ed. Hegla Tawil Souri and Dina Matar (London: Hurst & Co., 2016).
30. M. Darwish, *Between Rita and the Olive Branch*, in Abdullah Al-Shahham, 'A Portrait of the Israeli Woman as the Beloved: The Woman-Soldier in the Poetry of Mahmoud Darwish After the 1967 War', *British Society for Middle Eastern Studies* 15 (1988): 28–49.
31. Verena Klemm, 'Poems of a Love impossible to Live: Mahmūd Darwīsh and Rītā', in Introduction, *Ghazal as World Literature, Transformation of a Literary Genre: Why the Ghazal?* ed. Thomas Bauer and Angelica Newwirth (Leiden: Verlago, 1996), 243–59, 255.
32. See Huma Baig's Chapter 6 in this book.
33. See Laleh Khalili, *A Habit of Destruction*, http://societyandspace.com/material/commentaries/laleh-khalili-a-habit-of-destruction/, last accessed 24 September 2014.
34. Al-Shahham, 'A Portrait of the Israeli Woman as the Beloved', 28–49.
35. In one of his last writings on love, Darwish writes about the impossibility of defining it: 'love is like meanings on the open road; but it is, like poetry, difficult. It requires talent, endurance and skillful crafting in order to head its many degrees ... love is not an idea. It is an emotion that burns and freezes, comes and goes. It is an emotion embodied in shape and form, with five, and more, senses. Sometimes, it comes upon us in the form of an angel with light wings that are able to lift us up from the earth. Sometimes, it sweeps us away in the form of a bull which tosses us to the ground and goes. At times, it blows like a storm whose trail of destruction is well known to us. Sometimes, it descends upon us like a dew in the night when a magic hand milks a stray cloud.' Mahmoud Darwish, *Fī hadrat al-Ghiyab* (Beirut: Riad El-Rayyes Books, 2006), 127–35. See the translated text by Mohammad Shaheen and Mahmoud Darwish, *Absent Presence* (London: Hesperus Press Limited, 2010), 87–92.
36. Marcel Khalifeh put to song several of Darwish's poems, including *Between Rita and the Eyes of the Rifle*.
37. Mahmoud Darwish, *Hiṣār limdāih al-Baḥr* (Beirut: Dār al-'Wdah), 163–72.
38. Roland Barthes, *A Lover's Discourse: Fragments* (London: Random House, 1977).
39. Subhi Hadidi, 'Mahmoud Darwish's Love Poem: History, Exile and the Epic Call', in *Mahmoud Darwis, Exile's Poet: Critical Essays*, ed. Khamis Nassar Hala and Najat Rahman Najat (Paris: Interlink Publishing, 2007), 100.
40. Fady Joudah, Introduction to Mahmoud Darwish, *The Butterfly's Burden* (Northumberland: Bloodaxe Books, 2007), xiii.
41. Ibid., 7 and 9.
42. Ibid., xiv.
43. See T. S. Eliot, 'Tradition and the Individual Talent', http://www.bartleby.com/200/sw4.html, last accessed 2 August 2015.
44. *We Were Missing a Present*, Fady Joudah (trans.). Darwish, *The Butterfly's Burden*, 4.
45. See P. Suzanne Stetkevych, *The Mute Immortals Speak: Pre-Islamic Poetry and Poetics of Ritual* (Ithaca, NY: Cornel University Press, 1993).
46. See Mahmoud Darwish, *Absent Presence* (London: Hesperus Press Limited, 2010), 87–92.

47 Darwish, *We Were Missing a Present*, 5.
48 See Stephen Melville's definition of deconstruction which applies to the case at hand: 'Deconstruction presents itself as, in general, a practice of reading, a way of picking things up against their own grain, or at their margins, in order to show something about how they are structured by the very things they act to exclude from themselves, and so more or less subtly to displace the structure within which such exclusions seem plausible or necessary. Like an analyst listening to an analysed, deconstruction attends to the other that haunts, organizes and disorganizes, a speech that takes itself to be in control of its meanings and identify. Deconstruction arises a certain commitment to flux and fluidity', Stephen Melville, 'The Temptation of New Perspectives', in *the Art of History: A Critical Anthology*, ed. Donald Preziosi (Oxford: Oxford University Press, 1998), 401–12, 401–2.
49 See Darwish, *The Butterfly's Burden*, 9.
50 Ibid., 27.
51 In Hadidi, 'Mahmoud Darwish's Love Poem', 102.
52 Darwish, *The Butterfly's Burden*, 35.
53 Frederic Jameson, *Postmodern Or the Cultural Logic of Late Capitalism* (London and New York: Verso, 1991), ix.
54 Darwish, *No More and No Less, The Butterfly's Burde*n, 47.
55 Ibid., 89.
56 Barthes, *A Lover's Discourse: Fragments*, 192.
57 Quran, 12/30.
58 Pablo Neruda, *Fully Empowered: A Bilingual Edition*, trans. Alastair Reid, A Condor Book (Souvenir Press, 1967), 13.
59 Adonis, *Selected Poems*, trans. Khalid Mattawa (Yale University, 2010), 60.
60 Darwish, *Who Am I Without Exile, The Butterfly's Burden*, 91.
61 Darwish, *Jameel Bouthaina and I, The Butterfly's Burden*, 93.
62 Jameson, *Postmodern Or the Cultural Logic of Late Capitalism*, ix.
63 A Mask . . . for *Majnoon Leila, The Butterfly's Burden*, 97.
64 Ibid.
65 A Lesson from Kama Sutra, *The Butterfly's Burden*, 103.
66 See Alshaer, Atef, *Poetry and Politics in the Modern Arab World* (London: Hurst & Co, 2016).

SELECTED REFERENCES

Abou-Bakr, Omaima. 'Abrogation of the Mind in the Poetry of Jalal al-Din Rumi'. In *Journal of Comparative Poetics: Madness and Civilisation*, 37–63. Egypt: American University in Cairo and American University in Cairo Press, 1994.
Abrahamov, Binyamin. 'Al-Ghāzālī's Supreme Way to Know God'. *Studia Islamica* 77 (1993): 141–68.
Abrahamov, Binyamin. *Divine Love in Islamic Mysticism: The Teachings of Ghāzālī and Al-Dabbagh*, 1–86. London: Routledge, 2003.
Adonis. *Al-sufiya wa al-suryaliya*. Lebanon: Dar al-Saqi, 1995.
Adonis. *An Introduction to Arabic Poetics*. London: Saqi Books, 2003.
Al-Andalusi, Ibn Hazm. *The Ring of the Dove*. Translated by A. J. Arberry and D. Litt. London: Luzac & Company, Ltd., 1953.
Albert, Edoardo. *Imam Ghāzālī: A Concise Life*, 1–82. United Kingdom: Kube Publishing, 2012.
Al-Ghāzālī, Abu Hamid. *The Book of Knowledge*. Translated by Nabih Amin Faris, 39–43. New Delhi: Islamic Book Service, 1962.
Al-Ghāzālī, Abu Hamid. *On Disciplining the Soul and On Breaking the Two Desires*, 156. Translated by Timothy Winter. Cambridge: Islamic Texts Society, 1997.
Al-Ghāzālī, Abu Hamid. *Deliverance from Error*. Translated by Watt W. Montgomery, 26–31. Kuala Lumpur: Islamic Book Trust, 2005.
Al-Ghāzālī, Abu Hamid. *The Alchemy of Happiness*. Translated by Claud Field, 1–85. New York: Cosimo Classics, 2010.
Al-Ghāzālī, Abu Hamid. *Marvels of the Heart: Science of the Spirit*. Translated by Walter J. Skellie. Louisville: Fons Vitae, 2010, 53–4.
Allen, Roger, K. Hilary and M. Ed de. *Love and Sexuality in Modern Arabic Literature*. London: Saqi Books, 1997.
Alshaer, Atef. *Poetry and Politics in the Modern Arab World*. London: Hurst Publishers & Co, 2016.
Alster, B. 'Marriage and Love in the Sumerian Love Songs'. In *The Tablet and the Scroll: Near Eastern Studies in Honor of William W. Hallo*, edited by M. E. Cohen, et al, 15–27. Maryland, MD: CDL Press, Bethesda, 1993.
Anderson, Benedict. *Imagined Communities*. London: Verso Books, 1991.
Andrews, Walter and Laurent Mignon. 'Ottoman, Azeri and Modern Turkish Poetry'. In *The New Princeton Encyclopedia of Poetry and Poetics*, edited by Roland Green, et al. Princeton: Princeton University Press, 2012, 1469–74.
Arkoun, Mohamed. *Islam: To Reform or To Subvert*. London: Saqi Essentials, 2002.
As'ad, Khairallah and E. Love. *Madness and Poetry: An Interpretation of the Majnūn Legend*. Beirut and Wiesbaden: Orient-Institut der Deutschen Morgenländischen Gesellschaft, 1980
Auberbach, Erich. *Memesis: The Representation of Reality in Western Literature*. Princeton: Princeton University Press, 2003 [1953].
Barry, J., E. Greenwich and P. Spector. *Be My Baby*. Philles Records, 1963.
Barthes, R. 'The Death of the Author'. In *Image, Music, Text*, translated by S. Heath, 142–8. London: Fontana, 1977.
Barthes, R. *A Lover's Discourse: Fragments*. Translated By Richard Howard. New York: Hill and Wang, 1978.
Bauer, Thomas and Angelica Neuwirth. Introduction: *Ghazal as World Literature, Transformation of a Literary Genre: Why the Ghazal?* Leiden: Verlago, 1996.
Bausani, Alessandro. 'Theism and Pantheism in Rumi'. In *Iranian Studies*, vol.1, 8–24. Taylor and Francis Ltd, 1968. Bodman Jr., Herbert L. '(untitled)' Rev. of The Alchemy of Happiness

Translated by Claud Feild and Revised by Elton L. Daniel. *Journal of World History* (Fall 1993): 336–8.

Bell, G.. *Syria: The Desert and the Sown*. London: Heinemann, 1907.

Berlant, L. 'Love, A Queer Feeling'. In *Homosexuality and Psychoanalysis*, edited by T. Dean and C. Lane, 432–51. Chicago: University of Chicago Press, 2001.

Biggs, R. D. *Šà.zi.ga: Ancient Mesopotamian Potency Incantations*. Texts from Cuneiform Sources 2. Locust Valley: J.J. Augustin, 1967.

Black, J. A. 'Babylonian Ballads: A New Genre'. *Journal of the American Oriental Society* 103, no. 1(1983): 25–34, republished in Studies in Literature from the Ancient Near East by Members of the American Oriental Society Dedicated to Samuel Noah Kramer, edited by J. M. Sasson. American Oriental Series 65. New Haven: AOS, 1984.

Bodman Jr., Herbert L. 'Review of The Alchemy of Happiness'. Translated by. Claud Feild and revised by Elton L. Daniel. *Journal of World History* (1993): 336–8.

Bowering, Gerhard. 'Review of Al-Ghazzālī's *Alchemy of Happiness*'. Translated by Claud Field, revised and annotated by Elton L. Daniel. *Journal of Near Eastern Studies* 54 (1995): 227–8.

Burgess, J. 'Recent Reception of Homer: A Review Article'. *Phoenix* 62 (2008): 184–95.

Butler, J. *Gender Trouble. Feminism and the Subversion of Identity*, 2nd edn (1st edition 1990). New York: Routledge, 2006.

Calder, Norman, Jawad Mojaddedi and Andrew Rippin. *Classical Islam: A Sourcebook of Religious Literature*. London: Routledge, 2003.

Cavigneaux, A. 'Prier et séduire'. In *Dans le laboratoire de l' historien des Religions. Mélanges offerts à Philippe Borgeaud*, edited by F. Prescendi and Y. Volokhine. Religions en Perspective 24, 496–503. Geneva: Labor et Fides, 2011.

CDLI: Cuneiform Digital Library Initiative, http://cdli.ucla.edu/ (last accessed 12 May 2015).

Chittick, W. *The Sufi Path of Love: The Spiritual Teachings of Rumi*. Albany: State University of New York Press, 1983.

Chittick, W. 'The Spiritual Path of Love of Ibn al-'Arabi and Rumi'. In *Mystics Quarterly*, vol. 19, 4–16. USA: Penn State University Press, 1993. http://www.williamcchittick.com/wp-content/uploads/2019/05/The-Spiritual-Path-of-Love-in-Ibn-al-Arabi-and-Rumi.pdf, accessed on 29th August 2021.

Chittick, William C. 'The Pluralistic Vision of Persian Sufi Poetry'. *Islam and Christian-Muslim Relations*, 14, 4 October 2003.

Christoph Bürgel, Johan. 'Theories About Love: How Love Manifests in Islamic Culture'. In *Art &Thought: Fikrun Wa Fann, Goethe-Institute, e.V*, edited by W. Stefan, no. 86 (11). August–October 2007. Berlin: Goethe-Institute.

Cleveland, A., R. Benson and M. Gaye. *What's Going On*. Tamla Records, 1970.

Cohn, N. 'Phil Spector'. In *The Rolling Stone Illustrated History of Rock & Roll*, edited by J. Miller, 148–59. London: Picador, 1981.

Cooper, J. S. 'Sacred Marriage and Popular Cult in Early Mesopotamia'. In *Official Cult and Popular Religion in the Ancient Near East*, edited by E. Matsushima. Papers of the First Colloquium on the Ancient Near East – The City and its Life held at the Middle Eastern Cultural Centre in Japan (Mitaka, Tokyo), March 20–22, 1992, 81–96. Heidelberg: Winter, 1993.

Cooper, J. S. 'Magic and m(is)use: Poetic Promiscuity in Mesopotamian Ritual'. In *Mesopotamian Poetic Language: Sumerian and Akkadian*, edited by M. E. Vogelzang and H. L. J. Vanstiphout, 47–57. Cuneiform Monographs 6. Groningen: Sty, 1996.

Cooper, J. S. 'Sex and the Temple'. In *Tempel im alten Orient. 7. Internationales Colloquium der Deutschen Orient-Gesellschaft 11.-13. Oktober 2009, München*, edited by K. Kaniuth, A. Löhnert, J. L. Miller, A. Otto, M. Roaf and W. Sallaberger. Colloquien der Deutschen Orient-Gesellschaft 7, 49–58. Wiesbaden: Harrassowitz, 2013.

Culcasi, Karen. 'Constructing and Naturalizing the Middle East, Geographical Review'. *American Geographical Society* 100, no. 4 (October 2010): 538–97. London: Wiley. See: https://onlinel ibrary.wiley.com/doi/epdf/10.1111/j.1931-0846.2010.00059.x (last accessed 20 July 2021).

Currie, B. *Homer's Allusive Art*. Oxford: Oxford University Press, 2016.

De Bruijn, J. T. P. *Persian Sufi Poetry. An Introduction to the Mystical Use of Classical Persian Poems*. Richmond: Curzon Press, 1997.
Dib Sherfan, Andrew. *Khalil Gibran: The Nature of Love*. New York: Philosophical Library, 1971.
Dijck, J. van. *Nicht-kanonische Beschwörungen und Sonstige Literarische Texte*. Vorderasiatische Schriftdenkmäler der Staatlichen Museen zu Berlin 17. Berlin: Akademie, 1971.
Diwān Majnūn Layla. *Beirut*. 'ālam al-Kutub, 1996.
Doors, The. *Light My Fire*. Elektra Records, 1967.
Durand, J. M. and M. Guichard. 'Les Rituels de Mari'. *Florilegium Marianum* III (1997): 19–78.
Dyckhoff, Chr. *Das Haushaltbuch des Balamunamhe*, Inaugural-Dissertation zur Erlangung des Doktorgrades der Philosophie an der Ludwig-Maxilians-Universität, München, 1999.
Ebeling, E. *Keilschrifttexte aus Assur Religiösen Inhaltes Bd. I*. Leipzig: Hinrichs, 1919.
Ebeling, E. *Literarische Keilschrifttexte aus Assur*. Berlin: Akademie-Verlag, 1953.
Edzard, D. O. 'Zur Ritualtafel der sog. "Love Lyrics"'. In *Language, Literature and History: Philological and Historical Studies Presented to Erica Reiner*, edited by F. Rochberg-Halton. American Oriental Series 67, 57–69. New Haven: Eisenbrauns, 1987.
Eksell, K. 'Genre in Early Arabic Poetry'. In *Literary History: Towards a Global Perspective, Volume 2: Literary Genres: An Intercultural Approach*, G. Lindberg-Wada, S. Helgesson, A. Pettersson and M. Pettersson, 156–98. Berlin: De Gruyter, 2006.
Encyclopaedia Britannica Online, http://www.britannica.com/EBchecked/topic/201463/fana (last accessed 23 February 2014).
ETCSL: Electronic Text Corpus of Sumerian Literature, http://etcsl.orinst.ox.ac.uk/ (last accessed 27 September 2014).
Fain, S. and P. F. Webster. *Secret Love*. Columbia Records, 1953.
Finkel, Caroline. *Osman's Dream: The Story of the Ottoman Empire 1300–1932*. London: John Murray, 2005.
Finkel, I. L. 'A Fragmentary Catalogue of Lovesongs'. *Acta Sumerologica Japan* 10 (1988): 17–8.
Foster, B. R. *Before the Muses: An Anthology of Akkadian Literature*, 3rd edn. Bethesda: CDL Press, 2005.
Foucault, Michel. *Madness and Civilization: A History of Insanity in the Age of Reason*. Edited by Vintage Books. New York: Random House, 1988.
Frahm, E. *Historische und historisch-literarische Texte*, Keilschrifttexte aus Assur literarischen Inhalts 3. Wiesbaden: Harrassowitz, 2009.
Frahm, E. *Babylonian Text Commentaries. Origins of Interpretation*, Guides to the Mesopotamian Textual Record 5. Münster: Ugarit-Verlag, 2011.
Freud, Sigmund. *The Psychology of Love*. London: Penguin Classics, 2006 [1905].
Freydank, H. *Beiträge zur mittelassyrischen Chronologie und Geschichte* (Schriften zur Geschichte und Kultur des alten Orients 21). Berlin, 1991.
Friemuth, Maha Elkaisy. *God and Humans in Islamic Thought: Abd al-Jabbar, Ibn Sina and al-Ghāzālī*. London: Routledge, 2006.
Fromm, Eric. 'The Art of Loving: The Theory of Love'. In *Art &Thought: Fikrun Wa Fann, Goethe-Institute*, e.V, edited by W. Stefan, no. 86 (11). Berlin, August –October 2007.
Frow, J. *Genre. The New Critical Idiom*. London and New York: Routledge, 2006.
Gelb, I. J. *Sargonic Texts in the Ashmolean Museum*. MAD 5. Chicago: University of Chicago Press, 1970.
Geller, M. J. 'Mesopotamian Love Magic: Discourse or Intercourse?' In *Sex and Gender in the Ancient Near East. Proceedings of the h Rencontre Assyriologique Internationale, Helsinki, July 2-6, 2001*. 2 vols, edited by S. Parpola and R. M. Whiting, 129–39. Helsinki: Neo-Assyrian Text Corpus Project, 2002.
George, A. R., 'Four Temple Rituals from Babylon'. In *Wisdom, Gods and Literature: Studies in Assyriology in Honour of W. G. Lambert*, edited by A. R. George and I. L. Finkel, 259–99. Winona Lake: Eisenbrauns, 2000.
George, A. R. *The Babylonian Gilgamesh Epic*. Introduction, Critical Edition and Cuneiform Texts. Oxford: Oxford University Press, 2003.

George, A. R. 'Review of Lapinkivi 2004'. *Bulletin of the School of Oriental and African Studies* 69, no. 2 (2006): 315–17.

George, A. R. 'Babylonian and Assyrian: A History of Akkadian'. In *Languages of Iraq, Ancient and Modern*, edited by J. N. Postgate, 31–71. London: British School of Archaeology in Iraq, 2007.

George, A. R. *Babylonian Literary Texts in the Schøyen Collection*. Manuscripts in the Schøyen Collection, Cuneiform Texts 4. Cornell University Studies in Assyriology and Sumerology 10. Bethesda, MD: CDL Press, 2009.

George, A. R. 'The Assyrian Elegy: Form and Meaning'. In *Opening the Tablet Box: Near Eastern Studies in Honor of Benjamin R. Foster*, edited by S. C. Melville and A. L. Slotsky, 203–16. Leiden: Brill, 2010.

George, A. R. *Mesopotamian Incantations and Related Texts in the Schøyen Collection*. Manuscripts in the Schøyen Collection, Cuneiform Texts 8. Cornell University Studies in Assyriology and Sumerology 32. Bethesda, MD: CDL Press, 2016.

Goetze, A., M. I. Hussey and J. van Dijk. *Early Mesopotamian Incantations and Rituals*. Yale Oriental Series 11. Yale: Yale University Press, 1985.

.Greenwich, E., T. Powers and P. Spector. *Today I Met the Boy I'm Gonna Marry*. Philles Records, 1963.

Griffin, J. *Latin Poets and Roman Life*, London: Duckworth, 1985.

Groneberg, B. '"Brust" (irtum)–Gesänge'. In *Munuscula Mesopotamica, Festschrift für Johannes Renger*, edited by B. Böck, E. Cancik-Kirschbaum and Th. Richter, AOAT 267, 169–95. Münster: Ugarit-Verlag, 1999.

Groneberg, B. 'Die Liebesbeschwörung MAD V 8 und ihr Literarischer Kontext'. *Révue d' Assyriologie et d'archéologie Orientale* 95, no. 2 (2001): 97–113.

Groneberg, B., '"The Faithful Lover" Reconsidered: Towards Establishing A New Genre'. In *Sex and Gender in the Ancient Near East, Proceedings of the XLVIIe Rencontre Assyriologique Internationale*, edited by S. Parpola, and R. M. Whiting, 165–83. Helsinki: The Neo-Assyrian Text-Corpus Project, 2002.

Groneberg, B., 'Searching for Akkadian Lyrics: From Old Babylonian to the "Liederkatalog"'. *KAR 158, Journal of Cuneiform Studies* 55 (2003): 55–74.

Groneberg, B. 'Liebes-und Hundesbeschwörungen im Kontext'. In *Studies Presented to R. D. Biggs, June 4, 2004*, edited by M. T. Roth, W. Farber, M. W. Stolper and P. von Bechtolsheim, 91–107. Chicago: Oriental Institute, 2007.

Gupta, M. G. *Maulana Rum's Masnawi*. India: M.G. Publishers, 1990.

Gzella, H. *A Cultural History of Aramaic. From the Beginnings to the Advent of Islam, in Handbuch der Orientalistik 1/111*. Leiden: Brill, 2015.

Hackl, J. 'Language Death and Dying Reconsidered: The Rôle of Late Babylonian as a Vernacular Language'. Version 01, in Imperium and Officium Working Papers, 2011, http://iowp.univie.ac.at/node/206 (last accessed 11 August 2014).

Hameen-Antilla, Jakkö. 'Abu Nuwas and Ghazal as a Genre'. In *Ghazal as World Literature, Transformations of a Literary Genre*, edited by Thomas Bauer and Angelika Neuwirth, 87. Baden: Ergon Verlag, 2005.

Hamid, Farooq. 'Storytelling Techniques in the "Masnavi-yi Ma'navi" of Mowlana Jalal al-Din Rumi: Wayward Narrative of Logical Progession', *Iranian Studies* 32, no. 1 (1999): 27–49.

Hanif, N. *Biographical Encyclopaedia of Sufis: Central Asia and Middle East*. New Delhi: Sarup Book Publishers, 2002.

Harrison, G. *Within You Without You*. Parlophone Records, 1967.

Harrison, S. J. *Generic Enrichment in Vergil and Horace*. Oxford: Oxford University Press, 2007.

Hasselbach, R. *Sargonic Akkadian: A Historical and Comparative Study of the Syllabic Texts*. Wiesbaden: Harrassowitz, 2005.

Hasselbach, R. 'The Affiliation of Sargonic Akkadian with Babylonian and Assyrian: New Insights Concerning the Internal Sub-Grouping of Akkadian'. *Journal of Semitic Studies* 52, no. 1 (2007): 21–43.

Hays, L. and P. Seeger. *Kisses Sweeter Than Wine*. Decca Records, 1951.

Hecker, K. 'Akkadische Hymnen und Gebete'. In *Texte aus der Umwelt des Alten Testaments NF 7. Hymnen, Klagelieder und Gebete*, edited by B. Jankowski and D. Schwemer, 51–98. Gütersloh: Gütersloher Verlagshaus, 2013.

Hecker, K. 'Ich zähle die Lieder'. In *Hymnen, Klagelieder und Gebete, Texte aus der Umwelt des alten Testaments, Neue Folge 7*, edited by B. Janowski and D. Schwemer, 54–63. Gütersloh: Gütersloher Verlagshaus, 2013.

Held, M. 'A Faithful Lover in an Old Babylonian Dialogue'. *Journal of Cuneiform Studies* 15 (1961): 1–26.

Held, M. 'A Faithful Lover in an Old Babylonian Dialogue: Addenda et Corrigenda'. *Journal of Cuneiform Studies* 16 (1962): 37–9.

Hilgert, M. *Akkadisch in der Ur III-Zeit, Imgula 5*. Münster: Rhema, 2002.

Hutchinson, G. 'Genre and Super-Genre'. In *Generic Interfaces in Latin Literature: Encounters, Interactions and Transformations*, edited by Th. D Papanghelis, S. J. Harrison, and S. Frangoulidis, 19–34. Berlin: De Gruyter, 2013.

KAR = E. Ebeling, *Keilschrifttexte aus Assur religiösen Inhalts*. 2 vols. Leipzig: J.C. Hinrichs, 1919–23.

Kennedy, D. *The Arts of Love, Five Studies in the Discourse of Roman Love Elegy* Cambridge: Cambridge University Press, 1993.

King, James Roy. 'Narrative Disjunction and Conjunction in Rumi's "Mathnawi"'. *The Journal of Narrative Techniques* 19, no. 3 (1989): 276–86.

Klein, G. and H. Hoffman. *Bobby's Girl*. Seville Records, 1962.

Klein J. and Y. Sefati. '"Secular" Love Songs in Mesopotamian Literature'. In *Birkat Shalom. Studies in the Bible, Ancient Near Eastern Literature, and Postbiblical Judaism Presented to Shalom M. Paul on the Occasion of His Seventieth Birthday*, edited by Ch. Cohen, V. A. Hurowitz, A. Hurvitz, Y. Muffs, B. J. Schwartz and J. H. Tigay, 613–26. Winona Lake: Eisenbrauns, 2008.

Kogan, L. E. '*ġ in Akkadian'. *Ugaritforschungen* 33 (2001): 263–98.

Kogan, L. E. 'Additions and Corrections to'*ġ in Akkadian'. *Ugaritforschungen* 34 (2002): 315–17.

Kraus, F. R. 'Das Altbabylonische Königtum'. In *Le palais et la royauté*, edited by P. Garelli, 253–60. Paris: Geuthner, 1974.

Kugle, Scott. *Sufis & Saints Bodies: Mysticism, Corporeality and Sacred Power in Islam*. Chapel Hill, North Carolina: The University of North Carolina Press, 2007.

Lambert, W. G. 'Divine Love Lyrics from Babylon'. *Journal of Semitic Studies* 4 (1959): 1–15.

Lambert, W. G. 'Divine Love Lyrics from the Reign of Abi-ešuḫ'. *Mitteilungen des Instituts für Orientforschung* 12 (1966–67): 41–56.

Lambert, W. G. 'The Problem of the Love-Lyrics'. In *Unity and Diversity. Essays in the History, Literature, and Religion of the Ancient Near East*, edited by H. Goedicke and J. J. M. Roberts, 98–134. Baltimore and London: Johns Hopkins University Press, 1975.

Lambert, W. G. 'Devotion: The Languages of Religion and Love'. In *Figurative Language in the Ancient Near East*, edited by M. Mindlin, M. J. Geller and J. E. Wansbrough, 21–36. London: School of Oriental and African Studies, 1987.

Lambert, W. G. 'The Language of ARET V, 6 and 7'. *Quaderni Semitici* 18 (1992): 42–62.

Lambert, W. G. *Babylonian Creation Myths*, Mesopotamian Civilizations 16. Winona Lake: Eisenbrauns, 2013.

Lapinkivi, P. *The Sumerian Sacred Marriage in the Light of Comparative Evidence*. State Archives of Assyria Studies 15. Helsinki: Neo-Assyrian Text Corpus Project, 2004.

Lapinkivi, P. *Ištar's Descent and Resurrection. Introduction, Cuneiform Text and Transliteration with a Translation, Glossary and Extensive Commentary*. State Archives of Assyria Cuneiform Texts 6. Helsinki: Neo-Assyrian Text Corpus Project, 2010.

Lewis, Franklin D. *Rumi. Past and Present, East and West: The Life, Teachings and Poetry of Jalal al-Din Rumi*. Oxford: Oneworld Publications, 2000.

Limet, H. 'Le texte. KAR 158'. In *Collectanea Orientalia: Histoire, Arts de l'espace et industrie de la terre: Etudes Offertes en Homage à Agnès Spycket*, Civilizations du Proche-Orient, Series

1, Archéologie et Environment 3, edited by H. Gasche and B. Hrouda , 151–8. Neuchâtel: Recherches et Publications, 1996.
Mabey, Juliet Introduction: *Rumi: A Spiritual Journey*. Oxford: Oneworld Publications, 2000.
Mafouz, Naguib. *Aṣdā' al-Dhākkirah al-Dhātiyyah*. Egypt: Dār al-Shrouq, 2006.
Mahdī Muhammad Nāsir al-dīn. *Diwān Jamīl Bouthina*. Beirut: Dār al-kutub al-'ilmiyya, 2009.
Maine, G. F. *Rubáiyát of Omar Khayyám Rendered into English Verse by Edward Fitzgerald*. Edited by George F. Maine. London: Collins,1954.
Mannani, Manijeh. 'The Metaphysics of the Heart in the Sufi Poetry of Rumi'. *Religion and Literature* 42, no. 3 (2010): 161–8.
Massignon, Louis. *The Passion of Al-Hallaj: Mystic and Martyr of Islam*. Translated by Herbert Mason. Princeton: Princeton University Press, 1994.
McCarthy, R. J. *Al-Ghāzālī's Path to Sufism: His Deliverance from Error*, 56. Kentucky: Fons Vitae, 2000.
Meinhold, W. *Ištar in Aššur – Untersuchung eines Lokalkultes von ca. 2500 bis 614 v. Chr*. Alter Orient und Altes Testament 367. Münster: Ugarit-Verlag, 2009.
Miller, James, *Examined Lives: From Socrates to Nietzsche*. New York: Farrar, Strans and Giroux, 2011, p. 283.
Montefiore, Jan. *Feminism and Poetry: Language, Experience, Identity in Women's Writing*, London and Chicago, IL: Pandora, 2004.
Mukhia, Harbans. 'The Celebration of Failure as Dissent in Urdi Ghazal'. *Modern Asian Studies* 33, no. 4, Cambridge University Press (1999): 861–81.
Musche, B. *Die Liebe in der altorientalischen Dichtung*. Studies in the History and Culture of the Ancient Near East 15. Leiden: Brill, 1999.
Nicholson, Reyold A. *The Mathnawi of Jalalu'ddin Rumi*. Cambridge: Luzac and Co., 1977.
Nissinen, M. 'Love Lyrics of Nabû and Tašmetu: An Assyrian Song of Songs?'. In *"Und Mose schrieb dieses Lied auf": Studien zum Alten Testament und zum Alten Orient, Festschrift für Oswald Loretz zur Vollendung seines 70. Lebensjahres mit Beiträgen von Freunden, Schülern und Kollegen*. Alter Orient und Altes Testament 250, edited by M. Dietrich and I. Kottsieper, 585–634. Münster: Ugarit-Verlag, 1998.
Ormand, K. *Controlling Desires: Sexuality in Ancient Greece and Rome*. Westport, CT, Praeger, 2009.
Ouyang, W.-Ch. *Literary Criticism in Medieval Arabic-Islamic Culture: The Making of a Tradition*. Edinburgh: Edinburgh University Press, 1997.
Ouyang, W.-Ch. 'Genre, Ideologies, Genre Ideologies and Narrative Transformation'. *Middle Eastern Literatures* 7, no. 2 (2004): 125–32.
Paul, H. C. 'Rumi: His Life and Genius'. In *The Maulavi Flute*, edited by S. H. Qasemi, 30–53. India: New Age International Limited Publishers, 1997.
Pedersén, O. *Archives and Libraries in the City of Assur. A Survey of the Material from the German Excavations, Part I*. Acta Universitatis Upsaliensis. Uppsala: Studia Semitica Upsaliensia 6, 1985.
Ponchia, S. *La palma e il tamarisco e altri dialoghi mesopotamici*. Venice: Marsilio Editori, 1996.
Pongratz-Leisten, B. 'Sacred Marriage and the Transfer of Divine Knowledge: Alliances between the Gods and the King in Ancient Mesopotamia'. In *Sacred Marriages. The Divine Human Sexual Metaphor from Sumer to Early Christianity*, edited by M. Nissinnen and R. Uro, 43–73. Winona Lake: Eisenbrauns, 2008.
Powell, M. 'Wine and the vine in Ancient Mesopotamia: The Cuneiform Evidence'. In *The Origins and Ancient History of Wine*, edited by P. E. McGovern, S. J. Fleming and S. H. Katz, 97–122. London: Routlegde, 1996.
Qabbani, Nizar. *Qisatī ma'al-Sh'ir*. Beirut: Manshūrāt Nizār Qbbanī, 1973.
Qasemi, S. H., 'Preface'. In *The Maulavi Flute*, edited by S. H. Qasemi, i–ix. India: New Age International Limited Publishers, 1997.
Quasem, Muhammad Abul, 'Al-Ghāzālī's Conception of Happiness'.*Arabica*, 2 (1975): 153–61.
Quasem, Muhammad Abul *The Ethics of Al-Ghāzālī: A Composite Ethics in Islam*. New York: Caravan Books, 1978.
Renard, John. *Historical Dictionary of Sufism*. Lanham, USA: Scarecrow Press, 2005.

Rich, A. *The Dream of a Common Language: Poems 1974-1977*. New York: Norton, 1978.
Rifai, Kenan. *Listen: Commentary on the Spiritual Couplets of Mevlana Rumi*. Translated by Victoria Holbrook. Maryland, USA: Fons Vitae, 2011.
Rodney, Deborah. *Love Creates Meaning*. 2014. https://www.strategyforuminc.org/ProVision_by_Rodney10_26.html (last accessed 25 April 2014).
Roger, Janet Afray, Paolo Gardinali and Cambria Naslund. 'Love in the Middle East: The contradictions of romance in the Facebook World', *Critical Research on Religion* 4, no. 3 (2016): 229-58.
Roth, M. ed. *Assyrian Dictionary of the University of Chicago*. Chicago: University of Chicago Press, 2009.
Rubio, G. 'Inanna and Dumuzi: A Sumerian Love Story'. *Journal of the American Oriental Society* 121 (2001): 268-74.
Safavi, Seyed Ghahreman. *The Structure of Rumi's Mathnawi*. London: London Academy of Iranian Studies Press, 2005.
Salma, Jayussi. *Trends and Movements in Modern Arabic Poetry*. Leiden: Brill, 1977.
Sanchez, M. *Erotic Subjects: The Sexuality of Politics in Early Modern English Literature*. Oxford: Oxfor University Press, 2011.
Schimmel, Annemarie. *Mystical Dimensions of Islam*. Chapel Hill: University of North Carolina Press, 1975.
Schimmel, Annemarie. 'Mystical Poetry in Islam: The Case of Maulana Jalaladdin Rumi'. *Religion and Literature* 20, no. 1 (1988): 67-80.
Schimmel, Annemarie. 'The Manifestation of Love'. In *I Am Wind, You Are Fire: The Life and Work of Rumi*, 173-194. London: Shambala Publications, 1992.
Schroeder, Eric. 'The Wild Deer Mathnawi'. *The Journal of Aesthetics and Art Criticism* 11, no. 2 (1952): 118-34.
Schroeder, J. and M. Hawker. *You Don't Know*. Columbia Records, 1961.
Schwemer, D. 'Ein akkadischer Liebeszauber aus Hattusa'. *Zeitschrift für Assyriologie* 94, no. 1 (2004): 59-79.
Schwemer, D. 'Magic Rituals: Conceptualization and Performance'. In *Oxford Handbook of Cuneiform Culture*, edited by K. Radner and E. Robson, 418-42. Oxford: Oxford University Press, 2011.
Scurlock, J. A. 'Was there a "Love-Hungry" Ēntu-priestess Named Eṭirtum'. *Archiv für Orientforschung* 36/37 (1989-90): 107-12.
Sefati, Y. *Love Songs in Sumerian Literature*. Ramat Gan: Bar-Ilan University Press, 1998.
Shakespeare, William. *Romeo and Juliet*. London: Shakespeare Library Classics, 1953.
Shehata, D. *Musiker und ihr vokales Repertoire, Untersuchungen zu Inhalt und Organisation von Musikerberufen und Liedgattungen in altbabylonischer Zeit*, Göttinger Beiträge zum alten Orient Band 3. Göttingen: Universitätsverlag, 2009.
Siddqi, Muhammad Zubayr. *Hadīth Literature: Its Origin, Development and Special Features*. Edited and revised by Abdal Hakim Murad. Cambrdige: The Islamic Texts Society, 1993.
Sigrist, M. and J. G. Westenholz. 'The Love Poem of Rim-Sîn and Nanaya'. In *Birkat Shalom: Studies in the Bible, Ancient Near Eastern Literature, and Postbiblical Judaism Presented to Shalom M. Paul on the Occasion of His Seventieth Birthday*, vol. 2, edited by Chaim Cohen, Victor Avigdor Hurowitz and Avi Hurowitz, 667-704. Winona Lake: Eisenbrauns, 2008.
Skellie, Walter James. 'The Religious Psychology of Al-Ghazzali: A Translation of His Book of the Ihya on the Explanation of the Wonders of the Heart with Introduction and Notes'. PhD thesis. Kennedy School of Mission, Hartford Seminary Foundation, 1938.
Sladek, W. R. *Inanna's Descent to the Netherworld*, Baltimore: Johns Hopkins University, 1974.
Smith M. *Muslim Women Mystics: The Life and Work of Rabi'a and Other Women Mystics in Islam*, 124. Oxford: Oneworld, 2001.
Soden, W. von and J. Oelsner. 'Ein Spat-Altbabylonisches Pārum-Preislied für Ištar'. *Orientalia Neue Serie 60, (with Plate CVI)*, 1991, 339-43.

Soden, W. von. 'Ein Zwiegespräch Ḫammurabis mit einer Frau (Altbabylonische Dialektdichtungen Nr. 2)'. *Zeitschrift für Assyriologie* 49 (1950): 151–94.
Soden, W. von. *Akkadisches Handwörterbuch*. Wiesbaden: Harrassowitz, 1959–81.
Spector, P.. *To Know Him Is to Love Him*. Doré Records, 1958.
Spector, P., J. Barry and E. Greenwich. *Da Doo Ron Ron*. Philles Records, 1963.
Sperl, Stefan. *Introduction: Classical Traditions and Modern Meanings*, 1–15. Leiden: Brill, 1996.
Sperl, Stefan. '"O City Set Up Thy Lamen": Poetic Responses to the Trauma of War'. In *Poetry and Warfare in the Middle East*, edited by H. Kennedy. London: I.B. Tauris, 2013, 1–37.
Stetkevych, Suzanne P. *The Mute Immortals Speak: Pre-Islamic Poetry and the Poetics of Ritual*. Ithaca: Cornell University Press, 1993.
Streck, M. P. and N. Wasserman. *Sources of Early Akkadian Literature*, http://www.seal.uni-leipzig.de/ (last accessed 27 September 2014).
Swift, T. *Am I Ready For Love?* no date. http://www.azlyrics.com/lyrics/taylorswift/amireadyforlove.html (last accessed June 2014).
Turkmen, Erkan. *The Essence of Rumi's Masnevi Including his Life and Works*. Lahore: Jumhoori, 1999.
Veldhuis, N. 'Intellectual History and Assyriology'. *Journal of Ancient Near Eastern History* 1, no. 1 (2014): 21–36.
Volk, K. *Inanna und Šukaletuda: zur Historisch-Politischen Deutung eines sumerischen Literaturwerkes*, SANTAG 3. Wiesbaden: Harrassowitz, 1995.
Wasserman, N. *Style and Form in Old Babylonian Literary Texts*, Cuneiform Monographs 27. London-Boston: Brill, 2003.
Wasserman, N. 'From the Notebook of a Professional Exorcist'. In *Von Göttern und Menschen, Beiträge zu Literatur und Geschichte des alten Orients, Festschrift für Brigitte Groneberg*, Cuneiform Monographs 41, edited by D. Shehata et al., 329–49. Leiden and Boston: Brill, 2010.
Wasserman, N. 'Piercing the Eyes: An Old Babylonian Love Incantation and the Preparation of Kohl'. *Bibliotheca Orientalis* 72 (2015): 601–12.
Wasserman, N. *Akkadian Love Literature of the Third and Second Millennia BCE*, Leipziger Altorientalische Studien 4. Wiesbaden: Harrassowitz, 2016.
Weeden, Lisa. *Ambiguities of Domination: Politics, Rhetoric, and Symbols in Contemporary Syria*. Chicago, IL: Chicago University Press, 1999.
Westenholz, A. and J. G. Westenholz. 'Help for Rejected Suitors. The Old Akkadian Love Incantation MAD V 8'. *Orientalia Neue Serie* 46 (1977): 198–216.
Westenholz, J. G. 'A Forgotten Love Song'. In *Language, Literature and History: Philological and Historical Studies Presented to Erica Reiner*, American Oriental Series 67, edited by F. Rochberg-Halton, 415–25. New Haven: The American Oriental Society, 1987.
Westenholz, J. G. 'Metaphorical Language in the Poetry of Love in the Ancient Near East'. In *La Circulation des biens, des personnes et des idées dans le Proche-Orient Ancient*, Actes de la XXXVIIIe Rencontre Assyriologique Internationale, edited by D. Charpin and F. Joannès. Paris, 8–10 Juillet 1991, 1992.
Westenholz, J. G. 'Love Lyrics from the Ancient Near East'. In *Civilizations of the Ancient Near East*, edited by J. M. Sasson, 2471–84. New York: Scribner's Sons, 1995.
Wilcke, C.. 'Liebesbeschwörungen aus Isin'. *Zeitschrift für Assyriologie* 75 (1985): 189–209.
Worthington, M. 'On Names and Artistic Unity in the Standard Version of the Babylonian Gilgamesh Epic'. *Journal of the Royal Asiatic Society Series 3* 21, no. 4 (2011): 403–20.
Wyke, M. 'Mistress and Metaphor in Augustan Elegy'. *Helios* 16 (1989): 25–47.
Zohary, D. 'Domestication of the Grapevine *Vitis vinifera* L. in the Near East'. In *The Origins and Ancient History of Wine*, edited by P. E. McGovern, S. J. Fleming and S. H. Katz, 23–30. London: Routledge, 1996.

INDEX

'Abbas, al-Mu'tamad bin 126
Abdülhamid II, Sultan 151
Abu-Nawwas 126
Adonis 128, 185, 236, 242
Akkadian 2, 6–7, 12, 14–34, 39–65
Allah 121, 140, 186
Amichai, Yehuda 95
Ammiditana 18, 39
antiphone/antiphony 18
Aragon, Louis 158
Assyrian 16–17, 26, 28, 42–5, 49–50, 64
Atatürk, Kemal 153, 154, 165
Auberbach, Eric 101, 108, 125
al-'Azm, Sāddiq Jalāl 240

Babylonian 7, 16–18, 23–8, 31, 37, 39, 43–65
Balqees (Nizar Qabbani's wife) 215, 219–23, 239
Barthes, Roland 12–13, 42, 126, 129, 229, 241–2
Behar, Almog 93, 99
Bialik, Haim Nachman 100
The Bible 38, 44–5, 67, 86–8, 91–100
Bluwstien, Rahel 88
Bombaci, Alessio 151, 166
Breton, André 159
Buthaina, Jamil 8, 102, 107, 111–12, 116–17, 120–2, 127, 129

Cleopatra 67
cupid 15, 22, 40

Darwish, Mahmoud 10, 213–14, 224, 240–2
Dramtis persona 188, 190, 192–4, 197–206.
Dumuzi 17, 23–7, 36–7, 39–42, 47, 50–1, 58, 62, 64

Egypt 2, 5, 7, 10–11, 66–86, 126–7, 148, 228

Einstein, Arik 93, 99–100
Ekrem, Recaizade Mahmu 151–2, 159–60
Eliot, T.S. 227, 231, 241
Eluard, Paul 156, 157, 159
Enki/Ea 27, 37, 38

Al-Farabi 136
Farrokhzad, Farough 8, 9, 188–9, 191–201
Freud, Sigmund 126, 128, 159, 181, 210

ġaraḍ (aghrad) 15, 19, 43, 110
Genesis 62, 87–8, 91, 93–5, 98–9
Al-Ghazali, Abu Hamid 4, 8, 131–50
Gibran, Gibran Khalil 1, 6, 10–11, 214, 238
Gilgameš 37–9, 49, 55
Goethe 10, 11, 171, 184
Goldberg, Leah 91
Grossman, David 91, 99–100

Hammurapi 30–1, 33, 53
Hathor 67–8, 70, 76, 78, 80, 82
Hazm, Ibn 108, 114–17, 127–9, 229, 234
Hikmet, Nazim 9, 152, 153, 155–7, 159–60, 163, 165, 167–8
Hordedef, son of Khufu 74
Horus 67, 68
Hutiah 68

Ibaḥī poetry *126*
Ibn Rabī'ah, Omar 126
Inana 20–1, 25–6, 38, 46–7, 49–51, 55
incantation 7, 16, 19, 20, 22–6, 29–30, 39–41, 46, 48, 49, 51, 55, 56, 58, 63–5
'ishq 9, 114, 128, 172–7, 185, 196
Ištar 17–18, 21–9, 31, 33, 36–45, 49–55
Išullanu 37–9, 55

Jameson, Frederic 235, 237, 242
al-Jawziyya, Ibn al-Qiyam 114

Keats, John 66
Kemal, Yahya 9, 152–5, 165–7
Kerem 156, 157, 167
Khairall, Asʿad 115, 118, 129, 196, 211, 240
Kurdish poetry 6–9, 166, 169, 171–3, 176, 181, 184

Labīb, Ṭāhir 127, 128
Layla, Majnun 3, 8–9, 102–8, 112, 119–30, 176–7, 188–90, 195, 200–7, 211–12, 237
Luxor 67

magic 7, 19, 22–4, 30, 39–41, 46, 48, 49, 56, 58, 63–5, 92–3, 95, 241
Malik, ʿAbla Bintu 108
Mohammad, Prophet 3, 61, 107, 109–10, 128, 196, 218
Mohar, Eli 93–4

Nanaya 25–33, 45–51, 56
Nasīb 15, 105
Nefertum 68
Neruda, Pablo 156, 236, 242
Neuwirth, Angelica 5, 11, 125, 184, 185
Nizami 9, 171, 190, 196, 203, 207, 211, 212

Ottoman Empire 3, 4, 11, 153, 154, 171, 182, 184, 187, 194
Ovid 15, 43

Palestine 2, 6, 89, 127, 213, 223–5, 227, 228, 241
Pepiankh 68
Pyramid Texts 7, 66, 67, 86

Qabbani, Nizar 10, 213–24, 227, 238–40
Ibn al-Mulawwah, Qays 104–5, 126–7, 190, 237
al-Qays, Imru 104–5
The Qurʾan 106–7, 110–11, 121–4, 129, 131, 134–9, 145–6, 148, 172, 174, 217, 233, 236, 242

Rabikovitch, Dalia 96, 100
Ramesses II 68
Republic of Turkey 152, 155, 163, 165
Rich, Adrienne 12, 22, 192
Rim-Sin 27, 45
Roman 13, 15, 41–3, 67, 68
Romanticism 151, 214
al-Rumi, Jalal al-Din 4, 8, 132–6, 139–50, 171

Saadi 3
Said, Edward 113, 128
Al-Saman, Ghada 195, 210, 211
al-Shabbi, Abu al-Qassim 214
Shaddād, ʿAntara Bin 108
Shakespeare, William 127–8
Shamlu, Ahmad 8, 188, 189, 192, 196, 205–6, 208–11
Shelley 68
al-Shirazi, Hafiz 3, 171, 184
Sina, Ibn (Avicenna) 4, 116, 138, 139
Sippar 29, 34, 52
Song of Songs 86–7, 91, 98
Sperl, Stefan 11, 107, 126, 127
Stetkevych, Suzanne 105, 126, 241
Sufism 131–4, 145–6, 150, 166, 170, 182
Šukaletuda 38, 55
Sumerian 6, 16, 18, 24–6, 42–64
Süreya, Cemal 9, 152, 153, 162, 164, 165, 167, 168

Tanzimat era 9, 151, 159

ʿUdhrī poets 8, 101–9, 112, 114, 118–19, 122–9, 216–19, 222, 227, 231, 232

Valley of the Kings 67, 68, 79
Veli, Orhan 9, 152, 153, 159–61, 164, 165, 167, 168
Verlaine, Paul 152

Yeni, İkinci 152, 162, 163, 165

Zimmerman, Beeri 94

www.ingramcontent.com/pod-product-compliance
Lightning Source LLC
Chambersburg PA
CBHW062129300426
44115CB00012BA/1863